Mary Edwards Bryan

Wild Work

the Story of the Red River Tragedy

Mary Edwards Bryan

Wild Work
the Story of the Red River Tragedy

ISBN/EAN: 9783743303607

Manufactured in Europe, USA, Canada, Australia, Japa

Cover: Foto ©Thomas Meinert / pixelio.de

Manufactured and distributed by brebook publishing software
(www.brebook.com)

Mary Edwards Bryan

Wild Work

WILD WORK;

THE STORY OF THE RED RIVER TRAGEDY.

BY

MARY E. BRYAN,

AUTHOR OF "MANCH."

NEW YORK:

D. APPLETON AND COMPANY,

1, 3, AND 5 BOND STREET.

1881.

TO

HON. ALEXANDER H. STEPHENS,

THE WISE STATESMAN, THE JUST COUNSELOR,

THE TRUE FRIEND OF HIS COUNTRY AND OF HUMANITY,

THIS BOOK IS REVERENTLY

Dedicated.

A WORD BEFORE.—BY THE AUTHOR.

"THE reign of the carpet-bagger"—a troublous, transition period—was rich in dramatic features. Abnormal conditions of government and society brought out unwonted lights and shades of character and gave rise to extraordinary incidents.

Particularly was this true of the States west of the Mississippi, where comparative freedom from social restraints fostered individuality and independence of character—too often to a lawless extent. There the Ku-klux proper, with its mask and mummery, was little known. The protest against the "carpet-bag dynasty" was there more boldly uttered. If at times it found expression in the violence of a mob, at other times it wrought through manœuvres that showed a genius for state-craft, and, in one instance at least, the results it brought about partook of the character of a revolution.

The author of "Wild Work" has sought to reproduce a few scenes of that time and region with an eye solely to their dramatic aspect, not distorted by sectional prejudice and not disturbed by political side-lights.

The incidents of the story are, however, not *all* photo-graphed from life. Some of these have their outlines of fact colored by imagination; others are wholly fictitious. The catastrophe in which the story culminates will be recognized as one which has a place in the Nation's rec-ords. There it forms the most tragic chapter in the history of reconstruction. It has been called the "blackest blot upon the South," and the blame of it has been saddled upon the people of an entire section. But, notwithstand-ing the researches of the Government's Investigating Com-mittee, the true nature of the tragedy was never unveiled. It remains a mystery. Accident had given the writer of this story a glimpse behind the veil, and it is believed that the theory of the *character* and *cause* of the tragedy which is developed in "Wild Work" is the true one, though a thread of romance is interwoven with the warp of fact.

"Wild Work," written while the scenes it reproduces were fresh in the author's mind, was first published as a serial in a literary paper—the "Sunny South." Two years after its publication "A Fool's Errand" appeared, and several newspaper reviewers of the book called attention to the similarity of one of its incidents—"A Race against Time"—to an incident in "Wild Work." This resem-blance was probably accidental, or it may be that the inci-dent in each case was suggested by the same real occur-rence, and that Judge Tourgee had heard of the Louisiana girl—known to the writer of "Wild Work"—who saved the life of a carpet-bag post commander by riding across a wild country at night to warn him of his danger. Only the Judge has seen fit to make the heroine of his spirited "Race against Time" a *Northern* girl.

Once more insisting that "Wild Work" takes its view of the carpet-bag era simply from a dramatic standpoint, and through no distorting lens of sectional or party feeling —out of place in a story—the book is left to find what friends it may.

WILD WORK.

CHAPTER I.

A RED sunset flamed over the great wall of woods that stood against the horizon in the distance, seeming to guard the acres of level, fertile fields that stretched from its foot to the steep bank of the river. Half the stream was lighted by the glow; the other half lay in the lengthening shadow of the deep bank. On the illuminated side, the bank exhibited in one place a natural terrace, beneath which sloped down a "second bank"—a sand-bar projecting into the river, sparsely fringed by willows and young cottonwood-trees. To one of these was tied a large flat for ferrying people and horses across the river, and through the trees that grew on the upper bank could be seen the cabin of the negro ferryman. Up to this cabin there rode a party of three, two young girls well mounted and tastefully habited, followed by a gray-haired negro attendant, mounted on a mule that seemed as ancient as himself.

Stopping in front of the cabin, the old negro uttered a "hello!" that was only answered by the echoes of the opposite bank.

Again and again he called, but without response; the old ferryman was either soundly asleep or absent. Getting

down from his mule, the old negro approached the cabin
to make investigations, while the two girls rode along the
path to the water's edge—the taller of the two, a lithe,
slender brunette, with a style in her movements and closely-
fitting black habit that bespoke intercourse with fashionable society, checked her horse and took from her pocket
an envelope, the seal of which was already broken. As she
took out and unfolded the enclosure, her companion touched
the closely-written sheets with her riding-whip, saying :

"You can't read that now. I imagine that to enjoy a
love-letter one must take it as the butterfly takes the blos-
som he likes—leisurely and daintily. You will have to
wait till we get home."

"Yes ; and it seems that will never be. Why doesn't
Uncle Jake come on with the ferryman ? Yonder he is
now, and nobody with him. Uncle Jake, where is the
ferryman ?"

"Lord knows, Missy. He door done locked ; and I call
him till my throat most split, thouten gitten' any answer.
Spec' I'll have to try to put you over myself."

"That's a good enough idea ; you can take us over, I
know, as well as any ferryman on the river. Let's hurry
and get in the flat. The sun has been down these ten
minutes," said the brunette, Zoe Vincent, springing from
the saddle, and stepping lightly with lifted skirts to the flat.

"It's hurry for true Missy, case de Monsoon's comin'
round de bend. Dat's her puffin' and snortin' so ; and
she'll be around in no time. De Monsoon ain't a boat to
fool wid."

"Best wait till she goes past," said Adelle Holman,
who stood holding a beautiful mare by the bridle. But
Uncle Jake demurred.

"It's powerful late, and I ain't had a mouthful since
brekfust, 'cept de cheese and crackers you give me, Miss

Dell. Dat Cohatchie's a mighty unneighborly place for to spend de day in. A gentleman kin stand round dere all day hongry, and not a soul'll ax him in to git a bite. We might as well be gittin' over here; I'll have to make two trips, anyway. I can't carry over all three o' dem hosses to onct; I'll take yer over and de mare, and by dat time de boat will be done gone by. Den I come arter old Sol and de Gray."

While he talked, he was unfastening the flat; lifting the chain, he threw it in with a resounding clang. Then he led in Adelle's mare, and the girls stepped in and stood in the rear of the flat, Adelle placing her arm around Zoe to steady her city-raised friend, who was less accustomed than herself to this mode of crossing water.

"Now be spry, Uncle Jake," she said, and the old man responded bravely; but he met with a difficulty at the outset in pushing off, for the flat was aground, and it required no little exertion and a loss of precious time to shove the unwieldy bulk off into water that would float it. When this was finally effected, the sound of the steamer's revolving wheels and the piff-paff of her escape-pipe sounded alarmingly near. Old Jake's knotty hands trembled nervously as they grasped the oars and pulled for the opposite shore. He did well enough until he struck the swift, strong current of the river; then, in spite of his desperate efforts, the flat made little headway. The current grew stronger every minute; the old man strained to the oars with all his might, but in vain. The flat was turned slowly sideways by the stream and began to drift down, instead of going across. Seeing the emergency, Adelle sprang to a seat beside the old negro, seized one of the oars, and, with an encouraging word to him, joined in his efforts to right the flat. For a moment, it seemed as if they might be successful, but the next instant the oar broke off short in the negro's hand ; he turned his black face in blank dismay upon Adelle. At the same instant, the signal lights of the steamer came into sight, as the Monsoon rounded the bend, and seemed to head directly for them.

"De Lord above ! We'll be runned over in three jumps of a rabbit, and I can't swim a lick !" cried old Jake, the perspiration streaming down his ebony face.

Adelle dropped the oar, and turned a startled glance upon the red and green signals. They seemed to glare ominously, as there flashed into her mind the stories she had heard of skiffs and flats being run over by the river steamers, whose night watch were not always as careful as they should be.

The sight had a paralyzing effect upon old Jake. Down he fell in a heap in the flat and began to pray. Adelle shook him by the shoulder.

"Get up," she said. "Take this handkerchief and wave it, and shout to the boat as loud as you can for your life."

Then, as he rose and did her bidding, she went back to the rear of the flat, where stood Zoe, with a white face, and the mare, with head erect and ears pricked forward, seeming to comprehend the situation.

"Zoe," she said, "if the boat doesn't stop, you must get upon Fleta and make her jump into the river. She will swim to shore, and, if you will only hold on tightly, she will carry you safe."

"And what are you going to do ?"

"Swim, if I can ; I used to swim a little. Here, I think you will have to try Fleta, the boat does not seem to see us," she continued, with her strained gaze fixed on the lighted monster bearing down straight in their direction as they drifted helplessly in the middle of the stream. No one was to be seen on deck, it being the hour for the early

supper of Western steamers, nor were there any signs that
the white signal had been seen, or that any one had heard
Jake's vociferous shouts of "Stop; stop; help; stop yer
boat dere. You'se 'bout to run over white folks. Hold
up, you dere!"

Then dropping his voice to a hoarse mutter, "Lordy
messy! Eder she won't hold up, or she can't. Here she
comes right down upon us, and yonder dem niggers in der
cabins at old Mr. Pyle's place, a eatin' der supper, and let-
tin' us be drownded before der eyes."

"Come," said Adelle, calm in spite of her white lips.
"Come, Zoe, and let me help you upon Fleta."

But at that instant her arm was grasped by Uncle
Jake in a sudden paroxysm of joy.

"Bless de Lord; we'se saved!" he exclaimed; "Look,
missy!" He pointed to a skiff rapidly nearing the flat
from the side of the river they had lately left. Sinewy
arms propelled it with a will, and in a moment it was
alongside them. The tall, active oarsman seized the chain
of the flat, and cried out to those on board:

"Jump in the boat; push the horse into the river, old
man; she will swim ashore."

His voice inspired confidence; he was obeyed at once,
and, pushing off from the flat, with a few long strokes of
the oar he sent the skiff out of mid-stream and presently
out of danger of the boat, that now bore down upon the
flat, crushing it under and sinking it, while the mare,
swimming gallantly, neared the farther shore. Under shelter of the opposite bank, the two girls, huddled in the skiff
that tossed on the agitated water, looked on with blanched
faces, and shuddered at their near escape from death. Zoe
hid her face in her hands; Adelle drew a deep breath, and
turned to the stranger, who had so opportunely come to
the rescue.

"We have been saved from death, I think, thanks to you, sir," she said, holding out her hand and looking for the first time into his face. What was there in that face to make her start and draw back her hand? He saw the movement, and smiled—a cynical smile, that had yet a touch of proud patience in it.

"Yes, thanks to de Lamb and to you, Mars Witchell, we'se 'scaped bein' squshed and drownded to death by dat very boat snortin so unconsarnedly down de river. You was sent here by de Lord for to help poor niggers; and you're doin your work."

"Never mind that. Here's the bank; get out old man, and take your horses to the next crossing."

"Next crossin's a mile above here; 'twill be awful late for de ladies to be a ridin'; and how's dey goin' to ride, I'd like to know? Miss Dell's mare done swim out on t'other side, and gone home like lightnin'. Won't dey all be wild, do, when dey see her comin' all wet, and wid nobody on her back? Gray, here, won't tote double no how, and old Sol won't let woman folks tech him, much less git on his back."

"My own horse yonder is not safe for a lady to ride," Captain Witchell said, pointing to a fine-looking animal, standing loose where he had leaped from him on riding down the bank and seeing the danger to those in the flat. "Where are you going, old man?"

"To Mr. Vincent's place—Miss Zoe's brother."

"Take the horses on to the crossing. I will row these ladies home in the skiff."

"Don't put yourself to that trouble, sir," interposed Adelle, icily, "we can manage some way with the horses, or we can walk home, if you will hand the oar to Jake and let him put us on the other side of the river."

"Miss Dell, ain't you shamed of yourself, talkin' to Cap-

tain Witchell like dat, and he just done save you from bein'
drownded to death! De Captain's not gwine to hurt you.
You better let him take you in de skiff; de massey knows
when you gwine to git home, onless; and your pa'll be dis-
tracted about you."

But Adelle had risen, and was preparing to leave the
boat.

"Sit down, if you please," commanded Captain Witchell. "I shall take you home. It is already dusk. To
cross at the upper ferry would throw you late in the night.
You need not look at or speak to me, and I shall have nothing to say to you. I shall land you safely at home; then
my duty will be done."

As he spoke he pushed the boat, from which the negro
had just stepped, away from the bank, and began to pull
steadily and swiftly down stream, after a word to Jake to
tell him to fasten his horse where the animal stood.

The trip was accomplished almost in silence. The girls
sat together in the back part of the boat, their eyes fixed
with a kind of fascination upon the straight, soldierly figure
that wielded the oars, his profile sometimes turned partly
to them, showing the bold outlines of throat and chin, the
firm nose, the close-set mouth, with the slightly scornful
lines about it, the thick light hair thrown back from the
well-poised head.

A full moon had risen over the dark rampart of woods
that bounded the distant prospect, and long streams of silver light glorified the murky river and eclipsed the lingering rosiness of sunset. Adelle's lovely face looked pale
under her dark riding hat, and changes of expression
passed over her sensitive mouth and eyes, which still kept,
however, the look of haughty reserve that had come over
them at first sight of Captain Witchell's face.

Zoe had her rich cheek buried in her ungloved hand,

that had a diamond flashing on the betrothal finger. She had turned her dark eyes wonderingly from her friend to Captain Witchell when Adelle had so coldly declined any further service from the man who had just rescued them; but a whispered sentence served to make her understand. She nodded her head acquiescingly, and remained silent, save for a murmured word to her companion, about the beauty of the night or her fears that the family would be alarmed on their account.

A turn in the river brought the Vincent plantation into close proximity. A little, whitewashed country store came first of the buildings. It was perched near the shelving bank, while behind it stood the stable, the corn crib, and "lot." Before the gate of this last, forms were seen moving about confusedly, and the sound of excited voices reached the ears of those in the boat as they neared the landing. The mare Fleta, dripping from her bath in the river, had a few moments before stopped in front of the stable, and Hugh Vincent was excited with apprehensions concerning the fate of his sister and her friend. As he caught sight of the boat he hurried to the bank, followed by the negroes who had been grouped around the trembling mare.

As the skiff grated upon the sand, Captain Witchell leaped out and held the chain to steady the little craft, while the girls got out. He offered them no other assistance, and he merely bowed when Zoe, stopping near him, could not forbear saying :

"I am very sorry to have put you to all this trouble. I thank you very much for the assistance you have rendered us."

Adelle's foot slipped as she stepped from the skiff; she would have fallen had not Captain Witchell's arm caught her and placed her firmly on the ground. Confusedly, she murmured her thanks. He inclined his head slightly in acknowledgment, leaped into the boat, and pushed off, as Mr. Vincent came down the bank, saying as he met the girls :

"I am glad, I tell you, to see you two back safe. Fleta came up a while ago with the saddle and bridle on, wet as a fish, and frightened me mightily. Lucky I saw you before the alarm was carried to the house, to scare your father, Cousin Dell, and my wife and Miss Floyd all for nothing. What has happened ?"

"We came near being run over by the Monsoon, as we were crossing at Watt's Ferry," explained Zoe. "An oar broke in Uncle Jake's hand, and he couldn't manage the flat. The boat was close upon us, when a man came to our assistance with a skiff, just in time to get us off before the steamer went rushing over the flat. The mare had jumped out and swum ashore ; the other horses we had left behind on the bank. Uncle Jake has gone to cross them at the upper ferry, and the man brought us home in the skiff."

"Did you ask him in to rest, and take supper with us ? You didn't ? Well, it was as little as you could have done after his risk and trouble on your account. Is that your city politeness ?"

"Cousin Hugh," interposed Adelle, "the man was Captain Witchell. We did not think he would be welcome."

"Witchell, the deuce ! That carpet-bag scoundrel ? I had rather you owed a favor to the blackest nigger about than to one of that set of thieves—jackals, that come here to fatten on the carcass of our dead liberties. I wonder you accepted an obligation from him, Zoe."

"Would you have had us drown, brother ? Besides, we didn't know the man until after he had rescued us. I had never seen him, and Dell was too much frightened to recognize him at first."

"Well, I suppose it could not be helped. Old Jake was the one to blame. It's like his thick head, trying to cross at dusk with a boat comin' round the bend; letting you two get under obligations to such a d—— —I beg pardon, Dell—such a rascal as Witchell. I'll row him up about it when he comes. Of course, he thinks it was all right. It was Mars Witchell—the god of every darky about here. I suppose he is on his way down here to organize a loyal league among the darkies and the scalawags. I hear they are to meet at the nigger church on the old Burns place to-night. A *dark* assembly it'll be, in every sense of the word; only two or three white skins among them, and they ashamed of their color, and apologizing for it with all their might. I can't see why Witchell is hugging the new voting power just now. He can't want more office after just being appointed District Judge by the Governor, without the formality of an election; but he is a shrewd, far-sighted scamp, and he means to fly his kite high, I imagine."

They had reached the yard gate—set in a low paling that was overrun with trumpet vines. The house was an unpicturesque, whitey-brown cottage, neglected-looking, like most of the buildings of that rich, alluvial section, where cotton-raising absorbs the energies and the money of the planters. But the yard was covered with velvety grass, and under a great walnut-tree swung a hammock, from which floated a mass of white drapery. The occupant who lazily swayed therein was singing the "Mocking Bird" to a guitar accompaniment, while several children stood around her listening. The music stopped; the musician turned around in her hammock.

"Truants!" cried a voice like a flute, "come here and give an account of yourselves. Why are you so late?"

"Oh! Floyd, we have had an adventure!" Zoe said, as they approached the tree.

"An adventure! what—in going to and from such a stupid little village as Cohatchie? Did old Gray stumble, and some shirt-sleeved knight of the plow pick you up out of the mud, or did the mishap take place in the street, and was it some hero of the yard-stick or the sugar-scales that came to the rescue?"

"Nonsense, Floyd!"

"By the way, I've been presiding over the scales and the yard-stick myself to-day, helping your brother in his store. He has had a run of custom of all colors—darkies from the plantations and swarthy Creoles from the swamps, and I've been weighing candy and measuring red ribbons as if to the counter born. Mr. Vincent declared I was a charming saleswoman."

She did not add that the young farmer and store-keeper had supplemented the compliment by the present of a pretty dress-pattern, now reposing in her trunk. Floyd Reese always took the goods the gods sent, without scruple or injudicious parade. The organ of secretiveness was fully developed in her handsome head.

"But about your adventure—what was it?" she asked.

And Zoe recounted the story of their escape, with more of picturesque detail than she had used in relating it to her brother. Evidently it was interesting to her listener. Floyd raised herself from her lazy, reclining posture in the hammock and leaned forward, looking into Zoe's eyes.

"Why in the world did you not ask him to come in?" she cried.

"Did you not understand, Miss Reese, that it was Captain Witchell, the Radical leader?" Adelle asked, her face full of scornful wonder.

"Judge Witchell, you mean, and may be future Governor

of the State," said Floyd, nodding her graceful head em-
phatically.

"Through unjust measures and an ignorant negro vote,
then," cried Adelle, indignantly. "What honor is there
in office so gained?"

"He is fast getting what is better than honors or office
—plenty of money—the stepping-stone to everything else.
Widow Ellis and Mrs. Delaney have had to turn their plantations over to him to manage, because they could not get
hands, or control them when they were got. He is coining
money out of the lands they had lying waste. Then the
appropriation he got from the State for cleaning out Lake
Wisteneau—that was a grand speculation."

"A grand swindling scheme," flashed Adelle; "thirty
thousand dollars for clearing out a few harmless snags. To
pass such a bill was an outrage."

Floyd laughed musically.

"No matter; they did pass the bill, and the Captain
has pocketed the money. Success makes right in this
world, my dear. A man who carries things before him
like this one, deserves consideration. Throw up your hat
for the powers that be; there goes mine in the Captain's
honor!"

She caught up from her lap her gypsy leghorn, stuck
full of purple flowers by the children, and tossed it up by
its ribbon string. Then she jumped from the hammock
with a quick movement that showed a shapely, slippered
foot, and sent a mass of warm brown hair tumbling about
her shoulders.

Even in the half light the charm of this woman could
be seen. The carmine glow in her cheeks and the gold
glints in her hair were not visible, but the outlines of a
most seductive shape—at once full and flexible, sumptuous
and sinuous—made apparent that charm of form so potent,

especially in the eyes of men who are no longer very youth-
ful.

" You were short-sighted not to have turned your adventure to good account," she said, shaking back her curls
and looking at Adelle.

" If I thought you were in earnest, Floyd Reese ! "

" Am I not, though ? It was a rare opportunity, and
you should have remembered your copy-book counsel, and
' improved your opportunity' in this instance ; I would, if
I had been in your place."

Holding the guitar with one arm, she put the other
around Adelle's waist and stood laughing.

The younger girl shrank slightly from the embrace—a
movement that did not escape the quick discernment of the
other.

" Pardon," she said, with a sudden change of manner.
" Of course, my talk is to be taken with the classic grain of
salt ; yet, if I should be tempted by a full purse and a bold
arm, it might not be so bad for me—a moneyless waif, with
none to help me fight my battles with the world. With
you it is different; you have the shelter of home and
love."

Her voice had lost its light ring, and was rich and sweet,
seemingly charged with more emotion than was expressed.
Her eyes were cast down ; one would not have thought they
had noted the approach of Hugh Vincent ; but there was
little that escaped the keen vision and wonderful intuition
of Floyd Reese.

Adelle was touched into forgetfulness of the distrust
that had made her shrink, and Zoe said, reproachfully :

"How can you be so unkind to your friends as to call
yourself friendless, Floyd ?"

The stoutly built, rather coarsely handsome brother of
Zoe suffered his eyes to dwell for a moment on the tableau,

whose central figure was Floyd, with downcast lashes and
picturesquely falling hair.   Then he said :

"Is it too romantic out here in the moonlight to speak
of supper, young ladies ?   It is waiting, my good wife says ;
and no doubt, Cousin Dell, you and Zoe are very hungry
after your ride and your rescue.   By the way, I would not
mention that last to your father, Dell.   It would worry him
uselessly, for I have sufficiently accounted for your staying
late.   He is so bitter against carpet-baggers."

"Against this man, especially.   Do you not know,
Cousin Hugh, that once, when he was Provost Marshal, he
had my father arrested, humiliated before him, and fined for
striking an insolent negro.   Think of it—my father !"

She said "my father" as proudly as though the plain,
Mossy Valley farmer had been some potentate of the land ;
and truly, if he had been, she could not have rendered him
more loving homage.   Besides being a kind father he had
a commanding way that became him well at the head of his
regiment in Confederate days, and still made him looked up
to with deference by his household and his neighbors.

His fine presence gave quite an imposing look to Mrs.
Vincent's neat tea-table, as the party from the yard entered
the supper room.   Adelle went up to him and kissed him,
as was her habit whenever she had been away from him for
a day or a night.   Then he bent his iron-gray head with a
fine grace to her companion, "Cousin Zoe," as he called her,
though the tie of blood between him and his host was not
very close—just enough to warrant the Colonel's stopping
here a few days with his daughter on their return from
New Orleans.

His notice of the girl who came in behind the others
had in it something more to be remarked.   His eye kindled with admiration as Floyd Reese took her seat at the
table just opposite.   Why was it ?   Miss Reese had not the

delicate, regular features of Zoe, nor the sweet, womanly loveliness of Adelle. But she had that picturesque, dramatic charm that excites curiosity and appeals to the imagination. It was seen in her movements, her postures, her looks, even her dress—not arranged with the orderly neatness of the two other girls, but having a negligent grace of its own ; from the full sleeves falling back to show the round arm, to the muslin folds caught low with a rose under the large white throat. The charm of the lawless and unfettered hung about her in spite of the air of queenly self-assurance which served to keep down any utterance of distrust from those who might secretly regard her with suspicion.

One of these, it was apparent, was the plump, sun-browned little wife of Vincent, who poured out coffee at the head of the well-supplied table. Her pleasant hostess's smile gave way to a half frown as Floyd came in talking with Vincent and smiling in his face. Miss Reese had the faculty of looking at every man in a way to convey to him a secret impression that she was especially interested in him ; and this, curiously enough, without being suspected by other men who might be present, each of whom was apt to believe that he alone was the object of the lady's interest.

Something of this flattery was even in the glance and nod she gave to a common-looking man, who came in presently and took a seat at the table—a carpenter hired by Mr. Vincent to work on his cotton-press, and just back from the town, where he had been to get a tool mended.

After the democratic fashion of the South, he was asked to eat at the table with the family. He was from the same neighborhood as Colonel Holman, and, as he stuck his fork into a ruddy slice of boiled ham, he said :

"Colonel, I saw your son Derrick in Cohatchie this

evenin'. He crossed over on this side, too, at the upper ferry—not half an hour before I did."

"You saw my son Derrick in town to-day? I can't imagine what brings him down here."

"I think I have an inkling what he's up to," returned the other with a knowing wink. "Derrick wasn't by himself. Half a dozen or so of the Mossy Valley boys were with him, and I heard it hinted they were going to have some fun to-night. Did you know, Colonel, that another of your folks was down here—no other than Captain Witchell? There's to be a big nigger meeting at the old Burns place, and the Captain comes down to organize a Loyal League. The boys, so I heard, were bound to interrupt the grand pow-wow and give it a scare, if no more. I hope they won't get hurt, nor into any difficulty."

Adelle saw her father's face cloud anxiously, but, straightening himself in his seat, the old man said stoutly:

"I should regret it, Mr. Davis; but if they should get into a difficulty—if blood was spilled—even my own son's blood, sir, I should not grieve, if it might be the means of rousing our people from their cowardly submissiveness. Forbearance in their case has long ceased to be a virtue. If they are down in the dust, need they grovel under the foot that crushes them? Here we are reduced to the most humiliating slavery that ever outraged a people—taxed beyond all justice, swindled on every hand, our political rights taken from us, our private business interfered with and disorganized by meddlers that set our ignorant African laborers against and above us; and we submit to it without so much as a protest! Better be dead at once!"

"That's true, sir,' assented the carpenter, rather gratified at the excitement he had caused; "but you, up in your parish, are better off in that respect than we are. From accounts, Captain Witchell must be the best of our carpet-

bag masters ; more just in administering affairs, and knows
how to do a generous thing sometimes."

"Yes, sir ; he knows how to lavish with one hand what
he has robbed with the other when it is policy to do so.
He is courting popularity with the ignorant whites ; why,
I don't know, since he seems to get all he wants, and no
thanks to them. He gets to be judge without a vote
being cast. But he will not be allowed to hold court, sir ;
never !"

The old gentleman's eye flashed : he pushed his cup of
coffee from him, half full, and rose-from the table. His
daughter followed him, and as he stalked up and down the
gallery she tucked her little hand under his arm and walked with him, trying to mollify his mood by her pleasant
talk. But, with all her affectionate prattle, she did not succeed so well as the syren who came out presently and sat
down where the moonlight fell over her and her picturesque
white drapery.

"Sing 'Nelly' for us, Miss Floyd," cried one of her two
little pupils, lugging up the inevitable guitar.

"Oh dear !" she said, but she sang notwithstanding
—old-fashioned songs, sweet in themselves and sweeter by
association ; gay little trills at first, and then songs of love
and parting.

"I'll play this old drawl for you, especially, Zoe," she
said. "Waft a sigh southward while I sing that venerable
lover's lament, 'Days of Absence.'"

Zoe merely smiled ; it was not worth while to blush at
allusions to her engagement ; she heard them so often ; and,
besides, her attachment to her young lawyer-lover was not
of the sort that effects blushes, being quiet and dispassion-
ate as it was sincere. She had no girlish shyness at hearing
their marriage discussed. She had looked forward to it so
seriously that she seemed already Royal West's wife, as in-

2

deed she would have been had not her mother's recent death postponed their marriage.

Soon afterward her home in New Orleans was broken up; her father went to Cuba to establish a business, and she came to live with her married brother at his river-side farm.

"Now sing something to suit Cousin Dell," the children cried when the dolorous "drawl" was finished.

"Yes, I will," Floyd said. "Lines to her who will understand them;" and she sang "Norah's Vow."

> "Hear what Highland Norah said,
> 'The Earlie's son I will not wed,
> Though all the race of nature die,
> And none be left save he and I.'
>
> .   .   .   .   .
>
> But Norah's vow is lost and won,
> She's wedded to the Earlie's son."

"How is that applicable to Adelle, Miss Reese?" Colonel Holman asked, stopping beside the singer.

"It is prophetic," she laughed, unmindful of the haughty look Adelle threw at her upon this allusion to their conversation this evening, and to an adventure, a knowledge of which she knew would destroy all her father's hardly regained good humor.

She quitted the group on the gallery and went into a room that opened upon it—Mrs. Vincent's room—where the little mother sat rocking her fretful baby to sleep with a weary look on her face. Adelle took the baby and soon succeeded, through her gift in soothing, in getting it to sleep. As she sat, with the little head against her bosom, a sweeter picture than Raphael's Madonna, she said:

"Cousin Monde, who is Miss Reese?"

"Ah! who is she, indeed?" returned the little matron, suddenly animated. "I would like to have that question answered to my own satisfaction. I never saw her before Hugh brought her down two months ago, to teach May and Rob; though I had heard bits of her history—her history, mind, according to herself, which may be true as gospel for aught I know. She suddenly appeared in the neighborhood above Cohatchie, one day last fall; went to see Judge Clark, who is a well-to-do, kind-hearted old gentleman, and made the Masonic sign of distress, and then told him her story—how she had crossed the river from the Texas side in the night—a stormy night, too—that she was followed and pursued as far as the river by her guardian, who was a very bad man, and wanted to get all her property for his own use. With this object, he had pretended that she was crazy, and shut her up somewhere. When she made her escape, he followed her. He had thought, so she hoped, that she had been drowned while trying to cross the river in the darkness and storm. It was her intention to stay in this State until she was twenty-one, and then return to Texas and prosecute her guardian, and recover her property. As she must earn her support till then, she begged Judge Clark to help her. He did; he enlisted the Masons and church members in her behalf, and obtained for her a school. But somehow she was dissatisfied; the school taxed her too much: she saw my husband and told him how greatly she would prefer to teach a few children in a private family; and he offered her a place with us. I trust he may never regret it."

"Is she not a good teacher?"

"Yes, she does well enough in that way, I suppose, though it's easy to see she is not used to teaching, and she is no disciplinarian; at one time romping with the children like another child, then cold and moody and cross. But it's not that I object to so much. She has managed to make herself first in the house—her wishes and opinions to be

considered first by servants, children, and even Hugh. No
woman likes to be made of second importance in her own
house."

"No; I should think not."

"Married women have cares and troubles enough, if
they do their duty faithfully. They ought, at least, to be
a sort of queen in their own little home—that's my idea;
but you don't always see it so; far from it, sometimes. Married life is not the honey-sweet cup that girls are apt to
think it. But there! I've no business putting a bitter
taste for it in *your* mouth beforehand, and you to try it
yourself so soon, cousin."

"I? who told you so?"

"Your father and I were talking about you to-day—in
here by ourselves—and he told me you were engaged, or as
good as engaged, to Richard Lanier—your near neighbor.
I used to know the family well."

"Papa told you that?" said Adelle.

She had turned pale, and she rose hurriedly and laid the
baby in his little crib. She tucked the soft white covering
around him to gain time, before she faced Mrs. Vincent and
said:

"Cousin Monde, don't speak of that again—to me or
any one, please. There is nothing settled, and I don't
think—"

"Why, your father seemed so pleased."

"Yes, I know. Richard's land joins ours; he is Derrick's friend—a brave, hot-headed fellow, but—I don't
think I will ever marry; I like my girl-life too well to
change it." She walked to the open window, and stood
there, wondering why the mention of Richard Lanier jarred
on her so. The picture of him that rose before her—the
slim, swarthy face; the small, keen eyes, so watchful of
her—was absolutely repugnant.

"I believe I am tired," she said, wearily; "I will say good-night, and go to bed. Zoe has already gone up stairs."

Zoe was re-reading the letter she had got from the Cohatchie post-office that day.

"Would you like to see how he looks, Dell?" she asked, holding up a small card-picture that had come with the letter.

It was a refined face that Adelle held to catch the lamp-light. It was a good face, too. The mouth was gentle, the eyes had a frank breadth between them and a steady, truthful look. Adelle liked the face, and said so.

"You think it the perfection of manly beauty, of course, Zoe," she said, playfully touching the girl's cheek, as she handed back the picture.

"No, I do not. I don't think it is manly enough. I like a strong, masterful face, even if it is a bit rugged. Dell, there is no harm in just admiring a face, and I own I like Captain Witchell's—just the face, mind you."

"Don't speak of him. Oh! how sorry I am that we got under any obligation to him."

"I don't think he will presume upon it—after the way we received it, Dell. You were very cold."

"He must have thought me dreadfully mean and un-grateful," the girl said, with a sudden rush of color to her forehead. "But it does not matter what he thinks," she added quickly, undoing her hair, and letting its dark waves drop down upon her shoulders, saying, as she threaded its mass with her fingers, "I wish our land could be rid of these aliens. I am afraid they will cause us terrible trouble yet. I shall not sleep for thinking of Derrick to-night, and fearing he will commit some rash act that will cost him his life."

She knew that Lanier was with her brother, but she did not speak of this.

CHAPTER II.

ONE who had only seen Floyd Reese in the presence of others, her face carefully guarded in its expression, would hardly have recognized her when she sat alone, as to-night, her brow bent, her mouth drooping, her eyes full of gloomy thought.

"No use to dwell upon that now," she said, rousing herself at length. . Then standing up, and clinching one of her hands, "But I must make a bold stroke somehow. I won't vegetate here any longer; I can't stand it. Besides, there's a storm brewing. Monsieur is growing sentimental; and Madame cross as a cat. Why will men always fall in love with me?"

Her eyes fell upon the looking-glass over the mantel.

"If they could see me now," she thought, with a little bitter laugh that yet broke up the hard lines about her mouth, and brought the color into her cheeks. Still looking at herself, she thought, "How strange that my eyes can be bright, my cheeks red, after what I have gone through! I hope they will stay so and tell no tales, for I must call up all my assurance and strike out somewhere. I was born to rule. I feel the will and the power struggling within me, and yet here I am, ruling two disgusting brats, and perhaps their commonplace father, whose devoted regards can never serve me any further than to keep me in bread and clothes until his jealous wife objects. I must fly for higher game. If I could attach myself to this bold hawk that is preying to such good purpose on my chicken-hearted states-people! Captain Witchell, if I could win your confidence, share your schemes, help you to outwit men, and rise with you to power and riches, it would be all my ambition would crave. It would fill my heart, too—

better than love can fill it. Love! Faugh! I have done
with love, or I ought to have done with it. It has been
my bane : if I touch it again, it will be to make it my slave
—a stepping-stone to power of some kind."

Still with her eyes on the glass, she smiled slowly.

"How my eyes shine just now!" she thought. "Is it
prophetic of some lucky fortune? This is one of my beauty-
moments. I am only pretty by flashes."

A sudden barking of dogs outside, followed by the sound
of horses in a canter, caused her to start from her seat and
approach the window. Coming along the road that ran
just outside the fence were three or four mounted men,
plainly to be seen in the moonlight. They slackened their
pace as they came near the house; a window was thrown
open, and the voice of Vincent was heard calling out, but
in suppressed tones, as though afraid of waking others :

"Derrick Holman, are you there? Open the gate and
ride in here for a moment."

The foremost rider wheeled his horse, unlatched the gate,
and rode into the yard and up to the window alongside
the tall myrtle bush, whose polished leaves glistened in the
moonlight. Holding out his hand, he said:

"How are you, Cousin Vincent? Father is here, isn't
he?"

"Yes, he stopped off the boat to recruit a little. He
had a sharp attack of cholera-morbus coming up, and it left
him too weak to bear jolting across the country to Malta
over your rough hill-roads. He heard to-night of your being here, and on what errand, and was very anxious about it.
He sent a man—Davies—you may know him, as he comes
from your neighborhood—with a message to you. Did you
see Davies?"

"Yes; and sent back word to the old man that he
needn't have alarmed himself."

" Was anything done ? "

" No," laughed the other—a forced, self-mocking laugh.
" The adventure was a farce from beginning to end. In
the first place, Witchell rode down here by himself, instead
of with the nigger body-guard or the posse of white scalawags that we expected he would take with him. We were
out in the woods, two or three miles from Malta, on the
watch out for him when he passed, and we saw it wouldn't
do. 'Twould have been fun to scare the lot, but we couldn't
fall on one man riding peaceably along—though he was a
rascally carpet-bagger. We rode on after him, thinking to
break up the meeting anyhow. We thought to get some of
the boys at Cohatchie to join us, but they fought shy when
we hinted our business. I believe you folks down this way
think every Yankee usurper—Witchell especially—is a kind
of fate or providence that it's no use kicking against. Well,
we came on ourselves ; crossed over and went 'round by the
swampy road back of the fields to the place of meeting.
There, again, we found things not as we had counted on.
Instead of closed doors and a nigger guard, the door was
open and we were invited to come in and take seats. We
marched into the aisle and stood there listening to what
Witchell was saying. He was making a speech ; he turned
and looked at us—he knew me, for I'd been in his way a
time or two before, and I was at the head of the fellows
who warned him, after he made himself judge, that he
needn't try to hold court. But he made no sign, and kept
on with his speech. It was for the negro, of course, but in
a kind of general way. There was nothing in it to give a
handle to get after him. The house was pretty full—black,
with a sprinkling of white office-hankerers, and among
them that arch rogue Yent, that's hectoring over everything down here, as he tried to do with us. He was sitting
there, pompous as a king among his nigger worshipers.

My hands itched to get hold of him, but I saw there was no chance for that. There were enough of them there to gobble up our little handful. I thought best to get out of the den at once, but Lanier, who had been drinking pretty freely, gave the lie to something Witchell said. Witchell turned and flashed his eyes at us. 'If you interfere here,' he said, low (we were standing close to him), I will order your arrest. You had best go before there is trouble.' Lanier struck out at him with his knife ; Witchell caught his wrist and held it. 'Let him loose !' I cried out, and laid my hand on my pistol. Witchell said nothing, but that coward bully Yent bellowed out: 'Pitch into 'em, drive 'em out boys ;' and the niggers came tumbling over the benches like a black hurricane. We stood a fair chance of being torn to pieces. Witchell ordered them back, and, when they wouldn't mind, he drew a revolver, cocked it, and held it out, declaring that he would shoot the first one that tried to pass him. You ought to have seen Yent fall back. I said to the boys, 'This is no place for white men ; let's go '; and we went."

"So Witchell really kept down a disturbance ; saved your lives, perhaps ?"

"No thanks to any good feeling on his part. He does anything for policy. He looks ahead. He has more of the fox than the wolf in him. I hear he is coming to cast his lot here with you on the river ; I don't congratulate you. He'll make his jack out of you, you'll find to your sorrow."

"Won't you come in and stay all night, and see your father and sister ?"

"No, I thank you. We are going to cross to-night. The boys swear the game isn't done yet. Witchell is to have a nigger guard to-morrow ; it will be good sport to give them a run and scare, perhaps something else. Sis, is that you standing there on the piazza, looking like a ghost in the moonshine? Come and kiss me. Don't you begin to scold. If you had been at home, I would have been there too. Why did you stay away so long? You might have known I'd get demoralized."

He said the last words, bending down to kiss his sister, his arm about her neck as she stood beside his horse. She had stepped down from the piazza and stood with her white dressing-gown wrapped around her and her dark hair loose on her shoulders.

"I was too uneasy to sleep," she said; "I heard your voice, and crept down stairs to see you and know that you were safe. Father was anxious; he walked about the room a long time after he retired, but I believe he is asleep now. Will you come in and see him?"

"No; I have no time; they are waiting for me; Lanier is among them; he has seen you, and is riding in."

"Then I will go; I do not want to see him. Goodbye," Adelle said hastily.

"No," her brother answered, catching her hands. "You must not go now. He will think you are running away from him, and be mad with you. You know how quick he is. Besides, he is a little—excited to-night."

"He has been drinking—that is nothing very unusual," said Adelle in disgust. The slender young man rode up to her side and greeted her with eager tenderness, grasping in a tight, nervous clasp the hand she reluctantly extended.

"You are well," he said, bending down and fastening his black, burning eyes on her fair face, in its frame of loose, soft hair. "You are enjoying your visit. We heard of you; Derrick, did you tell her what we heard to-night?"

"No; I never thought of it. Besides, I did not believe it. Adelle, a negro told us that you came across the river in a skiff with Witchell. It was not so, of course."

"Yes, it was!" the girl said, faltering and feeling her

cheeks flame. "It was an accident. The flat we were in was run over and sunk by the Monsoon. He came up in the skiff just in time to rescue us."

"I had almost rather you had drowned," muttered her brother, with an oath."

"Oh, Derrick !"

"No, I don't mean that. But it was unfortunate. However, you need not recognize him afterward. You thanked him, and that was an end of it. Yes, I am coming this moment," he said, in answer to an impatient call from his comrades on the other side of the fence. "Good-bye, Sis ; I will send the carriage for you and father to-morrow. Come, Lanier !"

Adelle's dark lover snatched her hand and carried it to his hot lips. The kiss seemed to burn there long after he rode away, and the small cavalcade had disappeared up the moonlit road that followed the river's windings. She pulled a catalpa leaf, wet with dew, and rubbed the place on her hand where his lips, feverish with liquor and the passion of his fiery heart, had pressed the kiss.

"Somehow, I shrink from him more than ever," she thought, in some distress. "He is leading Derrick into all this. Oh ! how I wish I had begged them not to do anything to Captain Witchell to-morrow. I meant to have done it. He might not interfere as he did to-night. That *was* magnanimous, let them say of him what they will. But then, as Derrick says, it was done through policy. Of course, a grasping, unscrupulous man like him can have no real nobleness of character."

Yet still, to her own vexation, the thought of him, the image of his proud face, and the half-sneering, half melancholy smile that curved his lips when she shrank from him, recurred to her as she lay watchful beside her sleeping friend.

Another was wakeful with thoughts of Captain Witchell and of the conversation she had overheard between Derrick Holman and his cousin. Floyd made a resolve before she slept ; and, with her, to plan impulsively and to execute boldly were characteristic.

CHAPTER III.

EARLY next morning Floyd Reese came out of the house and took her way to the stable. Leading out Fleta, she took down bridle and saddle from the pegs where they hung and put them on the mare. Fleta was hers—her only possession. The mare's fleet limbs had saved her once in a desperate race for life, with a mob following like famished wolves behind. Floyd would not part with her, she said, as long as she could help it. A good price had been offered for her, but Floyd refused it. "Not till I need bread ; even then I will hesitate, and starve a little first, so long as the grass will keep her from famishing."

Vincent had the use of the mare now for her keep, but she was seldom ridden by any but Floyd, and her sleek coat and bright eye testified to greater care than is usual in Western stables. Floyd caressed her pretty neck a moment before she mounted to a seat in the saddle. She rode away just as the master of the house came out upon the piazza. Seeing her, he called to her and came eagerly toward her, but she only nodded her plumed head to him and waved her hand as she cantered swiftly up the road. She had no idea of being hindered in her purpose this morning by listening to the flattering speeches of a man whose admiration could be of no use to her—no help in getting her out of the dull routine of life which her restless, ambitious soul hated.

Briskly she rode through the broad fields bordering on the river, the murky stream rolling between its steep banks on one side, the long rows of flourishing corn or cotton upon the other; fields all the way, with dividing fences, whose big gates she had learned to open. Looking back, she saw galloping toward her a lank negro astride a diminutive white mule.

"He probably went to the meeting last night, and can tell what I want to know," thought Floyd, and purposely dropped her riding-whip.

"Pick it up for me, please," she said to the negro, who tumbled down, delighted to serve a handsome and stylish lady. As he handed it to her, she further pleased him by a smile and a gracious "Thank you."

"You are out early this morning; you are not just now coming from the Loyal League meeting, are you?"

"No, ma'am."

"Was it a good meeting?"

The negro hesitated, and looked at her doubtfully. Any allusion by a white Southerner to the negro's newly-acquired political relations disturbed the latter's equanimity, and made him draw into his shell of suspicion. But Floyd's smile was irresistible, and suspicion was disarmed.

"It was a mighty fine meetin', ma'am. Captain Witchell and Mr. Yent spoke beautiful."

"I am glad of it. We heard that a foolish attempt to break up the meeting was going to be made. I hope Captain Witchell will not go back alone. It would be unsafe."

"He oughtn't to, ma'am, that's a fac', and some of our people made up to guard him, but he sent word he didn't need it, and wouldn't 'cept it no how."

"And so he has gone?"

"Not yit. He's goin' to cross up here at Tenk's landin'. De flat's outer fix at Mr. Brown's, where he stayed las' night."

"He stayed at Mr. Brown's, the store-keeper's, last night ?"

"Yes ma'am, he did that. Mr. Brown writ a note and specially axed him. Mr. Brown knows which side his bread's buttered on. He's goin' to make fair wedder wid de Cap'n, and all de white uns better do the same. Cap'n Witchell mout help dem, same as he do we, and he's mighty good at helpin'."

"Mighty good at helping himself," Floyd thought, as, having gained all the information she wanted, she began to hum a tune and cut with her whip at the young corn blades, while the negro lifted his battered hat, said 'Good-morning,' and rode on ahead.

Half an hour more brought Floyd to the crossing spoken of, and, riding down into the strip of woods that here fringed the river, she dismounted, tied her mare to a limb, and, leaning against an old ash-tree near the path that led to the river, she waited for Captain Witchell to appear.

The birds twittered in the young leaves overhead, the yellow butterflies drifted over the blossomed herbs and dewy berry-vines at her feet, the river flowed below with a cool gurgle, but Floyd's thoughts were not in tune with these. They were confused and unquiet. The purpose she had in view seemed more and more absurd in her eyes, more desperate and unlikely to result in anything but failure. Still there was a chance of success. "Nothing risk, nothing get," Floyd said to herself. "He must remember me with some sort of interest. He can hardly have forgotten my face—ghastly as it was with terror, and covered with dust from that awful race. Those wretches must have told him everything, but he may not have believed them ; he may have credited my story and pitied me. He was so good afterward. It is natural to think kindly of one we have helped, more than of one who has helped us ; and, if I can rekindle his interest and keep it alive, something may come of it."

While such thoughts coursed through her brain, she heard the sound of horse's hoofs on the upper bank.

"It is he ; and, thank fate, alone," she said, looking up. Leading his horse by the bridle, Captain Witchell was descending the path to the flat. His head was bent in thought ; he did not see her until she made a step forward. He stopped ; a surprised look came into his face. Then he lifted his hat courteously, and was passing on, when she detained him by a gesture.

"Captain Witchell," she said, her hand held out, her eyes full of eager light. He bowed and took her hand, but his look was still puzzled and unrecognizing.

"You do not know me. You have forgotten me." Her voice had a pained thrill, and the light died in her eyes.

"I know you now. Remember, we only met once. I hope you have had no ill fortune since that night."

"When I was so sorely beset, and you saved me ? No ; my enemies have not found me out. They really thought me drowned. Thanks to you. I have not forgotten you. I have thought of you daily, hourly. But for you, I might now be in the cell of a mad-house, or in my grave, more likely ; for that man—my guardian—has no conscience."

A curious look passed over Captain Witchell's face. Floyd's quick eye caught the incredulous, half-sneering expression, and her hopes sank. The Texans had told him, then, she thought, and he believed their story and not hers.

"I did you a service at no cost to myself," he said ; "you owe me no thanks."

"Thanks are poor payment for what you did for me.

If I could only do something to prove my gratitude. If I were a man, I would give you my life-service; I would follow your fortunes, watch out for the dangers you despise, the enemies you are too busy to guard against. You need such a friend."

"Do you think so?"

"I know it. I know what you aim at. I know what your ambition would compass; and I know the difficulties, the dangers in the way. You have a strong will, and circumstances give you a power outside your own strength; but other circumstances are working against you—growing stronger every day. The people have been paralyzed, but they are recovering; opposition is waking up; hatred is growing active; the people are getting furious at seeing the negro used as a tool to keep them down, and at seeing all the money and privileges of the country going into the hands of men that are not of them—men like you. They hold themselves imposed upon, over-taxed, swindled; and they will not endure it long—not here, at least, in this section of the country, where law has never pressed hard, and restraints of any kind have been few. Already there have been secret meetings—"

"At which you were the chief spokesman?" Witchell asked, with quiet sarcasm. "Judging from the speech you have just made, you might have been the leading spirit—the exponent of the people's rights."

"No, I have no leaning that way. I am not patriotic. I believe that might makes right. I would do as you are doing, if I had the power. I would make the most of my opportunities—take all I could get—knowing that money brings power. I have spoken of the opposition against you because I don't think you feel it enough; you don't see the difficulties you must meet. You think you have everything in your own hands; your mind is full of your own schemes; you do not see what pitfalls are being dug in your path. You think too little of personal danger. For instance, you are going to travel alone to-day, and there is a party of men following you to do you harm."

"Harm! what! that handful of harum-scarum boys, who don't know what they want? I have no fear they will do anything—not the least. Is it only to tell about them you have stopped me?"

"No, there may be nothing to fear from them, as you say, but such demonstrations are forerunners of something more serious. They betoken the opposition that is gathering—that may cut short your career before you get the fortune and the power you aim at. You have need to be watchful, and to have devoted friends; and you stand alone."

"You mistake; I have friends."

"You have a few men whom you have yourself put in office and made all they are. They will look out for themselves, serve themselves, and you, perhaps, as long as they can make it pay well—no longer. Larger pay on the other side would make them desert and betray you. You need one about you devoted to your interests, heart and soul, capable of sympathizing in your plans, of encouraging, of inspiring them; of being watchful and argus-eyed in your behalf, looking out for possible small dangers and plots and treacheries, while you are busy with your schemes."

He looked at her with keen, curious inquiry. She was beautiful, with that heightened color, that lifted eye, standing under the old oak-tree with the shadows and sifted sunbeams quivering over her. The audacity of the venture she was making gave her an eager, vivid grace.

"It is hardly possible to find a man so devoted," he answered, at last.

"But a woman! Only a woman can be so unselfishly

devoted to a man, can so watch over his interests, enter into his plans, scent danger with woman's keen instinct, and help guard against it with woman's tact and finesse."

"Where will you find such a woman?" he asked, curiosity conquering his impatience to be gone.

"I could be such a one—to you!" she said, softly. Her voice faltered, blushes dyed her face, for womanly shame was not dead in her, and the hand she laid on his arm, the look she raised to him, was in deprecation as well as appeal.

He, too, reddened with embarrassment and surprise, perhaps with passing gratification, for the woman was beautiful, and her words and looks were full of intoxicating flattery.

"What can you mean?" he half stammered.

"That I am as ambitious as you are—that I too have a genius for ruling men and daring fortune by bold measures —only, unfortunately, I am a woman. I can act only through some man. I understand your aims; I appreciate your powers; I see the difficulties in your way; I would help you, if I might; I would devote myself to that purpose; I would be eye, and ear, and hand to you."

Her earnestness confused him. He tried to put her offer in the light of a jest.

"The days of page and squire are over," he said. "You don't mean to make me out a knight, and put on male clothes, and ride by my side as my armor-bearer?"

"That would be infinitely better than dragging out the days in woman's drudgery—sewing seams, teaching brats to spell," she said, bitterly. "No, I don't care for the male clothes. I would not need to lay aside my woman's dress and nature to be all I have said to you—devoted friend, helper—"; if *wife* was the word she tried to speak, it died on her lips. He was silent, and she went on hurriedly, dropping her eyes under his searching look.

"You don't know what I am, or anything of my past ; that matters little. It is unfair to judge any human being by their past. As to what I am, I will prove that. Try me."

"You make a strange request," he said, at last. "To be what you ask would require that you should be near me all the time, and I have no home for you. And, if I had, it would not look right for you to be there."

"Look right ? I thought you disregarded looks. I thought you defied these people."

"You thought wrongly. I want to conciliate them, and gain their confidence and esteem. I want them to feel that I am one of them—that I have their interests at heart, as I have."

"Very likely," she retorted, stung by his coldness. "All tyrants and extortionists have expressed the same exalted sentiments, from Napoleon down—"

"To myself. Quite a descending scale. So be it. If you have done, I will say good-by. That old darky yonder has smoked his pipe out, sitting in the flat waiting for me. I thank you for the interest you have expressed in my welfare, but I think I can manage to steer my own boat. If it goes to pieces, nobody will suffer but me. Stay ; here is something of yours I ought to restore. I picked this up on the river-bank, where you dropped it, I think, that evening. I forgot to speak of it in our hurried interview afterward. Indeed, I was not sure it was yours. I had not looked at it *then*."

If he had been in doubt as to whether the letter was hers, he could be so no longer. A sight of her face was enough. It turned ghastly in an instant. She stretched out her hand mechanically for the bit of crumpled paper ; her fingers closed convulsively over it.

"You said you had not read it *then!*" she gasped. "You did read it afterward ?"

"I did, but no one else saw it; no one else knows or shall know from me. Good morning!"

"One moment!" she cried, in a stifled voice. "Let me explain; let me—"

"No," was the cold answer, accompanied by an impatient wave of the hand. "No explanation from you is needed. I have lost too much time already." He tightened the reins he had been holding. "Come, Zep," he said to his horse, that had been chafing the bit and pawing the ground for the last five minutes.

The woman made a quick step toward him, a malignant, snaky gleam springing into her eyes.

"You prefer to believe the lies against me," she cried. "I understand now why you refused my friendship. But you shall repent this; I swear you shall. You think I have no power; you will find your mistake. You think I can not injure you; you will find that my hand shall stir up a storm that shall sweep you from this country or into your grave."

"So this is woman's gratitude," he ejaculated. Turning round with a coolly sardonic smile he walked away, leading his horse.

But a strange, uneasy feeling (prophetic, though he knew it not) shivered through him, as he caught the baleful look in her eyes—the look full of the rage and hate of a woman who finds that she is known at her worst; who feels she has humbled herself uselessly; that her game has been seen through and despised as more contemptible even than it was, for there might have been some real honesty in that offer of devoted service to Captain Witchell. The woman had a thirst for power and a passionate admiration for any who had won it. She had a restless desire to be or do something out of the commonplace, and she was shrewd and daring. Moreover, she had a grateful remembrance of what Captain Witchell had done for her. He might have found such a woman a valuable ally. He would have hesitated before he turned her into an enemy, had his been a nature to take cognizance of minor causes and influences. But, preoccupied with big schemes, he lost sight of smaller policies. He had but little hypocrisy in his nature, and but little softness or flexibility. Having heard her story from the Texans who had pursued her to the river's brink, and having had the story confirmed by that picked-up letter, and her looks at receiving it, he thought of this beautiful woman as a sort of human leopard. He shook her from him as such, and went on his way, thinking he had done with her for ever, foreseeing not that, with more of the wolf than the leopard's nature, she would track him with her revenge. It was not only because he had met her overtures with scorn that she hated him, but because he knew her secret—he alone. To all others, the woman Mabel Waters was dead. "He might not have believed what he heard, had he not seen the note," she thought. "Why did I not destroy it? Because it was poor Morris's last words, I must thrust it in my bosom instead of tearing it to pieces."

She crushed it in her hand as she spoke. Then she opened her fingers and looked down at the bit of soiled paper, with the blurred penciled lines upon it. Her mood changed, a shadow of remorseful agony swept over her face, and she sank down at the foot of the tree, and pressed her hand, still holding the crushed letter, over her face.

If Captain Witchell had seen her then, he might have softened to her in some degree, he might have felt some of that pity which had made him ready to help her that August day eight months ago, when, preparing to ford the shrunken river, he had heard the gallop of a horse behind him, and turning saw a woman, wild-eyed and dust-stained, urging toward him a horse covered with foam, and panting as if its sides would burst.

"I am pursued," she gasped ; "men are following me to take me, imprison me, kill me. They are close behind, and my horse can go no longer. Help me, hide me, for the love of God !"

He sent a hurried glance around. All about were broad fields, not a house, not a tree nearer than the swamp that stretched back of the fields—nearly a mile away. Yes, there, just across the river, were the woods—a belt of thick growth—and, farther back, the cabin of a negro.

"Your only chance is to cross the river," he said. "It is low—can be forded here, but the water is deep in places ; you must seek the shallowest. I will go first ; it may swim your horse, as she's not tall. Come—"

But, looking down at the panting, trembling mare, he saw this would not do.

"She can never carry you over," he said ; "she will not hold out."

"Then let me drown ; it will be better than to be taken. My God ! I hear them coming. They shall not take me. I will drown myself in the river."

Distractedly she tried to urge the horse down the bank.

"Stop !" he cried, springing to the ground. "You shall ride my horse. He knows the ford, and will take you over safely. Now go at once."

He had put her in the saddle while he was speaking.

"Off with you, Zep !" he cried to the horse. The tall, strong animal took the water with long strides, while the mare, stooping her head, drank as if famished with thirst. As Captain Witchell ran back up the bank, the sound of approaching horses reached his ear. Far down the lane leading up from the woods he saw four men coming at a slack gallop, as if their horses were badly blown. A glance across the river showed him the woman safely landed on the opposite bank, and making for the covert of the woods. In the same glance he saw, to his surprise, that the mare had followed her mistress, and was nearly half way across. Already the water was running over her back.

"She will have to swim, and the current will be too strong for her," he thought.

The next moment the men had caught sight of him. They rode up, and the foremost one cried :

"Have you seen a woman on horseback pass this way ?"

A thought seized him.

"Yes," he said, and waved his hand carelessly toward the river. All eyes turned in that direction. There was the mare struggling gallantly with the current.

"But there's nobody on her," cried the man.

"Nobody ? There was a woman just now."

"The current swept her off, and she's drowned, then. There's nothing to be seen of her."

The eyes of the group were strained for a breathless interval upon the river ; then the first speaker looked round on the others.

"She's drowned, boys, for a fact," he said. "There's an end of her ; and he loosed his feet from the stirrup and seated himself more at ease.

"No harm done," muttered another. "She's cheated a rope, that's all. It's a better end than she deserved."

"Why ?" asked Witchell.

"Why ? Because she's been the death of as good a man as ever a woman fooled—her own husband, too. Yes, Waters was a good fellow, paid his debts, lived honest, a splendid shot, and free-handed as could be—too free-handed for his own good ; it kept him poor. He wasn't as young as a wife might like, nor as neat-looking, maybe, but he just loved the ground that woman walked on. He took her up out of the dirt, married her when she was a slip of a girl, and sent her to school and made a lady of her.

"A rich fellow, Morris by name, from Louisiana here, had refugeed to our parts durin' the war, and Waters, who'd known him where he came from, give him house-room and pasture, and let him have provisions. When the fight was over, he kept a sayin' he war goin' back to his own farm on the Bayou Teche or his property in New Orleans, but he kept puttin' it off, and bimeby we found out why. He was waitin' to take Waters's wife with him, and they made up to put the husband out of the way. The overseer was hired to do the job. Morris got Waters to go out huntin' one day, and the overseer shot him, and he and Morris buried him. It was found out, and the overseer got away, and Morris dodged us for three days. We caught him at last, as he was sayin' good-by to his lady at night, not far from her house. He had hung around to see her agin, and it cost him his life. He danced a jig with no floor under his feet next mornin'. He made his will beforehand, and left her all he had. Then, when he was about to be hung, he begged leave to write a note and send it by a woman that was cryin' and takin' on over him. He was jes' the kind o' chap that women are soft upon. We told him to go ahead, and down he sat on a log with the rope round his neck, and writ the note and gave it to the woman, whisperin' something in her ear. We all thought afterward that it was Waters's wife he sent it to, and that he wrote her word to get away as fast as she could, as he had heard us swearin' vengeance on her; for when his job was done, and we went for her, she had gone—run off on Morris's fast little mare. We gave chase, and would er got her, ef that ther accident hadn't happened."

"It's well enough as it is," said another of the men, laying his leg comfortably over the saddle-bow, and refreshing himself with a chew of tobacco. "I'd hate mortally to slip a noose round a woman's neck, deservin' of it as she might be."

"How do you know that she deserved it? Are you sure she knew they were going to murder her husband?" asked Captain Witchell.

"Didn't she meet Morris in the woods after her husband was killed? There was evidence, too, in plenty to show she'd put 'em up to it, though Morris swore to the last she was innocent as the babe unborn, and took all the blame on himself. That counts for nothin'. He was so mad over her, he'd done anything to clear her skirts."

"Come, boys," said another, "the game's over; let's get down and cheer up, and rest our horses a spell before we turn back."

They got down; the horses began to crop the grass; the men drew out a "tickler" and "cheered up" all around, proffering the cheer to the stranger, who declined it, left them, and crossing the river in a "dug-out," at a point lower down, made his way to the cabin at the ford, being a little apprehensive about his horse and curious to know what had become of the woman. He found his horse quietly grazing in the little yard, and in the rear of the house, hid by a clump of young trees, he found the woman he had heard called Mabel Waters. She had been feeding the mare whose speed had saved her life, and was standing with an arm about the animal's neck, and her head drooped upon it. When she looked up, he saw her black eyes were swimming in tears.

"You are safe," he said. "They have gone back. They saw your horse swimming over without a rider, and thought you were drowned."

She brought her hands together convulsively; her eyes glistened.

"That is good! that is good!" she said, under her

3

breath, and began to thank him eagerly for his timely help. Seeing his grave face, she broke off with a sudden question:

"You saw them and spoke to them, they told you— what?"

He was silent.

"It does not matter. I do not care to hear what they told you. It was some lie, of course—a trumped-up story to excuse their pursuit of me. They were my guardian, his brother, and his sons. They want my money between them. They pretended I was mad; they locked me up and I made my escape. I will yet have my rights. In a little while I shall be of age. I will go back, and they shall suffer punishment for the wrong they have done me."

She spoke with such clear-toned, steady-eyed assurance that he almost believed her story.

An hour afterward, when he was pursuing his journey miles away, he chanced to put his hand in his pocket, and felt there a folded paper he had picked up from the river bank when he saw the Texans approaching. Opening it, he deciphered the agitated, scarcely-legible handwriting. It was the note Morris had written to Mabel Waters a few moments before he was hung. It implored her to fly the country at once, to ride his Mexican mare, and get out of the State. It expressed undying love, and bade her an impassioned farewell.

CHAPTER IV.

SUMMER was abroad over the land—a summer unusually rich in leaf, and flower, and fruit. Especially was this the case in the swamps and the rich, level lands lying along the river and bayous. Here vegetation ran riot. Corn stood in solid, dark-green phalanxes, the great ears pushing against each other, the thick stalks matted with convolvuli and coral-berry vines. Cotton, overtopping the tallest man, interlocked its heavy-bolled branches across rows; weeds sprang up thick and rank everywhere; trumpet-vines and poison-oak embowered every stump and tree, and grass and wild clover and parsley spread a matted carpet over the ground.

Yet the summer that was so kind to the plant world was no friend to man. The atmosphere, so stimulating to vegetable forces, held germs and exhalations noxious to human life. The season had been unusually sickly. Fevers had grown gradually more malignant as the summer advanced, until the deadly swamp fever made its appearance, chilling and burning its victims by turns, and tinging them a saffron deep as that of the helianthus, whose bloomy mass burned like a flame beside the bayous; swamp fever, near akin to, and often the prelude of that yellow scourge, so much dreaded along the Western watercourses.

This summer everything along the river was favorable to the propagation of the pestilence; the atmosphere, the human system, deteriorated by malaria, were ripe for it; only the seeds were wanting. But not long. In September, a boat, with a yellow-fever case on board, stopped at a near landing; the germs escaped, fastened themselves upon their human food, and propagated and spread with terrible rapidity. A number of the dwellers upon the river and the fertile swamp fell victims to the scourge, and then the planters and their families made a hurried exodus, refugeeing to the hills, carrying a portion of their household effects, and getting into outhouses, or stretching tents along the lakes, where the fish and game were abundant. Crops were left to the care of the negro laborers, who seemed to enjoy an immunity from the disease in its fatal form. Of the whites there remained on the river only a few old veterans, who considered themselves fever proof, and some enthusiastic young planters, too full of life and youth to fear death, and too eager for big harvests and heavy money returns to leave their farms at this critical time, when those indigenous rebels, weeds and grass, were fighting for the mastery over King Cotton.

There was sickness on the hills at the same time, but not of the malignant type that raged in the alluvial regions. It was severe enough, however, to occasion no little uneasiness. It broke up, for the time, the prosperous little school in the town of Malta, in which Adelle Holman was teacher. Very unexpectedly to herself and her friends had Miss Holman come into this position. The cherished daughter of the well-to-do Mossy Valley planter had no need to leave her parents and her pretty home to teach grammar and rhetoric in a country town. Adelle could hardly have analyzed the motives that induced her to accept the post urged her by the principal of the school, her warm admirer and her father's old friend. She knew that the unrest which had lately taken possession of her had something to do with this desire for change and for absorbing work, as had also an increasing repugnance to the marriage her parents seemed to expect and desire her to make; but the cause of this unrest, and of this dislike to a union she had not before actually opposed, she could not herself understand. She only knew that the old home pleasures had grown tame and wearisome—her garden, her dairy work, her walks and rides through the summer woods, her evening readings aloud to the household, or singing to her father the old-fashioned ballads he loved—all these, that had filled up her young life satisfyingly enough before, failed to do so now.

Lanier found her moods very puzzling, but her increased reserve, dreamy indifference, and sometimes haughty repellence, only served to fan his passion into more eager flame. His farm joined her father's, and his chestnut stallion prancing impatiently under the great oak in front of the Holman gate was an every-day sight. Adelle had grown to dread seeing that slim figure spring from the saddle and come hastily up the avenue, followed by two or three hounds, the swarthy face lighting up as he caught sight of her sitting at her sewing in the shaded piazza, or at the window behind her geraniums with her pet orioles chirping in the swinging cage over her head.

She always found some household task that called suddenly for her attention in time to break up the *tête-à-tête* she hated. But even in these self-imposed tasks he would insist upon helping her, following her about the garden, among the pea-rows and raspberry vines, or in the poultry-yard among the pigeons and bantams, with the assurance of an accepted suitor. His passionate love talk exasperated her sometimes. She could not respond to it, but neither dared she silence it, for she had a reproving consciousness that she had listened to and tacitly encouraged it in days gone by. To her parents everything seemed to go on smoothly. Age is seldom keenly observant. Colonel Holman thought this young man—the son of an old war comrade—quite well suited, in spite of a little wildness and a rather fierce temper, to be the husband of his beautiful daughter, with her fine, pure, yet passionate nature.

"When are you and Lanier going to make it up, Dell?" he would ask her sometimes. Her brother, in one of his last visits (he was farming to himself this year as an experiment) took her to task.

"Seems to me you are treating Lanier rather coolly, of late," said the young fellow. "I don't know much about such matters, but I'm sure I would like my betrothed to be a little more affectionate."

"I am not his betrothed. You know, Derrick, there never was any positive engagement between us."

"Wasn't there? Well, there was a promise pretty well understood, if not made in form; and I suppose you intend to marry him one day—don't you?"

"Never! That is, I think not. I do not believe I can."

"Dell, you don't mean to say you've been flirting with Lanier all this while? You can't deny you encouraged him."

"I am afraid I did—once. I really thought I liked him well enough to— But I know my feelings better now. I seem much older, somehow. Like all foolish girls, I found it pleasant to be made love to. I am very sorry. I don't know what to do about it."

"I am sorry, too. I hope you will get over this non-sense, and behave to Lanier as you ought to. He'll make you a devoted husband, but he's not a fellow to be fooled with, I can tell you—gay and light as he seems."

Adelle felt sure of that. Lanier had a careless, pleasant way about him, but she had more than once caught a flash of those small, keen black eyes that told her there was a lurking serpent under that surface-deep *bon hommie*. Exacting and fierce in his love, she was sure he would be jealous and revengeful, if he had grounds to be so. Hitherto he had had none. No other lover had been bold enough to contend against him for the favor of the Mossy Valley belle —this girl, whose shy smile and dreamful eyes told of hidden sweetnesses of heart and soul that had never yet been called out.

"Don't scold, Derrick," she said, putting her arm around his neck, and laying her cheek against his shoulder. "Remember you are going back to-morrow, old fellow. I do wish, though, you had never taken that river place.

You are looking thin and sallow already. Good crops won't make up for chills and fever, and nobody to nurse and coddle you as I always did. I know you miss me, but not as much as I miss you. I get quite cross and beside myself, sometimes."

"You need a change; why don't you pay that visit to Birdie Deal you promised her? I'll go through Malta and take you there to-morrow. I want an excuse to stop and see Birdie, anyhow."

"That would be nice. And they could spare me, now that Aunt Mitt is here to help with the housekeeping. Malta is always so pleasant in the spring, and so many new people have come in since I was there last summer."

Her cheek flushed a pretty pink as she spoke. Perhaps the presence in Malta of some one of these "new people" gave a special secret attraction to the place—an attraction she would not have dared to confess to herself, much less to that fond, but fierce, prejudiced young fellow at her side.

The visit so suddenly planned was really made. Adelle's father, looking at her keenly, declared she had been mopy and drooping of late, and bade her go and stay as long as she liked, so that she brought back the roses and bright eyes he missed, which was self-denying on his part, seeing that "daughter," as he loved to call her, was the delight of his heart.

When Lanier came next day he found the sitting-room window unadorned by the pretty figure in cool-tinted prints, whose little hand he had been wont to grasp so warmly as to make the red drop from her cheeks and a shiver run through her frame. He was very angry when he found she had gone, and, though Mamma Holman improvised a little message of farewell from the flown bird, he received it in sullen silence, and mounting his horse galloped away in high disgust.

CHAPTER V.

NOTWITHSTANDING good Mrs. Holman's consoling assurance to Lanier that Adelle would soon come home, the
weeks went by and she did not return. Instead, came a
letter to her parents, dutifully asking their consent to her
acceptance of a situation in the Malta Academy, and sug-
gesting so many reasons why the place would be pleasant
and advantageous for her that they plainly saw her heart
was set upon staying. The desired consent was accorded
in Squire Holman's precise old-fashioned hand, though he
could not help intimating his surprise that she should prefer the drudgery and confinement of a school-room to the
ease and liberty of her own home, the society of her parents,
and the proximity of a devoted lover.

It was almost as much to her own surprise as to her father's that Adelle had been led into accepting the situation.
The little lady who had filled it for two years was now about
to be promoted to the control of a widower's household, and
good Dr. Wheatley—the school principal—was at a loss
how to supply her place. He was deploring his dilemma
one evening at Mrs. Deal's tea-table, when Adelle, who sat
opposite, looked up from her strawberries and cream, and
half playfully proposed to take the vacated place herself—
a proposition which was quickly taken up, and resulted in
her receiving next day from the academy trustees a formal
offer of Miss Black's situation and salary.

Adelle felt that in some respects the place would be
good for her. The regular work was what she needed,
and, if she was hearing parsing lessons in the little academy
under the oak-trees, she would not be listening to Lanier's
half-whispered love speeches, or flushing uncomfortably
under his fixed gaze while she tried to sew.

She need never see him alone. When he came to Malta, she could easily persuade good-natured Birdie to make a third party in the parlor and in the walks which she would do her best to avoid. Placed under this restraint, the hot-tempered young man would not be apt to avail himself of Mr. Deal's hearty invitation to prolong his visits. Mr. Deal took quite a fancy to him. Lanier had the reputation of being a bitter and daring opponent of the new *régime*, and the old fire-eater, notwithstanding his hospitable disposition, cherished an undying prejudice against everybody that had worn the blue in the late conflict; and more particularly against those who, since the war, had been quartered upon portions of the conquered country, ostensibly to keep the peace. The presence in his town of some of these *ex-militaires*, now holding civil offices by appointment or through negro votes, was an eyesore to the hearty old rebel. Especially was this so in the case of Witchell, and the old gentleman would never believe otherwise than that the Radical judge's choosing to board next door was done as a personal aggravation to him.

Witchell, having sold his landed property on Lake Wisteneau, and bought a valuable plantation in the rich river region which he would come in possession of at the end of the year, was now busy maturing large plans for the future. His first aim was to have himself made a State Senator, representing three large and important parishes. This, in the existing condition of politics, where the people had little or no voice in choosing their officials, could be easily done. After this, foreseeing that the party he belonged to would not always have such smooth sailing as now, and that its sway in the State was destined to be interrupted and weakened by dissensions and discords among contending cliques, he determined to make himself independent of it by acquiring popularity forcing the people to respect his qualities as a leader, while he earned their good-will in more personal ways. He would further strengthen himself by gathering around him some strong and daring spirits, whom he would bind to him by ties of gratitude and interest. By this means, he aimed to make himself the head of a faction, wiser, wilier, and more politic than any of those which were now tacitly organizing through the State, so that, when the time came for a change in the chief State officers, he might be strong enough to seize the supreme prize—the chief Executor's chair, now filled by the adventurer Warmoth, the shrewd, daring, and unscrupulous.

Money, always such a mighty lever to success, Witchell knew was all important in attaining his ambitious ends. He had already made money, but he looked on this as merely the nucleus of the colossal fortune he saw opportunities to acquire in the future.

He had an eye to acquiring money, as well as to gaining influence with the people, when he determined on his change of location. The point on Red River which he had fixed upon as his home was full of promise. Not only was it in the midst of a rich cotton-growing section—a section, too, where the negroes, who worshiped him, were numerous, and in many instances well-to-do, but it was near the little riverside town of Cohatchie, now a mere handful of houses, but destined to play an important part in Witchell's programme. He meant Cohatchie to be the base of wide-reaching operations. He had decided it should be the county site of a new parish which he would create. The people in this section had long ago—even in the antebellum times—eagerly desired a division in the over-large parish of which they occupied an extreme end. They had never failed to instruct their representatives to obtain this for them, and had hitherto been disappointed so often, they despaired of ever obtaining their right. He would gain it for them, and earn their gratitude and good-will, while he laid the foundation of a fortune for himself in the prosperity that would attend the new county site. He would take this under his special charge, buying lots for a song, selling them at high figures to the people who would gather in to the young town, the public buildings of which he promised himself should be as elegant as the gratified new parishioners would bear being taxed to build.

Such schemes of self-aggrandizement floated through his brain, gathering the consistency and system of an organized plan.

Adelle could see him sometimes thus occupied with his ambitious thoughts from the window of her room, which commanded a view of his across the paling and the narrow strip of yard that intervened. His blinds were often open for the sake of cool air, and she could see him walking the floor with that firm, military stride, or seated at his reading-table, his head thrown back against the high chair, his eyes looking intently forward, as though at some vision of the To Be.

Sometimes he had company. There were two men especially whom he counted on to be of use to him, one from his daring and persistence, the other from his shrewd judgment and financial sharpness. One was Morton Carls, a former sugar-planter in Cuba, now a rabid office-seeker ; the other was Devene, who had early become a satellite of Witchell's, and owed to his influence his seat in the Legislature as representative of the parish in which they lived, the Democratic member having been ousted on the principle that might makes right. Devene had already been useful to his friend. The bill appropriating thirty thousand dollars for the cleaning out of Lake Wisteneau had been got through the Legislature by the new member. The cleaning out that was done was a sham, but the appropriation money which found its way into Witchell's pocket was a solid reality.

These two satellites were sometimes to be seen with Witchell in his room. Even with his friends, he did not condescend to familiarity; but, though he kept on the mask of reserve that prevented over-intimacy, and confided his plans to no one, he could be genial and companionable. Adelle had glimpses of the three sitting at the small table, across which the bottle and glasses were occasionally pushed about, not pausing before Witchell, however, for drinking was not one of his vices. He was temperate almost to austerity in his appetites.

Adelle saw little of him, beyond these glimpses caught through half-open blinds. Occasionally, she had met him, but he volunteered no sign of recognition; and she, confused by consciousness of obligation to him, which she had ungratefully received, felt her cheeks flame and her eyes involuntarily avert themselves when they met.

Only once had she spoken to him. She had gone to evening church service, escorted by a physician, who had been called off on a professional errand before service was over. In a whisper, he excused himself to her, and knowing that Miss Deal and her father were at church, she felt no uneasiness about the way in which she should get home.

When the benediction had been pronounced, and the people were streaming out of different doors, she stood waiting for her friends to come out with the rest. But she waited in vain. Not knowing she was alone, they had gone out at another door. The church was empty before she became convinced her friends were gone, and, hurrying out, she found everybody walking away at some little distance. She stood annoyed and perplexed, turning her head from right to left, in a fluttered way. Mr. Deal's house was at some distance from the church, and the social code of Malta made it a great breach of propriety for a woman to walk alone at night.

"Can I assist you?" asked a voice. A man's figure stepped out from the shadow of the church wall and stood before her. Too much confused to know in the dim light whether it was an acquaintance or a stranger, she answered that she was lost from her party, and disliked to go home alone. He seemed to hesitate after hearing her voice, but the next instant he proffered his escort, adding, "Perhaps we can overtake your friends before they reach home."

There seemed nothing for her to do but to accept his attendance, and she walked on by his side. They walked so rapidly as soon to overtake the hindmost groups, and the glare of a street lamp just before her showed Adelle the familiar figures of a gentleman and lady, who lived near her boarding-house.

"It is Mr. Medlock. I need not trouble you any longer, sir. Thanks for your kindness."

This is what she was *going to say*, as she turned to look in her escort's face.

But that face drove the words out of her mind and the blood into her cheeks. It was Captain Witchell. Instead of saying what she had intended, she stammered some incoherent words, and hurriedly withdrew her hand from his arm. His lip twitched; he smiled in a bitter way, as he had done that time she shrank from him in the boat.

"You did not know it was I; neither did I know who you were when I offered to accompany you. I think you have no longer any need of my escort; you have come up with your friends. Good evening!"

He turned off before she could speak. Her first impulse was to call him back. What a lack of common courtesy he must attribute to her! But then, what right had he to expect civility from her—he, her father's and her country's enemy?

Yet she was troubled; her voice was agitated when, joining her acquaintances, she explained that she had been left in church by her attendant and had failed to get with her friends.

"One dislikes to be rude and ungrateful, even to a carpet-bagger," she wrote to her friend Zoe, that night. "Does it not seem that Fate tries to throw Captain Witchell for ever in my path? Did I write you that I had found out it was he who kept papa's old hound Nero from being killed? He had followed papa up here when he came to see me, and had got left. He was disconsolate because of it, and howled about the streets so that the people thought he was mad and were going to kill him, when Captain Witchell interfered and took him with him, fed him and kept him until he could send him home by a negro. The negro would not tell who it was had cared for the dog, but I have since found out. Really, there must be some good in the man. The poor people around Lake Wistencau and about here say he is very kind to them—gives them corn and other provisions—'robbing with one hand to give with the other,' papa says, like Robin Hood and Rinaldo Rinaldini, only our freebooter is a licensed one, and, with his inflexible figure and sandy locks (they are *almost* red, Zoe), he looks more like a Highland chief than an Italian brigand. And he has the Scotch love of lucre, my dear."

This letter Zoe got from the Cohatchie post-office, as she and her brother's family were on their way to the hills —refugees from the yellow fever that had now broken out upon the river. Adelle was exceedingly anxious about her brother until she had a note from him, telling her that he was camped on Clear Lake with his gun and dogs and a half-dozen young fellows, and might have a fine time, if it did not hurt him so to think of his crop being left to the devastation of stock and negroes, just as the cotton was bursting open and the corn was getting ripe enough to gather.

She sent this note to her father, with a few lines from herself, saying that the school was suspended at the end of the week because of sickness, and they might look for her to come home in a little while.

One afternoon, a few days afterward, she was sitting in the shaded piazza, watching the clouds that piled themselves in the sky, and noting the hot, hushed stillness of the hour, when a negro rode up to the gate, got off his mule, and, coming up to the paling, said :

" Step here a minute, Miss Dell."

She recognized Jake—an old negro that had once belonged to her father, but, since "freedom came," had cast his fortunes on the river, and was staying on Mr. Vincent's place when she saw him last spring. The adventure of the flat and her rescue by Captain Witchell came vividly to mind as she walked up to the paling, and greeted the old negro with her usual friendliness.

" Do you come from the river ? " she asked.

" Yes, I do, missy, but I dassent let it be known. Dey halts me eberywhere, an' ax, 'Ain't you come from de yaller fever country ?' and I swars I ain't been nigh de riber in a year. Bound to do it, or git stopped, and I come on an arrant of mussy, myself. I come to git a doctor for de sick ; dem our way is done give out."

" Did you get one ? "

" No, missy. I went to two, and, when dey heard what I wanted, dey jumped up from de wind side o' me, an' say, 'Ef you don't git out'er dis, you raskil, I'll sit de dogs on you.' What's to be done ? Our doctor is jes' worn out wid ridin' and tendin', and de fever's on de increase."

"That is dreadful! And you black people are the only ones to nurse the sick?"

"Yes, missy; but de black folks gittin' scurt deirselves now, scnce Big Sam tuck de fever un died, atter waitin' on Captain Levin; and now you kin hardly git um to nuss de sick or to bury de dead."

"God help the poor sufferers! Why did they not leave the river before it was so bad? I am glad my brother got away in time."

"When you done hear las' from your brudder, Miss Dell?" the old negro asked, eyeing her in a peculiar way.

"Only four or five days ago I had a letter from him. He is camped on Lake Clear, enjoying the hunting and fishing, only he says he can't help being anxious about his fine crop on the river, and wanting to run down and see about it."

"He did run down."

"Is it possible he has been so imprudent? I hope he did not stay an hour. When did he go back."

"He ain't gone back, missy."

"What! Is he there yet? My God! Uncle Jake, please do ride back as fast as you can, and tell him, for my sake, to come away this moment. Ride fast, Uncle Jake."

She put her hand over the paling, and laid it on the old negro's arm in entreaty. He took it in his wrinkled fingers, and looked at her pityingly.

"De Lord help you, Miss Dell," he said, sadly, "he can't git away, chile. It hurts me to tell you sich bad news, but—he's got de fever; tuck it yesterday, bad."

She turned ghastly in a second; she grasped the fence with trembling hands.

"Don't faint, missy; don't take it to heart so. He's in de Lord's hands."

"No," she said, hastily, "I won't faint, Jake, for I

must go to my brother now—this moment. I will go with you."

"Better not, Miss Dell. You'd jest take the fever yourself, and break yer pa's heart. I thought you might use your 'suasion to git a doctor for him up here and a nurse. Me and Brudder May will 'tend him as bes' we kin, but we'se boff ole, and it takes mighty strong hands to wait on de yeller fever. You couldn't do much good, Miss Dell; and 'tain't 'spected of you to go. When young George Glaston was tuck, dey sent up for his ma and his sister what was gone to dere hill place, and der 'lations wouldn't let 'em come, nohow. Miss Annette's sweetheart, he come down hisself, poor fellow, and nuss'd George like a brudder, and now he's down, and no hope for him. Dey sent George's body up to be buried in the fam'ly graveyard, on de hills, and a party o' men rode outer de woods jes' t'other side de riber swamp, and drawed up in de road fifty yards ahead o' de wagon dat had de corpse in it, and hollowed to de black folks dat was gwine 'long wid it, to stop right dare, and dig a hole an' bury de body in it, or else git shot like dogs; kase dey shouldn't take a yaller fever corpse troo de country, and dey shouldn't go troo it deyselves. Dat'll show you how dreadful folks tink de yaller fever is."

"Dreadful!" echoed the girl, absently. "I must go to him at once. I won't tell them here where I am going, for fear of being hindered. I will let them suppose I have been sent for to go home. They will lend me a horse. While it is being saddled, Jake, you go to Dr. Pritchard, tell him I sent you, and beg him to go to my brother. Come back immediately. Don't tell any one where I am going."

She was ready to mount the waiting horse when Jake rode back, having failed in his mission. Dr. Pritchard said he was sorry, but he dared not venture on the river, where the disease was so virulent. He had a family to whom his life was important. Besides, he would lose all his practice here, if it was known he had visited a yellow-fever patient.

They set out by themselves, riding leisurely until out of sight of the town, for Adelle was fearful of being delayed by arguments against the step she was taking, if her friends found it out. Once away from the town, they increased their speed to a gallop. As they rode, Adelle said : " I trust they will not hear of this misfortune at home. Father and mother would come, and it would probably be their death. Uncle Jake, did you charge Dr. Pritchard not to tell any one that Derrick had the fever ? "

" Yes, missy, I told him you was afeard his ma would hear it, and she was sickly like."

"And have you told no one else ? "

"Not a soul—yes, I'm tellin' a lie—I told Captain Witchell. I met him jes' dis side o' town, goin' toward de riber. He 'trected me to de doctor."

It was a long, weary ride. It seemed to Dell that they would never reach their journey's end—never leave the pines and oaks of the " Hills" behind. It was near sunset when they entered the river-swamp. Adelle felt the difference in the atmosphere the moment that, after crossing a small bayou, she rode under the great ash-, and gum-, and cypress-trees, hung with huge, festooning vines, with a carpet of grass underneath.

The shadow and stillness of death seemed to brood under those great trees and knotted vines. Not a bird sang—the rustle of a snake among the grass—the stealthy flap of an owl's wing, as the bird, wakened from his drowse on a limb overhead, flew away, skimming his level flight among the huge tree-trunks—these were the only sounds that broke the gloomy silence.

It was strangely still, too, out in the broad fields and

cleared pasture-lands which they soon came upon. These were green with riotous growth, but they bore a look of neglect and desertion. The cotton bolls were bursting open, here and there, and thickly in patches, with none to pick them ; the fodder hung brown and ungathered upon the corn-stalks. Labor had become paralyzed in the presence of death. The negroes did nothing but wander from one plantation to another—in some instances nursing the sick with attentive kindness, but usually hanging about the plague-smitten houses, fascinated, after the manner of their kind, with the horror of death and suffering, and pleased with the chance to gossip and idle, and the opportunity to steal ; at one moment holding vociferous song- and prayer-meetings, and shedding tears over the delirous patient ; the next, slipping out to rob his hen-roost, his pig-pen, or his smoke-house. Such is the contradictory nature of this people.

As Adelle and her gray-haired but active and garrulous companion wound their way down to the river, old Jake pointed to a fresh mound not far from a river sand-bar, and said :

"Dere's where de steamboat Belle Bowling stop las' Sunday night, and buried a young 'oman what died on board wid de fever. Dey buried her 'bout midnight. Tony Watts seed de lights, an' comed down. He sed dey took her out mighty easy, fer fear of waken' de passengers. Dey never does let 'em know dare's any fever on board, 'fraid o' der leavin de boat."

The shrunken, muddy river flowed sluggishly between its steep banks ; the poisonous night-fog was beginning already to rise from it, and from the half dried-up sloughs filled with rank grass, tall blossoming weeds and croaking frogs.

In answer to Jake's prolonged "Eh-o-o-o," a thick-lipped, stupid-looking negro brought over a flat. As he stepped out of it upon the sand, Adelle asked :

"How is my brother—how is Mr. Holman ?"

"I hearn a while ago he was d-e-a-d," drawled the negro, pulling at the chain of the flat in a leisurely way.

"Dead !"

"Well, no'm. 'Twant him ; I dunno how he is. 'Twar Major Copley, down de river. He's had to gib up de game at las', Jake."

"He has ?" returned Jake, and explained that when "de fever comed, de major shut hisself and his man Dank up stairs in de ole house, wid a bar'l o' whisky, and swore he'd stay and tough it out. Yallow Jack 'd never come his way. Whisky 'd kill him dead'n a cottonwood stump, if he did. Well, Yallow Jack struck him las' Monday, war'nt it, Bill ? and de fus' ting he done, when the lirum tuck him, was to jump up outer de bed and stave in the whisky-bar'l. Den he paddled and splosh about in de licker over de floor, and holler out he's in de lake o' fire and brim-stone."

"He's dere now, sure enuff," Bill said, shaking his stupid head wisely. "Died a cussin', and a hollerin' out de debil had 'im !"

This cheerful conversation, added to her suspense and distress, set every nerve in Adelle's body to quivering so that she could hardly keep her seat in the saddle when they had remounted on the other side of the river, and were riding the quarter of a mile that lay between the crossing and the house where her brother lived. The road ran near the bank, with the stream on one side and the fields (unfenced) upon the other. But now, both field and river were hid by the ranks of tall weeds that grew on either side, crowding close to the narrow road, in which nothing but the constant trampling of horses ridden by negroes had kept them down.

At last they were at the gate of the old weather-beaten, moss-grown house in which Derrick had set up his bachelor's hall. An enormous pecan-tree shaded it at one end, fennel and coffee-weeds grew up to the door-step, the gate swung open on its broken hinges, and hogs and little negroes were feasting on the fallen peaches in the grass of the orchard. A couple of negro women were despoiling the garden of the few cabbages that dared to show their heads among the weeds.

With that cowardly dread that assails us when suspense is about to be exchanged for certainty, Adelle shrank from asking the negroes how her brother was. She would rather solve the dreadful doubt with her own eyes.

She jumped from her horse so hurriedly that her foot received a wrench which made her fall to her knees with keen pain. In a moment she had mastered it, and rising to her feet she turned to enter the gate. But a man's tall form barred the way, and Captain Witchell's voice said calmly :

"Miss Holman, you must not go in."

She looked at him in haughty surprise.

"Do not dare forbid me," she said. "My brother is ill ; I must be with him. Let me pass, sir."

"Not till you have listened to a word of reason. Your brother has the fever, but it is not necessarily fatal. With good nursing he may recover."

"I have come to be his nurse."

"You have no idea of the sort of nursing a person with yellow fever requires. Calmness and physical strength are needed. You are not fitted for the task. Then you are more than likely to take the fever yourself. The fatigue and anxiety you are suffering this moment predispose you to take it at once. Then we would have two patients instead of one. If your brother should recognize you, anxiety on your account would make him worse. The least thing tells against the patient in this disease."

"Captain Witchell, I came here to see my brother, to be with him while he is ill; do you think I can stand here and know he is suffering yonder, and yet keep away from him, through consideration for my own safety?"

"Your parents deserve also to be considered. What would they suffer, knowing that you both are in danger? But, if you could do your brother any good—"

"You have said that good nursing may save him."

"It may, and he shall have it. I will myself be his nurse."

"You? You will do what his sister must not? You will expose yourself to danger when she draws back—you, a stranger, an—"

"Enemy, you would say, but I have no enmity for him, nor any of these people. In the end it will be proved. But let that pass. I shall not risk much by attending on your brother. I have been several times in the midst of yellow fever; I have experience in nursing it; it requires constant watchfulness to see that the patient does not uncover himself in his delirious tossings. The bed-covering must be held down by force. Much depends upon this."

"Is my brother delirious? Oh, how he must suffer! Captain Witchell, stand aside, I will see my brother, if I die for it."

"No, Miss Holman, I will not let you see him. The doors of that house are locked; the keys are in my pocket. I will not permit you to enter."

His determined look made her falter. That look on a man's face—the look of knowing what he is about, and being resolved to hold to it—usually masters a woman, and turns opposition into trust. But she tried to stand firm against it.

"What do you mean, sir? What right have you to oppose me?"

"The right of common sense, Miss Holman. I have told you I shall nurse your brother, and that he shall want for nothing. I have sent a messenger to N—— for a physician. I know him, and he will come for me. The negroes will help nurse your brother. They are frightened, but they will obey me."

"But I can not go back and leave my brother this way, not knowing what his fate may be; indeed, I can not. Let me at least stay near here; and promise that you will let me know if he is worse."

Witchell thought a moment.

"You can not, indeed, go back to-night. It is already nearly dark. But where can you stay? I think there is not a white woman left in this part of the country. Both those houses yonder are deserted and shut up; in that one there, the corpse of a young man has lain since yesterday.

He pointed, as he spoke, to different plantation houses which could be seen along the windings of the river across the level country.

"What can I do?"

"You must not stay out any longer. It is dangerous, now that the sun has set. There are nothing here but the negro cabins, but there is one of these you might stay in to-night, at least. It is only occupied by an old negro woman. She is eccentric, and the negroes shun her, and call her a witch; so that they will not intrude upon you. One of her hobbies is to be always washing and scrubbing, and you will find everything about her perfectly clean. You will be better there than anywhere I can think of now. Let me take you there at once. It is advisable that you get in out of the evening air; and I must go back to your brother."

She hesitated, and stood half bewildered. It was all so strange. This country, so gloomy and waste-looking in spite of its wealth of green ; that old weather-beaten house, lying among the weeds like a stranded wreck ; death all around ; death in the air, and her only brother lying yonder, delirious of the fatal fever, nursed by a man he hated, and this same man getting the mastery over her, making her look up to him, and trust to him to plan for her safety.

It all seemed strange. She put her hand to her brow in confused thought. As it fell again to her side Captain Witchell took it quietly, drew it within his arm, and, without a word, guided her steps away from the house toward the row of cabins that faced the river farther up. One of these was isolated from the others, and stood back under a tall cottonwood-tree. Before the door of this cabin several fires were blazing and crackling, sending up bright sparks through the dusk. Distinct in the glare stood the tall, withered figure of an old negro woman, who was heaping on the fires the brush and cypress knees she had brought up from the swamp. She wore a big-flowered cotton dress, faded and fantastically bepatched, but clean ; a strip of red shawl was tied about her head, under which shone her small, keen face and sharp little eyes. Captain Witchell pointed to the figure standing among the smoke and glare.

"If you should ask me, with Banquo, 'Who is this—so withered, and so wild in her attire ?' I would make answer, It is Aunt Margaret—the reputed conjuress—who is herself desperately afraid of being 'conjured.' She is a queer character, a little crazed at times, but perfectly harmless ; and there is usually a method in her madness. Those fires, for instance ; she has kindled them every evening since the fever made its appearance. I can't tell where she got the idea, but it is a good one. The heat kills the floating germs of the disease, which are especially active and plentiful in the still air of evening."

She took no notice of their approach, but, passing from one little fire-heap to another, pushed up the crackling brush and muttered her satisfaction as the tongues of flame leaped up, and the sparks flew out. Captain Witchell touched her on the shoulder, upon which she turned and courtesied in a stately way. But, on his explaining Adelle's situation, and his wish that she should find shelter for the night in her house, she shook her head, declaring : "Can't let nobody stay in my house. I might be blind, or stiff-dead in de mornin' ; too many tryin' to put bad eye on ole Margaret."

Fear of being "conjured" haunted this old creature continually, and it was not until after much persuasion from Captain Witchell, aided by the silver piece he pressed in her hand, and supplemented at last by a stern declaration of authority, that she was induced to promise Adelle a shelter in her house, and kindness and attention at her hands.

"She will keep her word faithfully when she has once given it," Captain Witchell said. "I have occasion to know she is stanch and honest, in spite of her crotchets. She will make you as comfortable as she can. And now go in ; I must get back to my patient. I will send you word to-night how he is."

He was gone, and she had said no word in acknowledgment of his kindness. Why was he doing this ? What was his motive for the generous deed he was performing ? Was it "policy" ? Was this merely a step toward gaining popularity with that better class of citizens who were so opposed to him ? Of course, nothing really disinterested and noble could be the moving principle of such a man, and yet—

"What time did Captain Witchell come down here ?" she asked old Margaret.

4

"I see him crossin' de ribber 'bout three hours by sun. Heard he had cum down to see Majer Kopley on business and found out he's dead, and dat dis one up here" —pointing to the house where Derrick lay—"was like to die, and his nusses scared and runned away—ole Jake fust one, do' he brags so on hisself, and make out he's sich a brave Christian. Jake's a 'sateful old hypocrick, but he's not much worse'n de balance. Bound he'll not go nigh dat sick young man, less Witchell makes him. *He* can make 'em all do anything he wants to."

"How?" Adelle asked, seeing that the old negro's face put on a look of mystery.

"Ah! dat's it. He's got de power." She pointed down, as if to signify that the "power" came from below.

Adelle obeyed Captain Witchell's injunction to go in doors. Seated in a rude poplar chair, that had been scoured to immaculate whiteness, she watched old Margaret flitting, witch-like, around her pots and ovens, lifting a "spider" lid to show the corn loaves turning a rich brown, and peering into an oven from which escaped a savory steam. A negro came to the cabin door, set down a wooden tray full of things, and with the words, "Cap'n Witchell sent 'em," vanished.

"Might 'er had manners to come in and set it on de table," grumbled the old woman, inspecting the contents of the various vessels that filled the tray. "Flour; where de lard to make it up wid, I wonder? Oh, here it is. Sugar; mighty scase of it; spec dat triflin' nigger been stuffin' hisself wid it on de way. Coffee; drefful little, shrively grains. What dat in de tin cup? A-h-h-h!"

The sniff she took of the contents of the cup had the effect of suddenly putting her in a good humor; and, after sweetening the "dram" to her taste and drinking it eagerly down, she was ready to fly around with an alacrity that

surprised Adelle. The odor of parching coffee soon diffused itself through the room, a little square table was
drawn out and spread with a clean, coarse cloth, a gayly
flowered plate, cup and saucer, were deposited upon it, and
then the covered oven disclosed its savory mystery—a rabbit baked crisp, but juicy—the brown dodgers were turned
out, and these, with a saucer of golden honey, the steaming
coffee, and a small, red-hearted watermelon, constituted the
supper to which Aunt Margaret invited her guest to sit
down. She herself took a seat by the hearth, pretending
to poke the fire, while she covertly watched Adelle with
satisfaction as she drank the coffee and ate a slice of the
bread and honey.

When the supper was over, Adelle drew her chair close
to the door for the sake of air, and old Margaret, having
replenished her fires outside, sat down on the door step and
puffed away at her pipe. The night was clouded, the moon
shone feebly ; through the stillness came sounds of people
talking, as they passed along the river-side road in front.

"It's niggers goin' to Little Dan's buryin'," old Margaret said. "Goin' to bury him to-night under de pecan-
tree in his cotton fiel', what he used to love to sit under an'
oversee his hands. Dey'll see. His sperrit gwine ter haunt
dat fiel' 'til judgment day, and dey dassent pass troo it at
night, or hunt another possum in it agin. Ought to buried
him in de fam'ly graveyard on de hills, only he told 'em he
didn't want to go dere—too lonesome in dat piney woods
for Dan. Dan born on de ribber, and he love de red dirt.
He tole 'em he didn't want to lie out o' hearin' of de steamboat's whistle. Poor Dan ! De black people grieved after
him mightily. Dey nussed him well too—nobody but dem."

"Had he no relations ? "

"Sisters, but livin' further down de river, and got sickness and death wid dem too. And Dan was always one to

himself, never had no wife, no sweetheart, nor went off
nowhere ; jes' stayed up yonder in dat old house, where
most all his folks died. He's lyin' up dere now—what of
him hasn't gone below."

" Gone below ? Why do you say such a thing ? "

" Cause it's so. He died awful. Dey all die so—hollerin'
and jumpin' out 'er bed, and sayin' de imps is after 'em."

" Because they are delirious, or crazed with pain. It
is the nature of the disease."

She shook her head incredulously. To her mind, and
the minds of her race, all who do not die happy, " go below."

" Him up yonder is hollerin' now ; I heard him," she
said presently, with a gesture of her head toward Derrick's
house.

Adelle started up in terror and self-reproach. Derrick
might be dying as Little Dan died, with no friend or rela-
tive near him.

" I will go to him," she cried.

As she reached the door, she came face to face with the
negro who had brought the tray. He put a slip of paper
in her hand and disappeared. She hurried to the light,
and read :

" Your brother is no worse. I have hopes, but the fever
must run its course. The crisis will not be reached before
to-morrow. You shall know when there is any change."

She sat down again, and strove to quiet herself. An
hour went by ; old Margaret nodded in the chimney corner ;
Adelle had thrown herself across the bed, over whose white
sheet had been spread a clean, faded quilt. She lay, looking about the little room with bright, sleepless eyes, and
listening. Presently, she thought she heard a cry. She
rose softly, undid the door-latch, and went out. The night
had grown gloomier ; thick fog lay upon the river ; Marga-

ret's fires had burned low. Looking toward the dwelling-
house, she saw the dull gleam of the sick-lamp in the upper
front room. So it was there her brother was lying. As
she looked, and strained her ears to catch some sound, the
light at the window was intercepted by a man's form. She
knew that tall, spare figure, that attitude, the arms folded,
the head slightly bent. He was standing, looking out at
the night. Presently, he turned quickly as if at a call
from within. He had gone to her brother's bedside—he
had promised to watch him faithfully; he would fulfill his
word; she had perfect trust in this. And he had said there
was hope; she clung to his words, even while she wondered
at herself for feeling such confidence in the man she despised.

Again she heard the sound that had first startled her.
It did not come from her brother's room. It was farther
off. Looking, she saw, across a bend in the river, torches
moving slowly, as in a procession; notes of wild singing
came to her ears. The negroes were burying " Little Dan "
(so called because his father, who was dead, had borne the
same Christian name); they were burying him in the middle of the cotton field, under the pecan-tree, where he had
loved to sit on the cool grass with his dog beside him, and
exchange friendly words with the hands as they passed up
and down the long rows wielding their hoes, or dragging
their cotton-picking sacks. They were burying him there
with none of his kin or color to see the rude ceremony, and
that wild, mournful strain was the sound of the hymns
they were singing as they bore him to his grave.

Heart-sick, Adelle went back to the cabin. Old Margaret was awake and had resumed her pipe.

" You'll catch your death out dere," she said, placidly;
" Yellow Jack likes de whitest skins de best. They'se
buryin Little Dan; I hearn 'em singin'. It's better'n dey

did by poor Tom Wallace back here in de swamp. Dey had got skeered ; and didn't like him much nohow. Most dey'd do was to dig a grave in one corner de yard, and knock up a cypress coffin, and slide it onto de gallery. His young wife and her father—him wid de fever on him, too— had to do de rest—to git de body in de coffin somehow, and den roll and push de coffin till dey roll it into de grave, and cover it theirselves."

Shuddering at the gloomy picture, Adelle lay down and buried her face in the pillow. Sleep came to her at last— the deep, sweet sleep that comes to the relief of over-wearied body and over-burdened brain. When she awoke, it was broad daylight. A breakfast of eggs and biscuits, fried chicken and fragrant coffee was smoking on the little table near her, and old Margaret stood by her bed.

She started up in dread. "My brother ! " she cried, looking wildly at Margaret. The old negress smiled grimly, and handed her another leaf of the little pocket note-book. She read on it :

" Nothing that can be called a change. The disease is approaching a crisis. Dr. Mercer is here. Have courage."

CHAPTER VI.

THE long September day seemed interminable. The hours dragged on—hot, still, suffocating. In the brooding hush, Derrick's cries more than once reached his sister's ears, as she sat on a bench under the cottonwood-tree, with her eyes fixed upon the windows of that front room in which her brother lay.

As the day drew to a close the heat became more oppressive, the aspect of the sky more threatening. Each afternoon, for several days past, the sky had darkened, and emitted lightnings, but now the clouds rolled up in larger and darker masses, shaded and streaked with lurid bronze. About the hour of sunset the earth and sky were suddenly bathed in a wierd, blood-like glow, that contrasted startlingly with the darkness of the clouds, shutting down, like a black lid, upon the horizon.

Adelle had walked down along the river bank till she came to a point in front of Derrick's house, that stood back some distance from the river—a black-looking hulk, stranded in a sea of weeds. She stood there on the brink of the steep bank and watched the ghastly glow reflected far along in the waters of the river. She watched it in awe. It seemed ominous of evil, and the vulture, circling slowly under the black sky in the midst of the bloody radiance, seemed to scent approaching death, and to luxuriate in the scent with a slow, languorous joy.

As she stood impressed with the wildness of the scene, suddenly she heard her own name called aloud in tones that pierced shrilly through the unearthly stillness. She listened; the cry came again; it was Derrick's voice—he was calling upon her in his agony. She could bear it no longer. She ran straight to the house. She found the gate fastened with a chain, and, while she was trying to undo it, Captain Witchell came out to her.

"Why will you persist in this?" he said, sternly. "It is useless; I can not let you come in."

"I will," she cried. "You dare not turn me away. My brother calls me. He is dying."

"He is not. There is hope for him, but everything depends on the next two hours. We are striving to keep him calm; the least excitement increases the restlessness and fever. The sight of your face, which it is possible he would recognize, might ruin all at this delicate crisis. All that can be done for him is being done. Will you still persist in being unreasonable ?"

"No; I will go back and wait. Forgive me; this anxiety is hard to bear."

She turned away, but looked back to say : "In two hours—will you then let me know ?"

He nodded his head in silence, and went quickly back into the house, fastening the door after him.

Before the two hours had fully passed there were confusion and terror in the little row of cabins along the river. The threatened elemental disturbance came in the shape of a storm of wind and lightning. The wind came in strong gusts, that swept roaring through the far forests, and bowed the young ash and cottonwoods on the opposite bank of the river to the very earth. The rotten old cabins rocked like cradles in the blast, and the frightened negroes rushed out of them and huddled together, shrieking, in the open, treeless space between the houses and the river. It was so dark that hardly the shadowy outlines of their figures could be seen, save when a flash of lightning lit up the group with momentary distinctness. The last gleam showed a strange sight—a lovely white face in the midst of all those dusky ones—streaming hair, wild, dark eyes, and a little figure swaying in the wind, as she clung fast to old Margaret to keep from being swept away. She did not see the light that was coming toward them from the house—a lantern borne by a man, who, battling with the wind, could scarcely keep his feet as he struggled to approach them. At last he reached the group, huddled and clinging together in front of their shaking huts. The light falling on him revealed the face of Witchell. A flash showed him Adelle. She stretched out her hands in involuntary appeal; he went to her, gathered around her the shawl she was trying hard to hold, and supported her with his arm.

"Are you all safe?" he cried, as a lull came in the wind. "I think there is only one of those houses that will go; the third one, there. Is every one out of it?"

"Yes, Cap'n," responded several voices. Then a woman shrieked:

"Where's ole Granny Betty? She was in dere, in bed, by de door. She couldn't git out."

"And she's in there yet? Good heavens! she must be got out at once. Quick, boys! The house will not stand another blast."

But no one moved. The danger seemed too great.

"Then I'll go myself—here," he thrust the lantern into the hand of a negro, and rushed into the cabin. At the same moment was heard the sound of the wind returning to the charge, shrieking as it tore through the woods on the opposite side of the river. It came; it struck the group cowering from it in the darkness; it hurled its fierce strength against the tottering cabins; there was a sound of timbers giving way, then a crash of boards and heavy logs.

"He is killed!" shrieked Adelle, but that instant a flash of lightning showed her Witchell coming toward her, carrying the old paralytic he had snatched from the falling house. He set her down near Adelle; there was silence for an instant, then the group sent up a shout of "Hurrah for Cap'n Witchell;" and the voice of the old negress could be heard in the lull of the storm, mumbling blessings on her preserver. The light of the lantern streamed over her withered form; the rain blew on her shriveled face and gray hair; her trembling hands were held out as if to ward it off. Adelle snatched off her shawl, and wrapped it around the pitiable figure. Captain Witchell moved forward, as if to prevent her, but he stopped short, and the next moment Adelle felt him throw something over her own shoulders draw it up about her head, and fasten it around her. It was his coat; he had tied it in front by the sleeves. She was about to speak in deprecation, when another burst of wind took away her breath. Instinctively, she clung to him, and with his arm around her he sustained her against the wind, that now came mixed with rain. The instant it had subsided, he removed his arm.

"This blast was less severe than the last one," he said. "The worst is over. You can all go back into your houses without fear. Take this poor old woman in, and send to me for some brandy for her. Come, Miss Holman, let me help you to shelter at once. The rain will fall in torrents, now that the wind has lulled."

"My brother, Captain Witchell, how is he?"

"I have good news for you. He is better; the crisis is past. He is sleeping in spite of the storm."

Clinging to his arm, she reached the cabin from which she had fled in such fright a short time before. Old Margaret followed, and knelt down by the hearth, bemoaning her scattered pots and extinguished fire. Captain Witchell laughed encouragingly.

"Let me see if I can not soon remedy it," he said, taking some matches from his pocket, and kneeling down by the hearth. In a few moments he had kindled a blaze, and, collecting the scattered brands and piling on more wood from a box in the chimney-corner, he soon had the little room lighted and warmed.

"Now, Aunt Margaret, you can make Miss Holman a hot cup of coffee at once; and see that she gets thoroughly dry. I hope she will rest in peace to-night, since her brother is out of danger."

"Out of danger? Are you sure?"

"Yes. Unless he has a relapse, which good nursing will prevent. He had been sleeping an hour when I left.

Dr. Mercer says when he wakes he will be in his right mind. You can go home, and feel little uneasiness. I will leave him with good nurses.

"Leave him? Are you going away?"

"Early in the morning. I shall not see him again, if it is as well with him as I believe it is. Dr. Mercer will stay all day with him, and, as I have said, he has two experienced nurses besides. He will not need me. May I trouble you now for my coat?"

"Oh! I had forgotten! And how chilled you must be!" Coloring deeply, she undid the knotted sleeves with agitated fingers. He drew the coat on, and buttoned it around his square-shouldered figure.

"I shall not probably see you to-morrow," he said, "as our roads lie in different directions, but you will receive an account of your brother. Jake will attend you home."

He ran his fingers through his rain-wet hair and turned toward the door. He was going, and she had not yet said a word in acknowledgment of his kindness. She rose to her feet and faltered:

"Captain Witchell, how can we ever repay you for what you have done?"

He looked down at her, a smiling light in his blue eyes.

"What I have done is only the duty one human being owes another. If you wish, you can repay it by not believing *all* the evil you hear of me. Even the devil is not as black as he is painted. And there is one more favor I wish to ask. Do not tell your brother that I was with him in his illness. He was delirious, and did not know me. The negroes will not betray me, nor will Dr. Mercer. Will you, too, keep silent?"

"Why should he not know?"

"He does not like me—hates me, as you are aware. He

will misjudge my motives; and he may think himself
bound in gratitude to me. I want nothing of the kind.
I have done only what humanity prompted, but he and his
friends may put a different construction on my actions. I
ask you, as a favor, not to speak to your brother or to any
one of my being with him when he had the fever."

"Since you ask it, I promise not to do so ; but—"

"That is well. I know I can trust you. Good night!"

He was going away without any other farewell, but
Adelle stepped closer to him and held out her hand.

She did not say a word, but her eyes, that were lifted to
his, swam in tears, and her lips trembled, and seemed to
struggle to speak. He took her hand, bowed over it respectfully, and left her.

When he was gone, she turned her back upon the peering eyes of old Margaret, dropped her face in her hands,
and cried heartily.

Little wonder she was unnerved. The reaction from
the terrible suspense of the last thirty hours, the recent
fright and exposure, were sufficient to account for her tears,
yet they had their source in part in other feelings—a half
painful, half pleasurable agitation connected with the man
who had just said "good night" as calmly as if he had not
felt that it was good-by for ever.

A special, unlooked-for circumstance had brought them
into brief association ; it was not probable that any event
would again happen that would justify a disregard of the
wide barriers that divided them. The two barks had been
tossed together for a moment by a storm, and it had been
forgotten that they bore unfriendly flags ; but it was only
for a moment.

Their brief intercourse had been outside the territory of
society—outside the world of reality, it almost seemed to
Adelle—in some dim region bordering upon dreams.

She thought with shame, and yet with a half guilty thrill of joy, of how his arm had held her in the storm.

Yet, *if* they should meet again when back in the world, he would not feel it permissible to recognize her, and would she dare by look or word accord him permission?

As she sat with her face in her hands, a touch fell upon her arm, and she turned around to see old Margaret holding out a cup of coffee, and eying her with mingled cunning and benevolence.

"I don't want it, thank you," Adelle said, motioning the coffee away.

"The Cap'n said you must drink it. It'll set you up after the scare and chill you've had. It'll brace you 'ginst de fever."

She took the cup and drained it of the clear, strong contents.

"Dere! I thought you'd do it," the old negress said, the mixture of kindness and malice deepening in her face. "You'll do what *he* says. What'd I tell you? He makes people do like he wants. Dat's his *power*. He puts his spell on 'em. He's put it on you. Dat's why you cry. You don't know it; but 'tis. You feel like somethin's happened to you."

"What nonsense! I cry because I feel unnerved and tired out, and because I am glad of Derrick's safety."

"And for somethin' else, too. No need denyin' it. Cap'n Witchell's put his spell on you, and you can't take it off. You'll follow him troo good and bad."

"You are crazy. Captain Witchell is nothing to me. I shall never see or at least never speak to him again. My people are no friends to him."

"Don't matter," retorted the old negress, sagely, nodding her head. "It's like I tell you. You'll fix your eyes and your heart on him, and he's got his'n fixed yonder

ahead on chists of greenbacks and silver, and crowns of
gold, and he'll push on after 'em and forgit to look round
at de one walkin' at his side."

"You old goose!" Adelle said, trying to laugh off the
uncanny feeling that came over her as she watched old
Margaret peer into the fire with her small, keen eyes,
while her skinny finger pointed forward as if at some sight
she alone could see. "There are no crowns of gold to be
won in this country."

"Grant, de big president-gineral wears a goldin crown;
I seen it one night; Witchell's pushing on after one; gwine
to get it too, onless," sinking her voice to a mysterious
mutter, "onless his foot slips up in blood. Yes; in blood.
I saw him one night swimmin' in blood—a river of blood,
and he strugglin' and throwin' out his arms, till of a sudden
dey both dropped off, and he went driftin'—driftin' down
de current."

"Your dreams are wonderful, truly."

"'Taint dreams. I see things—plain as I see you. Do
you want to know how I saw *you* last night?"

She craned her long neck so as to bring her wierd face
close to the girl's.

"No," cried Adelle, drawing back. "I think there is
no import in your dreams; but I do not care to hear them.
I am tired out. The wind has died down, but how the
rain falls! I will try to sleep."

CHAPTER VII.

THE time of terror was over; the scepter of the scourge
was broken. The white angel of the frost had descended,
and the air was purified of its poison. The refugees came

back ; life went on in the homes from which the dead had
been carried—in the fields and places that would know them
no more.   The yellow-fever time was looked back upon as
a dreadful nightmare—a period of confused horror, too
painful for thought to dwell upon.

Before the coming of the frost, Derrick had gone to
Mossy Valley to recruit his strength in the pure air and
through the nursing and petting he would be sure to get
from his mother and sister.

He had lost color and flesh, but he bade fair to get them
back, for his appetite was such as to delight his mother and
astonish the old cook.   They had never heard at home
that he was ill, until the news came in a scrawl in his own
handwriting, the first time he had been permitted to sit up
in bed.   He had made light of his sickness then, to prevent
anxiety at home.   As soon as he was able to travel in a
slow, easy way, the carriage had been sent for him with
enough pillows and blankets to smother a dozen young
fellows of his size, and with his father, armed with camphor
and brandy bottles, to take care of him.

Adelle's visit to the river had never transpired.   Neither
her parents nor her brother knew anything of it.   Jake had
kept silent, and the great package of delicacies he had carried back from Malta to the sick man had been a mysterious
gift, so far as Derrick's knowledge extended.   She had gone
back to Malta after leaving the river, and her friends there
supposed she had paid a short visit to her parents, and wondered somewhat, when, only the next day, the Holman
family carriage came to convey her home.

When, upon the first evening of Derrick's arrival at
home, as he sat in the big chintz-cushioned invalid's chair,
sipping his wine negus, he detailed to his attentive listeners
all he could remember of his illness, Adelle discovered
that the doctor and the negroes had kept Witchell's secret.

Derrick knew nothing of his having been attended, during the most critical period of the fever, by the man whom he hated.

Several times afterward, the revelation, coupled with reproof, came near bursting from her lips. It was when she had heard her brother join his father and Lanier in denouncing Witchell as a heartless, unscrupulous scoundrel—an adventurer, who cared for nothing so that he mounted to wealth and station over the prostrate rights of the people.

Such denunciations of the Radical leader were more than usually frequent and severe at present, for Witchell's name was before the people as candidate for the office of State Senator, with almost certainty of election, taking in account his power with his own party and his popularity with the negroes and "poor whites," together with the opportunities for controlling elections possessed by the "Carpet-bag Ring," who managed the registration of voters, the balloting at the polls, and the counting of the returns.

The bitter feeling against the "Ring" had increased among the more aristocratic of the people. There was a class who, with an eye to favor or protection, openly courted the ruling powers, and were ostracized from their own set in consequence; and yet another class, who truckled to them, but in a sneaking way—obsequious to officiousness when they could be so on the sly, but joining with the enemies of the "carpet-baggers" in abuse of them behind their backs.

It was a stirring time with Witchell, this eve of his election and of his removal to his new home, around which he purposed should gather so many lucrative interests, so many important industries—the building up of a town, the conducting of a paper that should absorb the public printing of that section, the erection of a factory, the establishment around him of his relations and connections from the North, who should hold various offices, obtained through his influence, and who should repay him by working for his interests and playing into his hand.

He carried these schemes, and other plans to which these were only preliminary, in his busy brain, as he went to and from the new plantation he would settle upon in a few months, and as he rode over the country, strengthening his interests here and there, organizing Loyal Leagues, popularizing himself with the laboring class, who, having had fewer interests sacrificed by the recent change in affairs (they had called the Southern rebellion a rich man's war and a poor man's fight), were far less bitter against the new *régime.* He kept meanwhile a keen lookout for openings to make money—speculations that promised well, estates forfeited for taxes, that he might buy up cheaply and settle his allies upon ; fine landed properties that might fall into his hands by a mortgage ; or else their owners' influence might be secured in his favor by indulgence granted them. There were plenty such embarrassed estate-owners throughout a country that was groaning under heavy taxes and under the difficulty of controlling negro labor.

Occupied with these plans and cares, it was not to be expected that the Radical leader had given many thoughts to the girl he had parted with in the old cabin that stormy night, not quite two months ago. Adelle had seen him but seldom since her return to Malta, and she had met him face to face but once ; then he had ridden on without turning his eyes in her direction, or seeming aware of her presence.

She was vexed with herself at the pang of disappointment that went to her heart, and at the consolation she drew from the after-thought that the reason he did not speak might have been the fear of putting her in an unpleasant position. There were others with her, and, if he had given her a recognizing bow, and she had acknowledged the attention, her friends would have been shocked at finding her acquainted with him, and annoyed her with questions. He must have noted the haughty, averted face of the tall woman walking with her—dressed in mourning still for the boy-lover who had been killed nine years ago in one of the last struggles of the Southern Confederacy; and he could have overheard the sneering remark of the gay girl who walked ahead, trailing behind her the coral-berry vine she held:

"Yonder comes the R. R. R." (Radical Rogue and Ringleader) she exclaimed, "mounted on a horse that is by far the better-looking animal of the two ; " and the response of her companion :

"Wonder where he stole it?" as she tossed up her little nose.

When such remarks as these were made in her presence, Adelle always felt a quick fear lest somebody would notice the effect they produced on her. She could not keep the flash from her eyes, nor the wounded blood from mounting into her cheeks. Yet she had never owned to herself that she loved this man. The most she had confessed to her heart was that she felt a pity for him in his isolated, ostracized position, and that she admired his courage and persistence in facing dangers and difficulties, and keeping calmly in pursuit of his purpose.

Yet the hope of seeing him had been, half-unconsciously to herself, the motive of her return to Malta. In her secluded home at Mossy Valley, in her twilight dreams in the old honeysuckle arbor, and her solitary walks through the Indian-summer woods, she had thought of him continually. She had woven around his image the passion and romance of her fervid nature. The abuse she heard of him on every hand could not impair this secret worship. It only deepened the pity that was a strong element of her love.

The necessity of concealment was another circumstance that wrought through her imagination upon her heart. Their short, unsuspected association—what a charm secrecy gave to it !—what a wild, sweet spell it cast over her recollection of those days upon the river ! She dared not speak his name aloud ; she breathed it the oftener to her own heart.

She had kept all the little notes he had written her on the river—those brief bulletins of her brother's condition, penciled on torn-out leaves of Witchell's pocket note-book. She had received one more soon after her return home. A negro, belonging in the neighborhood, had ridden up one afternoon and handed her an envelope, on which she instantly recognized Captain Witchell's peculiar handwriting. The negro had refused to give the missive into any other hands than hers, a circumstance which excited the jealous suspicion of Lanier. He was present, and watched her covertly as she received the letter, and saw that she blushed deeply and turned away to hide her emotion as she read it. It contained only these few lines :

" I have just shaken hands with Dr. M——. He reports our patient out of danger, and fast getting well. As a negro from your neighborhood is here, I take occasion to send you the Doctor's good report."

Lanier insisted on knowing who had written the letter, and grew angry because she refused to tell him, declaring his determination to find out. He was sullen for days afterward, but presently Derrick came home, and the cloud seemed to pass away.

The intercourse of the tacitly engaged pair was much pleasanter when Derrick was with them than when they were by themselves. His presence checked the angry doubts, the passionate declarations, and above all the searching questions that poor Adelle could not answer as her lover

desired. As soon as frost came, and Derrick returned to
the river, she went with him as far as Malta, where her
school had already reopened.

Once more in her little room upstairs, she turned her
eyes first of all to that apartment in the next house which
could be seen from her west window. But the blinds were
closed. Captain Witchell came now but seldom to Malta.
He was often absent in different parts of the country, and
he spent days at his place on the Lake, which he had sold,
but would not give up until the end of the year.

CHAPTER VIII.

It was a festive evening at Malta. The town-hall was
wreathed in evergreens, its central chandelier ablaze, and a
stage erected at one end. The hall was crowded with the
citizens and neighborhood people, who had come to witness
a school exhibition, postponed since last summer, and to
enjoy afterward a supper furnished by the Academy patrons,
and an hour or two of social intercourse ; or, as the printed
programme expressed it, "a varied entertainment, by the
young ladies and gentlemen of the Academy, comprising
recitations, dialogues, charades, speeches, tableaux, and a
POLITICAL SATIRE, written by one of our cleverest lawyers,
all interspersed with instrumental and vocal music. Afterward, an elegant banquet, prepared by our fair townswomen,
and a social reunion."

Adelle had helped to conduct the rehearsals of the pieces
comprising the stage entertainment, and she trusted that
Witchell might not be here to listen to them. Several of
the original recitations and dialogues contained references
to the wrongs of the people and the outrages of carpet-

baggers, while the satire was a rather clumsily written but scathing lampoon upon Witchell and Devene—their names slightly disguised, but the allusions too pointed to be mistaken. Witchell, styled the Prince of Appropriationists, was held up to public hate as a creature without a conscience—a political vampire, fattened by the blood of the people.

When Adelle had heard this rehearsed in the summer, it had grated on her feelings; how much more did it do so now, when her heart had gone out to the man it lampooned, and every word spoken against him hurt her like a blow!

" Thank Heaven, he is not here," she said to herself as she looked out over the audience from an aperture in one of the little apartments curtained off at each end of the stage as dressing-rooms. But on looking once more, in the middle of the performance of the lampoon, she saw him. He occupied a position at the very back of the hall, standing—for there was scarcity of seats—with his back against the wall, his straight figure and leonine head calmly erect, as though he were not the target of the sneering looks and hisses of the more reckless among the audience, excited by the piece that was being acted.

His steely blue eyes beat back the stare of the people with cold, proud patience; his set mouth, his folded arms, his whole attitude, spoke eloquently, not of vulgar defiance or self-assertion, but of a purpose that might not be shaken, and of calm, half-sad endurance.

Adelle, whose nature was given to idealizing, and whose solitary, brooding fancy had surrounded the man with such a glamour that she saw only his virtues—Adelle, looking at him as he stood there listening to the abuse from the stage, and feeling the many unfriendly eyes turned upon him, thought of a picture she had seen of Christ standing calm and thorn-crowned among the mocking multitude.

While this passion of indignant pity was upon her, it came her time to sing. She went out, and, controlling herself by an effort, gave the opera selection named upon the programme, and, being encored, touched the keys of the piano, and sang that old tender melody of the Irish bard, "The Stricken Deer." Never was more fervor given to the impassioned words,

> " I know not, I ask not, if guilt's in that heart,
> I but know that I love thee, whatever thou art."

She trembled and blushed at her own earnestness—at the passionate impulse that had carried her away. She felt almost as if she had addressed the words to Captain Witchell himself. She dared not send one glance at him to see the effect of her song. In the midst of the applause she arose and quitted the stage.

Witchell had been on the point of going as she came out to sing her first song. Devene, who had a seat in the window close to where he stood, had touched his arm, saying:

" Come, we have had enough of this, don't you think ? I've stood it 'till I'm boiling over, while you look as cool as Diogenes in his tub. Let's go."

" Stop," Witchell whispered, for Adelle Holman had taken her seat at the piano, her sweet face pale except for the pink flush slowly spreading in her cheeks.

Her beautiful arms and shoulders shone like polished ivory through the transparent white material of her dress. He had a sudden, vivid sense of having encircled that fair form with his arms, of having wrapped it in his coat for protection from the storm, of her having clung to him like a child in her terror.

When she began to sing again in answer to the encore, and to interpret the poet's words in such impassioned strains, he listened absorbed, and his cold face thawed.

Devene, leaning toward him, whispered:

"She sings that song *con amore ;* I'll be hanged if she don't. The little girl has likely got a sweetheart that's not in the church—a naughty fellow that she's fond of, and her pa objects to."

Witchell frowned, and when Devene said, "That's about the last, I believe. Will you go now ?" he answered, "Not yet. Don't wait for me." And Devene went away, wondering what had come over his chief, that he should take the whim to stay to the "reunion," after he had expressly declared he would not ; that he only went to hear the "satire" and its strictures upon himself.

"I want to show my good friends that I can listen to their compliments without blushing," he had said, laughing in his quietly cynical way.

<hr>

CHAPTER IX.

ADELLE thought Captain Witchell had gone away after the performance. She saw nothing of him in the crowd, nor of Lanier and Derrick, who had promised to be there. But she did not lack admirers in her *fiancé's* absence. She had just left the refreshment room, and returning to the hall had missed her fan, and her attendant had gone back to hunt for it, when she caught sight of Captain Witchell not far from her.

He was sitting in the recess of a window, apart from the stream of promenaders and groups of talkers. He had a little girl on his knee whom he had lured to him with the present of an orange. He had peeled the fruit and was breaking it apart, listening to her prattle with evident amusement, when a larger girl—a sister of the other, from the likeness between the two—came looking here and there for the little one, and spying her called to her sharply.

The child slid from Captain Witchell's knee and joined her sister, who, snatching her hand, said crossly :

"Ain't you ashamed of yourself, talking to *that man?* That's Captain Witchell. Ma will give it to you for sitting in his lap."

He overheard the remark. Adelle saw his moustached lip twitch ; then he raised his head with that slight, bitter-sad smile she had seen twice before. His eyes met her own, and the color rushed to his face. He knew that she, too, had overheard the words so smarting from a child's lips. Obeying a sudden impulse, she walked straight to him, and held out her hand. It had not occurred to her what she should say to him, and she uttered confusedly :

"Captain Witchell, I hardly expected to see you here. You look lonely. Why are you not amusing yourself ? "

"I have been entertained," he answered.

· He had looked surprised that she should speak to him ; but he took her hand, and the slight pressure he gave it showed that he appreciated her notice.

"How must I amuse myself ? "

"Oh, by going to supper or promenading, I suppose."

She was only intent on saying something, that the attention might soothe the wound his feelings had received.

"The supper I don't want, and the promenading—who would be my partner ? Even the babies are punished for smiling on me, you see."

"Will I do for a partner ? "

"You ? Are you sure *you* would not be punished ? Look at those horrified eyes turning toward you already."

"Let them. Captain Witchell, will you promenade with me ? "

He looked at her for a second without answering; then he said:

"It was for *your* sake I hesitated. Nothing could give me more pleasure," and he drew her little hand, trembling through its glove, within his arm.

But it was too trying—that ordeal. To walk around the lighted room, the cynosure of all those amazed and scornfully disapproving eyes. She felt faint and sick under them.

"Let us go out on the piazza," she murmured.

But there, too, were promenaders. She glanced outside at the graveled walk a step below. The moonlight flung the shadows of the cedars across it; the air was soft as in May.

"Shall we go outside?"

Her look answered him; he took the light shawl that hung on her arm, and folded it around her. The next moment, the moon was tracing their shadows together on the white sandy space. They walked up and down without interchanging a word. Then Captain Witchell said:

"The last time I saw you, the scene was quite different from this. Margaret's old cabin—you in my wet coat in the big poplar chair, I on my knees before you, kindling the fire for your coffee. Have you ever thought about the queer picture?"

"I have thought of it often, thought of everything that happened then. But that was not the last time I saw you. I met you once here in town—and you did not speak."

"But you knew the reason why I did not? You knew I feared to subject you to ill-natured remarks on my account, as, alas! I am doing to-night. Besides, I thought, if I spoke, that you would not speak to me in return.

"You thought that? You thought that, after all you

5

have done for me, I would refuse to speak to you because
others who were present would blame me ? Never. If all
the world should turn against you and speak evil of you,
I will believe in you, honor you, be your friend."

The girl was utterly unconscious of the fervor with
which she spoke, but her looks and tones were a revelation
to Captain Witchell. He stopped still, and looked down
at her eyes lifted to his, at her hand she had laid on his
in her earnestness. He read her secret then ; he knew that
this little, pure-minded, country-reared girl loved him, the
world-stained man, with a fervor that consumed the barriers of prejudice and pride. He knew that the passion in
the song she had sung to-night was for him.

Did the knowledge give him more pain or pleasure ?
It was hard to tell. Pleasure came first—the throb of joy
that the consciousness of being loved always brings. It
was followed by something like a pang at the thought of
such love being lavished—wasted, it seemed—upon him—
upon one who could give no fit return. She had cherished
his image all this while, and he, with his mind busy with
schemes of personal advancement, had thought of her only
casually, as one remembers the scent or sight of a flower
he has seen as he hurried along the dusty highway.

He had no fresh feelings to match with hers. Once,
years ago, he had held a fair woman to his breast, and
thought nothing could come between them. But time and
absence brought change and estrangement. She grew tired
of waiting for the ambitious boy to accomplish what he had
planned. She married a wealthier suitor. In the hour
that he heard of it, a change came over him. He hardened
his heart against women's attractions ; he paid no court to
them ; his life was filled with other things, with the hopes
and efforts, the disappointments and successes of a man
who struggles up from obscurity and poverty. And now,

just as he was nerved and stripped for the goal that seemed at last in his sight, the flower he had ceased to hope or care for was flung in his path. Should he take it up? Was there room in his heart to shelter it? Had he time to caress it? Would it be right for the flower's sake? Should he ask this girl to turn her back upon her parents and relatives—upon all her friends for him? Would she? Yes; her face spoke for her, but should he accept the sacrifice? Should he break up the sweet peace of her life, bring into it dissension, separation from all dear ties and old associations? No; he determined no. He would do nothing to encourage this impulse of affection. But her sympathy was balm to him. Looking with grave kindliness into her face, he raised to his lips the hand she had impulsively laid upon his.

"I thank you," he said. "I accept your friendship as frankly as you have offered it. I shall never forget your brave kindness to-night—you shall see—"

His words were cut short by the sound of excited steps behind. Two men were hurriedly approaching.

"Scoundrel!" cried Derrick Holman's voice, as he rushed upon them. "Cursed Radical dog, how dare you touch my sister; how dare you speak to her?"

Grasping his sister's shoulder, he dashed her aside, and faced Witchell, his teeth set, his eyes blazing. His clinched hand was upraised to strike, but Adelle flung herself between him and Witchell. She caught the descending arm, she clutched it, and held it with all the strength of both her hands.

"He did not speak to me first," she said; "I spoke to him. I asked him to walk with me. He has done nothing."

"You asked him to write you letters, too, did you? and send them by his negro allies? Let go my arm, Adelle; you have disgraced yourself and me enough. Let me go, or I will strike you down."

"Do so. Make a scene here, and draw a crowd around us. Break up this peaceful assembly with a disgraceful scuffle. Proceed, you and Lanier, in your fisticuff exhibition. You will soon draw all these negroes into the entertainment, and get taken to the lock-up. Yonder are a dozen ladies looking on from the gallery. Have you no regard for their presence; none for me, or yourself, or for common decency?"

Her stinging words had the desired effect. Derrick's face lost a portion of its fierce determination. He wrenched his arm loose from her at last, and roughly pushed her away. To Lanier he said:

"Stand back. I told you not to interfere unless I called you. It was my place to thrash this scoundrel for his impudence. A horsewhip, if I had it, would do the business, but I don't care to mix myself with his nigger friends in a scuffle, and with women looking on. I'll have it out with him in another way. Witchell, you are not worth fighting a fair fight with, but, as my sister has given you her society, I may as well extend the family condescension. I challenge you to fight with me to-morrow, at what hour and with such weapons as you may choose."

"I will not fight you, Mr. Holman."

"You are a coward, then."

"I am no coward, but I will not risk my life in a foolish encounter. And, besides, I honor your sister, and I will not injure her by trying to kill her brother or to make him a murderer."

"You refuse, then, to fight with me?"

"I do."

"It's a d—— cowardly subterfuge," burst in Lanier, whom Derrick had, with difficulty, restrained; "you can have no such excuse in my case. I am not the brother of this young lady, that you have such high consideration for. You shall fight me, or I'll tear your Yankee heart out."

Exasperated by the cool, contemptuous eye that Witchell turned upon him, he sprang at the officer like a cat, aiming to seize his throat. Throwing himself back to avoid the shock, Captain Witchell caught his assailant's arm in his powerful grasp, and, seizing his shoulder with the other hand, hurled him to the ground, where he lay stunned and senseless.

Several men, who from their stand on the piazza had had their attention drawn to what seemed a dispute bidding fair to come to blows, now rushed toward the group, and the negroes hanging around the building came running up excitedly, one of the foremost flourishing a pistol and crying out, " Here, Captain ! here ! "

"Put it up instantly !" called Witchell. "Go back and keep quiet, all of you."

He turned and strode from the spot, till reaching his horse, that was fastened not far off, he mounted and rode leisurely away.

Lanier was only stunned. He raised himself on his elbow, glared around, and then leaped to his feet.

"Where is he ? I'll follow him. I'll have his life for this. Let me go," he cried to Derrick, who had hold of him. But others closed around him, and he was restrained until his anger had partly vented itself in curses, and he was cool enough to listen to Derrick's advice not to make a fool of himself ; that to follow Witchell was useless ; he would be sure to have his adherents, white and black, close at his heels ; "and you'd have the pleasure of looking at life behind a jail-window, my boy. No doubt, I'll have a black mark of remembrance set down against me for this. One can't resent a personal affront from one of these fellows, without being punished for it as a political offense. I am sorry I was so hasty, for my sister's sake," he went on, going up to her and drawing her trembling arm through his. "I don't blame her. Witchell forced himself upon her, I am sure. He happened to render her an important service not long ago, and now he presumes upon her gratitude and her womanish dislike to hurt feelings. Adelle, shall we go back into the hall, or would you not like better to be taken home? Your nerves are shaken, you are trembling, poor little girl! Come, let's go home. Lanier, wait here for me. I want to see you again to-night."

Adelle knew by the look in her brother's eye that this affectionate address and this exoneration of her from blame were all for a blind. They were to keep down gossip; for, unlike his reckless comrade Lanier, he had regard for appearances, and he smarted under the thought of his sister's name being spoken in any connection lowering to the family pride. This feeling made him hate Witchell still more, and he reproached Adelle savagely as they walked to her boarding-house.

"You shall stay here no longer; I will take you home to-morrow," he said.

"I have done nothing wrong. I will not go," Adelle answered, pride restraining her tears.

"You have ruined yourself. This town will be a-buzz with your name in connection with Witchell's. Haven't you sense enough to see what a humiliation that is?"

"I don't feel it so."

"No; and you don't feel what a blow it will be to my father, do you? How disgraced he will feel to find that you have been receiving letters from Witchell (Lanier found it out), and walking publicly with him—a man known to have insulted your father, and done a thousand dishonorable things besides. My poor father!"

That strain touched Adelle instantly. She could not bear to think of her father looking at her in anger.

"I will go with Derrick to-morrow," she said to herself; "I will be the first to tell my father; I will tell him everything, and he will know that Captain Witchell is not the heartless being he thinks him now."

CHAPTER X.

But, when Adelle reached home the next day, the story had already been told. Lanier's horse stood before the gate. No one came out to meet her except Nero, the old dog that Captain Witchell had protected. The servant she met in the hall looked at her in a shy, troubled way as she said:

"They're all in your ma's room, Miss Dell."

She found her mother in tears; Lanier leaning against the chimney-piece, a dark scowl upon his face, her father walking the floor, his heavy tread and his hands clasped behind his back betokening unusual discomposure.

She went to him and embraced him, but he did not return the caress. He put her back from him, and looked at her sternly.

"You have been forgetting whose daughter you are. You have forgotten that your mother is a gentlewoman and your father an honest white man. You have been consorting with an insulter and robber of your people. Girl, I did not look for such a mortification to come from you."

He turned from her, but she clung to him.

"Listen to me, father, listen to me, mother," she said, and she repeated the story of her rescue from the flat. She told what she had overheard Derrick say of Captain Witchell's interference to prevent the negroes, at the insti-

gation of the bully Yent, from falling upon the handful of
rioters, among them Derrick and Lanier, who had come to
break up the meeting of the Loyal League. She told even
of Witchell's kindness to old Nero, and she hinted at a yet
greater service he had done for Derrick, for them all, which
she was not yet permitted to speak of. When they knew
this, they would feel that Captain Witchell's magnanimity
was not mere impulse. Did they not know of his kindness
to poor people, and why should all those good acts be ignored
and the man branded so mercilessly? Then she told of the
unsparing lampoon directed against him, which he had
listened to at the exhibition, and of the child's words that
had hurt him so.

As she talked with one arm around her father's neck,
and her face close to his, his expression changed, his look
grew softer.

"Tut, child," he said, "don't talk to me of Witchell's
magnanimity. Cold-blooded policy, every bit of it. He
wants to make himself as strong as he can. Every dime he
spends on the poor is a seed planted, from which he expects
a harvest of good for himself. But I see you have not been
so much to blame as I thought. It was only that soft, pitiful little heart that was in the wrong. You were grateful
to him, and sorry for him. It was weakness; I looked for
more firmness and consistency from you. But you will be
more guarded in future; you have now done enough, and
more than enough, to satisfy your idea of gratitude. You
will not allow him to speak to you again, I am sure."

It was half an assertion, half a question, and his eyes
looked searchingly into his daughter's. But she said low,
yet with firmness:

"Father, I shall never refuse to speak to Captain Witchell. I shall always esteem him; I shall always be his
friend."

"Say at once that you love him, that you are engaged to him," cried out the sharp voice of Lanier, who had been listening to Adelle from his stand by the fireplace, watching her with a yellow, cat-like gleam in his black eyes. "Why do you not say that?"

"Because it is not true. Captain Witchell has never uttered a word of love to me."

"Never written one, I suppose?" Lanier said, leaving his post and coming close to her.

"Never."

"Will you tell your father and brother what were the contents of that letter Witchell sent you through one of his negro emissaries?"

"A letter! What does that mean, Adelle? Is it possible Witchell has written to you?"

"A few lines only, father. It was only to tell me about Derrick's recovery."

"What had he to do with that? And why did you hide what he had written to you?"

"I will tell you hereafter. I must see him first, and ask him—"

"See him! By the God above me, you shall never see him again. Listen to me. If I ever hear of your communicating in any way with that scoundrel, I'll fling you out from my house, as if you were a snake that had crawled into it. I will disown you forever; and your mother there shall never speak to you again. Do you hear that?"

She bowed her head, but did not speak. "If you have done, I will go to my room," she said, after a silence, broken only by a sob from tender-hearted Mrs. Holman, who could not bear to hear her darling scolded, though feeling that Adelle had really done a dreadful thing.

"Go; but remember that what I have said I will abide by."

The next day and the next were days of gloom. Adelle, although her own heart was sore, tried to bring some brightness into the house ; but in vain. Coldness and melancholy met her efforts to please. Her father hardly noticed her ; her mother sighed, looked at her reproachfully, and, when she spoke to her, used an aggrieved tone. Derrick avoided her. He had not returned to his river farm, but he was seldom in the house. His mother said plaintively that she was afraid Derrick was about to get on one of his sprees again. Trouble and fret were apt to make him drink. He was nearly all his time at Lanier's now; and Lanier, poor fellow, was drinking, no doubt. He had enough to drive him to it.

Adelle had not spoken to Lanier since the evening of her return home. Whenever she caught sight of him, galloping up the avenue with Derrick, she shut herself in her room. The erratic movements and disordered appearance of both gave color to her mother's fears that they were "on a spree." Lanier always kept the best liquors in the old-fashioned sideboard at his bachelor home, but it was rarely that he drank to excess.

There seemed to be some unusual pressure upon the two men. On the third morning after her return she saw them riding up with two other young men, as reckless-looking as themselves. They dismounted, came in, and followed Derrick to his room. Presently she heard successive reports of a pistol. They were firing off a charge out of the window.

Half an hour afterward she sat in her room—a pretty little apartment down stairs, open to the orchard and garden. She was sitting by the window, her book dropped in her lap, her thoughts far away, her arm lying on the window-sill, with the hand dropped listlessly outside. Suddenly she felt some one grasp her hand ; she turned quickly. Startled, she saw Lanier's dusky face and bloodshot eyes close to her. He stood on the ground outside, his chest on a level with the frame of the low window.

"Where is the ring you once wore upon this hand—our engagement ring?" he asked hoarsely.

"It was not an engagement ring; I never considered it one;" she said, trying to withdraw her hand.

"It was—and you know it. What have you done with it?"

"It is in my box; I will get it for you, if you will loose my hand."

He loosed his grasp, and she got up and brought the ring. As she dropped it on his palm he asked:

"Will you let me put it on your finger?"

"Not if it means engagement; I am not engaged to you."

"You lied to me, then."

"I did not. I never promised to marry you. I tried to love you for my parents' sake. Once I thought I did love you; I knew better afterward, and tried in every way to let you see my feelings. I ought to have told you plainly."

"You knew better, I suppose, when you fell so madly in love with some one else. That cursed Witchell is at the bottom of this. You have broken faith with a gentleman —the son of your father's best friend—to fling yourself at the head of a Yankee poltroon."

"Richard Lanier, I will not listen to your insults. Go away; I will close the window."

He dashed the ring to the ground.

"There goes all my belief in women, curse them! I'll care for none of them from this out. I'll care for nothing but to make them I hate feel my sting. That I'll do. I'll have revenge. You'll hear from me, you saint-faced piece of falseness."

Casting a look of fierce menace upon Adelle, he flung himself away from the window.

"Lanier, Lanier!" she called, in anxiety that was almost terror. But he did not look back. A few moments afterward she saw him riding away from the house at his usual reckless speed.

Directly after, her brother and his two companions came out of his room. They were flushed and excited. One of the young men carried Derrick's repeating gun, and Adelle caught sight of navy pistols under Derrick's coat.

"Going hunting, boys?" asked Mrs. Holman's quavering treble as they passed her door.

"Yes, mother, we're after game," called back Derrick, with a discordant laugh.

"What'll you do for the hounds? Nero and Bull are with your father at the mill."

"We won't need the dogs."

"You're going to still-hunt, then?"

"Yes, ma'am, we're going to still-hunt," Derrick answered, with another laugh that sent a cold shiver through Adelle.

CHAPTER XI.

TWILIGHT was settling over the prospect of russet fields and woods upon which Adelle looked as she sat by her window, having hardly changed her position since she watched, from this post, her brother and his companions riding down the road an hour ago. The crimson streak the sunset had left on the cloudless sky had darkened into a dusk red, almost the hue of the autumn woods with which it blended.

The twilight was becoming gloomy in Adelle's room,

still she did not light her lamp or close the window, out of which her eyes went in a far look that seemed to rest upon the rim of a distant hill.

Suddenly the line of her vision was broken.

A head popped up above the window-sill—a sandy-haired, sallow-faced head, with abundant freckles and two small, ferret eyes. She started back, and the figure waved a deprecating hand.

"Miss Dell, don't be scared, it's only me—Piper. I've got something to tell you. May I come in?"

She recognized a waif, who had found lodgment for two years past on Lanier's place, where he did odd jobs about the house and yard, and received victuals and clothes, and kind words or cuffs from his employer, according as it suited Lanier's capricious mood. His caprice could not affect Piper's dog-like devotion to him, and the boy was as meek after receiving a sound cursing as if he had been listening to his praises, though he was spiteful to the negroes, who disliked him and imposed upon him.

Adelle had done him a service once. She had released him from a steel trap that had clamped him as he was robbing her father's melon patch. She bound up his wound and kept his secret. He never forgot it, and had more than once declared that he would fight for her to the last drop of his blood; an assertion which Adelle, who had seen him take to his heels when assaulted by a turkey gobbler, had a right not to rely upon.

"Come in," she said, feeling a presentiment that she would learn something connected with the uneasiness that had been weighing upon her since hearing Lanier's words and noting her brother's reckless looks and laughter.

The slim, lank figure sprang nimbly over the window-sill.

"Lock your door, Miss Dell; I am afraid somebody will

see me. I come through the orchard. I knowed I could git to your window by stoopin' down as I run through the shrubbery, 'thout any them pryin' niggers seein' me."

Adelle locked the door, and came back to him.

"Now, Piper, what is it?"

"Promise me you won't let nobody know what I'm goin' to tell you, Miss Dell."

"I can't promise that until I know what it is I am to hear."

"Well, will you promise not to tell who told it to you?"

"Yes; I think I can promise that. Go on."

"Well, it's jes' this. There's goin' to be bloody doin's 'twixt now and sunrise, and I'm mighty sorry Mr. Richard and your brother Derrick's got a hand in it, for they'll git hurted, sure."

"What do you mean? O Piper, tell me at once!"

"I will. You see, I've noticed Mr. Richard's been actin' curus ever sence he come back from Malta. He's all the time on the go, and nothin' pleases him, and he's fonder'n ever of bringin' me to my senses, as he calls slingin' the tongs or the blacken-bresh atter me. Then, I reckin, 'tween him and Mr. Derrick, I've had to fill up the whisky bottle a dozen times. I couldn't make out what was to pay, but las' night it come out. Two more fellows come, and atter eatin' supper and emptyin' the bottle twice, they set down in Mr. Richard's room, where I was makin' a fire. Soon's 'twas burnin' Mr. Richard told me to go out and go to bed, and then he locked the door. That put me up to listenin', and what does I do but go in the next room and git down on my hands and knees by the partition where there was a crack in the plasterin' betwixt the chimney and the wall, and I puts my ear to the crack and hears every word they was talkin' about, I did."

"What did you hear?"

"Why, them four is goin' to-night with masts over their faces to Captain Witchell's house on the lake, and take him and Devene and hang 'em high to a tree. That's it; I heard Mr. Richard tell the whole plan to them others they had sent for to come and go with 'em. He said Captain Witchell wouldn't fight fair, and didn't deserve to have a white man fight fair with him nohow; and so they'd just take law in their own hands and give him the hangin' he's been earnin' for these many months, and Devene with him; and 'twould be a good riddance for the country and a right and just act. That's how they put it."

"Why did you not come and tell me of this at once?"

"Well, 'twas in the night then, nigh on to ten o'clock, and I aimed to come nex' mornin'. But what must Mr. Richard do but set me the bigges' kind o' task o' thrashin' peas, and I've been hard at it all day; jest got through when they rides up, and I gits Bob to take the hosses to water and pull the saddles off, while I runs over here as fast as my legs could carry me. I come to you bekase I thought the squire would interfere if he knew what was goin' on; or you might work on your brother, and git him to give it up. It's no use tryin' with t'other one. Mr. Richard is dead bent on devilment. I see it getherin' in him ever so long. See that fresh scar on my head? He give me that day before yesterday for just little or nothin' (give me a vest, good as new, nex' day to smooth over my feelin's), but I declare I thought he was goin' to kill me, his eye flashed so. It done the same las' night; I seen it through the crack, when one of the men laughed, and said: 'You're so hot after Witchell, Lanier, bekase he cut you out.' You ought to seen Mr. Richard jump at him, and your brother had to part 'em an' make peace, and then he said to the fellow : ' Never do you dare to 'lude to my sister in such connection agin. She's got nothin' to do with this affair. We're goin' to rid the country of a blood-sucker (with a cuss word in between, Miss Dell), that's all. To be sure, one of the many scores I've got against him is his pre-sumin' to speak to my sister, but that's my business, and no—' "

" Stop, Piper," interrupted Adelle, who had listened in pale distress while the boy, tugging at the patch on his old jacket, delivered himself of his information. "At what time to-night do they aim to make the attack ? "

" Late. After midnight, I think ; jes' before day. I heard Mr. Richard say that was the time sleep was soundest and niggers was hardest to wake. They was 'fraid the darkies on the place might interfere."

" Then we will have time to warn him. Piper, you will go, I know. You can ride my horse, and I will pay you well, Piper. You know where Captain Witchell lives. You were with us the time we had the fish-fry on the lake, and camped near Captain Witchell's place."

" No ma'am, I wasn't. I had fever un ager, and never went. But, if I knew where he lived, I dassent go there to-night."

" Why ? "

" Why, Miss Dell, Mr. Richard'd miss me, sure. He'd come upon me, or he'd find out about me goin', and he'd hang me then, certain. 'Sides, I wouldn't go 'way there at night by myself for the biggest bag of money Captain Witchell's got. I never could go about at night. I'm scared to go back home now, close as 'tis, and it not dark yet. I must go right away."

" Stop, Piper ! For my sake, I beg you to go. You will not be found out ; nothing will hurt you ; I will stand be-tween you and harm. I will write a note, and help you to get off without any one finding it out. And you shall have ten dollars, Piper."

" Miss Dell, I'd do it for the love of you without your money—*ef* I could. But I dassent. I know Mr. Richard 'ud find it out. He always finds out everything I do wrong. He'd run upon me ; and there'd be somethin' worse'n that scar on my head. He'd break every bone in my skin. I oughter be back home this minnet, to feed them horses. Miss Dell, do you want me to carry any word to your brother ?—somethin', you know, that won't let on about my havin' told you anythin'. You 'member your promise.

" Yes, there is something you must tell Derrick for me. Tell him to come to me at once ; that I am sick ; that I have just heard bad news, and want him immediately. Tell him to come right away, Piper."

"I will certain, sure, Miss Dell," the boy said, as he jumped out of the window like a cat, and took his way across the orchard. He meant to do as he said ; but, on reaching home, he was met by his irate master, who rated him roundly about having carried off the corn-crib key, and not being there to feed the horses at the proper time, and Adelle's message was quite frightened out of his head. When it came to his recollection, he was afraid to deliver it to Derrick, lest Lanier should find out what it was and suspect him of having eavesdropped and given information.

Meantime Adelle waited with agonized impatience for her brother to come. She forced herself to sit down to the early tea, and to eat a few mouthfuls and talk as usual. Her father seemed in better humor than he had been for some time. He even said to her at the table :

" Come in after a while and read me a chapter of Livingston's " Life. " The print is too fine for my eyes."

The thought came to her :

" I will tell him. It is possible, he may use his influence to prevent this crime. He never would restrain Derrick in anything he did against the Radicals. Now, it will be worse, since he thinks he has a fresh cause of hate to Captain Witchell. But I must, I will tell him. If Derrick does not come in fifteen minutes, I will tell my father and implore him to prevent this wicked murder."

She went out on the piazza and walked up and down, stopping often to listen if she could hear the tramp of an approaching horse. But no such sound came to her strained ear. The clock struck eight. She turned and went into her father's room. She found him comfortably settled in his favorite arm-chair, smoking his pipe, that he always emptied of tobacco before going to bed. Her mother was nodding softly over the stocking she had been knitting.

"Wake up, mother!" said the old gentleman, touching her cap-strings; "here's Adelle going to read something about Livingston's tribulations in the land of apes and snakes, hyenas and Africans—the last, the worst beasts of all. And a nice time he had trying to Christianize these cannibals! I wish every Yankee and Radical was there in the middle of Ujiji. They'd have their fill of their sweet pets then."

This was an unfortunate beginning; Adelle's hopes sank almost to zero, but she had determined to make a trial.

"Father," she said, "there are other barbarians besides the Africans, and other people who commit crimes besides the Radicals. What would you think of a party of men falling upon a helpless man in his sleep, dragging him out of bed, and hanging him to a tree without judge or jury— . would not that be a crime?"

"It depends upon who the man might be that was hanged. If he was some carpet-bagging tyrant stained with sins against the people, who had no other way of redress than by punishing him themselves, because law and justice had ceased to be, then I say let him hang. But what are you driving at? Some particular case, I suppose, from your pointed question. What is it?"

"It is this, father. Captain Witchell is to be fallen upon to-night and murdered, and my brother and Lanier will be chief assassinators?"

"How do you know that?"

"I know it; I need not tell you how I heard it, but it came direct—"

"I don't believe it."

"It is true, father. Derrick came this afternoon and got his gun and pistols. O father, send for him; go to him, forbid his doing such a crime."

"I'll do nothing of the kind. Derrick's of age and can take care of himself. If there's anything in this big mare's-nest that you have discovered, it's only that the boys want to tar and feather the rascal, and he deserves that, and hanging besides."

"Is it possible that you would be willing to let my brother commit a murder?"

"Murder, indeed! Do you call freeing the land from a Radical vampire a murder?"

"Father, listen to me. Only let me tell you what Captain Witchell has done for Derrick. Last September, he—"

"Silence, and go away from me, Adelle; I am sick of that villain's name; you shall not call it in my presence again. If Derrick gets into any difficulty about him, you may blame yourself. You are the cause of all this trouble. Go."

He pushed her from him, and when she turned to her mother, who had begun to cry, he sternly ordered her from the room.

She went ; her heart swelling with misery, but her eyes dry, her brain throbbing, active, her purpose to save Captain Witchell unshaken.　She would go to the negro quarter and find some one that she might hire to take him the warning in time.　She ran rapidly along the path that led to the quarter, situated at the foot of the hill on which the dwelling-house was built.　The night was clear ; there was a glory of stars overhead ; later, there would be a moon.　It was profoundly quiet ; the sound of a horse stamping in the stable not far off sent for an instant a thrill of joy through her veins.　She thought it was Derrick coming at last.　Oh, if he would only come !　She thought she might influence him, if she could see him alone ; she might work upon his feelings and induce him to give up this wicked project ; but to go there—to Lanier's house, with Lanier and those other men all heated by drinking—to seek him there would be madness ; it would only inflame his anger against her, and strengthen his purpose.

She reached the quarter, a long row of log cabins in a grove of hickory-trees.　In the days of slavery they had all been occupied, but now, with the exception of three or four, they had fallen into dilapidation—the pig-pens, the chicken-coops, the little gardens that had been wont to exhibit rows of the inevitable long-legged collards, were no more ; the shutterless doors gaped wide, and the dirt chimneys had fallen.

Into one of the cabins, whose curling smoke gave token of habitation, Adelle entered.　She found a negro woman patching a ragged garment while she sang a hymn and rocked a baby to sleep with her foot upon the rocker of the rude pine cradle.　Another child lay stretched before the hearth asleep, his head nestled close to a sleeping hound.　The dog waked and barked, the woman looked up and saw Adelle, rose and courtesied.

"Where is your husband, Phillis?"

"Gone over de creek to de sugar-bilin' on Dr. Winstor's place, Miss Dell."

"Where is Ben, and Miles, and Harry?"

"Gone dare, too. Ebery hand on dis place gone, wim-min and all, 'cept me and Sis Silvy, and Mag and Aunt Kate."

"When will they come back?"

"Dey went 'bout sundown ; can't come home till day-break, case de creek so full it's dangersome to cross it at night."

"Then you couldn't go there after Willis for me."

"To-night! Law sakes! Miss Dell. It's three miles, and, if the creek warn't up, I'd be 'fraid to go, anyhow. I never travel about any of nights 'thout there's men-folks with me."

"Would Silvy go?"

"Silvy's sick a-bed, and you know Mag wouldn't stir a step out of de house at night to save life. She was born wid a caul over her head, and she sees sperits and gits scared outer her wits. I'm mightly sorry they'se all gone. What fer did you want Willis, Miss Dell?"

"To take a note to a friend away off ; but I see I must try some other plan to get it carried. Good night, Phil-lis."

And baffled once more, but still resolute of purpose, she hurried back to the house, revolving in her mind what could be done. There seemed now but one alternative. She must herself take the note to Captain Witchell, warning him of the attack that would be made that night. She ought not, anyhow, to trust a messenger less interested than herself. Such a one might prove treacherous, or he might be too slow, or he might take too little heed and lose his way. Negroes especially were not to be relied upon.

"No," she said, as she drew near the house, "I must go myself. At nine o'clock, father and mother will be in bed; I can saddle Bayard and get away without any noise, and I can ride to the lake in two hours, or two and a half at most. But oh! if I should be seen on the way—if I should be found out—what would become me? what would be said of me? My reputation would be lost for ever. And, if some negro or lawless tramp should attack me in one of the deep woods and lonely places I will have to pass through—spring out and grasp my bridle-rein, and drag me from the horse, as I have heard so often of their doing. Oh! I can't risk it; I can't go! But can I not risk something, sacrifice something to save a life—to save *his* life? I will. I will disguise myself in some of Derrick's clothes; that will guard against the worst danger. Captain Witchell will not know me; I will send the note in to him. He will not even see me. But I must hurry—hurry; it must be nearly nine o'clock. I hear father locking the front door."

She met him in the hall as she passed on to her room. He looked hard at her, but did not speak. She heard him lock the back door and return to his room. When she heard the click of the bolt, she opened her own door and slipped out, and stole across the entry to Derrick's room, where she possessed herself of a dark suit of clothes belonging to him. Returning across the hall, she took down the stable key that hung there on the wall. Once more in her room, she secured the door, and wrote, as legibly as her trembling hand would allow, a note that ran in this wise:

"CAPTAIN WITCHELL: An attack will be made on you to-night. Four men will come, between midnight and day, for the purpose of taking your life. Guard against them, but avoid bloodshed. For the sake of the friend who warns you, kill no one of them. It would be best to leave the house secretly, and take refuge in some unsuspected place. To do this would be a wise precaution against violence.

"A True Friend."

This written, she hastily dressed herself in Derrick's clothes, that fitted her sufficiently well, buckled a strong belt around her, in which she thrust a little repeating pistol that her mother had worn as a means of protection during the troublous days of the civil war, threw around her a black talma and fastened it securely by its tasseled cords. Her long hair she bound up and tucked under a velvet riding cap of her own, from which she had torn the plume, that it might look like a man's cap. Putting the note and the stable key into her pocket, she approached the open window, and, after listening intently for a moment, noiselessly dropped herself down to the soft flower-beds a few feet below.

The stable was almost back of the house. She reached it, unlocked the door, and, going in, soon found, despite the partial darkness, bridle and saddle hanging in their accustomed places, and put them on her pet horse, Bayard.

"You and I have work to do to-night, old fellow," she whispered in his ear, as she led him from the stable. She dared not take him to the road by the ordinary outlet. It ran too near the house on that side where her father's room was situated. So she led him through a gate on the other side of the house, into the orchard and across it; then, by letting down a low fence, she had him close to the road, fifty yards past the house. There, in a little thicket of pine saplings, she mounted into the saddle, and rode slowly until she descended the hill and the house was out of sight. Then she quickened her horse's gait, and rode with a firm pace through the silence. In the first deep-shadowed hollow she caught her breath in fear, for she heard steps behind her. She looked and saw nothing, until, on mounting the unshaded crest of the hill, she saw a dark object trotting behind her.

"Nero," she called, and a pleased whine answered her, as the dog ran forward to the side of the horse.

"I am glad you came, old boy ; you are some protection anyway, though I shouldn't have dared to call you."

She rode on ; her father's fields were passed. The die was cast. She had set out on a strange, wild errand ; it might save the life of the man she loved : it might cost her more than life. But she threw fear away from her as she rode, till Lanier's house came in sight. It sat back some distance from the road in a grove of oaks, but a broad walk led down to a gate that opened almost upon the road. What if Lanier or Derrick should be sitting there on the fence, smoking their cigars in the starlight, as they were fond of doing ? They would recognize the horse, the dog, and through these herself. She would have ridden around to avoid going near the house, but there was a high fence on the other side of the road. There was nothing for her to do but to ride straight on at a quiet pace. She hardly breathed as she passed the gate, but no one was there. The sound of a loud laugh reached her ear as she passed, and, in the light that came through the windows, she caught sight of dark figures standing and moving about on the gallery. She reached the end of the lane, and was about to urge her horse to greater speed, when suddenly the animal started ; the dog gave a sharp bark ; she thought she heard a rustle in the woods close to her on the right. She looked in that direction fearfully, but her eye could not penetrate the gloom. She saw nothing—unless—could that be some dark object hiding behind the great oak tree close to the end of the fence ?

"On, Bayard!" she said, low, to her horse, and away he sped. Lanier's farm was left behind, and she breathed more freely. On and on—over hills, and down into hollows threaded by streams that babbled under the shadows. The loneliness of the road, the calmness of the night, began to give her courage. She ceased to start when a twig crackled under her horse's feet, or the night-prowling raccoon, skunk, or 'possum rustled the fallen leaves of the wood.

It grew late; the lights were out in the few farmhouses she passed. The face of the country had altered; she was sure her journey was more than half ended; and yonder was a gibbous moon rising and gleaming through the trees. She struck a match, and looked at her watch. Eleven o'clock. She had been an hour and a half on the road. In less than an hour more her mission would be accomplished, or it would have failed. If nothing happened, she would be in time; he would be saved.

But what of her return? Might she not meet Lanier and the others on her way back? She would not think of it. When she heard them coming, she could ride out into the woods until they passed. She would not let the thought of it disturb her yet. The night was cool, the air fresh, the skies brightening overhead, her horse still in excellent wind. Upon each height he ascended, his mistress mercifully slackened his speed. Once she was resting him for a moment on the crest of a hill, when she saw him prick forward his ears and seem to listen. She herself listened and heard a sound like that of a horse galloping on the road far behind. Was she pursued, or were they coming already to do their work of death? Again she listened. Yes, unmistakably she heard that sound, like the quick, steady strokes of a horse's hoofs upon the hard earth.

Off she started again, putting Bayard to his best mettle. Away, through strips of denser wood, into deeper hollows,

6

past richer fields white with opening cotton, stopping only once to listen for that sound and hearing it again, but more faintly.

CHAPTER XII.

At length the last hill was passed. She descended into the Lake Swamp; the undergrowth vanished. Great tree-boles rose like the masts of a giant vessel; huge vines swung from them like the ropes of the ship. The light of moon and stars only here and there flickered through the umbrageous gloom. For the first time the chill of the night struck through her veins, and she shivered with cold and fear.

"Nero," she called, to break the silence that frightened her. The dog answered by a reassuring bark.

At last she came upon cleared fields, and caught a gleam of the lake lying under the moon. She looked to the right. There should be a path here leading to Captain Witchell's house. Ah! here it was, and yonder the glimmer of a lamp at an upper window of the house. Now the outline of the building was seen, dark against the sky. Two minutes more, and, with wildly-beating heart, she drew rein before the gate of the low fence that inclosed the yard. Light streamed through a half-opened window; she saw a man standing by the fireplace; she heard a voice speak, and another one reply. At the same instant her ear caught the tramp of an approaching horse. She must lose no time. Summoning all her courage, she called out hoarsely, "Halloo!"

A man came to the window; the spare, straight figure was Captain Witchell's, and it was his voice that demanded:

"What do you want?"

"To see you a moment."

"Won't you come in?"

"No; I must go back at once."

"Very well, I'll come."

"Better not, Captain," said Devene's voice. "Be on your guard. This might be a stratagem to get you out for no good."

"There's only one man; I'm a match for one man, I think," said Captain Witchell, carelessly, as he came out. He walked directly to the paling where Adelle sat trembling on the horse, the velvet cap pulled over her face, the note in her hand. She held it out to him the moment he came within reach, and, fearful of being recognized, was wheeling her horse to ride away, when Captain Witchell asked:

"Is any answer needed?"

"No."

She could not keep her voice from trembling; she felt that his keen eye was upon her. She did not know that in trying to hide her face with the cap she had drawn it too far from behind, and that a tress of her long hair had escaped. He saw it in the moonlight.

"Do you come from Malta?" he asked, with a view to hearing her speak again.

"No. Good-night."

While she spoke, a horseman had ridden up. He could not be the one she had heard behind her. This one came from another direction. He was a negro, riding Captain Witchell's noted horse.

"The doctor wasn't home, Mars Witchell," he said. "Be home by daybreak; I lef' word for him to come right on. Is Sampson any worser?"

"No; I've just been down to the cabin to see him. Go

there, and make sure his wife gives him the medicine I left.
It is time now for him to take it. Fasten Zep where he is,
and leave him for the present?"

Adelle heard this colloquy as she rode away. With one
look at her retreating figure Witchell hurried up to his
room and read the note. One instant his brow contracted
in thought, then he rose with an air of decision, glanced
from the window, and saw in the dim moonlight the disguised messenger nearing the end of the path that led
through the cleared meadow, and about to enter the woods.

He threw the note over to Devene. "We are to be at-
tacked to-night, you see. Get the guns and pistols from
the *armoire* yonder; load them up. Call up Ben and Joe
Harris from the quarter; make them fasten up doors and
windows, and watch in the hall. I'll be back in time for
the reception. I'm going to follow that messenger and find
out something more."

"For God's sake, Witchell, don't go out by yourself in
that way! You may meet them any moment. It's madness
to expose yourself so."

"I'm not afraid. I'll be back directly."

"You are not going unarmed? Here, take my pistol,
at least."

"I have my stick; I'm all right. Don't be exercised
about me. Go back, and do as I told you.'

Mounting the horse that stood at the gate where he had
directed the negro to leave him, he was soon clattering at
full speed down the road, determined to overtake Adelle,
whom he had recognized from that truant tress, as well as
from the voice she had vainly tried to disguise, and from
the glimpse he had of oval cheek and delicate chin under
the slouched cap. He felt how much she had risked for
his sake; he could not let her ride back alone and unprotected. He would follow her, and, without betraying that

he knew her, find some pretext to ride with her, or at least so near her as to be at hand if any danger befell her.

She had already left behind her the road through the moon-lighted, cleared space, and entered into the shadowy swamp. Fears began to assail her lest she should meet some of the wild clan who might be coming to reconnoiter the spot where they meant, later, to do a lawless deed. What had become of the horseman she had heard following her when she was on her way to carry the warning?

Her horse was beginning to show signs of fatigue. She patted him encouragingly. The swamp road was not so gloomy as it had been when she rode there half an hour before. The moon had risen higher—gleams of light penetrated the frost-thinned boughs of ash and hackberry.

Nero, running ahead, began to sniff the air suspiciously. Suddenly he uttered the sharp bark that betrays a near presence. Adelle's horse stopped and threw his head around, A man on horseback emerged from the woods, and rode straight to her. Her first impulse was to turn and gallop back to Witchell's house, or at least to the open meadow beyond these dark woods. She wheeled her horse around, but the man was already alongside. His hand grasped her bridle rein.

"Off with your visor, Sir Knight," cried Lanier's mocking voice, as he struck off her cap and sent her long hair tumbling about her shoulders.

He laughed hoarsely.

"Let's have a better view."

He struck a match across his saddle bow and held the blaze close to her. It showed him a face pale as death; the lips firm, but the dark eyes dilated like a startled deer's. A wilder fear leaped into them when she saw his look. A sinister gleam gloated in his blood-shot eyes. Rage and revenge, fevered into delirium by liquor, glared close to her

in that bluish light.   She saw, with a shudder, that she had
to deal with a man beside himself.

"Brave knight," he began, tauntingly, but his voice
dropped to a hissing whisper as he leaned close to her ear,
"I saw you, I knew you, and followed you.   I would have
caught up with you and spoiled your fine purpose, if this
cursed beast had held out as he ought.   So you've warned
your precious lover.   He's ready for us yonder, is he, with
his guns and his nigger guard ?   You've spoiled our game.
Do you think you shall not pay for it ?   You shall.   You
shall pay dearly for this, and for having played your tricks
upon me—fooled me, and cast me off for this Radical hound.
He shall never have you ; no one shall ever have you, nor
care to.   You shall be a mark for scorn—Aha! that's
your game, is it ?"

He caught the pistol he had detected her in drawing
from beneath her cloak.   He tried to wrench it from her
hand, but her slim fingers seemed all at once to be steel.
Suddenly, she let go the weapon.   He had released his hold
upon her bridle in the struggle, and a word and a quick
blow made her horse bound forward in the direction in
which she had wheeled him in her first fright—the direction of the lake and of Witchell's house.

Before Lanier had recovered from his surprise at this sudden movement, she was some distance ahead.   He dashed
the bloody spurs into his horse's flanks, and started in pursuit.   She was going to Witchell to seek protection from
him.   He would follow her ; he would kill them both.
Rage and jealousy maddened him.   He was not a brave
man.   Cool resistance could back him down in a little
while ; but he had a species of impetuous frenzy when passion or strong drink, or both combined, heated his blood.

He gnashed out a curse when he saw her approaching
the clearing.

"Stop, or I'll shoot," he called out to her. Directly he heard her utter a cry of joyful surprise; he saw a man riding toward her, meeting her; he heard her excited exclamation, "Captain Witchell! Thank God!"

On hearing that name Lanier experienced an involuntary check. A portion of his mad impetuosity died out. Whenever an animal, whether brute or man, has once been whipped, he afterward, in the presence of the superior power, instinctively recognizes his master. Lanier felt a burning rage against his rival, but his nerves also gave token that they remembered that good blow Witchell had dealt him once. While he hesitated to proceed, he heard a horse approaching from behind. He turned, and gave a peculiar whistle; it was answered in kind, and a moment after Derrick rode up beside him.

"Lanier," he demanded, "what the deuce did you mean by slipping off in this way, letting nobody know when you left?"

"I had reason to think that news was being carried to Witchell. I came to reconnoiter. I expected to have gone back before this. Where are the others?"

"Coming on behind. You took that notion to reconnoiter very suddenly. What have you found out?"

"That it's all up as to our plan to surprise them. Witchell got hold of it."

"How the devil could that be? Who knew of it but ourselves?"

"One other found it out. Love's eyes and ears are keen. It was your sister that gave warning to Witchell. She rode here by herself, dressed as a boy, and went to his house."

"Adelle! my sister! to Witchell's house! Take that back, or you shall repent it."

"It's true; you can see for yourself. Yonder they are;

she was coming back, he riding with her. They have dismounted, I see, for some cause."

Derrick looked, and saw two horses and two figures standing in the moonlight, just beyond the edge of the swamp. His comrades, Verne and Wylde, were just riding up. He turned to them. "Yonder's my man," he said; "I have an account to settle with him. Don't interfere with me. I want neither help nor hindrance."

He spurred his horse in the direction in which the two were standing—Adelle leaning against a tree to support herself; Witchell standing by, holding her hand, and looking at her with deep concern. At the instant when, flying from Lanier, she had met Captain Witchell and stretched out her hands to him with that cry of joy, she had felt her brain whirling and her strength failing her. The fatigue and anxiety she had undergone, the terror, the feeling of relief succeeded by the sudden sense of shame, were too much for her. She reeled in the saddle, and Captain Witchell reached her side barely in time to prevent her falling. But she did not faint. A dash of dew from a broken bough in the hands of Captain Witchell revived her. She gently pushed him from her, and leaned against a tree for support; she hid her face in the dark mass of her hair, and sobbed in shame and distress. He looked at her, and hesitated. Then he ventured to lay his hand upon her arm.

"Miss Holman!"

She dropped her hands from her face and wrung them passionately.

"O Captain Witchell, what must you think of me?"

"That you are a brave and true woman, Miss Holman. That in all probability I owe my life to you."

"Your life!" she cried suddenly, brought to a recollection of his danger. "O Captain Witchell, they may take your life here at any moment. They will fall upon you here, and you have no help, no defense. That was one of them you saw following me just now. Where is he? He is only waiting for the others to come up to attack you. Captain Witchell, go at once. Ride to a place of safety, or get into your house and arm your friends. Go!"

"I will not leave you, Miss Holman. Let me help you to mount your horse. How cold your hands are, and how you tremble! Do not be afraid any more. I will not leave you; I will ride with you to your home."

"But you—it is you who are in danger! I tell you they will be upon you in a few moments. There! do you not see them yonder? They are coming this way. O Heaven! that is Derrick."

As her brother leaped from his horse, she sprang to meet him. She saw that he held a pistol in his hand, and that his face was white and rigid with determination.

"O Derrick, listen to me!"

He pushed her aside, and pressed on to where Witchell stood.

"Villain, your time has come," he cried, raising the weapon.

Before he could take aim Adelle threw herself in his arms and clung to him.

"You shall not, you shall not kill him," she cried. O Derrick, he saved your life! He cared for you while you were so ill with the fever. He watched you day and night when you were delirious. He got the doctor to come to you—the negroes to wait upon you. You would not kill a dog that had saved your life, Derrick."

"No thanks to him for my life. Better be dead than dishonored. A villain who has ruined my country, and now has taken away the good name of my family. Curse him! Nothing can keep me from having it out with him now. Get away from me, girl."

"Derrick, for my sake—"

"Your sake! Yours! What are you to me now? A wretch that has disgraced me. What are you to me any more after this night's work? Get away with you—outcast."

These cruel words staggered her worse than blows would have done. She loosed her hold of him, and tottered back. Witchell stepped quickly to her side; he put his arm around her; facing her brother, he said:

"You shall not speak to her in this way. You may abuse me as much as you please, but you shall not say such words to my wife."

"Wife?" echoed Derrick, the pistol he had half raised dropping to his side in his astonishment.

"My wife that shall be to-morrow. She had a right to do what she has done to-night for my safety. Derrick Holman, listen one moment to common sense. You need be in no hurry to shoot. I am unarmed and have no one in call. Hear me a moment first. In your mad passion you would only burn your own house. You would kill me . and fix a stigma on your sister. That is not necessary. You say that after to-night she shall be an outcast from your home; she shall be received in mine as my honored wife. Is not this better for her—for you and your parents —than if you killed me and left her no refuge? If her brave devotion to-night is to draw reproach upon her, let me forestall it by a marriage.

"A marriage with a Radical carpet-bagger! That would be a fine amendment," Derrick said, with an acrid sneer.

Captain Witchell bit his lip hard. He was controlling himself by an effort, for the sake of the girl by his side. He answered calmly:

"It might hurt your pride; it would not hurt your honor. I am considering *her* first. You may disclaim her,

but would you not prefer to know that she was happy?
Have you not so much natural affection for one of your own
blood?"

The appeal had its effect upon Derrick.

His real love for his sister, his pride in her good name
and in the good name of his family, the knowledge of Captain Witchell's past kindness, the sense of his generosity and
fearlessness on the present occasion, all operated to influence
his action. He stood looking at the two for an undecided
moment, then he thrust his pistol back in its place, and
without a word was turning to remount his horse, when
Adelle caught his hand, and looked beseechingly in his face.

"O Derrick, put all this enmity out of your heart,"
she pleaded. "Be friends with Captain Witchell."

"Friends! Have you lost your senses, girl? I trust
to God I may never see his face again. Marry him, go with
him, but remember that afterward you have no brother, no
father, no mother—you have only *him*. Remember that—
and be happy—if you can."

He mounted his horse, then turning as if a thought
struck him, he said to Adelle:

"Get into your saddle. I can not leave you here. I
am going now to send those others on. I shall be back for
you directly."

He rode off and rejoined Lanier and the others, who had
waited where he left them, wondering greatly at hearing no
report of a pistol, or other signs of combat.

"There is nothing to be done," he said gloomily. "I
can not kill my sister's husband. Ride back. I will follow
you in a little while. Lanier, let me speak a word in your
ear."

Between the two he had left there was silence for a moment. Adelle's bosom swelled with conflicting feelings.
At last she turned to Captain Witchell:

"Why did you say that?" she said; "I will not have it so. There can be no marriage."

He answered gravely: "I hoped otherwise. I know it was presumptuous to infer your consent, but I thought it for the best. The circumstances were such—I thought—"

"You thought I would shelter myself from blame by marrying a man who—"

"Whom your family hate, whom your friends vilify, who is misunderstood and maligned. It *was* too much to expect."

She had sat down upon the trunk of a fallen tree; her face was turned from him.

"No, it is not that," she said, low. "That was not what I meant to say; I mean that I will never consent to take what was offered in generous pity. I will bear the consequences of my own act. I came here to-night through a good motive. I dressed this way because I thought it would protect me from insult. If I lose friends and home because of it, let them go. The world is wide, and I can find—"

Her voice broke and a sob came. He sat down by her. He put his arm around her.

"So the world is wide, and you can find a nest somewhere, little dove? Why not in my arms? Why do you refuse to come to me?"

"Do you think I do not know you said that to my brother only to shield me? I will not make it true; I will not accept such a sacrifice."

"You will not marry me?"

"No."

"Not if it is no sacrifice? Not if I love you?"

"But you do not love me."

He drew her to him. "Not love you? How could I help loving you; brave, kind little heart, tender eyes, sweet, true mouth?"

He put back the hair from her face, and kissed her wet lashes, her cheeks, that lost their paleness under the rush of burning blushes.

"Will you marry me now?"

There was no answer, but she did not draw away from him.

"Do you not love me, Adelle?"

"Yes."

"But not well enough to see parents and friends and the little world around you turn their backs on you for my sake?"

"You are all the world to me," she whispered, hiding her face against his shoulder.

He was silent, gently caressing her soft hair. He felt that he had the destiny of this girl wholly in his hands. She was his to the heart's core, to make happy or miserable, as he chose.

Presently he said: "I will go for you to-morrow; will you be ready to come with me?"

"Yes, but—"

"What is it?"

"If I could be married in my father's house."

"That rests with them; we will see. Let me put you upon your horse now. I hear your brother coming. Wrap your cloak well around you; it is growing cold."

He lifted her to a seat in the saddle and stood by her until Derrick rode up.

"I have a word to speak to you, Mr. Holman," he said, going up to the young man as he sat in the saddle. Derrick nodded haughtily.

"I wish to marry your sister to-morrow. She prefers that it should be at her own home. It is best, for other reasons."

"Under my father's roof, sir? Never."

" He is also her father. She has been a beloved daughter, a dutiful one, except in one instance, where she obeyed the promptings of her heart. She has certainly a right to as much consideration for her feelings as a marriage under her father's roof would imply. But it matters little. A marriage anywhere else will be as well."

"Stay, sir! Come to my father's house prepared to make Adelle Holman your wife. Bring your witnesses; you will find none there who will witness this marriage."

"Very well." He turned to Adelle.

"Does this please you?"

She gave him her hand in silence.

"Come," called her brother, sharply.

They rode away, leaving Witchell standing there in the moonlight, looking after them, feeling almost as if all had been a dream. Could it be that in a few moments so great a change had taken place in the future he had mapped out for himself? To be married in a few hours—married to the daughter of his bitter enemy—a girl of whose nature he had had only glimpses, of whose more hidden and subtile traits of character he knew nothing. Could he make her happy? All that money or kindness could do should be done to supply the place of what she must lose through him. As for love—"

But how sweet her face had looked in the moonlight when he had lifted it to kiss her. The eyes that shone through tears, the red lips that quivered so, the little, delicately molded chin, the white neck under its veil of hair? How her heart had throbbed against his! And that little, earnest, thrilling, yet timid, whisper:

"You are all the world to me." Its remembered pathos touched his heart.

"I will try to be all to her. She shall not miss the love of father and mother, and the society of friends," he said, as he stepped upon the piazza of his house. He had almost forgotten the plotted attack. The bolted door and barricaded windows reminded him of it. He knocked on the door, calling out :

"It is I ; open."

Within, a dim light was burning. Three negro men with guns in their hands stood there, looking at him inquiringly.

"Go home, and to bed," he said. "There is to be no attack ; I have settled it."

They asked no questions. They were accustomed to think Captain Witchell could do whatever he wished. They believed he bore a charmed life. He had been in danger so often—shot at, threatened by mobs—without harm coming to him.

Devene was not so easily satisfied. "What did you do ? How did you settle it ?" he asked, when they were alone in their room.

"I saw the ringleader, and induced him to forego his fun for to-night. Instead of being hanged, I am only to be—"

"What ?" asked Devene, in suspense.

"Sit down. Take a cigar, and hand me one. What, only one o'clock ! How many events can crowd into a little hour !"

He stirred the rich bed of wood coals and threw on a fresh pine-knot. Then looking across at his companion through a cloud of tobacco-smoke, and smiling in his peculiar way, he said :

"Devene, you must put off your trip to N——; I want you to go to Colonel Holman's with me to-day. I am to be married."

CHAPTER XIII.

THE slant afternoon sun was shining upon the little riverside town of Cohatchie, upon the white cottages with bright green blinds, the new brick stores, side by side with wooden shanties, and the cupola of the really handsome court-house. The town had the irregular appearance that marks a new place, but the bales of cotton piled before the warehouse, and the amount of freight in boxes and barrels which a steamboat, petulantly puffing at the landing, had just discharged, told of thrift and business.

Captain Witchell's scheme in this direction had succeeded. The new parish had been created, the new court-house erected, the new town built up rapidly around it, drawing the produce and trade of the rich alluvial region above and below it, and of the thrifty "Hills" lying at its back. Witchell's town bade fair to become of considerable importance. His plantation was two miles above it and on the opposite side of the river—an ample, old-fashioned house in a grove of trees with broad fields lying back of it and stretching along the river on either hand. Having perfect control of the negroes, he could, through their labor, make these level, fertile acres yield the splendid returns of cotton that had brought their former owner a princely income in slavery days.

Various industries which had sprung up about the plantation under Captain Witchell's management bore evidence to his New England activity and enterprise. A mill with the most improved machinery turned out lumber and ground the plentiful grain of the neighborhood, a well-stocked storehouse furnished customers, mostly the negroes belonging to the place and to neighboring plantations, with provisions and other merchandise suited to their wants;

various offices and outbuildings gave a village look to the
place ; a printing-press, almost in the very yard, absorbed
the public printing, and turned into Captain Witchell's
hands the public money appropriated therefor.

These industries, circling more immediately around his
home, were carried on at the same time with outside enterprises of a broader scope. Contracts for the erection of
public buildings in the new county site he had created ;
the improvement and sale of lots therein ; the buying in
and turning to good account of real estate sold for taxes or
for debts ; the extension of his influence with the people
of the section and with his party at large ; these schemes
fully occupied the time and brain of the energetic member
of the State Senate. They were regarded by him as merely
the beginning of greater things.

He was becoming rich and influential—he was paving
the way to greater power, to more extended opportunities
of building up a vast fortune. He confided his plans to no
one, not even to Adelle, devoted wife as she was, making
him her loving but painful study ; nor yet to the members
of his own family, whom he had gathered around him and
made sharers in his prosperity and strengtheners of his
position. Two of these were his brothers-in-law—young
men, full of hope and activity, eager to make their fortunes, but fully under the control of Witchell, whose experience and firm will gave him perfect mastery over them.
He had obtained an office for each of these. Mark Hollin
was appointed supervisor of registration, and settled with
his pretty, fair-haired wife upon a plantation below Cohatchie which Witchell had bought for him. Wallace,
the husband of another sister, was made a magistrate,
and given also the supervision of the numerous interests on
Witchell's estate.

Both were prepossessing young men, calculated to make

friends for themselves and Witchell, and to wear off gradually the edge of aversion with which the Radical ring was regarded. But the one upon whom Witchell relied most was his only brother. Young Omar Witchell was not brilliant, nor was he masterful like his elder brother. Reserved in general society, though to his friends he talked with a candid almost childish earnestness, quiet in manner and grave of face, except when he smiled ; tall, dark, deliberate of speech and action, impressing you with the idea of a kindly, unsuspicious, loyal nature—this was Omar Witchell ; as unlike the ordinary type of New-Englander as one can imagine, and the direct opposite of his brother, who with his incisive eye, sanguine color, thin lips, and firm chin, seemed born to sweep away obstructing circumstances, not to be patient under them.

But there was hardly a being in the world that Marshall Witchell believed in as he did in this quiet young brother.

It was not wholly a selfish gratification in having secured a trustworthy assistant that made him so delighted when welcoming Omar to his new home. As he folded the young fellow in his arms, the night when he stepped from the steamboat upon the soil of the stranger country, it was a pure emotion that stirred under the worldliness that incrusted the elder man's nature. A tenderness almost paternal thrilled in his voice, as, putting his hands on Omar's shoulders and looking into his clear eyes, he said :

" Old fellow, it does me good to see you. I hope, Omar, you'll do well here. I believe you will, or I shouldn't have got you to come. I trust you may never have cause to regret it."

Omar Witchell had been appointed tax-collector, and on this sunny afternoon he sat in his office at Cohatchie. The breeze came in at the open window and stirred the dark locks on his temples, and freshened the two or three flowers that bloomed in a little glass beside him as he sat leaning his elbow on his desk, and resting his chin in the hollow of his hand in a brown study. He did not hear the rap of a cane on the threshold of his open door, and looked up in some confusion as a finely-formed man, with a keen eye, but a look of benevolent humor about his mouth, tapped him upon the shoulder.

"I beg your pardon, Judge Pickenson. I did not see you."

"No; your thoughts were off wool-gathering. How far, eh? No farther, I imagine, than a certain cottage where I saw somebody sitting at the window as I came along."

"Oh, a good deal farther, sir. 'Over the hills and far away.' It's not often I get homesick, but to-day something—the scent of these flowers, may be, or the look of the white clouds piled up yonder—has set me to thinking of the mountains, and longing to see them."

"The mountains, or the maid of the mountains?— 'The girl I left behind me?'" queried the Judge, playfully. "But really, Omar, honor bright, how do you like our folks here in Dixie?"

"Better than they like me, I am afraid. I have two or three good friends here, but the others—when I come where they are—seem to freeze up as if I carried an arctic atmosphere along with me. They look at me as if they expected me at any moment to develop some sinister aspect."

"The horns and hoofs of the Old One, probably."

"That hurts me, you know. I don't like to be looked upon with suspicion. I feel very friendly toward the people here. They seem so pleasant with each other; all the more I hate being left out in the cold. But I hope I may succeed in making them like me yet."

"I think you will. They have thawed wonderfully to

you. They have been badly treated, no doubt about it, and still have deep grounds for grievance. I have run on your party ticket, Omar, partly because I had bitter need of the income the office would bring, for my children's sake, but more because I hoped to do some good by restraining on one hand and conciliating on the other ; but, for all that, I don't endorse the present policy of the Government toward my country. It's founded on ignorance of our people's wants and dispositions, or on revengeful disregard of their rights; but come ; don't let's talk about any such crabbed thing as politics this lovely afternoon. I hope all will come right after a while. I think things would right themselves slowly here in this district, if there wasn't a secret, disturbing influence beginning to work just now. Something is brewing, mark my words. And disappointed avarice is the leaven of the ferment. Some men that have been loudest in denouncing Captain Witchell's plundering, as they call it, are mad as Lucifer because they can't get his chance."

"What has my brother done to make them denounce him so strongly, Judge Pickenson ?"

"Oh, no more than others in the same position have done and are doing. He has carried out the policy of his party with regard to upholding the negro, and he has made use of the opportunities his position gave him to enrich himself."

"Legitimate opportunities, of course ?"

Judge Pickenson evaded the young man's questioning eye, and went on :

"Others right here are precious anxious to secure the same opportunities, or even to go shares in what they are pleased to call the spoils—Democrats and leaders of the opposition though they pretend to be. You know Colonel Alver ; what do you think of him ?"

"He seems polite, and even suave, of late. But there seems every now and then a false ring in his voice, and his cold blue eye contradicts his friendly speeches. But this impression may be unfounded and unjust."

"No; it is nature's warning. It tells you to beware!"

"By the way, I have an invitation to a little party at his house to-night."

"So have I; and it's funny. He hates me like poison, because I succeeded in getting the office I hold; he hates Witchell, and has until lately openly abused him. Awhile back, he would not speak to any member of the Radical party; now he has suddenly grown friendly. I guessed the secret before I saw your brother last Friday; I found out from him that Alver has been making overtures in a delicate way. He wants to be admitted into the ring of the 'Plunderers.' He is anxious to get in, and asks a small slice of the booty. By and by, he would want the lion's share. He is a tyrant by nature. The position he had as head of a regiment in the late war pampered this love of ruling men and overriding them. Then he came here, when this little town first began to grow. He put up a store, and went into business. He aimed to monopolize all the trade—to make himself the big man of the town—the Great Mogul. The Lisson Brothers also put up a store at the other end of the town. Their real cleverness drew better than Alver's surface politeness. Trade flowed chiefly to the Lisson end of the town. When Witchell was ready to build the new court-house, each rival party put in a bid to get it built at his end of the town. The bids were in lots; Messrs. Lisson outbid Alver in the number and desirability of lots they offered Witchell as inducements to erect the court-house on their portion of Cohatchie. It was built there, the warehouse also put there; and a friendly relation, some say a business un-

derstanding, was established between the Lissons and Witchell. This drew the negro trade—an important item here,
where darkies handle so much money—to Lisson's store—
the quarter that Captain Witchell seemed to favor. There
grew up two factions, and it was 'under which flag, Bezo-
nian? speak, or die!' Alver and his clique were hot
against Lisson and his friends—the Radical ring, as they
called them. The Lissons shrugged their shoulders in
good-natured contempt. You saw plenty of all this, Omar,
after you came. Lately, you must have remarked a change.
Alver has altered his tactics. He has grown mild, almost
affectionate. The secret is that next year there will be an
election, and Alver means to make a desperate effort to get
into the ring he pretends to scorn. He has made numerous
friendly advances to Witchell in private; now he comes out
openly and extends the hand of amity. He wants to receive
something besides good-will in return. You will see him drop
the sheepskin and show the true wolf when he is refused
admittance into the fold, as he is sure to be, for Witchell
understands him. He will take no man into association
with him, overbearing as he knows this one to be. When
Alver finds out there is no use to knock any longer at this
door, look out for a change of strategy. He will return
to his old position, and be a more bitter opponent than
ever. He will be more cunning and cool though, and work
with more system. He will try to undermine; he will set
secret wheels to work; he will not rest until he has wrought
mischief."

Omar looked down on the floor; his face was clouded.

"The game does not amuse or even interest me," he
said. "It seems wrong and mean. I trust no harm will
come to Marshall. I am sure my brother's aims are good.
He looks forward. He means to do what he can to restore
the people to prosperity. He will spend the money he has

made right here in enterprises for the public good. How he made the money, I have not asked him. I don't understand the mysteries of finance or politics. I don't comprehend the secrets of trading and speculating; Marshall does. He has a head for all these things; and then he has a heart —you do not know what a heart he has. Even his enemies own he is helpful to the poor, but they, and even his friends, even you, think that money-getting is his passion. If you knew his earlier history, you would understand him better. When my father died, fifteen years ago, our income died with him, and a large, helpless family was left upon my brother's hands. I was too young to be of any use ; the others were girls, my mother an invalid. It was a heavy burden for a boy's shoulders. How nobly Marshall bore it ; how he worked, economized, sacrificed ; how he put aside all temptation to self-indulgence, personal ambition, and love—yes, a strong first passion that tempted him more than anything ; how he gave up all these for the duty of supporting his mother, of educating and providing for his sisters and brother ; all that would make a long story, if I should tell it. When war came, he had succeeded in making us comfortable. He went as a private soldier ; afterward, his good conduct raised him from the ranks. He sent us regularly nearly every dollar of his pay. The war closed ; as a reward for his services he was given a post here. He was successful, and made money. Sickness and other misfortunes had brought debt and distress at home. He released us from that bondage. He made it possible for my sisters to marry the men of their choice. At length he has brought us all here, where he feels our well-being still a responsibility upon him. Can one wonder he has made money-getting something of a passion ? It had been a binding duty so long, it is not strange it should become second nature. Circumstances forced his thoughts into that one channel so long ; and now he is making it minister to his ambition."

"And to his love. That's a sweet woman he has married at last."

"Adelle ? She is the tenderest, the most devoted creature I ever saw. I wish, from my soul, Marshall had met such a woman and married her earlier. You knew her as a girl, Judge Pickenson ; was she gay, light-hearted ?"

"She was merry enough. There was always a touch of gentle dignity about her, and a shade of romance—just enough to give a depth and sweetness to her nature. She is changed. I saw her last week. She is pale, and looks absent and preoccupied. She ought to go more into society."

"She ought. Marshall must insist on it. Even when they go to New Orleans he says she is almost as much of a recluse as she is here. The truth is, *he* is her world ; her thoughts all center in him. When he is away she watches for his coming, and her color rises as soon as she catches sight of him. Poor girl ! Her parents will have nothing to do with her ; her brother treats her like a stranger ; she has given them all up for Marshall. It seems to me, if I were he, I could never show my appreciation of her enough. He loves her, I know ; he is kind, too. But you see he is occupied with other things. This is all between ourselves, you know. I could not discuss Marshall's affairs with any one but his friend—his true friend, as I believe."

"You are right ; I *am* Captain Witchell's friend, or I should not have associated myself with him. He has done some things I have not approved of, and I have told him so, as friend to friend. I have advised him, too—but no matter. He is a sharp fellow, and luck is with him. He may be able to ride into the port he aspires after, on the present high tide of fortune, over the breakers that I see ahead. No more of that now. Lock up your books; get your hat, and come with me for a long walk. Let's go and get a late paper off the Marie Louise. She is still at the landing discharging Alver's freight. Look at Alver, standing yonder on the plank, directing matters and hectoring the deck-hands. To order roustabouts is better than not to order anybody. He ought to have been born across the water—a Russian Count, with a parcel of quaking tenants under his thumb."

"Is that his wife holding a little girl by the hand who has just come up to him?"

"Sly rogue! you know it isn't. You are very well aware that it is Miss Reese—the fair Floyd. I saw her at a window as I passed Captain Alver's, posing as if for a picture. She's not the usual style of schoolma'arm at all, at all. More like a stage-queen. Alver shows his taste in female looks in choosing a governess, though I fancy he appreciates her excellence in that line more than his wife does. But I must take care; I believe you are attracted in that quarter."

"So far as to think Miss Floyd Reese a handsome woman, with fascinating ways. But my heart is safe, for I left it in the Green Mountains. I have told you so much of my family affairs; I may as well confide this secret. I am engaged to a dear little girl at home—another schoolma'arm—and I shall marry her soon. We have waited five years; now, thanks to Marshall's goodness, I am able to marry her. She is not as handsome as Miss Reese, but a dear, bright, little woman, and will make a good wife."

"Well! she'll have a good husband, Omar. I hoped you might have married one of our Southern girls, as your brother did—not Miss Reese, though; she's fine to look at, but when one thinks of her as a wife there comes a dash of cold water on his enthusiasm. Stick to your little Yankee

7

girl ; bring her down here, and put her in that pretty little house you are having built. We'll adopt her as one of us. Hi ! there goes the Louise's whistle. What lady is that who has just got off the boat and is coming up the bank ? Why, it's Miss Zoe Vincent. She has come up to the party at Alver's to-night, I imagine. She lives three miles below here with her brother. Do you know her ? "

"Yes ; she is Adelle's friend. She came to see her not long ago. I have never seen Adelle show so much pleasure at meeting any one. She seemed quite glad and girlish for a while. Miss Vincent is beautiful ; such a glorious black eye, such a proud poise to her little head ! You needn't look at me in that quizzical way, Judge. She is engaged as well as I am. Adelle told me so."

"Yes ; so I heard three years ago, when she first came here. To some young lawyer in New Orleans, and they were to marry right away, said Madame Rumor. Odd, no such match has come off yet. To a girl like her it must be awful lonesome down there on her brother's plantation. But I think she lives a great deal in 'dreams and stately-stepping fancies.' She is not like the average girl; has more soul ; plenty of nerve, too. I saw that tested two years ago. I was with her on the steamer Alethea when it burned up, just above Baton Rouge, and when most of the passengers—she among them—would have been lost if it hadn't been for the coolness of one fellow, a long haired Texan, quick as a cat and sinewy as a buffalo. He got a lot of us safely off in a boat, but somehow Zoe was left behind, and he swam ashore with her. She had a chill after she reached the bank ; and you ought to have seen the Texan taking care of her ; respectful and delicate as if he had been a gentleman instead of a gambling dare-devil. We had to stay on the bank all night ; no boat came along to pick us up. Vincent, Zoe's brother, was drinking (some of our best fellows *will* get on a spree when they go to the city), so Zoe was left pretty much to the Texan's care. I saw him fairly carrying her across to the boat when one at last came along.

She must have had a civilizing effect on him, for he drank no more that trip; he had his beard trimmed, and he only let slip an oath now and then. Vincent had lost money to him at poker on the Alethea; now he let him win it back, and more besides. We all saw he only played to lose. He sent fruits and ices to Miss Zoe, and charged the waiter not to tell where they came from. About an hour before the boat would reach Vincent's place, whom should I see in the ladies' cabin but that Texan, begging Zo e for a song. He had got into a black coat and wore a subdued, really gentlemanly look. When we landed at her brother's home, Vincent was seeing after his freight, and asked me to help his sister off the boat. I went up to offer my services, but the Texan was there. He glared at me as though he would like to call me out, and seized Miss Vincent's hand. She blushed red, but did not look displeased. I heard afterward that he was a noted desperado."

"How do you know, Judge, that this little adventure is not the secret of Miss Vincent's failing to marry the New Orleans lawyer?"

"Pshaw! a fellow like that. She has hardly thought of him since. Omar, you are as romantic as a girl."

"Miss Reese is looking at us; shall we go up and speak to her?"

"Not I. She is standing by Alver. I never seek his society. I sha'n't go to his house to-night."

"I do not think my brother will; nor shall I, I believe."

"You'll change your mind after you have spoken to Miss Floyd. There she is, beckoning you with her fan. Go and speak to her."

As Omar walked away, Judge Pickenson's eyes followed him with a shrewd yet kindly look.

"Good-hearted but simple fellow," he muttered. "Looks on that sharp brother of his as a sort of demigod; will make a capital cat's-paw. I don't like the notion of his getting burnt, though; and he will get burnt, I am much afraid."

The sun had set; the townspeople strolled to the river bank. Judge Pickenson soon had a knot of his friends around him. He was liked by many, despite his position as the only prominent Southerner of the district who held office under the Radical administration. His independent character, his well-known courage, and the consideration he had won as captain of a daring Confederate cavalry corps in the war, made even his enemies treat him with outward respect, thought they cursed him behind his back as a "hanger-on of the robber ring." He did not condescend to defend his position. He held that he had a right to accept office, and to treat his Northern fellow-officials as human beings. No doubt some of the "carpet-baggers" were rogues and rascals. Rogues and rascals were to be found everywhere. No doubt others, fairly sound in principle at first, had been over-tempted by the wide opportunities for arbitrary power and extortion that the abnormal condition of things at the South threw in the way of office-holders. Didn't they know of good Southerners who would be tempted to fleece the flock, if the gap was let down to them in the same way?

"The temptation to play the autocrat is mighty strong for the human worm," the Judge would say, lying back philosophically in his chair, his hands locked behind his head. "And the temptation to make money by ways that are dark is stronger still—has the fascination of freebooting and smuggling. Why, I have had to have 'Deliver us from temptation' framed in big capitals over my bed-foot;

and now I find myself getting up without opening my eyes."

There was one man of the " Ring " whom Judge Picken-son would not affiliate with. This was Yent, the burly, brazen sheriff of the parish. Yent's nationality was uncertain ; he was a sort of interloper in the Radical camp. He had won his way into it, partly by his persistent assurance, and partly by the capability Witchell had seen in him of impressing the negroes and ignorant white voters. His big, imposing form, always well dressed and well mounted, his bass voice, his fine condescension, the straightforward facility with which he could flatter or lie, and his ready knack of rolling out wordy information and advice made him seem a marvel of wisdom and honesty to his ignorant worshipers.

He impressed the negroes with the belief that he was Witchell's right hand, and that it was their interest to stay and work only where he said. In this way he got planters (widows particularly) under obligation to him, which he turned to account by inducing them to intrust the sale of their cotton to his superintendence. He pocketed the stealage accruing from this trust with such bland assurance that his victims (more especially the widows) were dazed into believing that they owed him a debt of gratitude. Indeed, he took bribes, swindled, and lied, in such a pompous, self-approving way, that it is certain a moral sense was omitted in his composition.

Witchell regarded him with growing disfavor. He would have taken away his office at once, but Yent had had glimpses behind the scenes, and would be a dangerous enemy. There seemed no other way but to throw sops to Cerberus ; and this Cerberus was capable of absorbing a good many sops.

The sunset crimson was fading into purple and gray.

Many of the loiterers by the river bank had gone home to their early supper. Colonel Alver carried off his guest, Miss Vincent; Floyd Reese, gayly calling out that she would follow in a moment, had lingered behind, talking to young Witchell. The fresh wind played with her half-curled hair and blew aside her light scarf, giving glimpses of her round, white arms.

All at once her bright look darkened. Only for an instant; the red lips caught up their smile.

"Yonder is your brother, the Captain," she said to Omar. "How well he looks on horseback!"

Captain Witchell had just returned from a day's ride through the "Hills," where many of the poorer farmers were his grateful adherents. He noticed Miss Reese by the merest nod, and motioned with his riding whip for Omar to come to him.

"What do you know of that young woman?" he asked.

"Only that she is a governess in Colonel Alver's family, and that she formerly taught at Mr. Vincent's and seems good friends with Miss Zoe."

"She has not always been a governess. I happen to know an episode in her history. I need not tell it to you. A word will be sufficient. Beware of her. She is not so angelic as she seems."

Omar looked his surprise.

"Very well. I will be on my guard," he said at last. "How is Adelle?"

"She is not so well, and that reminds me to be going. She was anxious I should be back early."

"Yes, go at once; she will be looking out for you. I had some flowers to give you for her, when you should come back by here, but—"

"But Miss Reese has got them away from you, I see.

Take care she gets nothing more important from you. Good-by. You are coming to spend Sunday with us, of course. Adelle told me to remind you of it."

CHAPTER XIV.

THE party at Colonel Alver's house dragged, in spite of the host's elegant politeness. His self-control was not so perfect that a sense of something having gone wrong—of some secret discomfiture—did not emanate from him and affect his guests. Only one present besides himself understood the cause of the cloud that came and went across his face ; and that one was *not* his wife—a gentle, sweet-faced lady, who patiently played quadrilles for some of the young people to dance, and who seemed wrapped in her children. She kept them by her at the piano ; when she was not playing she threaded their curls with her slim white fingers, and looked into their faces with wistful tenderness.

Presently, when they had looked long enough at the dancing, she carried them off to bed, leaving the part of hostess to be filled by Miss Floyd Reese. That young lady, though only a governess, was at home in dispensing courtesies here, and was treated with much consideration by Colonel Alver and his friends. Dressed in black gauze, with her fine arms bare, and Omar's wild pinks in her hair and on her bosom, she eclipsed every girl there, except Miss Vincent. Zoe's face, perfect as a medallion cut in ivory, her coils of black hair, her slender, graceful shape, were in accord with the simple dress she wore—white all over, except for one dash of vivid color at her throat, where a red rose was held in place by a diamond cluster.

But Floyd had a score of alluring coquetries of manner

that Zoe could not, or would not use, and she managed to have a larger share of admirers about her. To have seen her, gay, witty, ready with repartee or adroit flattery, one would not have guessed that she too was disappointed to-night, and that the bright glances that seemed to be carelessly sweeping the room were really watching the door with feverish eagerness. But, had one been noticing, he would have seen a peculiar look come into her face as Omar Witchell entered the room at last, quite late, and having with him only young Hayne, and Devene, the tax collector of an adjoining parish, the younger brother of that Devene who had been Captain Witchell's right-hand man during all his political career, and who still held a place in the Legislature.

After leaving Judge Pickenson's, Omar had gone to Devene's room, where he found Hayne and Devene smoking by the open window. Devene was giving a comic description of his "tribulations as a tax collector in an unreconstructed corner" of the neighboring parish.

"They gave me hail Columbia," he said. "The men got down their old shot guns and tried the triggers; the widows got after me with broomsticks, the children set dogs upon me, the very donkeys brayed defiance at me from their little pole-pen stables, and the damsels were proof against all my blandishments. They made satirical remarks about my appearance quite loud enough for me to hear, and one pretty red-cheeked girl broke my heart by characterizing my mustache (my best point, as I thought) as an old coon tail. I was told several times, 'Never mind; when you go to Morefield you'll get it. Folks there are not going to stand such tax papers as these—and from radical carpet-baggers. They are fixing up for you in Morefield.' So, before I start for Morefield, I'll have my will drawn up, boys, and make you my heirs.

I advise you to take the same precaution, Omar. You've only had to deal as yet with the people round about here, and this section is pretty well under the Captain's control. It's the best reconstructed parish in the district, thanks to your brother Marshall. Even Alver has come around lately, which is quite a triumph. By the way, are we going to his house to-night? I should say it was time we were there. Are you waiting for Captain Witchell, Omar?"

"No, he is not going."

"He is not? Why, I thought his policy was to conciliate."

"So it is; but in this case he has his reasons for staying away. Hayne, my dear boy, put down that bottle. You've had enough this evening. I don't want the finest waltzer in the country to do discredit to his reputation to-night. No, indeed; I'm in earnest. Here she goes into the lock-up;" and firmly, but with an air of affectionate playfulness, he took the bottle of brandy from the handsome deputy sheriff, whipped it into Devene's *armoire*, and turned the key. Many a time he had interfered to keep the self-indulged young aristocrat from drinking more than was good for him, and from throwing away his money at cards.

The young Southerner was a pet among the Radical officers. Witchell had given him a place at first through politic motives, but his gay, indolent humor, and frank, improvident ways, had a fascination for these colder and more rigid New Englanders, and Hayne became a favorite among them.

The three young men were not a bad-looking trio as they entered Colonel Alver's parlor ten minutes afterward.

Omar was the least striking. He was slender, and he

had a slight stoop of the shoulders, but his smile gave a charm to his grave face, and his eyes set you to wondering at their childlike earnestness.

Miss Reese left her partner and came to meet him with her sweetest smile, and a chiding for his being so late. He answered her pleasantly, but she knew, by some subtile change in look and tone, that something had happened since she talked with him at sunset on the river bank. His brother had warned him against her. Had he told him all he knew of her ? No, he would not do that. He had promised not to tell that bit of black history which had come to his knowledge the evening of her hurried advent into the State. But he had warned Omar against her. It was for this he had called him from her side. And he refused to accept Alver's invitation. Her game was blocked in this direction, She set her sharp little teeth hard together.

" I'll pay him for it," she thought.

Then she turned to her partner.

" I beg your pardon," she said graciously. " I believe you asked me what I thought of our State Senator's younger brother. He's quite stupid and ordinary. His looks have not even the knavish distinction of the Captain's. He looked so owlish I thought he might be wise, and was at some pains to draw him out, but I soon found there was nothing to draw. He is ' a blank, my lord, a blank.' No, Captain Witchell did not come. He showed his discernment. He was only invited for courtesy's sake. His wife and Mrs. Alver are old acquaintances. The Colonel is relieved, I know, to find that they have had the good sense to stay away."

The company went away a little after twelve. Mrs. Alver had long since retired. Floyd took Zoe up to her room, helped her lay aside her dress and comb out her splendid hair; then, stooping to kiss her as she sat robed in the snowy, ruffled gown, she said:

"Go to bed *petite*, and keep your eyes bright for to-morrow. I'm going down now to count the spoons; I'll be back directly."

Down she went, noiseless as a cat, but not to the pantry. A single light was burning in the parlor, and Colonel Alver sat there—gloom in his looks. She went and stood at a little distance in front of him, her hands crossed before her, her eyes fixed upon him.

"Well," she said, with a little flicker of mirth about her lips, "you look as Napoleon may have looked after Waterloo. You have not lost a battle—only made a false move—an unimportant one."

"A mean, sneaking, asinine move that it humiliates me to think of—a move you were the cause of. But for your persuasions I would never have stooped to conciliate these men."

"There is no great harm done; you have been checked in one little diplomatic move; the question is now, what shall be your next?"

"My next move? I will make none. I will not keep up this farce of good-will any longer. The mask of the hypocrite stifles me. I will fling it off. I hate Witchell and his set, and I'll let them see and hear it when they please, but this is all I can do. I can't supplant them; it's folly to think about that. They have too firm a hold here, and they have had it so long now that it seems a thing of course for them to be our masters, to absorb all our offices, to make money out of us, and to whistle up the bayonets if we dare expostulate. It is one of the many contemptible qualities of men that they soon become servile after they have once been cowed. I was a fool not to have left this land of slaves as soon as the war ended and gone to Honduras, when I had money and energy to begin life over again. Now I must content myself to be a village store-keeper to the end of the chapter, with my poor chances of trade crippled by Yankee interference."

"Is it possible you so soon give up? Where is your ambition?"

"Ambition? Talk of running a race to a man who is tied hand and foot. Don't you see I can do nothing here. Witchell has this parish completely under his thumb. He is daily becoming stronger here. He will be reëlected for the Senate, unless he thinks the time is ripe for him to snatch at a bigger office, for he aspires to be governor of the State, and he will be. But he will manage to quarter his needy kin upon us here, world without end. I have humbled my pride, and acted on your suggestion that the only way to get rid of them was to get in with them, learn their secret tactics, beat them at their own tricks and mount over their heads. But that plan doesn't work, you see. Witchell has given me the cold shoulder. He will have nothing to do with me. He knows I would not make a good tool in his hands. I would not be satisfied to have a petty office flung to me—a crumb from a full table. For this reason he don't want me, and it is as well, for I could never submit to his dictation. So there's an end to a foolish dream—partly inspired by you, for I had become almost a 'good citizen,' as the 'Ring' call these cowardly boot-licks, until I knew you, and your words fanned the smoldering fire into a flame of hope. Let it die down now in ashes."

"A poor flame it must have been to be so easily quenched. If it is a true flame it will burn through these obstacles. I tell you, there is no ground for giving up hope. Your prospect of success is as good as ever, if you will believe it."

"Pray, what would you have me do? Woman-like,

you have some impracticable plan in your brain. You hang
out rainbows, but fail to show us how to get the treasure
at the end of them. I suppose you would have me go
down on my knees to Witchell and beg some deputy office
or other. He absorbs all the rest himself. He is representative, tax-receiver, magistrate, and everything else. I
will not stoop to him again."

"Nor do I want you to. I can see that there is no use
to move farther in that direction. But you must not drop
your mask, as you call it, altogether—at least for a while.
You can work best for a time behind it; and work against
him you must; secretly for a while, and then as openly
as you please. You have time to do much between now
and the next election. Institute a secret society in opposition to his 'loyal league,' extend its branches into the
country around. Make speeches at the meetings. You are
eloquent and impassioned; you can stir up the people
against this man; you can break through this numbing ice
of submissiveness."

"You forget that the people, as you call them, do hardly
half the voting now. The negro predominates under Witchell's registration."

"You may work upon the negro also through one
man."

"You mean Yent?"

"Yes; he is secretly Witchell's enemy, and he has full
as much control over the man and brother as Witchell has.
I found that out, and some other things, in a private talk
I have had with Yent."

"A private talk—you? Floyd, and you know Yent's
reputation?"

"I am not afraid of him. Don't be jealous, my Cæsar
of the yard-stick, my eagle caged and clipped. I am working in your interest. Leave Yent to me. He shall not

suspect you in the case. He shall work cautiously and
for himself chiefly, as *he* will think. At the last moment
he may be the means of bringing over no mean number to
your party."

"My party! I have none."

"But you must have. Set the ball rightly in motion
and it will gather as it rolls. Organize a party of opposition, secretly at first, as I have said. Such an organization grows faster under the shadow of secrecy. Curiosity
and mystery stimulate its growth. When it has attained
a formidable size, bring it out into the light."

"How plausibly you talk! As if there were any use of
organizing an opposition that would be certainly crushed
when it came to the test of election. The ballot-box is
wholly in the hands of this Ring. They can manipulate
there as they please. If fraudulent registering and fraudulent casting of votes do not do the work, fraudulent counting of returns will set them all right."

"You must make them afraid to practice such unlawful
tricks. You must watch them so vigilantly, hold them to
account so boldly, that they will grow timid, hardened as
they are in assurance. Get a mouth-piece here in opposition to theirs—a newspaper—that, when the time is ripe for
open opposition, shall begin the war in the most fearless fashion; shall make wit, abuse, and satire its unsparing weapons. Scatter abroad scathing truths, withering exposures.
Rake up old scores and light them with fresh fires of hate.
I can worm many of their evil secrets from Yent. Show
these up in vivid colors. Throw sneers at the people, who
have so long stood these things, and encourage them to
stand them no longer."

He looked at her with admiration.

"What a leader you would make!" he said. "Floyd,
you ought to have been born a man."

"Oh ! if I had been," she cried. "As a man, I would act ; now I can only inspire others to act. I would command fate. I would fight against dull mediocrity. I would rise above the heads of the common crowd, or die in the attempt. I would stickle at nothing, fear nothing, care for nothing but power. Ah ! to feel such a will—throbbing, struggling inside your heart, and know it must be kept in, restrained for ever by the *woman's* bodice."

She trembled with the strength of her emotion. This passion for power was a mania with her. It had been her ruin. Since she *must* rule by the need of her being, she had sought to rule hearts—dangerous and explosive things. Had she been a man, she might have ruled *heads*.

He was silent for a moment, looking at her ; then, as she sank slowly into a seat and leaned her elbow upon the marble table, and dropped her eyes, he said :

"Floyd, I wonder, with your ambition, that you did not attach your hopes to the winning clique."

"Because I did not believe it would continue to be the winning party. My woman's insight tells me that it is doomed. It seems flourishing now, but there is rottenness within. I had rather launch my boat on the low tide that is just beginning to rise than on the high tide that is beginning to ebb. A reaction is at hand."

"I can not see it. Our cause never seemed darker than now."

"It is the dark hour that comes before the day. The pendulum must swing to the farther end of the arc before it begins to return."

"And it is this foresight that makes you prefer rather to buoy a stranded ship than to float with one whose timbers are giving way ?"

"That is one reason."

"And you have another ?"

"Perhaps I have—a woman's reason," she said, her expression changing. "Perhaps, instead of seeking to bask in the good fortune of this lank, lucky Yankee adventurer, with his

> 'Heart that is cold
> To all but gold,'

I prefer to cheer and inspire a—"

"A cropped-winged eagle—a Cæsar of the yard-stick, as you contemptuously characterize him."

"Hush," she said, rising and putting her little hands together, her favorite gesture. "To inspire a man who, in spite of his fallen fortunes, is a king among men; who was born to superiority, who aspires, and may succeed if he wills it—a man whose wrath can make men tremble, whose voice can persuade or command, and whose smile is —fascination."

Her burning eye—her voice sunk to such a thrilling whisper! He started toward her, but she sprang back a step, light as a bird. She stood there, looking in her gossamer black dress and red flowers, with her long, white neck, and bright eyes, like some bird of the tropics, conscious of alluring you, yet ready to fly if you approach too near. But when she saw he had controlled himself she came up of her own accord and laid her hand on his arm.

"Promise me that you will do what I have asked," she said, looking into his eyes. "Promise me that you will not give up in this weak fashion, that you will supplant these men that are your own bitter enemies as well as the enemies of your country."

"I am ready to promise anything *you* ask."

"Do not speak that way. I am in deep, bitter earnest. Promise that you will follow the plan I have outlined, filled in by your superior judgment."

"I promise you I will. I only follow out my own

strong inclination when I oppose these tyrants. Justice, patriotism, as well as desire to redress my individual wrongs, make it right to use every means to root them out. Every *honorable* means—dishonorable means I will not be a party to."

She bit her lip with a quick expression of impatience, but she bent her head to hide it the next instant.

"Very well," she said. "Thanks; I will count on you. You will succeed."

"I have scarcely a hope of it. By next election we will be calling our little play 'Labor Lost.'"

"By next election much may happen," she said eagerly. All this opposition we are to sow broadcast must break out in some result; with all this scattered gunpowder, the least spark will produce an explosion that shall send our enemies to destruction."

He looked at her earnestly in silence.

"Or," she went on, "some trap may be set into which they shall walk blindfold, and which will crush—*kill* them."

"Floyd, would you advocate such measures?"

"Yes, I would fight Satan with fire; I am afraid it is the only way in this case. It is the only way to rid our section of this pest. Witchell has fastened upon it with the cold-blooded persistence of the devil-fish. Lop off one tentacle, and he will put out another. No lopping or crippling, then, but *crushing*. And if not by fair means, then by foul."

"There I can not follow you. I said I would use all *honorable* means. Assassination, and traps, and dark plots are not honorable. I would stop this side of these. So far, and no farther."

A scowl of disappointment and contempt darkened her face. Then she laughed mirthlessly.

"All's fair in war, you know," she said carelessly. "Spare me that frown, just Cato. I was only testing your integrity. Of course you will do nothing but what is honorable, nor would I wish you to. Could you not see I was not in earnest? I only gave you a touch of my histrionic powers. Am I not a good actor?"

"You are, indeed. You looked the murderous Borgia then. I wonder now, as I have often done before, why you have not gone on the stage."

"I preferred a wider scope for my powers—a real stage. Some day I will act a real tragedy—or inspire one. Or, perhaps," with another of her quick changes, "it will be only a melodrama or a love idyl."

She gave him a kiss of the hand and a courtesy. "Goodnight. I told Miss Vincent I was coming down to count the spoons. She will have a poor opinion of my arithmetic."

She reached the door and looked back.

"I have recorded your promise *here*," she said, laying her hand upon her heart. "I shall not forget it."

Outside the door, she paused and stared at the low moon, seen through the glass around the hall-door.

"So far and no farther," she repeated to herself. "Oh! what weak, squeamish things some men are! Honor and conscience and pride are bugbears for ever in their path.

"Well, we'll see. He shall be blinded and led farther before he knows it—if there is need of it. I will not give up—no not if I have to play a lone hand. I can not rest until Witchell is out of the way—the man who has scorned me, humbled me, as no man ever did before—the man who alone knows my secret, who watches me with such cold, cruel contempt in his eyes, who may at any moment expose me, and put my life in danger."

The moon sank behind the forest line. Floyd stole

noiseless as a gliding serpent up the stairs. She cast a glance at the sleeping Zoe, undressed, and crept to bed, lying down with her brain full of wild, whirling thoughts and dark memories that *would* steal in—by the side of the white-souled girl asleep with the smiling shadow of a dream on her parted lips.

The man she had left sat awhile with his brow contracted in thought, his eyes fixed upon the door that had closed behind the beautiful woman.

"So far and no farther," he too repeated. Captain Pickenson had been mistaken in his estimate of him. He was not fit for "treason, stratagems, and spoils." He was too proud and hot-tempered. He hated his foes with all the strength of his fiery heart, and he was intensely ambitious—more ambitious than Witchell (though without the New Englander's cold, plodding earnestness of aim), for he loved power for power's sake, and he only cared for money as a means to increase his influence.

He was a born autocrat. He had reigned like a feudal baron among his many slaves; he had commanded a regiment with the pride and zest of a Russian Prince. No wonder he chafed in his narrow sphere. But, for all his hatred of his enemies, his resentment at the injuries he held they had inflicted upon his business, and his desire to supplant them, he revolted at using underhand means to accomplish his end. He would have despaired of attempting any systematized means had it not been for the persistent suggestions of the girl who was so mad for the overthrow of Witchell, and the accession of another, in whose prosperity she might have some share. He was under the influence of the wily charmer. She bewildered and attracted him; but she adroitly held him at arm's length, and increased her power over him by preserving his respect for her as a woman.

CHAPTER XV.

THE Legislature was in convention in New Orleans. It was a busy session. Besides the legitimate State business, there were issues affecting the party in power, and there were questions of vital personal interest to some of the members. Most actively interested of any man in the Assembly was the member of the Senate from the —th district. Yet Marshall Witchell's activity was never outwardly shown. His bearing had its usual self-collected, almost stoical quiet. The firm mouth, the cold, keen eye kept the secret of the busy brain that was on the alert to avoid false moves, to seize all the points of advantage that were offered by this occasion—an important crisis, as he rightly judged, in his political destiny. This year his term as member of the Senate would expire. He determined at least on reëlection. He had hoped for a higher office, and there was no reason why he should not obtain it. In intellect he was superior to either of the two other men who were pointed at as the possible prospective governor of the State. Financially, he was able to cope with them, and politically his influence was as wide as theirs; he had as many friends, and they were stanch ones. There was only one drawback. Both the other aspirants for the highest office of the State resided near New Orleans. They were identified in a manner with the city that was the political and business center of the State. The influence they could wield was from this circumstance stronger. Then there were tricks that the Metropolitan Political Ring was up to which Witchell, with all his acuteness, had not yet learned. He was learning them, however. His energies were bent to the task of extending his influence, bringing his views into prominence, conciliating those in any way unfriendly to him, and trying to understand the tactics of his opponents and to set in motion secret springs that might circumvent them. He found there was disaffection in the Republican party; a complaint of mismanagement and of unfair distribution of favors. The disaffected ones would rally around Witchell. They would be willing to have New Orleans thrown out in the approaching nomination, and all the higher offices given to men from the country. Witchell saw this disposition, and he saw his chance to be the political leader of the State. He set his sails to catch this favorable wind, but he gave no sign of his intentions to the other side. While he based his hope on this half secret split in the party, he appeared to enter heartily into the formation of what was known as the Republican Alliance, which consisted in the Republicans banding together to meet the Democratic opposition which they foresaw; binding themselves to do all in their power to uphold their party and to check the rebellious spirit that began to be rife in the air. Every parish was to be newly organized by all the negroes being sworn in, and as many of the whites as could be induced to ally themselves with the party that seemed at present all powerful. Witchell's cupidity and his ambition were alike fired by the prize he saw in the future. He saw power and a fortune of millions ahead of him; but his hand did not shake as he prepared to grasp it. Coolly, systematically, and with great *finesse* and strategy, he set about paving his way, preparatory to the Convention of nomination that would meet in the summer.

The work in hand absorbed his thoughts and occupied his time; he had none to spare to his invalid young wife. She was with him in the city in elegant apartments, but she felt almost as far removed from his daily life—his thoughts and occupations—as though she had remained in her quiet, catalpa-shaded home on Red River. Her husband had taken pains that she should have every attention that money could obtain.

She had a physician and nurses, a carriage was at her disposal, and fresh fruits and flowers were daily sent to her room. But those attentions that only watchful and devoted love can give—these the poor, sick heart missed and pined for. To have him sit by her and hold her hand and look with tenderness into her fading face, and say cheering words, adding the balm of affection to the cordial of his electrical presence—this would have been happiness to Adelle. But though he daily left a kiss on her lips, he was too preoccupied to notice how feverish they were, and how wistfully they trembled. He did not see, when he parted the hair from her temples, that her forehead grew wanner and the blue veins more apparent every day. Her complaints of loneliness, her little tender appeals to spare her an hour from daily business or night committees annoyed him sometimes. Could she not see he was working for her? She would be the richest and most honored lady in the State; she should have her winter mansion near this beautiful city, her summer home among the mountains of his native land. Why would she not go out more into society? His mother, for whose opinion he had the highest regard, had told him before he and his wife left "Starlight Home" on the river that Adelle was hysterical and babyish. She had been too much petted when a girl. She must be dealt with kindly but firmly, and taught some womanly strength of character. If she would mix more with people, go more into general society, it would make her realize the dignity of her position, and keep her from pining because she missed the petting of the father and mother and the brother who had cast her off. Her illness, declared the strong, wiry New England woman (who forgot *she* had once been an invalid), arose from this weak grieving over the estrangement of her family and from childish craving to be petted and caressed by her husband. If she could get over this, was Mrs. Witchell's decision, Adelle would soon be perfectly well. Witchell, who knew little of the secret and delicate mechanism of a woman's heart, tried to act upon his mother's suggestion. Her plan might have answered with a colder and shallower nature, but it did not answer with this girl, to whom love was the fountain without which, if once dried, all her physical being must wither and perish.

She did pine for the home friends, and the fond home care and watchful tenderness—the kind old face of her mother, the stern, but to her (in the old days) always tender eyes of her father. Oh! how could they harden their hearts so against her? How could they refuse to see her, to write to her in answer to her imploring letters all this long, weary while? She had heard that her mother told a friend she knew "Adelle needed her old parents no longer; that she was rich now, and she had the husband she was so anxious to forsake every one else for; she was flattered, followed in society, and had a fine house and jewels and dresses, and her husband's mother and kinsfolk to care for her. No doubt she never gave a thought to her old home."

Not give it a thought? How often Adelle, in the midst of her fine surroundings, yearned with inexpressible longing to rest her languid form under the old honeysuckle shaded porch at home? The scent of the pinks; the twitter of the martins in their gourd nests, hung aloft to swing and rattle in the wind; the coo of her pigeons; her mother's voice, singing as she sewed or knitted,

"How do thy mercies close me round?"

Her father's whistle as he worked away at putting up a trellis for a grape-vine, or at hanging a refractory gate; the

monotonous song of the little kitchen darky in the back
yard as he plied the churn-dasher under the mulberry-tree
and pleaded

> " Come, butter, come,
>   Here stands Miss with a free good-will ; "

Derrick's laugh and his quick step behind her, and his
hands put over her eyes while he drew back her head to
drop ripe huckleberries in her mouth—all these sights and
sounds of the sweet, lost country home came so vividly
over Adelle, as she lay in her elegant bed, or sat by her
window, looking out into the street full of strange, hurrying, self-absorbed people, that the tears would come in
slow drops and roll down her pale cheeks, and the hired
nurse (a French woman, cross and tyrannical when alone
with her charge) would say impatiently,

" Now you are crying again, madam, and making yourself worse. What will the Captain say when he sees your
eyes all red ? "

At this the poor girl would hurriedly wipe away the
tears and beg the maid to remove their traces with pearl
powder, for she knew Captain Witchell was always annoyed
at her weeping. His nature was utterly dissimilar to hers,
and he could not understand why she should not be happy.
He was more to her than the parents or the home she had
lost ; but, alas ! to her sensitive, sick heart, she seemed to
have lost him also. She counted for so little in his busy
life—she had so little part in it. It would have been a joy
to her to help him. But he seemed so sufficient to himself.
He asked no sympathy ; he confided none of his hopes and
plans.

Neither understood the other, but Adelle tried faithfully to please her husband, although the weakness conse-
quent upon ill health made her efforts fitful and languid.

When she felt able to be up, she dressed sometimes and went with him to dinner at the houses of men whose wives had left their cards on her center-table—men whom Captain Witchell wished especially to please. Her delicate beauty and sweetness of manner always rendered her a favorite, but it was at sad sacrifice of her own feelings that she made these efforts.

Zoe Vincent came to the city with her brother, who brought his cotton to exchange for plantation supplies and goods for his store. She went to see Adelle at once, and the poor little patient brightened under her nursing and her cheering presence. A delicate pink came into her cheeks, unlike the feverish hectic that sometimes burned there. One evening she was greatly better; she was going to the opera with Zoe and Royal West. She hoped to persuade her husband to go with her, and she waited for him with childlike eagerness. Very lovely she looked in her dress of pale silk with ermine-trimmed opera cloak and dainty hood that only half covered her little shapely head, whose dark tresses she had made the French hair-dresser arrange in curls, because she had often worn them so in her girlhood, and she fancied Marshall liked it.

He came at last; a glance at his face told her he had brought his business cares home with him, but going up to him she timidly preferred her little request. Would he go with her and her friends to the opera to-night? She would not enjoy it without him. Her spirits sank as, without noticing her pretty toilet, he said:

"I am sorry; I have a business engagement to-night; I am chairman of a committee—and of course can't go. Mr. West will fill my place as escort, and Miss Zoe will keep you in spirits."

She went with her friends, but all pleasure in the entertainment was gone for her. As she sat in a side box many

8

eyes were turned wonderingly to her beautiful pale face and large melancholy eyes.

In the midst of the prima donna's mimic grief Mrs. Witchell fainted. She soon recovered consciousness, but she looked so wan that Zoe hurried her home, and sat by her until Captain Witchell came, while Royal waited in the parlor. Zoe was strongly moved by the change in her friend.

"It all comes from love," she thought. "Let me take warning."

During the drive to the hotel she was altogether silent, and when, Royal having dismissed the carriage, the two sat secluded and quiet in the bower-like balcony that over-hung the street, she still remained silent and *distrait* in spite of the balmy air, the myriad stars overhead, and the softened light that came through the windows of the draw-ing-room. She started as Royal, laying his hand over hers, asked the cause of her silence.

"I have been thinking what a mad thing it is for a woman to stake her happiness for this world upon a man's love," she answered, drawing away her hand as she spoke.

"If it be a mad thing, you will never deserve a strait-jacket for any such insanity," he said sardonically.

"I was speaking generally. I do not like to have my remarks applied to myself by another," she responded haughtily, half rising as she spoke, and then added : "It is late. I had better say good-night."

"Excuse me ; it is not so late. Sit down. I must have some words with you in private. I have had no oppor-tunity of speaking them since you came. You have seemed to me to plan that I should not be alone with you. Pardon me if I wrong you, but I can not help believing that your engagement to me is no longer agreeable to you ; that your heart is not in it. You have put me off from time to time

until months have grown into years, and, now that no
shadow of pretext is left for you to postpone our marriage,
you seem to avoid the subject altogether ; you shrink from
being alone with me. What does it mean ? "

For a while she was silent, then she said deprecatingly :

"You know my reasons for postponement, Royal.
First, it was my mother's death. I could not think of
marriage while that sorrow was so fresh in my mind."

"But it is now three years since that happened."

" I know ; but I have been of such use in my brother's
family, teaching his dear little children, he often declares
he could not spare me ; and, besides, I hated to come to you
as a burden ; and you know the little fortune my mother
left me is to stay in the hands of trustees until I am twenty-
one. You agreed with me—or you ought to have—that it
would be more prudent to wait until then."

" I agreed to nothing of the kind. You tried to reason
me into agreeing to such an absurdity, but I told you we
wouldn't need your money. I had a fair income from my
profession ; I had saved money and invested it to advantage.
I am now about to purchase a handsome house, which I
will furnish comfortably. If any prudential reasons once
existed why we should not marry, they exist no longer. I
am tired to death of boarding-house life, and, to be frank
with you, I am tired of your dilly-dallying in this matter
of our engagement. To-night I must have your positive
answer. When will you fulfill your promise, Zoe ? On
what day, or week, or month at farthest will you marry
me ? "

He felt her hand tremble as he took it in his, and he
could see how pale she was.

" I have been too impetuous in my way of speaking to
you," he said gently. "Pardon me, and give me the answer I ask—my best love."

"Am I really your best love?" she retorted quickly. "Do you love me better than you do any one else? better than you *could* love some one else if you were to try, Royal? There are so many beautiful, accomplished girls here in the city, and you might win any one of them; I am sure you might."

"Thank you, I know that there are scores of handsome women here, and that I am looked upon as a good catch, in their parlance, but I can not see what that has to do with the question I have asked you. Certainly I loved you only, or I would not have asked you to be my wife."

"But people change."

"Do they? I have not. Over three years ago I engaged myself to you, with the approval of your father, and the full sanction of your mother who is now in heaven. I have looked forward constantly to our marriage. I have worked hard with that incentive, wishing to give you the social position you deserved. It is rather late in the day to ask me if I love you, Zoe. I will retaliate and ask you the same question. Zoe, do you love me?"

She made a movement as if she would withdraw her hands, but he held them firmly. She tried to laugh at his earnestness.

"How like a lawyer you put that question, and how sharply your eye takes me up; you make me feel like a veritable prisoner at the bar."

He did not smile; his face grew sterner instead.

"Zoe, I will not bear any trifling with me now. Speak; I insist upon your answering me. I know that you are truthful. You will not tell me a lie."

"No, I will not," she said with impetuous emphasis, as though she had conquered in a struggle with herself. "You ask me if I love you, and I must answer, I do not know."

"Not know? Your ignorance in that matter is recent. *Once* you seemed to have no doubt on that score."

"I had not—then. I esteemed you. I felt sure that I loved you—but, since—"

"Since then you have lost your esteem for me."

"No, not that. I—I have seen—"

"Ah! you have seen some one else you had rather marry. I might have known what all this reluctance meant."

"I have seen no one I had rather marry."

"Then what do you mean? Be calm, Zoe; speak coherently, and to the point, please."

"I will, so far as I can. I can hardly make my feelings clear to you, for they are not clear to me. If they had been I would have spoken before now. It has pained me to feel as if I were imposing upon you. You shall hear all; you can understand, perhaps, what I hardly comprehend myself. I have met a man in whom I feel a singular and unexplainable interest. No matter where I met him, or what his name may be. Indeed, I do not know his real name, or his family, or anything scarcely of his past life; but—I think of him always. I am filled with anxiety for his fate, for he is what may be called an outlaw. I remember every word I ever heard him speak. I recall the look in his eyes, the touch of his hand; no other look or touch ever thrilled me so. You see, I am holding nothing back," she said, lifting her eyes that had dropped to the floor. The deep flush that burned on her cheeks witnessed at what cost she was making this confession.

"And you wish to marry this man?" asked her lover with forced calmness.

"No, oh! no. I would not; I could not marry him. No woman of gentle blood could promise herself happiness in marrying such a man. He is rough; he is reckless, fierce at times. Something in his life has happened to make him so."

"An unprincipled desperado, like many who are coming to the front just now."

"Unprincipled! No, Royal, no, he is not unprincipled. He has a high sense of honor; I have seen it proved, and he is brave; there is no hero in old days that was ever braver; yet he can be tamed by a soft word."

"Ah! I know the style of man—a modern Red Rover. He rendered you some service. You saw him in some position that excited your pity; you saw him do some act of cheap bravado, and straightway your imagination painted him a hero—especially after he told you that he loved you."

"But he did not tell me so, unless in some wild, impulsive words that probably meant nothing. He rendered me a service, it is true, but it was not until after I had seen him and—felt for him as I have told you. Do not be sarcastic, Royal; listen to me. I do not know how to analyze the feeling I have for this man. I could never marry him; my judgment would oppose it—and what would my father and my brother say? He himself said he would wish any woman a better fate than to marry him. I shall, in all probability, never see him again, for he has gone, as he told me, to the outskirts of civilization—to Mexico or Utah, I imagine. I have not seen him for months. Now I have told you all."

"All?"

"Everything, I think."

"And it was the interest you took in this desper—I mean in this man that caused you to put off fulfilling your engagement to me?"

"It was. I could not think it right to marry you, feeling as I did about another man."

"Yet you do not respect him; you would not marry

him ; you have never spoken a word of affection to him or listened to any avowal of love on his part. You never expect him to cross your path again—all this is true, is it not ?"

"It is."

"And you still care for me ?"

"I do ; as much as I ever did."

"Zoe, depend upon it, your feeling for this man is a mere romantic fancy—the impulse of an imaginative, sympathetic girl. Banish it. Think no more of such a man. Forget that you have met him, and I will forget it as well. The engagement between us that has lasted so long, until you seem almost my wife, shall still exist—unless you wish it to be broken. Do you ?"

"No," she said, after a pause. "I will fulfill my promise, since you still wish it after what I have told you. I will try to forget as truly as I regret having ever met this man."

"I am sure you will. I love you for your truthfulness in telling me what you could have easily kept back. I know it has been painful to you. I will not trouble you any more to-night. To-morrow, if you will, you shall name the day when you will make me happy by giving me this little hand."

He raised her hand to his lips, bowing as he kissed it, and left her.

She admired his good sense and kindness in dealing with her unfortunate "fancy"—and yet—oh ! contradictory puzzle of woman's heart ! she would have liked him better if he had been unreasonable and jealous—had gone into a passion over her confession, and upbraided her in violent terms.

But she admired and respected him ; she thought how good and talented he was—how perfectly nice, from his morals to his person—his well-kept hands, his glossy hair,

his immaculate shirt-fronts and perfectly fitting coat and
boots. What a contrast to that other one—that long-limbed
"desperado," as Royal had called him, and as, perhaps, he
deserved to be called.

CHAPTER XVI.

In the spring, now close at hand, it would be two years
since Zoe met this man who had taken such a hold upon
her sympathy or her imagination as to make her feel it a
duty to tell Royal of her interest in him. She had then
been in New Orleans waiting the departure of the steamship that would take her to Havana to visit her father, who
had gone there a year before, and, entering into the tobacco
business, had endeavored to repair his damaged fortune.
He had had yellow fever the fall before, and had ever since
been rather weak in health and depressed in spirits. His
usually cheerful mind was clouded with presentiments, and
he longed to see his daughter. In this mood, but without
frightening Zoe by any gloomy expressions, he wrote to her
to come to him—for a visit, if she should not fancy living
on the island, or the climate did not agree with her. It
would be a pleasant trip, and she would be well taken care
of by any of the captains of the three United States packets
plying regularly between New Orleans and Cuba, and touching at various ports along the gulf coast to put off freight—
much of it supplies for the United States troops stationed
at various points on the coast or along the railroad line in
the interior. He knew the commanders of those government vessels; had had business transactions with them,
and found them gentlemanly and honorable.

Zoe had come down to the city in company with some

friends, had found the Lavaca in port, and advertised to leave on next Tuesday. The Captain, who called on her and gave her a letter from her father, assured her his vessel would leave promptly on time. He had the brusque manner of a seaman—a tall, lean, sandy-haired giant, with quick, blunt speech, active and shrewd—Yankee to the core, which did not prevent him from being struck with Zoe's dark southern eyes and dusky bloom.

Tuesday, at the hour announced for the steamer to leave, Zoe drove up to the levee, but on looking from the carriage window she saw no sign of preparation on board the Lavaca; no smoke issuing from its chimneys, and no hurrying sailors. Instead, she saw groups of people turning away from the boat with disappointed looks. The Captain saw her, and, coming up to the carriage, apologized for an unexpected delay in the time of his vessel's leaving. She could not get away before the next morning, owing to the fact that a portion of her cargo had not arrived, and he had received orders by telegraph to wait for it.

"Government stores, I presume," said Royal, who, with his sister, had accompanied Zoe to the ship.

The Captain bowed, but he looked embarrassed. In spite of his very reasonable explanation of the cause of his ship's detention, Zoe could not help feeling that there was some mystery about the Lavaca's delay. She did not find out what it was until next day—some hours after the vessel had left the harbor of New Orleans, and when it was just leaving the mouth of the river and entering upon the broad, blue gulf. Zoe had gone to the rear of the ship for an undisturbed view. On the deck, in front, there were a number of strange passengers and some United States soldiers, under a burly Lieutenant, whose staring regard annoyed her. Here she leaned unmolested on the railing and gazed in calm enjoyment at the lessening shores—the expanse of colorful sea, ruffled with light waves that here and there were flecked with foam.

The chatter of some birds behind her drew her attention, and she turned round and admired the plump little creatures, hopping about their rough cage, with green-blue backs, white breasts, and short bills, red as coral—"Jamaica sparrows," so the old sailor, who was feeding them, called them. He himself was not an unpicturesque figure —a little wiry, weather-beaten man, in a red shirt and tarpaulin cap, but with a shrewd, bright eye set like a black bead under his browned and wrinkled brow. He laughed merrily at the frolics of his pets, let them peck bits of banana from his mouth through the bars of their cage, and scolded them for not having taken their bath.

"I wish all captives could be as happy as your birds are," Zoe said, amused at their antics.

"Yes, miss, so do I; for instance, them poor prisoners here on board with us. If they could take more kindly to their lot, 'twould be better for them. Their stubborn ways will only provoke the Lieutenant in charge of 'em and our Captain, what's none too good-natured already."

"Prisoners on board this vessel! What do you mean?"

"What! you don't know about 'em, miss? Maybe I oughtn't to spoke then. I knew 'twas a secret on land, but I don't see how it can be hid here when we're all in one 'hollow oak' together, as the song says. The prisoners was fetched to the city last night, and brought on board here after midnight for fear of there being a row and a rescue by the mob if they come through the streets in the day. It was in the night, too, that they took 'em out of jail in some town in Alabama, where they had been since they was first arrested. It was feared there'd be a rush to get 'em and set 'em free if they took daylight to bring 'em out."

" What had the prisoners done ? "

"Went to the house of a man that was teaching the darkies, miss, and rode him on a rail, tarred and feathered him, and sent the purty bird back to his country, where he set up such a croakin' as scared and angered the big bugs so they ordered the bunch of law-breakers clapped into jail ; and, when they got afraid there'd be a row, they telegraphed to the Lavaca to hold on and get the prisoners, and take 'em on to the Dry Tortugas—the black rock in the middle of the sea, miss, where they've got Dr. Mudd for splintering the leg of the chap that killed President Lincoln."

" Where have the prisoners been put ? "

"In the ship's hold, miss, a dirty, close box, for the likes of them. I'm told they belong to good families, all seven of them."

" Then there must be some mistake as to their offense. Southern gentlemen would not maltreat a man simply because he taught negroes."

The man looked at her shrewdly from under his old cap. Then his little eyes twinkled with pleasure.

" I see you are not U. S., miss. So I don't mind telling you. You see this steamer's a United States packet, and everything aboard her is U. S., the Captain most of all ; he's the strongest Rad you ever saw. Well, most of them chaps below are real gentlemen and good fellows, miss. One of 'em was my lieutenant in the Confederate navy during the war, and I got a chance to speak with him last night.

"They're takin' 'em to Dry Tortugas for givin' a scalawag thief a ride on a rail. They reported him to the law, and got insulted for their pains. Nigger school-teacher was what he pretended to be, but he was a rogue, and he lived by robbing the planters, getting the niggers to steal cotton and corn from their employers, and bring them to

him in the night and get whisky and tobacco for them.
He bought a little cotton for a blind, and packed and sent
off his bales by the dozen.   The planters had stood it a
long time, with only a little cursin' and threatenin', that
just tickled the thief, when a fellow, a Texan, happened
to stop in the neighborhood, and put them up to taking
the law in their own hands, and getting clear of the rascal
in the way I told you of.   He wasn't hurt ; only scared out
of his cowardly wits, and thought he'd do a good job by
playing off as a martyr to Southern prejudices.   That's the
prisoners' story, miss, and I believe every word of it.   They
don't look a bit like rowdies, not even the Texan, though
he's all torn and bloody."

"Bloody ?"

"He fought before he'd let 'em take him, miss."

"Was he wounded badly ?"

"I can't tell.   He doesn't talk any, but he won't eat,
and he looks dreadful.   Them handcuffs are bad for him
in his fix."

"Handcuffs !   Have they got chains upon them ?"

"You bet they have, though one of them soldiers told
me the handcuffs was to be taken off as soon as we were
fairly out at sea, and only put on when we stop in port or
go near the shore.   The Texan, though, is to have 'em on
all the time, to punish him for—Whist ! here comes the
Captain.   Be mum about the prisoners, miss," and the old
sailor turned off and began to whistle unconcernedly as the
Captain approached.

It was probable that the commander did not wish his
passengers to know the nature of the "Government stores"
he had delayed his vessel to take on board, but it had
already transpired, and his passengers had been besieging
him to give them a sight of the prisoners.   He told Zoe he
had just had the hatchway thrown open, "and now," he

said sarcastically, "I suppose you too have your feminine sympathies excited, and want, besides, a chance to rail at the Government and the Yankees. So will you come and see my show ?"

She hesitated a little before she went round with him to the forward part of the vessel, where the heavy iron-clamped door of the hatchway had been thrown open, and a group of men and women were standing around the oblong opening looking down into the hold. Mrs. Moss—a pretty young married woman, the pet of a husband twice as old as herself—was down upon her knees dropping flowers to the prisoners. "Flirting with them already," the Captain said sardonically.

He pushed a gentleman aside and made room for Zoe and himself near the edge of the hatchway.

"There are your high-toned countrymen, Miss Vincent," he said.

The men below heard the sneer. Eyes were raised, and flashed defiance at the speaker. Others stood in stoical quiet, a curl of contempt just perceptible on their lips. They were no common outlaws. One could see this in spite of their soiled, disordered looks. Their handcuffs had been taken off, and lay in a pile at the feet of the soldier who had been sent to remove them.

"Here are only six men," said some one to the Lieutenant, who was puffing at a cigar, and staring with bold admiration at the unconscious Zoe. "Where's the seventh ?"

"Yonder he lies. His bracelets are not to be taken off. He is too important a personage."

"The lead wolf of the pack," put in the Captain. "Fought, and nearly killed a good soldier before he'd be taken. Stir him up. These ladies want to see the whole show. Make him come out from under that hat, can't you ?"

The man spoken of sat, or rather lay, apart from the others upon an old wooden chest, another box covered by a coat propping his head. His shirt-sleeve was torn and bloody, his manacled arms were folded on his chest, his hat slouched over his face. He did not move when the Captain spoke, nor when the soldier touching him said : "Look up, Hirne."

"Stop," cried the Captain, and, taking up a long bamboo cane that lay on the deck, he reached down and tipped off the prisoner's hat from his head.

The man leaped to his feet ; his eyes blazed upon his insulter with the glare of a caged and maddened lion. The Captain recoiled under the sudden fury of that look.

"Yankee coward," said the prisoner between his set teeth, "you would not dare insult a man unless his chains made it safe for you."

The Captain was furious, but the Lieutenant prevailed on him to say no more.

"You brought it on yourself by noticing the fellow," he said.

That night the Lavaca reached Pensacola, and lay at anchor for some hours in its magnificent bay ; and the next afternoon she was lying at the wharf of the Navy Yard. It was warm and sultry. The hatchway was open, and passing near it Zoe saw that the men were handcuffed again, as the old sailor had said they would be whenever the vessel approached the shore. A tall, bony woman, in black bombazine and green spectacles, with the look of a female lecturer, was standing up under an umbrella, close to the edge of the opening, haranguing the unfortunates below upon the error of their ways, and dropping down upon them a shower of tracts. Most of them sat passive under her eloquence ; a few smiled disdainfully as they took in their manacled hands the tracts that fluttered down to them. As

she turned off out of breath one of them returned thanks
with humorous unction ; another read the title of his tract,
"Bread of Life."

"Considering our short rations, I'd thank the marm a
little more if this was literal instead of figurative bread,"
he said.

"If it was, be sure the close-fisted Yankee wouldn't be
so quick to give it," responded the sardonic voice of the
man with blood on his sleeve as he turned his head on his
hard pillow and smiled grimly.

A small schooner from Cedar Keys loaded with oranges
and bananas had come alongside the Lavaca. Zoe bought
the finest bunch of yellow bananas in the lot, and got the
old sailor, Jack Barnes, to take them down to the prisoners.

"With the compliments of a true-hearted girl, my boys,
who wants you to know there's one friend you have on
board, if no more," said Jack as he deposited his luscious
burden on the floor and looked up to see that none of the
ship's officers were in hearing.

"Thank her for us, Jack, and beg her to let us have a
glimpse of her," said one boyish young prisoner. "She's
even nicer than her bananas, I dare swear."

"And you wouldn't be wrong either, my hearty—
Whist ! there she is !" he broke off as Zoe stepped near the
edge of the hatchway and glanced down. Instantly all eyes
were lifted, all heads bowed—all but the sick man's. He
did not see her ; he had turned away his head and closed
his eyes again.

"Will not your comrade try some of the fruit ?" Zoe
asked, indicating him by the direction of her eye.

"He's feverish, miss, and doesn't care for any," said
one of the prisoners ; whereupon the man spoken of turned
his head and nodded, saying : "But he thanks you all the
same."

He smiled, too, a smile that lit his stern features into singular attractiveness. His bronzed cheek was flushed with fever, his eyes watery bright, but the forehead, from which the hat had been pushed away, was broad and white, though it had lines of care upon it. It looked a totally different face from the one she had seen before with the scowl of sullen endurance or the flash of fierce resentment upon it.

As she walked off she said to the sailor :

" He looks to be suffering. I wish I could do something for him."

" It is his wound, miss. It is an ugly bayonet thrust in the shoulder ; the heat frets and fevers it, and I don't think it's been half dressed. The ship's surgeon is sick— or, to tell the truth, he's on a spree. It's hot and close down there, and the flesh flies are swarmin'."

Zoe shuddered.

"I *must* try to help him," she said. " Does he complain ?"

" Only of thirst, miss ; the water is so bad."

" And there is plenty of ice on board. At least he shall have a cool drink."

Going into the cabin, she sent for iced lemonade. It came in a glass pitcher, looking cool and tempting. The Captain accompanied the boy who brought it.

" It's nice," he said ; "I made it myself."

" Thanks. As you made it, I will drink a little of it, though I intend it for another—the poor wounded man down stairs. He has fever, and is consumed with thirst."

" If I had known that, I certainly would not have made the lemonade," the Captain said gruffly. " Miss Vincent, do you make it a point to encourage law-breaking ?"

" No, Captain Lester ; but I try to follow the law of the highest Law-giver, which enjoins upon us care for our fellow-creatures. That prisoner is suffering from neglect, and want of proper food and medicine. His wound may mortify, and death ensue."

"I can't help that; it's the place of Osborne and his fellows to see to their prisoners. If I had my way I'd toss the lot of them overboard, and save expense to the Government."

Zoe made no reply, beyond a look under which the Captain changed countenance, though he affected to laugh. Presently she asked:

"Will you not at least speak to Lieutenant Osborne about the sick prisoner?"

"No, Miss Vincent, it's no business of mine, and the fellow has been insolent to me."

"Will you introduce me to Lieutenant Osborne?"

He gave her a quick glance out of the corner of his eye, and made no answer on the instant. At last he said:

"I can introduce you; but I warn you that Osborne is not a man that a girl traveling without her friends ought to know."

"I am not afraid he will do me any harm. I can take care of myself," she said coldly.

"Oh! in that case I will give you the introduction. Here, Osborne, come this way. Here's a young lady who wishes to know you. You're in luck, you see."

The officer came up at once, and with a flush of anger on his forehead the Captain introduced the two in his curtest way, and, turning on his heel, left them. The burly Lieutenant, much flattered, bowed low and began an elaborate compliment, which Zoe cut short by telling him at once her reason for wishing to speak to him, and pleading the cause of the sick prisoner with so much gentle earnestness that Osborne, with his fat hand on his heart, promised the man should be looked after at once—a promise which he made it convenient to forget, or the fulfillment of which he indefinitely postponed.

That evening, while most of the passengers were eating their early supper in the cabin, and the Captain, the Purser, the Lieutenant, and some ladies, whom Lester had invited to sup with him, were enjoying oysters, lobster salad, and wine in the officer's private mess-room, Zoe, who had declined the Captain's invitation to his supper, took the opportunity to stroll about the deck; to look out over the sea where, low in the west, the sunset fires had not yet died.

The hatchway door was down, and she heard nothing of the prisoners. Presently, however, confused sounds from below came to her ears, and in the midst of them Jack Barnes came running toward her, having come up from that lower world by some ladder and trap-door in another part of the ship.

"Hirne has a fainting fit; he looks like death. I believe he will die if he is kept down there," he said to her.

Shocked and distressed, she ran to the door of the mess-room and called Lieutenant Osborne. The officer, bowing gallantly, tossed off the glass of wine he had just lifted to his lips, and, coming out to her, was told of the prisoner's condition.

"Let him be brought up here and his wound attended to," pleaded Zoe. "If there are extra charges for his being brought up here I will pay them, and I will stand for his good conduct."

Then, as she saw his hesitating, indifferent look, her indignation flamed up. Coming close to him, she said: "If you do not do this, sir, I will report you. I can not believe that your orders were to treat your prisoners worse than brutes."

He flushed. "Look here, miss," he began, excitedly, but he calmed down and took on an injured tone. "Miss Vincent, I hope I know my duty to my fellow-man as well as to my country," he said. "I don't need to be badgered about that prisoner. If he's sick I'll have him attended to. There's so much infernal shamming about his sort it takes a smart one to know when there's anything real the matter."

He gave orders to have the prisoner brought up and laid on deck under the canvas awning that had been put up during the day as a protection from the sun. Zoe found him there when she came with water and ice. He was lying on a blanket, and, kneeling down, she put her folded shawl under his head. The light of a lantern, flashed over his face, showed that he had recovered consciousness. His hands, as Zoe touched them, almost scorched her, so hot were they.

"Take off these handcuffs for the love of mercy," she said; "they are a mockery in his condition."

"Better let them be; he's only playing possum," sneered the Captain, who stood looking on; but the Lieutenant gave orders to have the manacles removed, and the poor prisoner gave a sigh of relief as they fell from his hands. The surgeon, still in no condition to attend the man, sent word that the dressing on his wound must be kept constantly wet in cold water, and cold applications must be made to his head. Seeing that no one else offered to attend to these directions, Zoe set herself to the task. The Lieutenant, perceiving that she took no notice of him, and the Captain, finding that she would not reply to his sarcasms, went off after awhile; and then the ladies, whom curiosity or compassion had drawn around the sick man, gradually dropped away, except the stewardess—an honest, good-natured woman—whom Zoe begged to stay with her. The two soldiers on guard hung the lantern near Zoe and withdrew to the railing where they could chew their tobacco and wonder when they were going back to the command. The stewardess talked herself tired, and began to nod. Zoe kept up unremittingly her applications of cold water to the bandages of the wound and to the hot forehead that throbbed so under her palm. He lay quiet; only at times he seemed to lapse into delirium and muttered incoherently. Once he started up and gave the word of command: "Forward, march," then stared around, met the soothing look of Zoe, seemed to gather consciousness, and dropped back upon his pallet.

Another time he spoke in Spanish, and once, when Zoe had her hand wet in ice-water on his forehead, he snatched it away, exclaiming:

"Off, snake! Women are snakes. They creep into your heart and sting it."

The instant after, as if vaguely remembering that he had said something unkind, he turned toward Zoe, and, taking her hand, put it mutely to his lips.

It was hours before the fever cooled, and he fell asleep. Zoe sat watching him. He looked much younger now, with the long lashes lying against his thin cheeks, his wet hair in dark rings on his forehead, and the bitter look gone from his mouth. At first sight she had seen a history written upon his face—a record of stormy experiences and strong passions; characters almost repelling in their fierceness. Now that sleep had softened these, one could see the fine points about the face—the breadth of the brow, a hint of tenderness in the mouth, of manly energy in the chin and round throat exposed by the open shirt. A broad breast was also laid bare, across which was seen a long, purplish scar.

Jack Barnes came up, being at last relieved of duty, and took Zoe's place beside her sleeping patient. At her direction he was covered with a blanket from the chilliness that was apt to set in as a reaction from the fever. Then leaving him with Jack, who promised to watch him till morning, she waked the stewardess, thanked her, and went into the cabin. The lights were turned almost down; she thought everybody had retired until Captain Lester stood before her.

"I have been waiting for you," he said. "Do you think your father would approve of this nocturnal devotion to an outlaw, a desperado who has worn the handcuffs before to-day?"

"I do not think my father would disapprove of my trying to alleviate the sufferings of a sick and friendless man, and I am sure my conscience does not."

"It's a great salve to conscience in such a case when the sufferer happens to be young and good-looking," the Captain said, with his short, sneering laugh. "Miss Vincent, good-night; don't refuse to shake hands. No doubt you think me a savage, but I only hate to see sweet meats thrown to dogs. There are others in this ship would give its cargo for the attentions you are wasting on that vagabond."

Early next morning, before any one but the sailors and soldiers on guard were stirring, Zoe was dressed and out on deck. The morning was fine, the sea was furrowed by a light wind, and in the blue distance the coast line was visible, just edging the horizon. Jack came up, cap in hand, and gave a good account of his patient. He had slept pretty well, and was now almost clear of fever, but very weak. He (Jack) had prevailed on the cook to make the sick man some soup, as he had tasted nothing since he came on board, it being impossible for him to eat the bread and salt pork rations of the prisoners.

Zoe went to him and found him quiet, but by no means rid of fever. He put out his hand to her, and the slight pressure of his fingers and the look he gave her touched her more than any word of thanks. He reported himself "better—almost ready again for the handcuffs and the black hold," and then, as he lay propped up, his eye went out over the sea to the shore-line not many miles distant, and kindled with an eager flash.

"I could swim it, I think," he said low; "and I'd make the jump and try it, in spite of this hole in my shoulder, if it wasn't that I know the bullets of those bluecoats yonder wouldn't give me half a chance. I don't want to die at last by a Yankee ball. My work is not ended yet."

"I hope you will not think of running such a risk," Zoe said, earnestly. "I know you will not when I tell you I made myself responsible for your good conduct. I pledged my word that you would not try to escape."

"Then your word must not be broken. I'll not abuse your confidence. You have been very good to me, Miss Vincent—disinterestedly good—and that's rare with women."

"Is it?"

"Yes; their goodness has usually dregs of selfishness. In your case there are none. You could have no motive but pure benevolence in being kind to a dirty, friendless outlaw, especially when your kindness to him drew on you the disfavor of your friends. I've seen that last well enough, and I don't want you to make such a sacrifice for my sake, young lady. Best avoid me; I am an unlucky dog, and I always bring trouble on the few that espouse my cause."

"I have no friends on board or acquaintances for whose favor I care. I will not avoid you, unless you wish it for your own sake."

Again he gave her the look that had seemed better than thanks. His blue-gray eyes, that could seem points of flame at times, had at other times a strangely soft and melancholy look. That look, in connection with the bloody sleeve, the wan cheek and throbbing temples, so moved Zoe's sympathy that she determined to give him every attention, unmindful of the Captain's sneers, the impertinences of the Lieutenant, and the gossip of the women. She sat by him all the morning, listening to him. He had just fever enough to excite him and make him talk—a little wildly and disconnectedly at times, but with such sudden flashes of quaint fancy, such wild, humorous, imaginative turns of thought, that Zoe, looking at him, asked impulsively :

"Did you never write poetry ?"

"Yes, once. Once I dreamed I was a poet—and wrote —things poured out of my heart."

"Where are some of them now ?"

"Where ? Oh ! that was long ago," he said, passing his hand over his forehead. "Long ago—it seems long— long. Before the simoom passed through my heart and dried all its fountains—before—"

His brow gathered into a tumult, his long, slender fingers grasped his temples convulsively as if to pluck out some memory that writhed within his brain.

The spasm passed ; his hand fell to his side, and he turned to Zoe with a smile of self-mockery.

"How grandiloquent that was ! I meant to say, young lady, that I wrote verses in my green and tender youth, and thought myself destined to the poet's crown. I have gotten bravely over that illusion, together with some others born of the same verdant imagination."

His talk gave Zoe glimpses into his past life. She felt that he had suffered some hard trial, some wrong that had warped his nature.

He was without ties of blood or of law ; neither parents,

brother, sister, wife, nor child, he said; nor any to care if his bones should be left to rot on the Dry Tortugas.

She was alone with him the greater part of the morning; others came up and stood or sat near for a while, but the stolid look that came into his face and the silence he maintained while they stayed were not encouraging, and they soon moved off. The soldiers stood out of hearing of his low tones, and Zoe paid no attention to their occasional glances in her direction, nor to their half audible jokes and occasional laughter.

Captain Lester came up sometimes, standing by with folded arms, and eying Zoe with a look of haughty displeasure, or uttering a sarcasm intended for her ears.

"His tongue wags all right," he said once to the Lieutenant. "If he can use his legs and arms as well as he does his tongue—and I believe he can—you'd better call up your jeweler. I see he has put the bracelets on the others. I hear there's a lot more of sympathetic females who have got wind of our precious cargo, and are coming from Appalachicola in the Shamrock this afternoon with pies and pound-cakes, bouquets and tears, and such like feminine incense for our martyrs. Confound such nuisances! I wish the blockhead Government had found some quicker way of getting rid of these fellows, or some other vessel to send them off on. If there's a thing I hate, it's to be annoyed with sympathetic women."

"Don't let your jealousy run away with your patriotism, Lester," retorted the burly Lieutenant with a chuckle. The Captain, affecting not to hear him, strode away.

The Lavaca was now anchored in the harbor of Appalachicola, half a mile or more from the picturesque little town. The bay was too shallow to admit of the steamship's nearer approach to shore, but a lighter—a little steamer called the Shamrock—was busy transporting the portion of the cargo that was consigned to this port.

Little boats, containing fresh fish and vegetables, came up alongside the anchored steamship. In one of them sat a nut-brown woman, with a basket of green peas on her lap, atop of which lay a bunch of fresh flowers. Seeing Zoe's lovely face as she leaned over the deck railing, the woman stood up, held out her bouquet, and, laughing till her white teeth gleamed from her brown face, she threw the flowers up into the girl's outstretched hands.

Zoe carried them with her to her seat, and gave a cluster of the English honeysuckles to her patient. She sat with the other flowers in her hand when the Lieutenant came up. He had been drinking ; his face was even redder than its wont ; he leered at the girl as his small, sensuous eye took in the grace of her figure, the ivory curve of her neck, the dusk bloom of her cheek as she bent over the flowers she was rearranging.

"Well, Miss Vincent," he said, "I've come to claim the fulfillment of your pledge. You promised to pay all extra charges if I would have your pet brought up here and give him the privilege of fresh air and the light of your lovely face. I've done so, and now I'm come to claim my pay."

Zoe saw the look that darkened over Hirne's face, and thought best, for his sake, to give a playful rejoinder.

"Will you take my roses in pay ?" she said, smiling, and holding out her nosegay. "Kind acts should only be paid for in flowers."

"I'd rather have one of the roses that bloom on your cheeks," he said, bending over her until his whiskied breath was hot upon her face. "Come, now, it's only fair, and there's nobody looking."

His arm went around her neck and tightened as she

9

struggled. The next instant he was stretched upon the deck, and Hirne was stamping him. Instantly three soldiers rushed up and caught the Texan from behind. He turned on them furiously, but, as he did so, he staggered, threw his arm up wildly, and fell back swooning.

The Lieutenant scrambled to his feet, panting and cursing as he wiped his perspiring forehead and felt of the spot where the Texan had planted the blow. Most of the passengers were in the cabin; only one or two had seen the incident, which had been all over in a minute. The Captain came up, and, quickly understanding what was the matter, seemed inwardly rejoiced.

"Now," he said, pointing to Hirne, who had recovered from his swoon, "I guess you'll have that fellow handcuffed, and send him below, as I told you to. You'll have him to account for, else. He's shamming for a purpose."

Hirne was taken below. He nerved himself to walk firmly, but Zoe could see that he staggered. As he passed her he held out his hand; she had just time to give him hers, to feel her fingers pressed in a convulsive clasp, when he was roughly pushed on by the soldiers.

Fresh blood-stains were on his arm and shoulder from his reopened wound; his face was ghastly.

"He will die," moaned Zoe, in the solitude of her stateroom. "I have killed him instead of helping him."

She saw him no more during the trip, save one glimpse she got of him by the light of the ship's torches as the prisoners were carried ashore at the Dry Tortugas. From her state-room window she was watching with strained eyes; she saw him come out supported by Jack Barnes and walking with difficulty. The light of the torch flared one moment over his pale face and over the gloom and barrenness of the island prison. Then the file of prisoners, and the blue coats and flashing bayonets of the soldier guard were swallowed up in the shadows of midnight.

CHAPTER XVII.

Zoe had returned to New Orleans in the early autumn. She had drooped through the long, hot summer in Havana. Even her brother's home on Red River, with its malarial dangers, which she had learned to guard against, seemed better suited to her health. She did not return in the Lavaca. Captain Lester had shown his preference for her in such rough fashion on the former trip that she had no wish to put herself in his company.

They passed the Dry Tortugas in the day. She learned that the Alabama prisoners had been pardoned through the intercession of friends two months before—all but one—the "ringleader of the mischief," said her informant, and she knew he spoke of Hirne.

" And where is he ?" she asked with forced calmness.

" Drowned or escaped, it is hard to tell which. He gave the guard the slip in the night ; a soldier saw and pursued him, and was close to him when he took to the water, exclaiming as he jumped in, ' Good-by, I'm going to Davy's Locker.' The man thought he had drowned himself, but some of the others knew him to be a good swimmer, and, as a schooner was lying becalmed three miles away, it is possible he may have got to her. They would have overhauled the schooner next morning, but a wind sprang up about daylight, and she was out of sight in no time."

Zoe stayed a month in New Orleans, where she had good friends besides the sister and mother of young West. It had been understood that she would marry Royal in December, but she urged her languid health and other considerations of a prudential nature as reasons to put off the marriage. Attached as she was to Royal, with no idea of breaking her engagement to him, she shrank from the thought of merging their pleasant relation into the closer one of marriage.

In November she returned home with her brother, who had made his usual fall visit to the city. It was during this trip that the steamboat accident took place, which Judge Pickenson had described to Omar Witchell. The boat, a slow old craft, loaded to her guards, was making poor headway against the current. The male passengers, bored with the confinement and the slow progress, took to gambling and drinking by way of diversion. Hugh Vincent was drawn into both—contrary to his usual habits. He lost money to a long-haired, black-bearded man, who called himself Karles—a fellow with devil-me-care manners —who played carelessly and seemed to be almost indifferent whether he lost or won.

Drinking and gaming were both running pretty high one night, when the boat struck a snag that tore a hole in her rotten keel. The pilot headed her for the shore, but the water was pouring into her hold, and in the excitement a lamp was overturned and a portion of the cabin was soon in flames. There was a rush for the two small skiffs belonging to the boat, and in a very few minutes they were launched and filled with passengers. Karles was the coolest man on board, and did good service in getting the women and children first of all into the boats. Vincent was in the first one, with his sister (as he fancied) by his side. She had been indisposed, and had kept to her stateroom ever since coming on board. When the accident occurred she was sleeping the heavy slumber that follows upon the exhaustion of fever. Her brother had gone to arouse her at the first alarm; but in the confusion of fright and the becloudment of liquor he had gone to the wrong state-room and brought out the wrong woman, so wrapped up that he did not find out his mistake. Zoe did not wake until the last boat was about pushing off. Karles, the last man to leave, was stepping into it when he heard a woman's cry, and, hurrying back into the cabin already filled with suffocating smoke, he saw Zoe standing in her white wrapper, her white face, surrounded by a mass of loosened hair, looming spirit-like through the glare and gloom. He started in amazement.

"Miss Vincent!"

She knew him in spite of his disguise of darkened beard and hair. His face glowed; with his arm around her, he hurried her out of the burning cabin; then he ran back to bring her shawl, and her watch and purse, that she had told him were under her pillow. He was gone only an instant, but, when he returned, he saw that those in the skiff had pushed off. Nor would they regard his command for them to come back. The skiff was already too full, they called out. Hirne looked at Zoe, and pointed to the shore, which was quite near. The water meanwhile had filled the lower part of the boat, and the flames were rapidly spreading.

"You will not be frightened to trust yourself to me," he said. "Luckily, you know me to be a good swimmer, else I would still be on the Tortugas. There, that is brave!"

He easily swam with her to the shore, but the water was cold, the night frosty, and Zoe, not well before, was seized with a chill that seemed like death. Hirne worked as hard as he had ever done in his life to keep warmth and vitality in her body.

Brandy and vigorous rubbing before a bright cypress fire that had been kindled in a wood-cutter's cabin—the

only shelter the gloomy swamp afforded—at last restored
her. Hirne, through the force of his will and his readiness
at resources, constituted himself her nurse.

"It is only doing as I was done by, and not so much,
for what comparison is there between my clumsy services
and your gentle ministration?" he said as she sat before
the fire next morning, dressed in the plain, dark clothes of
a lady who had saved her valise in the boat.

The two brawny wood-cutters, whose hut had given
shelter to the unfortunates, were early astir, and, ransacking their small stores, got ready a breakfast of hot coffee,
bread, bacon, and wild honey, of which the hungry passengers of the luckless Alethia partook with zest.

It was noon before a boat made its appearance; coming
up and being hailed, it rounded to and took on board the
little party standing forlornly on the bank.

Vincent had lost but little by the catastrophe. His
freight had been shipped by his merchant on another boat—
the same which had now taken them up.

Hirne had learned, to his surprise, that the man whose
money he had won was Zoe's brother, and, knowing he
would not accept it back as a gift, he induced Vincent to
play with him again, and permitted him to win from him
more than he had lost.

At the next town where the boat landed Hirne went
ashore and came back in a more civilized dress, with his hair
and beard shorn of some of its savage luxuriance. He sent
to ask Zoe if she would see him, and, receiving her answer of
"yes," he came that evening into the cabin and talked with
her in a quiet, dimly-lighted corner. Cynical and erratic
as some of his talk was, it was undeniably picturesque and
original. He was no ordinary man, Zoe felt, and she set
herself to persuading him to put his good gifts to use, to
quit the vagabond life he owned to leading, and come into

the ranks of useful work and social intercourse. Half laughing, he had said to her as Festus said to Paul, "Almost thou persuadest me to be a Christian"; then more earnestly, "Would *you* care really to have me become a domestic animal? If—I thought that you—" He broke off short with a quick gesture of self-scorn, but, meeting her eye, he leaned suddenly near her, and said:

"When you sang that little song just now, I told you it was as though you had felt the passion with which it was charged, and I asked you if this was so. You made no answer, yet my question was not an idle one. I had a reason for asking."

"And I had none for refusing to answer," Zoe said, while she grew paler with her effort to conquer a temptation. "I ought to understand the feeling expressed in that little song, since it was given me by the gentleman to whom I am to be married."

She did not, she could not look up to see the effect of her words. He turned off from her and walked away. Coming back in a few moments, he stood before her, looked at her in silence, then said abruptly:

"I was an idiot to dream it. I might have known there could be no hope in life for me."

Touched by his look, she said earnestly: "Do not say that; there is hope for you every way. You will come out from under the cloud of the past; you will put up the sword of hate into its scabbard and use the brighter weapon —mind—to carve you a worthy place in the world. You will love, marry, and be happy."

"He laughed scornfully. "Marry! I shall never do that. I wish any woman a better fate than to marry me. And as for your civilization, I'll have none of its narrow laws and hollow customs to fetter me. I shall go into the wilderness, as far from its sounding brass and tinkling cymbals as I can get. When that palls, there's always fighting somewhere to stir the blood, or to stop its circulation for ever. I can join the starved handful of red-skins that stand at bay against the trained West Pointers. Their savage instinct of hate is at least more honest than most things I can find in the world that calls itself civilized."

And with these reckless words he turned away.

That night the boat reached Vincent's plantation, and, while he was superintending the discharge of his freight, Hirne came to assist Zoe off the boat. He almost carried her up the steep bank. At the top, and withdrawn a little into the black shadow cast by a pecan tree, he took her hands in his, pressed them to his lips—and left her—not having spoken a word.

She had not seen nor heard from him since that silent parting.

This was the man of whom she had at last found courage to speak to Royal. The impression he had made troubled her; she could not throw it off. She found it hard to reason herself into the belief that it was a mere fleeting interest, born of sympathy and imagination. It was a relief to her that Royal thought it so. She wished to be faithful in heart as in deed to her betrothed. She was sure she loved him ; not, indeed, with that absorbing devotion that one reads and hears of, and more rarely sees, but then it was better so—better that her regard was of a calmer and more practical sort than this intense worship which, when thrown back on itself, consumes hope, energy, life itself, as in the case of Adelle. Poor Adelle! How her eyes had followed her to-night when she came away— how hollow, how wistful they were ! "I must be with her more ; I must go to her to-morrow," was Zoe's last thought.

CHAPTER XVIII.

SHE went to see her next day. She was met at the door of Adelle's chamber by Witchell's mother, an angular, grim-looking personage, who resumed her knitting the instant she sat down.

"What is this Gorgon doing here?" thought Zoe, as she looked at the hard face and cold eyes. Adelle was sitting up, but she seemed unfit to be out of bed. As she kissed her, Zoe felt her lips quiver, and the next instant the poor girl had her friend round the neck and was crying with suppressed sobs. Mrs. Witchell looked up disapprovingly. "Adelle is very nervous to-day," she said. "If she would exercise any self-control it would be better for her, and pleasanter for her friends. It was a mistake, her coming here in this noisy city; with all this excitement she can not be so quiet as she ought."

Adelle dried her tears, and, bidding Zoe sit by her, made an evident effort to talk about pleasant things, but her thoughts seemed to wander, and she broke off her sentences abruptly. Zoe glanced rather savagely at the Gorgon. Did she intend to sit by in that stiff, silent, yet observant way all the time, and exasperate one by knitting —knitting imperturbably as did the knitters of the Revolution while the axe of death did its work? The axe was at work upon this life, Zoe felt, as she looked at her friend. The hectic color on her cheeks could not hide how they were wasted. Her respiration came in labored breaths through her parted, feverishly-red lips, and Zoe's eyes detected the blood-stains on a handkerchief that had been thrust half under the sofa cushion to hide it. She looked wistfully at her friend, as if her heart were full of some grief she could hardly keep back. At last, to Zoe's relief, the old lady went out of the room to interview the man who had brought the coal, and tell him what she thought of his high charges. Then Adelle, stretching out her arms to her cousin, said :

"O Zoe! he is going to send me away from him. His mother is to take me away with her. This is why he has sent for her. I know it; I heard them talking together. She says I am in Marshall's way ; that he can not attend to his affairs here, I weary and trouble him so. O Zoe! won't you tell him you think I am better; that I will not trouble him—no, not one bit ? That I will not fret any more about his going out to night committees ? I will be satisfied only to know he is near me, that I can see him, and he will speak to me sometimes. But up there—away from him—at that lonesome place! Oh Zoe! I should die. His mother does not like me. She is kind, but it is in such a way. She looks at me as if she thought I was a spoiled child, and my sickness was only pretense. Then, not to see him—when it is my only happiness! He is my life—my all."

A fit of coughing cut short the panting whisper. When it ended there was blood on the fresh white handker-chief.

"That is nothing," she said, as Zoe, who stood over her, with her friend's head leaning against her, took up the handkerchief and looked at it sadly. "I have been having these little hæmorrhages a long time. Give me that glass of salt and lemon juice ; that will stop it; I am stronger than you think. I am determined to do without any more nursing. I am going to go out every day, and you must go with me. Velvine is altering my blue silk. It has got too large for me ; I always do lose flesh in the winter. Zoe, you must stay to dinner. You will see Marshall, and tell him you think I am improving, and that the city agrees with me. Hush! there comes mother Witchell. Hide that handkerchief, please."

She insisted on dressing for dinner, though she could hardly stand the fatigue of the operation. The fever flush was fading, and she bade Zoe put rouge on her cheeks, and arrange her hair so that it should hide the sunken temples. Zoe, who was clasping her bracelet, noticed how she trembled when she heard Witchell's step in the hall. The next moment he came in, greeted Zoe with his usual courtesy, spoke to his wife, and, tossing off his hat, ran his fingers wearily through his hair. Adelle went up to him and put her hand on his arm, and looked up at him, smiling.

"Don't you see how well I am?" she said.

He looked down into her face, sweet still as a faded rose. He passed his hand caressingly over her hair, and kissed her with more than usual tenderness. In spite of her efforts, tears rushed into her eyes. He frowned with an annoyed expression.

"You are such a child," he said; "do try to have more self-control, Adelle."

During dinner she exerted herself to seem gay and well. Zoe saw how she struggled against languor and pain, and was not surprised to see her, after their return to the sitting-room, suddenly turn white, and lie back nerveless against the chair. No one saw it but Zoe, and, rising quickly, she said:

"Dell, don't you need a little rest now? I have something to say to you in private. Come."

She put her arm around her as if playfully, and half supported her into her bedroom, and made her lie down.

"Not a word from you," she said, placing her hand over the languid eyes. "Sleep now, or at least be quiet."

She sat by her awhile, and, leaving her resting if not asleep, returned to the sitting-room. Witchell was speak-

ing to his mother as he walked back and forth in the room.
She heard him say :

"Yes, I have decided upon it. It's best for her and
for me. I ought to be free to give all my attention to the
work I have here."

Seeing Zoe, he said :

"Is Adelle asleep so soon ? I think of sending her
home with my mother, Miss Zoe. She will be so much
quieter there."

"Will you go with her, sir ?"

"No ; it is impossible for me to leave."

"Then do not send her away from you. It will be bad
for her. It will—let me speak plainly—it will shorten her
life."

"How absurd !" spoke up Mrs. Witchell, quickly.
"As if Adelle were really in any danger. Half of her
sickness is nervous irritation and low spirits. Miss Vincent, you ought not to humor your friend's childish
whims. She will be much better on the plantation, where
there is nothing to excite her. She can have a good physician at hand, and my own attention. Then my son is to
be considered. He has business it will not do for him to
neglect ; a sick wife claims his time, and is a burden on his
mind."

"Let us think of her first," said Witchell, and he no
doubt thought he was speaking from his heart. "I am
sure the change will be to her advantage."

"It will kill her," Zoe burst out impetuously. Then,
fearing she would injure her friend's cause by saying too
much, she hurried out of the room.

Next morning she had visitors, and could only send a
note to Adelle. A message was returned that her cousin
was "as well as usual." Rather late in the afternoon she
went to see her, and was surprised to find the doors of her

apartments fastened, and seemingly no one inside. Turning away, she met the mistress of the boarding-house and learned from her that Adelle was gone. She had left on the five o'clock boat with Witchell's mother.

"Gone, and she was so opposed to leaving! Did she seem very unwilling, Mrs. Rose?"

"Poor dear, she didn't seem to be more than half conscious of what was being done to her. Mrs. Witchell told me herself they had given her a quantity of morphine to quiet her. She looked quite dazed-like when they brought her down; not much more life in her than in a corpse. And the driver tells me they took her on the boat the same way. Captain Witchell knows best, of course. But, if it had been me, I could never have sent her off that way; I'd been afraid I'd never see her again; and she loves him so, poor child."

"He's a cold-hearted wretch," cried the impulsive Zoe.

"I think you are unjust, miss. He thinks it's best for her. He looked sorry, but determined. I saw him holding her in his arms in the carriage. He looked at her tender-like, but his mouth was shut together in the way he has. He seemed to be doing something against his heart."

It was true. The man had had a struggle with himself. Greed of money and power had taken possession of him. He felt he could gain a point by having all his faculties free to work to his ends in these last days of the legislative session, and he determined to remove the obstacle that his sick, clinging wife, with her exactions on his time and attention, presented. He had quieted his conscience by assuring himself that his wife was not dangerously ill, and that she would be better out of the city; but, when he carried her into her state-room, and, shutting the door behind, stood looking at her as she lay, so pitiful in her youth, her faded loveliness, her death-like whiteness, the battle in his heart had to be fought over again.　She was only half conscious of what was going on, so powerful had been the quieting potion given her.　She hardly knew she was going anywhere, and she had no idea she was leaving her husband.　She was soothingly conscious of his presence ; her eyes had opened and lighted on seeing him bending over her.　She stretched out her arms and clasped his neck. He feared she had roused to a sense of what was going to be, but she only whispered, "You wouldn't send me away without you, would you, dear Marshall ?"　He spoke soothingly to her, and presently she drifted away into sleep. The boat-bell rang ; he gently undid the wasted arms, kissed her softly, and crept out, with a guilty feeling at his heart.

He never saw her living face again.　When she recovered from the effects of the opiate, and knew that she had been betrayed, that her husband had sent her away from him—to die, as she bitterly said to her heart—she sank into a listless, hopeless state.　She never complained, she never spoke about her husband ; she seemed to be convinced at last that she filled but a small part of his life, and she strove to put the thought of him away from her. She grew weaker daily, and still her strong, stirring mother-in-law, who nursed her energetically, but with a lack of that tender, forbearing sympathy that only comes from love, refused to believe she was ill unto death, and insisted she would grow strong if only she would eat more and try to brighten up.

Omar was away upon business, else his affectionate attention would have soothed that sad pillow, and he would not have been prevented from sending at once for his brother.

One morning Mrs. Witchell came into Adelle's room, and as she stopped by the bed the girl laid her white ghost of a hand upon her mother-in-law's, and, looking up at her with her hollow eyes, said :

" Won't you send for mother ? I want to see her before I die."

" Stuff and nonsense !" the old lady said ; " you are not going to die, child. You will soon be getting strong."

Nevertheless, she shuddered ; that voice and look went through her with strong conviction. She read death in those eyes. She went straight and wrote a letter to her son, telling him to hasten home, and dispatched it on a boat that passed down that morning. There was no telegraph line, and it would take two days for the letter to reach its destination. She also sent at once for the mother of Adelle, even permitting the messenger to take the poor half legible line the dying girl had traced as she lay on the pillow.

" Mother, father, you must forgive me now—for I am dying. Come to me.   ADELLE."

Colonel Holman was not at home when the messenger arrived. His wife did not wait for him ; she came at once, trembling, weeping, praying it might not be so ill with the daughter whom she had not ceased to love and yearn over, though kept away from her by the stern will of her husband.

When she entered the room, turned to the bed and saw there the wan wreck of her beautiful child, she dropped on her knees as if pierced to the heart. Her bitter self-reproaches, sobbed out with her gray head bowed on her daughter's hands, were heart-rending to hear.

She never left Adelle's bedside any more. When, five days afterward, at the fading of a peaceful sunset, the young life passed away, father, mother, and brother were around her bed, holding her hands, watching with strained

looks of mute agony the faint smile of love that shone on
them to the last.

She had watched the door ceaselessly that morning, and
they knew she hoped to see her husband enter ; but after
awhile she sighed deeply and turned away her head, resigning the last hope that had power to agitate her. She had
only spoken of him once. In the middle of the last night
of her life she woke suddenly from a disturbed sleep with
a faint scream. As her mother leaned over her she drew
her close to her and whispered :

"I had a fearful dream. I saw Marshall swimming in
a bloody sea, with a bloody mist above and around him.
All at once, as he swam, both his arms dropped away, and
the cloud shut him from me. It was terrible ! And once
—before he married me—an old negro—old Margaret Sted-
man—dreamed the same thing, and told it to me. Is it
not strange ? "

"You remembered it, child—and it came to you in
your sleep. Dreams are idle things."

"Old Margaret said this meant evil to him. God
protect him from danger ! Margaret told me things
that came true. She said that I would only be a clog
to him, and he would tear away from me at last. That
has proved true—yet I loved him. I love him still. I
am glad, though, that he will be free. I know I was only
a hindrance."

While the body of what had been beautiful Adelle Holman lay dressed for burial in white robes with white flowers on her breast, the keen whistle of a steamboat at "Starlight Landing" told that he whom she had so mutely longed
to see had come—too late. He leaped from the boat and
hurried into the house ; went past every one without speaking, and stood in the presence of the dead woman, who had
loved him so well. Stood looking at her with arms locked

tightly over his chest, and a tumult working on his brow; then knelt and buried his head in her cold bosom, while a storm of remorseful agony shook his frame.

CHAPTER XIX.

A HALF-MOON hung in the sky. The summer air was full of the scent of night-jessamine and oleander. The little town of Cohatchie seemed asleep, for few lights gleamed from its scattered houses, and in a grove not far from Colonel Alver's pretty home a whippoorwill thrilled the silence with its cry. The still sweetness of the night wrought even on the restless pulses of Floyd Reese, and her step became slower as she paced the walks in the rear yard, with the perfume of flowers coming to her, and the shadows of the shrubbery falling now and then over her figure, clad in thin, dark gauze, with a black lace mantle over her head, through which gleamed her fair brow and throat and her wonderful bright eyes, whenever she passed into the moonlight.

No one was astir in the house, and the lights were out, except the lamp that twinkled in her own room. Mrs. Alver, whose health was delicate, had gone to bed at the persuasion of Floyd, who had made her a cup of tea, and insisted on her drinking it and lying down.

"Colonel Alver will not come home until late," she said. "I heard him tell you so. I will wake Rose and send her to open the door for him, or I will open it myself. I shall sit up late writing."

The step of a horse approaching in a quiet walk was heard, and Floyd stopped by a summer-house, overhung with multiflora vines, and stood just within one of its green-arched doorways. The horseman stopped at the stable, dismounted, led in his horse, and, emerging, locked the door behind him, opened a gate at the lower end of the back yard and came up through the shrubbery. He stopped by the summer-house where Floyd waited.

"I am here," she said softly from the shadow. "You are late."

"Yes, it was nine before the meeting broke up, and the road over the hills is terribly rough."

"What success?"

"As good as I could hope for. The meeting was largely attended, but many are holding back. Slaves! Witchell has bought them with a few bushels of corn and a little meat, or else empty promises."

"Did you address the meeting?"

"I spoke again and again, was called for with enthusiasm. They seemed fired up to any point I could wish. There is certainly a wonderful change in the last few months. The people are shaking off their paralysis. Hopeless submissiveness is gone. They begin to believe that Witchell is not necessarily their destiny, and they his slaves. At least a majority feel this way, and are ready to band together to resist the Radical clique, but the poorer class on the Hills belong to Witchell, body and soul, and these, with the negroes, will beat us at the polls, even if the voting is fair, which it will not be. Yent pretends he is bringing the negroes over, but I see little sign of it. He never tried to do it before Witchell dismissed him from his office of sheriff, and now he can not. Curse and expose Witchell as he does with all his wordy fury, he can no longer lead the negroes. He has lost his prestige of office. They look on him with suspicion. They are shrewd enough to suspect that all his denouncing of the Radicals is mere spite."

"Still you may use him other ways. He is a slippery tool, and requires that you keep your hand firmly upon him. Did you urge the measure you promised to propose ? The time is ripe for it. The Radical Convention is close at hand."

"The time is ripe for it, and I did propose the measure. I brought it out in artful climax. After I had shown how we were tied hand and foot by tyrannical laws enforced at the point of the bayonet, how we were made to accept the rule of corrupt men, who insulted and robbed us, I asked what should be done ? The laws, the Government, gave us no redress ; should we not rise up as a body, and shake our-selves free from this incubus ? Should we not force these men to resign, even at the muzzle of the shot-gun ?"

"And how did they receive this ?"

"They responded warmly, but I am afraid of their timidity when the time comes to act. If the movement could be unanimous, I would not fear, but Witchell has too many friends here and in other parishes as well. When I spoke to the White League in N—— last week, and proposed that that parish should force its scoundrelly officers to re-sign, there was vehement approval, and a resolution passed that the measure should be put in force. I believe that it will be. The Radical officers in that parish are not the chosen of Witchell—the friends and the kin of this man— curse him !—who has such a devil's power of blinding igno-rant people that he can make them believe his black record is as white as snow. But will they oust *him* from office ? Will our own parish dare to rid itself of the men—his tools and his blood—that he has fastened upon it ?"

"It will ; it must. It must force them to resign before a month is over. Your White League must be kept full strung. There must be no let down. If N—— thrusts out its officers, that will give our parish courage. You have worked well, you have gained much ground ; it is too late to give up now. You must fight it out. These men must be rooted out, even if they have to be *destroyed*. If they were made away with, you would have nothing to fear ; no other Radical set would dare to live and rule here. No other Radical leader can ever take the hold upon the people that Witchell has. Destroy them—it will be a just deed—and leave the way clear for better men."

Four months ago this suggestion had horrified him. It did not do so now, so morally undermining had been the gradual subtile influence of this woman. And he now felt the excitement of one who engages in a game or a combat. He only said :

"To destroy them would be to ruin our cause. It would be to rot in prison."

"Not if they seemed to bring their destruction upon themselves. The people are fully charged with indignation ; it needs but a spark of aggression on the Radical part to make it take fire. The end would justify a little irregularity in the means—would it not ? "

"In Witchell's case, yes. I am sorry for the others—for one or two of them, at least. I think they are innocent."

"Innocent ! when they work into Witchell's hands ? When they are his tools, his confidants ? "

"His tools they may be, but hardly his confidants. That brother of his has not worldly sense enough for a shrewd man to confide in. He seems a gentle-hearted young fellow. I saw his bride for the first time yesterday. They were standing in the gallery of their little home, feeding some tame mocking birds. She is a small, demure-looking creature, and looked up in his face, as I passed, with innocent adoration. Devene, too, is going to marry ; a Southern girl who befriended him at Morefield, where he had gone to collect Witchell's swindling taxes. It would be a pity for these young creatures to be waked out of their happy honeymoon by a storm of ruin—perhaps blood—in which the innocent would suffer with the guilty. No, that must not be. Reform must stop short of blood, or I will draw out of this movement."

"You can not. You are pledged to the movement. You have set it going. It must achieve its mission. It carries all your hopes—remember that before you let your weakness get the better of you. What if these men suffer ruin? They have ruined hundreds. What would even their death be? A small sacrifice to freedom. No great wrong can be righted without some sacrifice. You must not think of the sacrifice. It is your duty to look only to the purpose you have in view—to keep eye and aim for that. Not to mind what worms you may crush."

The moonlight, by some weird quality of its own, brings out the evil in a face better than the less subtile daylight. A ray, glancing through the vine-leaves, fell across Floyd's face, and he thought how hard and cruel it looked. He turned from her.

"You are no woman ; you have no heart," he said.

"No heart! You say this to me—you for whose sake I have steeled my heart and merged every feeling into sympathy with your interests ?"

There was no hardness now in her melting glance.

"Yes, you who despise me as weak because this soft night, the scent of flowers in your hair, the sweeter perfume of your breath, your warm, beautiful presence close to me here, soften my heart—make me feel a moment's sympathy for the young loving pairs that may soon taste misery and ruin."

"Then it is only a momentary weakness. You have no thought of giving up your purpose ?"

"I have not. It is now knit into my very life. All my hopes are staked upon it, even that of love. If I lose, I know you will despise me ! If I win—but you have never yet given me a promise—never one womanly token of affection—not one touch of that ripe mouth, not one throb of that white breast against mine—nothing."

"But I will," she whispered, shrinking back from his arms, and catching his hand firmly in hers. "Have I not promised? This is no time for love dalliance; but when the fight is won—when the parish is free from its tyrants—when Witchell is hurled from his seat in the Assembly, when Alver is placed upon it—Alver, whose genius and force of will shall make him the political power of the State—then all the kisses of these lips, all the throbs of this heart, shall be too poor to thank him for having been so true to himself, so brave, so deserving the worship of a proud woman."

His eye, ordinarily so cold, glowed with blue fire under his light lashes.

"Meantime?" he said, drawing her to him.

She did not struggle; she fixed her eyes steadily upon him.

"Meantime, he will forbear caresses and give his mind to the work in hand. Listen," she went on, stepping back from him. "The Radical Nominating Convention meets in two weeks. It is time to take some decisive step. What do you mean to do?"

"Call on our parish officers to resign. Demand Witchell's resignation through committees from the different parishes he represents."

"And if he refuses?"

"Press it upon him; threaten him."

"And if he still refuses?"

"We have gone no farther in our programme."

"But I have," she whispered. "Listen—" the sound of a clock striking one—always a solemn sound—made her start.

"Not to-night," she said, hurriedly. "It is too late;

I must go in. I will go first; after a few moments you can knock, and I will open the door."

She glided up the shadowed walk in her dark dress, entered the back door, which she had left slightly ajar, and went noiselessly up stairs to her room. She went down again presently, taking the lamp with her, to answer Alver's knock.

"What frauds we are!" she whispered, laughing as he came in and took the lamp from her hand. Then aloud: "Be as quiet as you can, Colonel; Mrs. Alver has headache."

CHAPTER XX.

It was a chill, rainy night. Judge Pickenson sat late by his wood-fire, comfortable, though it was midsummer. He could not sleep; he was troubled with conjectures and misgivings. To-day the Convention for nominating Radical officers had opened its session at N——. There were rumors that it would not be allowed to sit. It was known that Witchell was almost sure to be renominated, and there was a growing disaffection toward Witchell. He had received two anonymous warnings that a plot was on foot to procure his downfall; that a trap was to be sprung on the members of the Convention, and the Radical officers required to resign their offices or give up their lives. He made light of the warning and rode off to attend the Convention, unarmed, as was his wont, soundly rating the posse of negroes he found waiting to escort him. He dismissed them, saying that he feared no danger and wanted no guard.

Judge Pickenson had not attended the Convention.

He had determined to withdraw from politics. It had become too turbulent to suit his easy-going nature. And he saw more serious trouble brewing. He mixed too intimately with the people not to be aware that a secret fire had been kindled within them, and that it grew more intense every day. He feared it would soon find vent.

He had heard no news from the Convention; all through the day a feeling of feverish expectancy had possessed him. It was still in his veins; he sat listening to every sound. Presently his ear caught the thud of horses' hoofs on the sodden ground. He rose to his feet, caught up the lamp and opened the door wide that the light might stream out into the darkness. The gleam showed two tall, dark figures coming toward the house. As they entered, Pickenson saw that they were Witchell and the elder Devene—the legislator—Witchell's most intimate friend. He received them cordially, and threw a fresh pine-knot on the fire to give them a welcoming blaze. He scanned their faces with his keen, rapid glance, to see if anything had gone wrong. They might not choose to confide in him now that he had drawn out from among them. Witchell's countenance was pale and stern; Devene laughed—a laugh more reckless than mirthful—as he threw off his wet cloak and drank down the whisky his host had set before him. Witchell had declined the liquor, and, throwing himself into a chair, gazed moodily into the fire.

"Something has happened," the Judge said at last. "Is the Convention broken up?"

"No," Witchell answered, "but the members have taken it into their heads that it will be broken up; that a trap is to be sprung, of which I am the object. Such nonsense! But nothing would do them but I must leave. They put the demand on the ground of their own safety. They think it is endangered by my staying."

"But you—you think there is no ground for their fears?"

"There may be a crude plot hatched by a handful of reckless agitators, stirred up by Yent, who is smarting at having been turned out of office. It is merely a local ebullition—a bluff game to try and scare out the Convention. That is the extent of the movement."

Pickenson sat silent, his mouth gravely compressed. Witchell eyed him with knitted brows.

"Do you not think with me?" he asked.

A slight shake of the head was the only response.

"Look here, Pickenson; speak out plainly. What do you think this movement means? I want a straightforward answer."

"You shall have one then, though you will not thank me for it. Nor will you believe it. The movement means more than a mere ebullition of personal hate. It is an extended movement—a part of the wave that is beginning to be felt throughout the South. It means that the people are worn out with being saddled by tyrannical, dishonest, or ignorant rulers. They have waited and forborne, hoping in vain for a change; now they are gathering determination for an active protest. A revolutionary tide has set in. Many who have given offense will find themselves stranded high and dry; others, who are innocent, will suffer, like the Tray of our spelling-books, for being in bad company. That touches *you*, my friend. Mind, though, I do not say that you are an altogether blameless Tray."

"Speak out your meaning, sir. This is no time for jesting."

"It is not. I will speak in sober sadness. For years you have held the destiny of this section in your hands. You started out fairly in your administration, but the doors of opportunity have been thrown too temptingly

10

wide. Greed of rule and money has grown upon you.
You have turned this parish, if not the whole district, into
an autocracy, governed by your will alone. The officers
under you are merely your agents. They carry out your
individual will. You have enriched yourself by means
that, if legal, are not fair, as fairness is regarded by honorable men."

"Do you dare tell me this ?"

"I do; because it is true, and because your conscience
has told it you before. I tell you in all sadness, for I feel
that you have thrown away a rare opportunity. You might
have made yourself the head and heart of this people.
You had done them many good turns; you possessed a
genius for governing which they were quick to recognize;
you had personal magnetism; you could have lived down
prejudice and made yourself a permanent throne in the esteem and the necessities of the people. Again, I tell you
what I do in order to give weight to my warning—a warning you will most likely disregard. You shall hear it,
nevertheless. There is trouble ahead for you. The flame
you think so little of will spread. The officers of N——
will be called upon to resign; then the officers of this parish—you, yourself."

"Stop, sir; you are certainly mad. Called on to resign? They would not dare. And, if they were fools
enough to make such a demand, who would heed it? Resign the offices they hold lawfully at the bidding of a lawless rabble! None but the veriest craven would do it. I
suppose, sir, you would counsel me to humbly accede to
such a demand."

"That is my advice; I give it in good faith, though
you ask it in irony. The wisest course for you and your
friends would be to give up your offices. You could still
live here and continue to make money."

"Thanks for the privilege. You are kind, sir. I am sorry I can not accept your counsel. I should despise my-self for a coward if I were capable of following it. I re-fuse to believe in the bugbear you have conjured up—"

"I differ with you," interposed Devene, who had lis-tened attentively, shrugging his shoulders with an uneasy smile at the Judge's unflattering comments. "Pickenson is not the man to imagine bugbears. He has borne pretty hard on us, but I believe he has given us an honest warn-ing, and that there are breakers ahead, as he says. All the same, I'm not prepared to take his advice about resigning. We hold our offices lawfully ; no set of men has a right to deprive us of them. They can not force us to give them up. If they arrest and imprison us, they know they will pay for it, and such violence would ruin their own cause. The proper course, Witchell, seems to me to be the one you refused when it was urged on you this morning—to go to Washington and negotiate for troops to be sent here to pro-tect us and to help us carry the—"

"Silence !" interrupted Witchell, sternly. "Have you no discretion ?"

He darted a meaning look at Judge Pickenson.

"Can't help it now !" returned Devene, with an an-noyed smile. "The cat's out of the bag. But I am not afraid of the Judge. He has never betrayed any of our secrets, and he knows many a one of them. Yes, it is pro-posed to have troops quartered here to keep things in order, if not now, then a while before the election. You look glum ; the idea don't strike you favorably, Judge."

"It is the worst remedy that could be resorted to. If it gave present help it would bring future ruin upon your chief, all of whose interests are here. A hint that troops were looked for would inflame the people to—"

"Let it," uttered Witchell between his set teeth.

" Since it comes to a question of force, they shall see what hand a wretched rabble can stand against the Government of this country. I rejected the suggestion about troops this morning ; I felt I could hold my own against any opposition now, or at the polls. But I have changed my mind. The troops shall come ; these people shall see that the Government backs the side of law and right. Devene, I heard a steamboat whistle at Cohatchie a while ago. We will go down to the landing before she passes here, and signal her to stop for us. I prefer to leave at night. I don't care to have my movements bruited abroad. Judge Pickenson, you have been a true friend in times past. I believe you were sincere in what you said to-night, but I will prove you a 'false wizard.' I will show you that my foot is but just on the ladder. I will mount it in spite of a people who do not know what is best for them, or what they really want."

He turned to the door ; Devene with his lantern had already passed out. Judge Pickenson hesitated an instant, then he strode up to Witchell and laid his hand on the Captain's arm.

" One thing more I must say, and I charge you to heed it as you care for your brother and your friends. You are going away ; take them with you. It is not best for them to stay."

Captain Witchell's face went a shade paler. " What !" he said, " do you know of any plot against their lives ?"

" No, I only fear."

" Are your people, then, assassins ?"

"They are not. And yet I would not answer for them or any other people when blinded by excitement and misled by the representations of a designing leader."

" Is it Alver you mean ? He is too hot-headed to be designing."

Captain Witchell stood irresolute, his brow furrowed by perplexing thought.

"If I dreamed that any danger threatened the lives of my friends here I would not stir from this place. But I believe nothing of the sort. I have instructed Omar and the others to give not the slightest pretext for violence. They will obey me, and their enemies will not venture upon cold-blooded outrage. The very utmost they can venture upon is arrest and imprisonment, and this will tell in our favor in the end. Surely, Pickenson, this wild night has set your imagination wool-gathering. You are as full of forebodings as old Howard, but you can not infect me. I have determined on my course, and I will not turn aside. I thank you, notwithstanding."

He was gone out into the rainy gloom. Five minutes after, Pickenson heard the whistle of the steamboat in answer to Devene's waving lantern.

"Whom the gods would destroy they first make mad," he soliloquized, lighting a cigar, and standing at the window to watch the colored signal-lights of the steamer.

A few days later Judge Pickenson wrote to Witchell:

"You have received the news of your renomination. It was a foregone conclusion. You have also heard that it has happened in our sister parish of N——, as I predicted. The officers have been forced to resign. Myron and Judge Boone fled here in hot haste and took passage for S——. A similar movement was urged here, but it fell through. You are still strong in the parish of your creation. There is little doubt that you will be reëlected, when you will have an opportunity to retrieve the mistakes you have made.

"I see no new demonstration of excitement. Our officers are quietly attending to their duties. They are cautious and guarded in speech and conduct. Omar seems to rely on his friends and to feel no alarm. I took tea with him and his bride last evening. The little madam is a number one housekeeper ; her muffins melted in my mouth. Devene was there with his lately married wife—a handsome, high-spirited girl, showing her Southern blood in her face. She seems passionately fond of her good-looking husband. You have heard (haven't you ?) the romance of their courtship. She was the daughter of the landlord of the hotel in Morefield where Devene was stopping when the Morefield tax-payers gave the collector that stormy reception. It was she who prevailed upon her father not to open the doors to the mob, and she contrived Devene's escape in a woman's ingenious way.

" Edgefield's love affair does not prosper, and the fellow looks a little careworn. He attends well to his business, though, and makes a capital sheriff—worth a dozen of his predecessor—that bullying humbug, Yent. It is a pity he has set his heart on that little flirt Auzete.

" Howard, too, looks down in the mouth, but it isn't love that troubles our sage District Attorney. The old fellow is scared. He has dreams and presentiments. He fears some terrible calamity is impending, and says there will be wild work in the parish soon. I must own I partake sometimes of his gloomy humor, and fear with him that— But you have already branded me as a 'soothless wizard.'

" However, you see I feel easy enough to write you gossip, and to put off no longer my trip to Texas, which I delayed—as I may tell you now—because I foresaw a possible ' little unpleasantness ' that I might help to restrain. I leave now in a few days."

CHAPTER XXI.

A COMPANY of merry picnickers from Lake Clear streamed into Cohatchie as the sunset was burnishing the low, red waters of the river. A steamboat lay idly puffing at the landing. The gay party, who had not yet had their frolic out, jumped out of buggies and wagons, and, going down to the boat, besieged the Captain—a well-known favorite among them—for a moonlight excursion. The jovial steamboatman was in high humor at having secured a good return trip from this point without having to go farther at this stage of water. He gallantly acceded to their request. He would take them a few miles up the river and back with all the pleasure in the world. They had good music on board, too; they could dance in the cabin, or on the deck by the light of the moon. He knew Miss Reese wanted to dance.

He looked at her admiringly as he spoke. Hers was always the handsomest face in any group of fair women. To-day its radiant looks betrayed nothing of the disappointment and anxiety that gnawed her heart. Two of her plans had miscarried in succession. But she did not despair.

An hour afterward, as she was waltzing with the Captain of the steamer, she suddenly caught an eye fixed upon her, looking from beneath a slouched hat. She gave a quick, furtive glance at the shabby figure leaning against the wall. That gray hair, that mouth covered with a grizzly mustache, were strange to her, but the hooked nose, the lowering brow, the small, yellowish gray eye, gleaming with a vitality at variance with the gray hair—these were horribly familiar. A sick feeling came over her. She stopped in the dance, saying: "I have waltzed too much.

I am a little dizzy.   Will you get me a glass of water, Captain ?"

Her partner 'moved away.   The shabby figure darted to a side-table, caught up a half-filled glass of wine and brought it to her.

"Here is something better than water," said a voice she knew too well.   "Drink to our renewed acquaintance, Mabel Waters."

Mechanically she extended her arm and took the glass. Her hand shook ; the red liquid was spilled on her white fingers.

"Wipe it off with your handkerchief.   It comes off easier than blood," whispered the hideous stranger with a meaning look.   "You start ; if you did not know me before, you do now.   Come out to me on the deck five minutes from now.   I will find a dark corner where we two old friends may talk of old times and future plans."

She made no answer.   Dismay had blanched her face and paralyzed her tongue.   But she was used to controlling herself.   She repressed her emotion.   She gave him a look that signified she understood and would obey him.   Five minutes after he had gone out and taken his stand in a retired part of the deck, she came up to him and stood near without speaking or looking at him.   He put out his hand to draw her nearer.

"Come closer ; we must have a little confidential chat. What, you draw back ?   You scringe as if my hand was a snake.   It's not the first time it's held yours, though I know well that no love for me made you let me hold these little, soft fingers.   No, you felt nothing but disgust for the swarthy, dirty overseer, but you wanted to use him. You loved another, or you loved his money and his high place in the world.   You thought if you looked sweet at me on the sly that I'd go mad for you and put your hus-

band out of the way; and you would marry your rich lover.
I understand it all now, though I didn't then. I was fool
enough to think you cared for me, and I gave poor old
Waters his quietus, while that chicken-hearted Morris
looked on with his knees shaking and his face as white—
as white as yours turned just now when I called you by
your right name. He didn't guess I was killing the
man for my own benefit; he thought he had hired me to
put him out of his way. It was along of him and his
cowardice that the killing came out on us; but I was too
smart for them. I got away, and he swung, as he deserved,
for being such a fool. I meant to come back and get you.
I had a compromisin' note or two of yours that would bring
you to taw, as I knew, but when I slipped back I found you
had been accused, mobbed, followed, and had drowned
yourself, as they said, in tryin' to ford the river. I thought
you dead from that day to this, and here I find you alive and
as handsome—yes, handsomer—than ever. You won't get
away from me again. You don't like the prospect. I
see it in your looks. I know I'm not particularly fascinating, especially with this grizzly wig and bleached mustache; never mind, you're pretty enough for us both,
and I've done enough to earn you. Then *I've got them
notes yet.*"

"You wouldn't dare use them," she managed to say,
huskily. "That would be to betray yourself. There's a
price set on your head."

"And on yours, too, my beauty. We can shake hands
there. We know each other's secrets; neither dare quarrel
with the other. That's a good enough bond for close
friends. I've just come from California. I wasn't caring
where I drifted to, but now I've seen you, we'll not part
company; I'll take you with me. Won't you go?"

He pulled her close to him. His sensual, savage eyes

gloated on her. She tried to free herself from that disgusting embrace.

"Loose me! loose me this instant! How dare you?"

"How dare I? That's a pretty question; you know why I dare. You give me the right, and you know it. You put it in my head to kill old Waters to get you."

"It is false."

"You didn't tell me to do it in so many words, but you put me up to do it all the same, and you knew it at the time. I know now; it was that you might be free to marry the other fellow—but he should never have had you. I'd seen you both swung first. Say, are you going with me? Better promise at once. Or I'll call up the crowd and introduce Mabel Waters to them."

A thought flashed into the woman's mind.

"Yes, I'll go with you, Cobb," she said, "on one condition. You must do a favor for me. I can rely on no one but you. It is something you can do, without risk."

"Not another bloody job, I hope. What's it? Let me hear."

"You shall hear it. Not now. There is some one calling me. They are hunting for me. Let me go. For pity's sake, loose me."

"One kiss, then," and the thick, ugly mouth pressed itself on her quivering lips, on her cheeks that grew dead-white with disgust. It was gall and wormwood to the woman whose fastidious taste was her only substitute for conscience, but fear forced her to yield.

"Shall I kill myself?" she thought as she hurried from him. "Shall I jump over this boat's side, and end this torturing fever of life? Or shall I kill him, after I have made use of him to effect my purpose."

She decided on the latter.

That night, after her escort had parted from her at

Alver's door, she went up to the master of the house, who
sat on the gallery, moodily smoking a cigar, and asked:

"Have you taken that fellow out of the lock-up?"

"Yes, I paid his fine—a heavy one. There was no alternative. His brother was after me, threatening to expose
everything. I'm disgusted with them both. Their cursed,
blundering stupidity yesterday has nearly ruined all. Devene saw through it, and knew they were put up to provoke a fuss. I am sure he did. The wretches got drunk
and blundered like idiots."

"They are not fit for the business any way. I have
found a man who is better suited to our purpose."

"*You* have found a man? Who is he?"

"He is a man I knew in Texas. I have met him to-
night—luckily, just as we needed him."

"And you told him—?"

"Nothing yet. I have appointed to see him."

"How do you know he will keep silent? You remember I have a hold on these Nolan men to compel their silence. I happen to know of that Colfax business of theirs."

"And I happen to have a similar hold upon this man.
I know of a secret episode in his life. I will tell you more
another time. Enough, that you can believe me, when I
tell you he is the right man for this work. He is cunning
as well as bold, and liquor has no more effect on him than
water, so he will not get drunk and overdo the matter as
these Nolans did."

Floyd went to her room, lit her lamp, and sat down by
it to pore over a letter she took from her pocket. She had
studied this half sheet of paper hours at a time since it
came into her possession. It did not come there honorably,
but that mattered little to Floyd, who permitted no such
immaterial obstacle as a sentiment of honor to stand in the
way of her will.

Witchell's absence at this important time aroused the suspicion that he had gone to ask for troops on the ground that they were needed to preserve order in the parish. The suspicion required to be confirmed, and Floyd would have given much to have had the handling of the post-office matter which might contain a confidential correspondence between Witchell and his friends. But the postmaster was an honest man, who could not be tampered with. He was careless and unsystematic, however, like most village postmasters, and sometimes permitted an overlooking eye while he shuffled over a package of letters in order to satisfy the monotonous inquiry, "Anything for me?" In this way Floyd's falcon eye had had opportunities of reading the superscriptions upon letters, but she had seen none she thought might have been written by Witchell until two days ago. That morning she saw from her window the "pony express" pass by bringing a well-filled mail bag from the distributing office at N——. She hastily threw on her hat and ran down to the post-office, arriving while the mail was being opened. She was permitted to "help," through consideration for her prettily-expressed eagerness to get an expected letter. She caught sight of an address that sent a tremor through her fingers. It was written in a disguised hand, but she thought it resembled Witchell's. She dropped the fan with which she had been playfully repelling the advances of a little terrier.

"Oh, my poor fan!" she cried; "Mr. Vaughn, your dog is devouring it!"

The postmaster made a dive after the dog. The fan was secured; so was the letter. It was safe in the half-loose sleeve of Floyd's walking jacket. She was all sweetness over the broken slat of her fan; she pouted prettily because she had no letter. She left a charming picture on the young postmaster's mind.

Safe in her room, she carefully opened the letter, which
was addressed to Mark Hollin—Witchell's brother-in-law—
who had a plantation and a "store" a few miles below
Cohatchie. As she unfolded the inclosure her face grew
blank; the letter was written in cipher. But this only
stimulated her eagerness to know its contents. She had
had some experience in deciphering cryptographs. She
called up her skill and her fertile imagination to help her
solve this one. She sat up over it half the night, but
without success. She bent over it again to-night, but not
very hopefully. All at once her color deepened. A chance
suggestion seemed to give her a clew to the puzzle. A
moment's further study confirmed her triumph. She had
discovered the key to the cipher. She read the letter
through.

But its meaning was still mysterious. Evidently it was
an appendix to a previous letter containing secret instructions, which had been sent by private hand. She read :

"By this time you have my letter sent by B——. I hope
you understand that the matter is confided to you alone.
The others must not know or suspect—least of all O——.
The measure is repugnant to me ; I would not employ it
if there was any other way to obtain what I want. But
let me say again that there must be no serious mischief
done—just enough to build a strong paragraph upon. *Employ none but a safe man*—one who is under obligations to
us. It would be best if you could get one of the numerous
Tonio family on the Hills. You know only the old man,
but they are all our stanch friends, and, being Spaniards,
know how to hold their tongues. This is a delicate matter ; to bungle in it would be fatal. I rely on your discretion."

Floyd studied over this letter for five minutes ; then its
significance flashed upon her.

"The troops have been refused him!" she exclaimed. "There is no ground for military interference, so one must be created. It must appear that the negroes are being oppressed; the new voting element in danger of intimidation. 'Mischief must be done,' just enough to 'build a strong paragraph upon,' which means that some prominent darky's fodder stack must be set afire or a shot fired down his chimney, that the hue-and-cry of Ku-klux may be raised. Here is a fine discovery; here shall be a fine exposure! This letter shall be made public at once."

But her exultant look clouded. After-consequences presented themselves. How would she account for the letter being in her possession? How would she prove its genuineness? how establish that it was written by Witchell? It was in a disguised hand and had no signature, and no address save on the envelope. It would be assailed as a malignant forgery. True, its publication might forestall Witchell's policy and prevent the coming of the troops, but even without the presence of these Witchell was almost sure to be elected. He wanted them mostly to impress the people with the sense of his strong backing, and to give his friends a fuller feeling of security in which to work for him.

But Alver should lay the letter before the League. *They* would not inquire too closely as to how it was obtained—and they would believe it; they were ripe for believing anything against Witchell. It would be fresh fuel to their fiery hate of him. Floyd was impatient of Witchell's injunction—that the others, Omar especially, should be kept in ignorance of the plot. She wanted them all implicated. It was in her programme to sweep the district free of them all.

"I ought to be able to do something better with this," she said, looking at the letter with contracted brow. She started up, and began to walk the floor with bent head and hands tightly clasped before her. At last her brow cleared, she threw up her head, her eyes shone.

"Witchell shall be 'hoist with his own petard!'" she cried. "It is all here in my head. This letter shall be resealed and put back in the office. Mark Hollin must receive it. The copy of it which the League will read shall have my own amendments, by which it will appear that Witchell's underlings here have received instructions from him to stir up a negro riot. Meantime Cobb shall go to Mark Hollin, represent himself as one of the loyal and manifold Tonios, and ask to be hired to him as a farm hand. He is safe to be chosen to execute Witchell's 'delicate job' of Ku-kluxing; and he shall stir up the negroes so effectually as to give color to a report that they are about to 'rise,' and afford a pretext for a grand rally of White Leaguers from the neighboring parishes gathered here to suppress a bloody disturbance instigated by Witchell. Excitement will rise to its highest, and on its tidal wave Witchell and his crew will be swept to destruction. If it is managed well the verdict will be: 'Served them right.' The game will be difficult and risky, but there is a chance for success. I play my first card to-morrow when I make Cobb pledge me his help."

CHAPTER XXII.

THE sun, low in the west, shone behind cloudy bars of rose and gold, a wind crept up from the river freshening the heated air, stirring the silver-lined leaves of the cottonwood, and moving the silky rings of hair on Zoe's forehead. She sat on the gallery of her brother's cottage, her sewing dropped in her lap, her eyes watching the sunset gleam upon the tops of the dark woods in the distance.

"Look!" cried her little nephew, pulling at her sleeve and pointing to the road where two men on horseback were approaching the house. They stopped before the gate, and the taller of the two inquired for Mr. Vincent, and, being told that he had ridden back in the swamp to look at some wood his hands were cording, he asked if Mr. Vincent did not need more wood-cutters, as their business with him was to get work, and wood-chopping would suit as well as anything.

Zoe glanced up at the two men, and thought they would not do much at the wood business. Their appearance showed none of the muscular development of men accustomed to heavy work. Both were young; the taller had a supple, slender figure, straight as an Indian's, a pale, beardless face (the fact of being without a beard being singular in the West), a small, pale, restless eye, hands tanned but slender, and a foot whose shapeliness could not be wholly disguised by the rough Texan boot worn outside the trousers. In his manner there was a mixture of carelessness and refinement at odds with his coarse, dusty clothes. His companion, lower and clumsier in build, had nothing of his easy, independent carriage and grace of look. He was swarthy-skinned, with an eye dull yet watchful—like an alligator's.

They alighted from their horses and came up to the house, the tall one seating himself on the step and beginning to play with the children, the other walking up and down in the yard whistling and humming a song, the refrain of which, as Zoe caught it, was:

> "O Mary! sweet Mary,
>   You're false and unkind,
>   I'll roam the broad prairie
>   Some peace for to find."

Hugh came at last, greeted them in his usual off-hand way, and was informed of their business.

"Wood-chopping," he said doubtfully, as his eye ran over their figures. "You're rather light for that work—and your hands! Are you used to work?"

"Certain we are used to it, like all poor devils. Give us a job, and you'll see chips fly."

"Where did you come from, and what are you doing here?"

"Crops failed for want of rain in Texas where we were, and we come here hunting work."

"Haven't I seen you somewhere? I recognize your faces. Stay! wasn't your comrade here the fellow that pitched into the Radicals so at Cohatchie last Saturday, abusing Devene and Omar Witchell to their faces, and swearing he could whip out the whole of them?"

"The same. It's Jim's way when he takes too much. He must show his teeth right away."

"He did more than show his teeth Saturday. He was on the bite, and no mistake. He was outrageously abusive, and I wonder Devene kept his hands off him."

"He wouldn't if it hadn't been for that meek, sheep-looking chap, Witchell's brother. He kept holding the other fellow's arm and telling him to be calm, and remember what Marshall had put them on their guard about."

"If your brother wanted a fight out of them he went about it too brash. He overdid the matter, and made them suspect he was put up to it."

"That's Jim's foolish way when the liquor's in him. I saw he was going too far, but I was bound to back him."

"He got taken up and put in jail, didn't he?"

"He did, and he got out too."

"Through Alver's influence, I heard. You are lucky

to find such a friend. I wonder he did not employ you upon his own place. Did he send you to me?"

A shade of embarrassment tinged the young man's face at the keen look and abrupt question. But he answered promptly :

"Not exactly. He said if we were after work we might try here, as you had a wood-yard, and he knew you to be a square man to deal with."

"I didn't think Alver would be so complimentary to me. Something must be in the wind. I've never joined his White League that they tell me has got to be such a strong organization."

"You're a Rad, then."

"No more than Alver is ; but, all the same, I don't want to bind myself by the rules of a clique got up by a man who's more after office than he is after principle, or the good of the people. But this is drifting away from business. You want a job of wood-chopping, and I can't give it to you. I've more choppers now than I want."

"Anything else, then? We're bound to stay around here. Our horses are too jaded to travel."

"I've nothing you could do unless you could get out shingles. I want a lot for my new stables, but I've half promised the job to some darkies. You don't know how to get out shingles, I suppose?"

The young fellow cut a quick, half quizzical glance at his comrade, who had taken no part in the conversation, but had stopped his walk and his whistle to listen to it, and stood rubbing the rust off the blade of a large knife with his dirty handkerchief. Zoe, who did not like his furtive, reptile eye, wondered if that might not be the rust of blood.

"Shingle-getting is our favorite profession," said the other. "We can take a premium on that any day. We'll do the work cheap, too, as any."

"Very well, I'll try you to-morrow, Mr. ——. You haven't told me your name yet."

"Nolan—Dan and Jim ; we're brothers."

"You don't look the least alike. Well, you can sleep in that little outhouse there, Mr. Nolan, in the corner of the yard, and we will send you your meals."

"Did your professional shingle-getters go to work all right ?" Zoe asked her brother the next day, when he returned from the woods.

"Go to work ! There's something wrong about these fellows. Wanting work is an excuse to hang around the neighborhood. They have gone and hired negroes to get out the shingles, and I found them out yonder where the hands were at work popping away at a mark. Rube says they have whisky with them. I must turn them off. They are up to some mischief likely."

That evening, after sunset, as Zoe and the children stood on the river bank, they saw approaching a wagon, driven slowly, with an excited group of negroes following it. A little darky, running on ahead, announced to them breathlessly that "dem two white men done fout, and one bus t'other's head clean open wid a axe, and he dead dar in de waggin."

Zoe hurried up to the vehicle, which had stopped before the outhouse. Jim Nolan and two negroes were lifting the senseless form of Dan out of the wagon. They put him down on the floor of the porch. His face was covered with blood, his head a mass of clotted gore. His brother stooped over him. He was only half sober ; his hands were stained, his face streaked with his brother's blood.

He raised Dan's head and put a bottle to his mouth, his hand shaking and the liquor spilling over the unconscious man's face.

"Come, now, Dan, stop this foolishness; hold up your

head and drink some of this. You'll be right in five minutes. Curse the blood, how it runs! It's only a scratch.
You give me a sight harder lick. You ought not to have
provoked me, throwing up that blunder. You know how
I am, specially when I've had liquor. But I'll forgive you
if you'll stop this darned foolishness. Open your eyes;
drink a little of this, now do."

He tried to force the neck of the bottle between his
brother's teeth. Zoe was horrified.

"Let him alone; can't you see he is dying?" she cried.

"Dying!" he turned on her with a red glare in his
dull-lidded eyes; "dying! he is not going to die. If he
does," he uttered with slow, hoarse emphasis, striking out
with his clenched fist, "I die too. He's my brother, and
if I've killed him I'll go too. I'll blow out my brains the
minute I see he's at his last gasp. Here's what'll do the
business." He brought up a pistol out of his pocket and
cocked it with a sharp click; then his roving, crazy glance
fell on his brother, and he saw Dan had opened his eyes.
Down he got over him again, the pistol was hastily un-
cocked and thrust into his pocket, and the bottle drawn out.
"You're coming round old fellow, I see you are," he cried,
fumbling about his brother's face with his bloody fingers.
"There wasn't much the matter. That's right, stop your
nonsense, and drink this and get up. Curse it, don't shut
your eyes again."

"Get away with your liquor, Nolan," Hugh said sternly.
He had just come up. "Rube, set that bucket of water
close to his head. Here, Zoe, run and get some big towels;
we must stop this bleeding. The doctor won't be apt to get
here before morning. Get back, Nolan; you can't do any
good; you're shaking like a man with the ague. Go and
wash your hands and face, for God's sake."

"You don't think Dan's in any danger?"

" Well, from the looks of all this blood, I should think he was, and I'd advise you to mount your horse and get away from here as quick as you can if you don't want to get nabbed."

"Never ; I'll never leave him in death or life. What'd I do without Dan ? I'd be lost without him. He's all I've got. If he dies, gentlemen, I'll go too, quick as hot lead can send me. But he ain't a going to die, not he ; he's had too many hard rubs to knock under for such a tap. Look, there's his eyes open now. Hello, Dan ! you're gettin' all right, old fellow. You don't like so much water round you, do you ? Want something stronger ; here it is. Get away, nigger, I know what's good for him. There, you see he swallows ; that'll bring him up. Put back the cloths," he cried, as the towels dropped away and exposed the swollen, spongy scarlet cut, from which the blood continued to flow. " Yes, you'll soon be all right," he repeated, springing to his feet and beginning to walk the floor rapidly, whistling, and at last breaking out with

" O Mary ! sweet Mary,
   You're false and unkind,
I'll roam the broad prairie
   Some peace for to find."

Such scenes were repeated all night. Dan Nolan lay in a stupor from which he occasionally roused and stared about and spoke. Once he sank into a kind of swoon, and Vincent thought him dead. Jim Nolan, down on his knees, felt for his pulse. Shaking his head, he said, coolly :

" Yes, he's gone," and, pulling out the pistol, cocked it and put it to his own head.

" Stand back, Squire," he said to Vincent. " Don't interfere, or I'll shoot you, sure."

" Don't you see your brother is coming to ? " shouted

Vincent. Those words arrested the would-be suicide and brought him to his brother's side. A moment after he was whistling " Mary, sweet Mary."

At daylight the doctor came, and, contrary to Hugh's fears, pronounced the wound not necessarily fatal, and the patient likely to live ; though, having lost so much blood, he would be very weak for a long time.

CHAPTER XXIII.

HE was ill a good many days, his brother nursing him unremittingly, and Zoe helping in some of the lighter services. Dan Nolan was a mystery to her. In his fine brow and mouth, in his tones, and his quiet, careless manner, there was a strange refinement, entirely wanting in his brother, and foreign to his own present pursuits. He had read, traveled about, mixed with artists and actors—perhaps been an actor himself—for he had locks of hair from the heads of not a few famous ladies of the stage. He carried a flute, too, in his knapsack, and a set of chess-men he had carved with much taste.

Once, when his brother had gone to town for medicine, Zoe was sitting by him as he lay on his pallet on the shaded back porch. He had been more than usually feverish, and she had bathed his head and face. He took her hand as she was moving away, and, looking at her, said :

" You are too good ; you don't know what a wretch I am. What would you say if I told you that the hands you have been bathing are stained with crime ? that they had even meant to do harm to you and yours ?"

" Harm to us !—Why ?"

" Hasn't your brother enemies ?"

" Yes."

" Especially since he refused to join the White League. Alver's motto is, 'They that are not of us are against us !'"

He would not say any more, but closed his eyes and lay back as if exhausted. Zoe's curiosity was excited ; her fears were slightly aroused. She felt herself justifiable that evening, after Jim's return, in stopping an instant just by the window when she heard the brothers speaking on the porch outside. Alver's name caught her ear.

" Did you see him ?" Dan asked.

" Yes, I came near breaking his neck, too. He treated me as if I was a dog. Told me he had no further use for us, that we had played the fool, and gave me twenty dollars. Said that was enough for such marplots as we had proved ourselves."

" Twenty dollars—the devil ! As if he didn't make a firm bargain for us to stay here till after the election at his expense ! I'll get up there pretty soon if it kills me, and I'll show him."

" Better not. He declared if I came up there again he'd have me arrested, whether for what I did to you, or for the old scores, I don't know. He said it would be healthy for us to get out of the parish."

" He's afraid we'll peach. He want's us out of the way. He has got somebody else to do that job for him."

" I believe he has. I am sure of it. The town is in a commotion to-day ; people standing about with their heads together talking. Something's going to drop pretty soon. An old fellow told me it was whispered they were looking for the negroes to rise, and pitch into killing and robbing generally."

" We understand that," Dan said, significantly ; " at least I think *I* do. If they can make believe the Rads started the riot, it'll be better than their first plan. There, you've hurt my head, old fellow; that was an awkward punch."

Zoe stole away from her place at the window troubled and perplexed. Her situation just now was peculiarly painful. Hugh had been taken down two days before with fever; her sister-in-law had a little babe not ten days old; the responsibility of the family rested on her young shoulders. She knew nothing of the two young men whom accident had quartered upon them. They might be rogues or murderers for aught she knew, and now she seemed to have got an inkling of some evil mystery with which they had to do. She had no neighbors on this side the river upon whom she could rely. "Every one for himself" was their motto. They were narrow, selfish people, with whom, moreover, her brother was not on friendly terms. His quick, somewhat rough temper had resented some petty meanness and meddling on their part. Then, too, he was looked on with suspicion because he had not joined the White League. True Southerner as he was, he had his own notions, and he held that it would fetter his freedom of conscience and of action to pledge himself to follow the lead of any organization controlled by a man whose ambition was his god.

Thus Zoe felt herself in a manner isolated. Her keen instinct had made her vaguely conscious that something was wrong—something unusual going on among whites and blacks. Crops were neglected; men rode about restlessly, crossed the river, and gathered in Cohatchie; negroes left their work to collect in knots around the house of some important character among them, and talk earnestly. To-day she had noticed that they seemed to be excited; their gestures were agitated; she was driven to remark their restless tramping and riding up and down the river. Hugh's own farm hands looked at her strangely and held aloof. Even the cook was reserved and sullen. Zoe felt the oppressing influence of all these things, but she had no time to indulge in misgivings. Her day's work and cares were not yet ended. She called the children to her, gave them their supper of milk and bread, and put them to bed. Then she saw to the comfort of her sister-in-law, lying white as her pillows, with her fat, rosy babe sleeping beside her. She administered Hugh's medicine to him, and, after freshly arranging his bed and room, she left him in charge of the old colored woman, who had been his nurse when he was a baby, while she went out on the piazza for the sake of the fresh air and to get a moment's quiet thought. Some one was sitting on the steps ; he called her name as she approached.

"Is it you, Henry ?" she said. "Have you been here long ? I did not know it. You must pardon me."

"I knew you were busy, Miss Zoe, but I wanted to see you a moment, if no more, so I waited."

He was a young farmer who lived across the river—a good-hearted fellow, very popular among the men, and deeply attached to Zoe, but quite timid in his worship. She liked him. His simple, merry talk made some bright spots in her dreary life in this place where people, wrapped in the culture of cotton, were like cocoons in their cells.

"You wanted to see me, Henry ; was it for anything particular ?" she asked, sitting down on the steps near him.

"I wanted to ask you not to go to the ball to-morrow night."

"The ball—what ball ?"

"Why, the ball that Colonel Alver gives in his fine new store that's just finished."

"I had forgotten. I believe, too, I was to have gone with you. So many cares and distresses have come upon me lately, that they have quite put the ball out of my head. I
11

should not go anyhow, but why are you so particular in requesting me not to be there ?"

"I can't tell you that, Miss Zoe ?"

"Why not, Henry ?"

"I'm pledged not to. But I may tell you this much, I think. There'll be no ball, no dancing of any account. It'll be broken up as soon as it begins."

"Henry, I insist on your telling me what you mean. There is some mystery floating in the air. I feel it, and it troubles me. What is it that will break up the ball ? Why are you pledged to keep it secret."

"We are pledged not to tell the secrets of the League to outsiders, and your brother is an outsider."

"But he is a true friend to his country."

"I believe that. And I don't see why this should be one of the secrets of the League. Everybody ought to know it, seems to me ; you especially, who are so unprotected on this place right now. Miss Zoe, I must tell you ; it may put you on your guard. They say the negroes are going to rise ; that the night of the ball they aim to surround the ball-room and kill the men and carry off the ladies."

"Oh, what a wild project ! Do you think the negroes would be such fools? What end would they have in view ?"

"It's the Radicals putting them up to it."

"For what purpose in the world ? How did it get out, Henry ?"

"It got out through a letter Witchell wrote to his brother, telling him to stir up a riot with the negroes to scare and kill the whites, so that the Radicals would carry the election."

"You saw that letter ?"

"No ; we heard at our last meeting (that is, a few of us

did) how such a letter had been intercepted in the post-
office at Cohatchie, and how, in some way, it had come to
the ears of the League leaders that the night of the ball was
the night chosen for the attack. The programme is that
we are to go there, as if we suspected nothing; only, we
are all to carry arms. A few know why, and are pledged
not to tell; the others suspect there is something in the
wind, and will come armed, because told to do so. The
Radical officers are invited. Captain Witchell himself may
be there. They are looking for him from New Orleans to-
night or to-morrow."

"It all seems strange to me. It is strange that the
Radicals should wreck their own cause this way Why, it
is their policy to make out the negroes are the most peaceable, best disposed citizens of the South; and now to incite
them to a riot on the eve of election ! Why, that is to sell
themselves, sure enough. Of course the riot would be
quelled. The few white votes that might be destroyed
would count nothing against the injury that would be done
the Republican party in the State—in the whole South.
And Witchell has been working hard to gain the confidence
of a portion of the whites here, and has quite a number of
friends. It seems strange. I can not realize that such a
thing can be intended. Do you really believe it ?"

"Oh! yes, Miss Zoe, I am afraid there is something
of it."

"It may be. I know there is something unusual going
on among the negroes. I have noticed they seem restless
and excited, especially to-day."

"Well, you know they are all stirred up. They are,
or they pretend to be, as scared as sheep the wolf has got
among. One of their big men—old Moses Clark—the
richest and most thought of darky about here, was killed
yesterday. Haven't you heard about it ?"

" I stay here and nurse children and sick folks, and hear nothing."

" He was called out just at dusk and shot down—the negroes say by a white man. It's a pity. He was a harmless, respectable old fellow. And now I hear to-day that the cabins of two more negroes have been fired into, that the negroes have been threatened by an unknown party, and have had one or two anonymous letters through the post-office, warning them to join together for protection or they would be trampled out. Old Rube tells me they have come to Levi Adams—here on your place—to know of him what they must do. I can't think who's been working this mischief to the negroes. I know it's not our League. They've always frowned down Ku-klux measures of any kind. Maybe all this is done by the negroes and Rads to throw dust in our eyes. If so, we'll be too sharp for them. They'll be a little disappointed to-morrow night."

" As well as the poor girls who expected to dance. Why do you not warn them all to stay away ? "

" We were ordered to keep silent. I have broken commands, but I was determined to warn you. Miss Zoe, you had better go to Cohatchie and stay with some of your friends. It'll be very unsafe for you here, with nothing but the swamp back of you, and so many negroes and so few white people around. You must go across the river anyhow. Come and stay with mother."

" And leave this sick family and these little children ? No, Henry, I shall stay right here. I hope this may prove a mere sensational story—an election canard. I know our people would not be so unprincipled as to incite a riot, and I don't think the Radicals are such fools ; and the negroes have not sense or courage enough to organize anything unless put up to it—unless, perhaps, if they are really frightened, to band together in an irregular way for protection.

That is little Ralph calling me. He will wake up his father if I don't go at once and tell him a bear story to send him to sleep again. Thanks, Henry, for coming to put us on our guard. But I trust your warning will not be needed. Good-night."

CHAPTER XXIV.

THE day following—the day of the ball—was still and warm, shining down on ripening cornfields and orchards burdened with fruit. But to Zoe the cloudless day had dark portents. Ominous signs met her eye. No negroes worked in the fields; no songs or laughter floated up from the quarter; no little darky came to beg fruit. Some negro men came to the house to ask Zoe to open her brother's store and sell them powder and shot to go hunting with. They seemed to resent her refusal, and muttered their disbelief of the excuse she gave. Early in the day she saw the mulatto, Levi Adams (the negro-leader), ride off from his cabin on her brother's place and take his way down the river. When he returned some hours later he rode up to a pecan-tree in front of his cabin and talked awhile, with much vehement gesticulation, to some negroes collected there; then he rode away again, this time up the river. As he passed Zoe, who was standing in her front yard, he turned in his saddle and gave her a sinister look. He was a remarkable negro—half-breed, rather, for he had Indian blood in his veins. He rode, leaped, swam, and dodged like an Indian. His skin was tawny red, his nose straight, his eye keen and watchful.

The chief ferry for the planters who lived below bayou Vincey was at Hugh Vincent's place. Before sunset they began to ride up to the ferry by twos and threes on their way to Alver's ball. Each man carried a gun and pistols—strange ball-room equipment. Levi Adams stationed himself on the bank, motionless as a bronze statue on his horse, and eyed attentively every group that crossed. Zoe could see the scowl on his dark face from the piazza where she stood. Dan Nolan, propped on his elbow as he lay on a bench close to her, observed the negro and said, quietly :

"That darky's got the devil waked up in him. He's scared and savage at once, like a grizzly that scents the dogs. He's going to try to do something, he doesn't know what. Jim Nolan," turning to his brother, "there'll be fun at this ball. Get your horse and go. Come back to-night and report. We might have had an invite ; yes, and led off the ball, if you hadn't played the deuce. I don't fancy you'll be welcomed there now by my lord. Never mind, go ; I want to hear the news."

At the same hour Floyd Reese was nervously dressing for the ball. Earlier, she had been down to the ball-room putting the finishing touches to its decorations. As she was walking back, in company with several ladies, they passed a shabby figure sitting on a barrel in front of a store, smoking a short-stemmed pipe. Pretty Mrs. Perrine pointed him out.

"Diogenes sitting *on* instead of *in* his tub," Floyd said, laughing. Nobody noticed that she held up seven of her slender, ungloved fingers—nobody but the shabby man on the barrel, who answered the signal by a motion of the eyelids.

As the clock was striking seven she came out upon the back veranda, already dressed for the evening. She walked there a little while, enjoying the perfumed dusk, then she stepped down into the yard and glided among the shrubberied mazes in her floating draperies. She cropped tea-roses negligently, and did not turn her head toward a shaded corner of the yard, where her quick eye had seen a figure pause outside the vine-covered paling. The figure stood there motionless in the deepening dusk. At last Floyd approached the tree-shadowed corner and began to twist off a flower spray from the vine on the paling.

"You have done well," she said, low.

"Glad you're pleased," muttered a voice outside. "'Twarn't a pleasant job, though. That old darky's sure to haunt me. He was a meek-looking cuss."

"Why did you deal with him as you did? Hurting him pretty badly would have sufficed. Alver wanted no killing. He is opposed to any bloodshed even—"

"No bloodshed, eh? It's just so with the other side. 'Mind, Tonio, there must be no bloodshed,' says Mark Hollin; and no doubt he's wild over what's happened. But when folks hire the devil to scratch their backs they shouldn't cry out if his nails go deeper than they bargained for. For myself, I think it's best as it is. It don't pay to do things half way; and dead men can't blab. If Alver's so squeamish, he hadn't ought to've begun a thing like this. That's not the last blood there'll be before this is through with. He has sense enough to see that, surely."

"He shuts his eyes to it. Let him. The thing has gone so far now it will carry itself through if you do your work well to-night. How are the negroes?"

"Stirred up to the right pitch; scared and crazy as bed-bugs, most of 'em; lookin out for somethin' they don't know what. Some of 'em's savage, too—primed with hate and whisky, and rubbin' up their guns for what may come. They're safe to make some sort of spurt. Some of the worst scared are goin' to Omar Witchell to-night to know what they must do and ask him to protect them. I put 'em up to that."

"It was smart in you. It will play into our hands. They will be found at his house to-night when the alarm is given. If all works as it ought, there will be no proof of a plot on our side, no suspicion of a trap even by those who helped to set it. Now, Cobb, be off. You know everything depends on to-night. It is nearly dark. You are first to go across the river and fire the blank charges from your repeating gun to scare Holcomb's messenger. Mind that no one sees or suspects you."

"Do you mean to say that none of the White League are up to this?"

"None but Alver. Even he does not know all that has been done, or foresee all that we intend shall happen. The others think they are coming to-night to quell a possible negro outbreak incited by Witchell's Ring. Go, now, Cobb. Remember I depend on you to bring things to a successful point to-night. Don't blunder, for heaven's sake."

"For *your* sake I wont. Heaven has mighty little to do with this thing, I take it. You know my pay has got to be *you*, and the money Alver promised, and a good share of the spoils. They will be pretty rich, I fancy."

"Yes, yes; go."

The figure moved off through the dusk, and Floyd hurried into the house. Half an hour later she was at the party. The long, wide room of Alver's new store made a good enough ball-room. It was well lighted and decorated with flowers. Hardly twenty ladies were present, but more than three times that number of men stalked about the room in costumes rather rough for the dance, and with looks that betokened a fiercer excitement than belongs to the ball-room.

Two or three of the Radical officers came in and walked around, saying a few words here and there. Their manner betrayed repressed uneasiness and distrust. Floyd Reese welcomed them cordially. Alver was unusually courteous, but they met cold looks from many of the others, some of whom had been their friends, and they soon withdrew. Ominous rumors had come to their ears. Omar, though troubled, put little credence in what he heard. Devene and Edgeville feared nothing. Hollin and Wallace were at their plantations. Captain Witchell and Ed. Devene had not returned. Howard alone was frightened. He had not the youth and bold spirits of the others. He would not desert his post, but he was a prey to apprehension. He was shut up in his room to-night writing to the one woman the old bachelor had ever loved—the woman who was to have been his wife in the long ago, but

" Whispering tongues had poisoned truth."

He had made his will, and left to the child of his old love the little savings of his life.

Edgeville's capricious ladylove gave him only a haughty little nod as she passed him in promenading.

A month ago he had thought she really cared for him, but "the tide has turned against us, and she has turned with it. Let her go," he said to himself as he moved away with bitterness at his heart.

An hour—nearly two hours—went by. It was near ten o'clock. Alver's eyes turned often to the door, and he bit his mustached lip impatiently. Floyd's laugh had a false ring, and spots of color burned on her cheeks. At last there was the sound of a horse galloping at full speed along the hard street. A moment after a young man rushed into the room, dripping wet, bare-headed, his face pale with excitement. He walked straight to Alver, his spurs clanking across the floor, his garments dripping streams of muddy water as he went. He took a leather pocket-book from his bosom, opened it, took out a folded paper and handed it to Alver, saying, breathlessly :

"From Uncle Holcomb."

The contents of the note were these :

"COLONEL : I got your note telling me of the rumor that the negroes would have a meeting at Brownton to-night, and I must keep a lookout and report to you by ten o'clock. There *is* a gathering of negroes here, whether of a hostile nature or not I can't say. They have been coming in by two and threes since dark. Levi Adams and a few others are armed, but you know they often carry guns. Levi never goes without one. I can't make out what they are after. I report according to request.

"Yours,   H."

Alver ran his eye over these lines, then looked at the young man who had brought the dispatch.

"You have something to report ; what is it ?"

"The negroes ! the negroes are in arms in Keener field, this side of Brownton. They fired upon me as I rode through the field on my way here. At least a dozen guns were fired at me."

"Did you see any one ?"

"I saw the heads of several negroes above the cotton. I think they followed me. I heard horses galloping behind me at a distance. My horse was scared. He ran for the river. I swam across, and came straight here to let you know."

"You did well," commented Alver. Then, advancing into the middle of the room, his tall figure drawn up to its full height, his eye flashing like a sword of blue steel, he said : "Gentlemen, you have heard what this young man says. The note in my hand tells me that the negroes are gathering at Brownton. Levi Adams, whom you know for a desperado, is heading them. They will probably march upon Cohatchie. They no doubt knew that this young man was a messenger sent to apprise us of their gathering, and fired upon him with intent to kill. We must immediately take steps to patrol the town, form ourselves into vigilantes, and arrest all suspicious characters."

"First of all, the d—d Rads that are at the bottom of this," cried a loud, harsh voice—the voice of Cobb—at the door. Loud shouts answered him. His words were echoed from mouth to mouth. A chorus of excited exclamations filled the house; men rushed pell-mell for the door. Alver's strident voice arrested them.

"Order!" he commanded. "A few of you see these young ladies home; the others must at once mount their horses and see to their arms. Some of you I wish to send in all haste to Morefield, Madden, Malta, and other towns, with dispatches asking for men to be sent to our assistance. We must be prompt. There is no knowing the extent of this movement, or what form it may take. We must suppress it at the *fountain-head*. Do you understand?"

"Yes, yes. The Radical fountain-head. We will suppress it," responded his listeners. "Go ahead, Colonel. We're under your orders."

"Thanks," said Alver. He was in his element—looked up to, giving command. His eyes lighted with quickened intelligence and energy. Floyd gave him a glance of admiration as she passed. She herself was pale as marble, but her eyes shone with hard, gem-like brightness.

Alver ordered everything with wonderful rapidity. Messengers riding swift horses were sent to the various towns in hot haste, carrying dispatches that the negroes, incited by the Republicans, had risen, and that Cohatchie was in danger of being burned and its citizens massacred. Parties of young men patrolled the town in different directions, stopping at negro houses, and calling upon the inmates to come out and give an account of themselves. Most of them seemed terrified and bewildered ; a few of the men were sullen and defiant. Some were absent from home, and their wives declared they had gone to Omar Witchell to find out from him what was the matter, and what they must do.

As the men rode from house to house in the moonlight, their guns gleaming, their voices challenging, suddenly there came a sharp report followed by a cry, " I am shot !" from one of the young patrollers. A bullet had pierced his arm.

The first blood spilled at such a time—it is a breaking of the seals of the vials of wrath and frenzy. It is the last charm thrown in the caldron. At once the excitement boils over, drowning prudence and reason in its flood.

CHAPTER XXV.

IT was ascertained that a negro—a vicious, hair-brained creature named Saul—had fired the shot which wounded the young man. He was arrested, and with him another negro who had been found in his company armed with a gun. They were brought before Alver and the conclave of excited patrolmen. They denied the shooting at first. Finally Saul said, doggedly, " I did fire one shot." He was asked if he was put up to it by the "carpet-baggers." He answered " Yes." His "confession" was proclaimed abroad. It flashed like an electric shock through the crowd. Excitement rose to frenzy ; indignation filled every breast. No one reflected that the negro's answer might reasonably be false—that, confused and terrified, the weak-witted creature might have sought to shift the blame of his rash act upon another. Or that both the firing of the shot and the accusing of the officers might have been instigated by some malicious schemer, who had promised protection and pardon to the ignorant tool in case he was arrested. The people were too wildly moved to think of these extenuating probabilities. They seemed to see the climax put upon their wrongs—a hideous plot of blood and outrage unmasked. They determined to endure no more. They would form themselves into a body of punishment; retribution should fall upon the guilty. They would clear the political atmosphere by a storm of vengeance.

When the sun rose upon the little town it looked on the scene of a miniature revolution. The excitement increased every hour. Armed men poured in from the neighboring towns and parishes. Men, with their families from the river and the hills, crowded into Cohatchie for protection. Strict military rule prevailed. A double guard encircled the town, and no one was allowed to pass out of its limits without a pass signed by Colonel Alver. Parties of mounted men visited all persons suspected of lukewarmness in the present action, and demanded that they coöperate in it, or render a valid excuse for not joining in the movement. The negro Saul and his companion were carried in a wagon to the outskirts of the town, a great crowd following. The wagon was driven underneath a gigantic oak, the ropes, which were around the negroes' necks, were made fast to a large limb, and the wagon was driven away, leaving them hanging. Up to this last moment they had not appeared to realize their fate. They seemed to expect pardon. Saul was heard to enjoin his comrade not to "git scared, it'll all come out right." Not till the ropes were being tied to the limb did a look of anxiety come into his half-idiot face. His eye roved in a wild search over the crowd, and he shifted his quid of tobacco from cheek to cheek. As the lashed team sprung forward, and the wagon rolled from under the wretches' clinging feet, they seemed for the first time to despair of pardon, began to tremble and shriek, and beg for a minute's time to tell "how it was."

The Radical office-holders, six in number, were arrested and imprisoned. In addition to Saul's confession there was the evidence against them that negroes, some of them armed, were found huddled about Omar Witchell's house soon after the alarm of a riot was given. The negroes' excuse that, frightened at the hostile movements of the whites, they had come to Omar to ask his advice and protection, was scouted as false. The officers were confined in a building in the center of the town ; a strong guard was put around it, as much to keep the excited crowd from getting to the prisoners as to prevent these from escaping.

The ones first arrested were Howard, Edgeville, Devene, and young Witchell (respectively, District-Attorney, Sheriff, Tax Collector, and Tax Receiver). Parties were then sent to the plantations of Hollin and Wallace (Magistrate and Supervisor of Registration). These brothers-in-law of Witchell were arrested and brought to Cohatchie and locked up in the room with the other officers.

Meantime a court had been hurriedly improvised, and a committee of citizens, with Alver at their head, sat in judgment upon the prisoners' case in a building not far from where they were confined. More than one of the incensed committee insisted on the death penalty for the imprisoned officers. It was noticeable that Alver did not give his voice for this extreme measure.

The prisoners met the crisis calmly. Even Howard was quiet. The old man sat with his eyes fixed on his wrinkled hands that lay on his knees ; only now and then he looked up pityingly at his five young companions. Wallace and Hollin talked apart in broken sentences. Devene wrote rapidly in a pocket note-book ; perhaps it was something to reassure his young bride, who had shrieked and clung to him so when he was taken. Edgeville walked the narrow floor, his hands locked behind him, his thin lips compressed with half scornful pain. Omar sat at a table, his face bowed on his hands.

Presently Edgeville stopped by him.

"Omar ?"

He raised his head slowly and looked at the young Sheriff. His eyes were red and moist.

"*You* losing pluck, old fellow ? Brace up ; don't give way. However this scrape may end, let's be game. What will be must be ; it's all in a life."

"It is well for you to talk so, Edgeville, you who have nobody else involved in your fate. You ought to thank God you are not married. I'd give my right arm never to have got my poor girl into this. Here she is among strangers ; think what she must feel ! I see her this moment, straining her eyes in this direction, seeing, hearing the mob, trembling and heart-wrung. God pity her !"

With a groan he dropped his face again in his hands.

Devene closed his note-book and beckoned to Edgeville.

"What are you going to do ? Resign ? They'll demand that at the very least."

"No, I'll die first. I will not be forced to give up my right."

"All the others have agreed to resign to save their lives."

"Well, let them. You have all got something to live for, unless it's old Howard, and his soul and body have lived together so long they hate mortally to part company.

Mine don't. I'd as lief have a bullet to cut the connection as to wait till old age wore the thread in two. It might be different if somebody else's fate was bound up with mine, as in your and Omar's case; but there's nobody."

He walked to the other end of the room, whistling

"I care for nobody, and nobody cares for me."

The door opened; one of the guard thrust his head in.

"Here's a book somebody sends to one of you named Edgeville. It's a Bible, I believe."

Edgeville rolled up his eyes in comic despair.

"Are they sending us Bibles already? I thought such attentions did not come until after the death-warrant."

"That'll come along soon enough, my hearty," said the guard. "Here, let me look through this to see if something contraband ain't slipped into it."

He took the back of the book between his thumb and fingers and fluttered open the pages.

"There's nothing," he said; "take it—small good it's going to do such as you, though."

Edgeville's face had changed as his eye fell upon the book—morocco-bound and silver-clasped. He took it and walked to the window with it; turning his back to the others, he looked through its pages eagerly. At the back, on a carefully sealed down fly-leaf, he found these words, in small, penciled characters:

"I do not believe you are guilty. Don't be reckless and willful. Do not refuse to resign, I beg you, for your safety's sake, for *my* sake. Yes, for my sake. I may tell you *now* I love you. Forgive my folly, and remember your life is dear to   Auzete."

He pressed his lips to the words. The color surged into his thin cheeks; his heart beat with great throbs. He walked back to Devene.

"I've changed my mind, Bob," he said. "I will not make myself conspicuous by solitary opposition. I'll resign with the rest of you."

"How do you know they will ask you?" sneered Wallace, who had overheard him. "Small good resigning will do any of us."

Howard echoed the gloomy prophecy with a shake of his gray head.

"Then we'll die jolly fellows together,"

Edgeville sang gayly as he turned on his heel. The precious Bible was in his breast pocket; he pressed his arms over it fervently.

"Your love comes late, my darling," he said to himself, "but it is a draught that sweetens all this gall."

CHAPTER XXVI.

THE trial of the prisoners went forward with some show of dignity and fairness, for was not Alver—the diplomatic—at its head? The officers under arrest were charged with going beyond the law in administering affairs—a charge that might easily be true, since they were the instruments of a man who made his own will the law of his conduct, and whose energy and personal magnetism made him the autocrat of the parish he had created, if not of the district he represented. Ostensibly, his only office was that of Representative in the State Senate, but he absorbed other offices. He levied taxes, received the money collected, influenced the legislation, and managed the judiciary of the parish, controlling all verdicts of consequence.

The blacker accusation, that the Radical officers had

instigated a brutal negro riot, was far from being proved.
There was nothing to show that an outbreak had been intended beyond the report of the Brownton messenger that
he had been fired upon as he rode, the shot fired by the
negro Saul (which might well have been the result of fright
or excitement, or a vicious prompting), and the fact that
several armed negroes were found near Omar Witchell's
house on the night said to have been fixed upon for the
riot. To a cool judgment this would appear but narrow
grounds for finding men guilty of a crime which no motive
was apparent for, and which would injure the Radical
cause throughout the State. But the committee at Cohatchie were not judging in cold blood. To their inflamed
vision the guilt of the prisoners loomed distinct and black.
The verdict might have been instant death but for Alver.
He poured oil upon the troubled waters ; he gave his voice
for milder measures.

He walked the floor nervously, and listened to the
shouts of the excited mob in front of the building that held
the prisoners. Was he dismayed by the violence of the
tempest he had called up ? He seemed relieved when at
length the question of death-punishment was set aside.
This was the arrangement substituted—that the Radical
officers should resign their positions and quit the State
within twenty-four hours, pledging themselves by oath
never to enter it again.

The verdict was carried to the prisoners. They understood well that if they refused to abide by it death was the
alternative. They consulted together and agreed to accept
the conditions provided they should be given a guard to see
them safely out of the State. Alver acceded to this at once.

There was some grumbling at the leniency of the judgment. To the men who had ridden in such hot haste to
quell a bloody disturbance in Cohatchie this seemed a tame

ending of the drama, an insufficient punishment of the men whose guilt they honestly believed in.

"Better, a long sight, string 'em up yonder alongside the niggers, and be done with it," muttered several voices.

In each instance Cobb's watchful eye singled out the speakers, and took a mental photograph of their faces.

"Let 'em go," growled a harsh voice behind him; "give 'em that guard, but advise 'em to insure their lives before they start. Something might happen on the way."

Cobb turned quickly and looked at the man who had spoken—a gaunt, swarthy man, half of his face hid by a black beard, his long hair streaked with gray, and a lurid gleam in his bloodshot eye. Yet in his face and carriage there was an indescribable hint of good birth.

Cobb dropped back alongside him.

"Here's my hand on them sentiments, friend," he said low. "What's your name, if I may know it?"

"Dick," returned the other.

"Nothing but Dick?"

"They put Cap'n to it on the Mexican border where I hail from. I used to have another name somewhat known in these parts, but never mind it now. Nobody seems to recognize me, and it's just as well. I've only come to see how time is serving some folks I have a particular interest in."

"The Radicals, for instance?"

"Yes, the Radicals, for instance—one of them in particular, The big dog of the pack is not here, I find. I owe him a debt with four years' interest. I'd have a chance of paying it now if he was here. But he's slipped off—the sneak—and left this small fry to pay for his sins and their own too. Let them pay, too, I say. A pretty thing it is to raise this great rumpus, and then only to send the scamps safely off with all their ill-got gains in their pockets."

" You are right. I must see you again. Meet me here to-night. These men won't leave till sunrise to-morrow. There'll be a crowd around here all night ; but we and some others will have a chance to get off aside and have a talk among ourselves. Have you a good horse ? "

" Yes, a capital little mustang."

"That's well ; meet me at this corner at seven o'clock."

" I'll be there," said the man, who was no other than Lanier, back from his four years' sojourn in Mexico—swarthier, thinner, and more sinister of look—with beard and hair prematurely gray. He had not been six hours in his native neighborhood, and had made himself known to no one when Alver's dispatch came, and, all afire with the hope of seeing himself at last revenged upon the man who had crossed him in the fierce desire of his heart, he rode in hot haste to Cohatchie, and cursed the luck when he found that the husband of the dead Adelle was not among the prisoners.

When Cobb turned off from the crowd collected around the building in which the officers were confined, he took his way down the street. He stopped a moment as he came to Omar Witchell's house—the neat little home he had built for his bride. Already there were about it tokens of woman's refined taste—the flower beds in the yard, the young vines trained across the piazza, the bird-cage among the pots of blooming plants in the window. But the singing of the canary was now the only cheery sound about the little home. The wives of the four married officers stood together on the piazza, but they were not speaking. They were waiting in agonized suspense for news concerning the fate of their husbands. Through all that dreadful day their anguish had been greater than that of the prisoners. Every shout from the mob rent their hearts. The trampling of the horses in the street as parties of armed men rode by, the noise of the crowd as they carried the negroes to the gallows, struck them with fresh apprehension.

Cobb leaned on the paling and looked at them. Omar's wife stood with her locked hands resting on the railing—her white face, her small, childish figure leant forward as if intent to catch some sight or sound that should convey a hope to her heart. Devene's young bride—her Southern nature less capable of control—walked the piazza wringing her hands and crying. The two sisters of Witchell were quiet. Mrs. Wallace, pale, with compressed mouth, stood at the back of the chair in which her younger sister sat. Mrs. Hollin had her arms about her child, holding him to her, her head, with all its golden hair disheveled, bowed upon the flaxen locks of the boy.

While Cobb looked on, the expected message came. A man galloped up on horseback. Mrs. Devene sprang to meet him, and returned, holding out a note.

"For you," she said, looking at Mrs. Witchell. "Shall I read it aloud, Minnie?"

A quick gesture of assent answered her. Mrs. Devene read:

"We have resigned our offices, and are to leave the State upon oath not to enter it again. There was no alternative. It was do this or die. 'Resign only to save your lives' was my brother's instruction. We leave to-morrow at sunrise. I trust to God we shall be permitted to see you and say good-by, but do not be disappointed if this is not to be. I will see Hayne if I can, and get him to intercede that the favor be granted us—the only one I shall ask—to go to you and say farewell. You can not come to us here through the mob. It would not be permitted, and you must not attempt it. I have not been able to speak to Hayne. He will not come to me, though I have sent for

him, and called him when I saw him in the crowd. And
I thought him my true friend. But do not fear for us ; we
will be safe. A guard of our own choosing will accompany
us, will see us safely out of the State. Don't distress yourself any more, dearest. Be brave and strong. Think of
the time when we will be reunited, and among our old
friends. Alver has given us his word of honor that our
wives shall be protected, and every facility allowed them
for joining us as soon as we are in a place of safety. I will
write to you to-night and tell you at length what to do
and what to send me. We have been furnished with pens
and paper, and will each of us write to-night. Don't worry ; all will be right. Yours, 　　　　　OMAR."

"Thank God ! it is not what we dreaded," cried the
wife of Devene. "Let them leave this country. Who
would stay in it after this ? I will follow Rob with all my
heart, or I will go with him. Why should we not go with
them ? "

"We may not even be allowed to see them before they
go," Mrs. Wallace said.

"I will see my husband. They shall not keep me back.
What, not let me tell him good-by ? Could any one be so
cruel ? "

Omar's little wife said nothing audibly. Her lips moved
as she sank into a seat. She motioned for the note, and took
it in her hands and fixed her eyes on the lines written by
the beloved hand.

Witchell's sisters moved off to the end of the piazza and
looked into each other's faces—a look of mutual, dreary
understanding.

"They will choose the guard themselves," Mrs. Hollin
said at last, with an effort at reassuring.

The older sister smiled bitterly. "They will choose ! "

she said. "What choice is there? Who among all those men yonder dare befriend them if he wished to? Hayne will not come near them—Hayne, whom Omar treated like a brother; who sat at his table and shared his purse. I have little hope from the fact that they will choose their guard."

"Your head's level there, my Yankee madam," Cobb said to himself as he moved off and turned into a street running back of the main or river street. Every house he passed had horses tied to the paling or to the trees in front, and men in groups in the yard or on the piazza. Most of these were carelessly or roughly dressed, dusty and travel-stained, boots thrust on over their trousers, and minus collars or other neck gear, showing in what haste they had leaped on their horses and ridden here in answer to Alver's summons. It seemed as though the old Confederate days had come back. Cobb's rough heart was stirred. "Halloo, boys! where's camp?" he said as he passed a group. When he reached Alver's house, the yard was full of men who had been eating supper at a long table spread for them on the back gallery. Floyd Reese was waiting on them. She was bringing out a large pitcher of milk as Cobb sauntered up and seated himself on the edge of the gallery. The loose sleeves of her blue dress fell away from her round arms, her dark gold hair was breeze-blown into little rings on her forehead. She looked a lovely Hebe, innocent of anything but gay and cheerful service.

"Give me a draught, fair ministering spirit," Cobb said as she passed near him.

As she stooped to pour it, he looked up into her eyes significantly from under his broad-brimmed hat.

"Here's to our Rads," he said low. "May they take plenty of money and their best horses with them on their trip to-morrow. It'll be all the better for us."

They were at the upper end of the gallery. There was no one within hearing of their low tones.

"Cobb," said Floyd, leaning toward him, "are you certain of being able to carry this out to-morrow ? There'll be a guard, remember."

"A fig for the guard ! If they don't help they'll not hinder. I've spotted a dozen fellows among these here that'll see me out in the business ; and we're looking for a livelier crowd to-night from over the Texas line. A dispatch has been sent there, and they'll be here to-night by the Bayou Prince road. Maybe they'll have a brush with the darkies down below before they get here, to whet their appetites for more fun."

"What do you mean ?"

"Why, word came just now that Levi Adams has gathered up a gang of negroes down the river on the other side, and has seized all the flats and threatens to burn and rob and kill generally, in revenge for the niggers hung here and the darkies and the Radicals we've got jugged."

"An exaggerated report, of course."

"No, I reckon it's true. Adams is a smart darky ; a leader among the negroes. They are stirred up to a perfect ferment with the news of the armed men in Cohatchie and the arrestin' and hangin'. They may do damage, though there's only a few white families down there now. All have come into Cohatchie that could get away. The fellow that brought the news is staying at the Vincents'. He says they are all sick there. He came to get medicine, but Alver will not give him a permit to return. He has arrested him and put him under guard for disorderly conduct. The fellow had taken a dram or two, and was a little noisy and talkative—that was all. I can't make out why Alver had him taken up."

"I can," said Floyd. "I know who the man is, and

why he was arrested. I thought we had got rid of both those fellows. If they can't be forced to quit the parish, they ought to be scared into holding their tongues."

Floyd gave not a thought to the distress and possible danger of the Vincents, who had been so kind to her. She only thought: "If the negroes do commit any violence there, all the better for my scheme; all the more color will be given to the pretext we are to render for the steps that have been taken." But another thought came into her mind:

"Have any of the men been sent down in that direction?" she asked.

"None; and it will be wondered at that nobody has been sent to the very quarter where it was first reported a riot was gathering. It's an oversight."

"Yes, parties must ride down there to-morrow."

"By that time," she thought, "it is safe to suppose the negroes will have made some demonstration."

They had spoken low, but eyes were turning in their direction, and she moved away with her pitcher. She turned back to ask:

"Have you seen Colonel Alver?"

"Only for a moment."

"I see him coming this way. Mind what I have told you, not one word to him of what will happen to-morrow."

"I shall mind; but, between us now, does he not know?"

"He does not. He may suspect, but, if he does, he has not said so even to me. Let it be so; we do not need his help. You have seen that the intentions he has expressed concerning the prisoners are peaceable."

"Hell's paved with such peaceable intentions," muttered the desperado with an unbelieving grin as he turned away.

12

It was growing dusk—nearly time for his rendezvous with the men he had picked out to-day with his sharp eye. The crowd was gathering more densely around the place of the prisoners' confinement. Voices, clashing together, rose from the dark mass moving there in the wonderful, clear light of the full midsummer moon that surely never shone so brilliantly as on this night and the one succeeding.

CHAPTER XXVII.

AT midnight on the night of the Cohatchie ball Zoe had not closed her eyes. She was sitting up with her brother. His fever was yet unbroken, and, restless and partially delirious, he required constant watching. Her sister-in-law was wakeful and nervous; the children's sleep was broken, and they called upon her frequently. She was worn with anxiety and fatigue; her little, delicately-featured face, usually so vividly tinted, rose colorless as a magnolia from her dark wrapper as she sat by her brother's bed. A tap fell upon the door, and Dan Nolan came in, carrying the little metal tea-pot that belonged in his room.

"I can't sleep," he said. "I've come to ask you to let me sit up with your brother while you take some rest. I've brought some hot tea of my own making. Drink a cup of it; it will refresh you; and lie down a little, Miss Zoe. I will do all that's necessary here."

"You?" said Zoe. "You look like it. You look as bloodless as a ghost, and you can hardly stand. How did you manage to make this tea? Thanks for it; it's just what I wanted. But I can't permit you to turn nurse so soon; you need nursing still yourself."

"But I can't sleep a moment longer. I had a dream—

such a dream ! My God ! I wish my life had always been
as innocent as yours, young lady. Let me sit here ; I won't
feel so alone. This still moonlight night seems full of horror to me. Somehow I'm a little uneasy about Jim. If
anything should happen to him, just let them—but I'm
talking too much in a sick room. Give me the fan,
Miss Zoe. There, go and lie down. Rest, if you can't
sleep."

He was persistent, and, giving him a few low directions,
she went into the next room and threw herself across the
foot of the bed in which the two younger children were
sleeping. She rested there an hour ; the clock striking one
aroused her.

Sitting up, she heard the sound of a horse being ridden
around to the rear gate. She went out softly on the back
piazza, where she found Dan already standing.

"It's Jim," he said. "Hear that everlasting whistle !
Your brother's asleep. I'll caution Jim not to make a
noise. I believe I'll go out to him and hear the news from
this queer ball."

He staggered as he descended the steps, so weak had
he been left by that fearful loss of blood. Zoe came to his
side.

"Lean on me," she said, "I too am eager to hear what
has happened to-night."

"What news, kagen ?"* Dan asked as Jim Nolan threw
himself from the horse.

"Gay," was the answer. "Gay, I tell you. I came
nigh not getting back. If I had waited until morning I
couldn't have come at all."

"Why ?"

"Why, the town is under martial law by order of Com-

* Creole term—contraction of Acadian.

mander-in-Chief Alver. He's worked things round to suit him, after all."

"Was there any disturbance?"

"One reported down this way. Haven't you seen anything of it? Fellow burst into the ball-room, wet as a drowned rat and white as a sheet, declarin' the niggers were in arms down here and had fired a dozen bullets at him as he came along. Then the pot bubbled over. Alver issued his orders sharp and quick as a rattling artillery match, the boys mounted and patrolled the town, a negro fired at one and wounded him, and got arrested with a lot of other darkies. Some of 'em will swing to-morrow, and the Rads too, I reckon. They are all to be arrested. There'll be lively times. I say, Dan, what a cursed piece of luck it was that I should have given you that tap on the head! Warn't for that we could have lots of fun, and some profit too, to-morrow. It'll be better than Colf—"

"Hush!" ordered his brother, sternly. "How did you manage to get out?" he asked, after a pause.

"Pretended me and old gray was lightning express, carrying a dispatch to Malta. Alver sent messengers everywhere. Two niggers—one a darky constable and the other a sub in the post-office—crawled out through the guard somehow and crossed the river just now when I did. Levi Adams met them down there in the road, and they told him the news—such a tale as you never heard! They declared every nigger in Cohatchie was arrested and certain to be hung, and that the whites were coming in full force to-morrow to kill out the whole race of blacks. 'There's nothin' for us but to take to the swamp,' whined the brave constable. 'Let me see you do it,' growled Levi. 'I'll shoot the first sneak that runs to the swamp. If we've got to be killed, let's fight to the last and die like men.' That fellow's got Injun blood in him, Dan. No nigger was ever

so plucky. He took the two darkies off to his house, and
I'll wager they're concocting some devilment right now. I
shouldn't be surprised if Levi got up a gang and did mischief here to-morrow. He's got a fair chance ; white men
all in Cohatchie, and can't get out."

"What would become of us ?" Zoe uttered, dismayed
at the thought of the helplessness of herself and her brother's family.

"Don't mind his croaking, Miss Vincent. Get to roost,
you raven of ill-omen. Put up your horse, and then to bed.
You, too, Miss Zoe, go and lie down and go to sleep ; I will
watch the rest of the night with your brother."

The next day dawned upon Zoe's unsleeping eyes, and
before the sun was an hour high signs of unusual commotion showed themselves.

From the east window of her little upper room she saw
across the level, intervening fields her neighbors on the
right moving about the house and yard, and saw a trunk
carried out to a carryall, that with mules attached to it
stood before the gate. She hurried across the passage into
the other room. There from the west window she saw similar preparations going on at the tall, dark-looking house
in which lived her neighbors on the left nearly half a mile
away, but plainly to be seen across those level, low-lying
fields. Before this gate stood two saddled horses, and a
cart and horse.

A halloo startled her. She hastened down and found a
man on horseback—the nephew of her neighbor on the
right—standing at the gate. She ran out to him bare-
headed, and was informed that they were all going to Cohatchie for protection, as it was feared there would be
trouble with the negroes. If Mr. Vincent's folks wished
to move, now was the time. There would soon be left nobody but negroes to help them cross in the flat, and it was

doubtful if the negroes would help. They were getting more sullen and impudent every minute.

"But my brother and sister are ill; we can not go," Zoe exclaimed.

The young man said that was bad. He was sorry, but didn't see what could be done.

"Will you not have the kindness to report our case to Colonel Alver? I hear he has charge of everything in Cohatchie, and ask him to send us some assistance?"

"Y-e-s," doubtfully, "I can tell him, but, as Vincent don't belong to the White League, I don't know if Colonel Alver'll bother himself about it?"

Pride overpowered Zoe's apprehension.

"Well," she said, "you need not trouble yourself," and she turned and left him without asking for any of the information he was burning to impart.

She watched them all go. By nine o'clock the four planters living near her had all crossed the river with their families, and were making their way to Cohatchie. Groups of negroes stood on the bank watching them. When the flat came back the last time, pulled over by a negro who had been well paid, Levi Adams rode down the bank and fastened the flat to a strong tree by its chain, and a padlock that he took from his pocket.

Hours passed. The stillness and brightness of the summer day lay all around her. A soft breeze rippled the fields of green cotton and stirred the tops of the great swamp-forest lying back of the cultivated front lands. The white grossbeaks, flying back to the low, fish-filled bayous, were the only specks that dotted the deep blue of the sky. It seemed hard to realize that any catastrophe was at hand. Zoe strove to conceal her anxiety from her sister, but she had heard enough of what was going on to throw her into a nervous state, alarming in her situation.

Then, too, it was Hugh's bad day. The disease—a bilious disorder—grew worse every alternate day; and now the fever rose to its climax, and his symptoms became so violent that Zoe was glad to accept Dan's proposal to send his brother for medicine or a doctor, giving him a note explaining the urgent nature of the case. The only three flats in the neighborhood had been seized by the negroes, but Zoe remembered a little skiff, or rather "dug-out," that it was likely they had not thought worth while to sink or fasten. "It lies in a little nook in the bank of Bayou Vincey, just where the bayou empties in the river. You can shoot across in it like an arrow," she said.

"I'll go, and come back too, if they don't put a ring of bayonets round me. Dan, old fellow, take care of yourself. I don't like to leave you here, and you so weak. But I s'pose it can't be helped. Good-by," and he walked away.

Riding was out of the question. He must cross in the narrow dug-out, and he must take his chances to slip out of Cohatchie unobserved.

CHAPTER XXVIII.

JIM NOLAN had not been gone an hour before Zoe regretted having permitted him to leave. It was hardly likely he would be able to get out of Cohatchie, and he was all the dependence they had in case the negroes should really attack them, for Dan had not strength to offer any but the feeblest resistance. Besides, her brother grew better. The fever, having risen to its greatest intensity, began to cool, and a deep sleep settled upon his restless limbs and disordered brain. The crisis was past. Zoe, who had so frequently seen diseases of this type, knew that the danger was over. She left his eldest child—a sweet little girl of twelve—to sit by his bed and brush away the flies, while she went out for a little change into the orchard. Standing there, with the great pear and apple-trees overhead, and the grass and clover under foot, she heard the young mocking-birds twittering in their nests above her, and saw the yellow wasps and brown bees feasting on the red pulp of the over-ripe figs and peaches that lay in the grass. The orchard was only a narrow space; the rich cotton lands were grudgingly spared to mere fruit or flowers, and fields of the favorite staple pushed up close around the little inclosure set apart for Pomona. Up to the very paling, covered with vines of wild morning-glory and trumpet flower, grew the wide-branched cotton, taller than a man's head, and clustered thickly with blooms and bolls.

Through those thick cotton rows came the rustle of some one approaching. A negro emerged from the mass of green, glanced furtively around, and then, coming close to the paling, beckoned her to approach. She knew him well. He was the husband of her brother's cook, and she had been kind to him and his family in various ways. She had always thought him a humble, stupidly inoffensive creature; what had changed the look of his face so completely? His expression now was a mixture of cunning and insolence. Deceit ill concealed the elation that lit his usually dull, pig-like eye.

As Zoe approached he asked :

"What did you send that white fellow up to Cohatchie for ?"

"On my own business," Zoe answered, shortly, for his manner was hardly respectful.

"No use flyin' off de handle. I jest wanted to tell you you needn't look for him back. If he gits out of Cohatchie 'twon't do him no good. Levi already sen' over and got de dug-out what he stole to cross in, and we've got a watch all along de river."

"What is that for? What is it, Tom, that you negroes intend to do?"

"I ain't said we niggers is goin' to do nothin'."

"I am glad you are not. I thought you had more sense than to attempt any riot," she answered, pretending indifference and moving away. Her assumed carelessness had the desired effect. It made him more eager to impart the news.

"You don't understan'. *Niggers* ain't goin' to do nothin'," he said, "but *colored men* is tired of bein' trampled on, and is goin' to make a defense if no more. No sense you say, hey? You think 'twould be sense, though, to set down here and let de white folks shoot and hang us like dey done Mose Clark las' week, and Saul and Peter in Cohatchie dis morning, and de Lord knows how many more by dis time. Word come to us a month ago dat dis rumpus was gwine to be. Strange man 'splained it to us. God showed it to him in his dreams, and told him to tell us we must stand stiff or we'd be run over and trampled out. We must hold our own, or we'd be buzzard meat afore we know it. But we jes' went on and didn't pay much 'tention till dey begun to fire in our windows an' down our chimleys, an' Uncle Mose Clark was shot in his tracks, an' den we begin to git worked up, and had meetins to talk over what we mus' do, and of a sudden we hear dis news from Cohatchie; soldiers pourin' in, hangin' and 'restin' dere, and coming down here to kill out our race. We made up a comp'ny las' night. I'm a ossifer—named a Cuppural. We're gwine to stan' up fur our rights if dey come over here atter us, and we're goin' to—but you'll know about dat soon enough. Only, I hear say you're packin' up your jewelry and money, and goin' to try to git away through de swamp by de Bayou Prince road, and I

thought I may as well tell you 'tain't no use. Levi ain't
agoin' to let no waggin start from dis gate. Our folks is
scattered all through de swamp, and ef you got in there
they'd stop you soon nuff. You couldn't get away in time,
neither, ef you had a chance."

"In time? Tom Ludd, tell me what you mean. Is
there an attack to be made on the white people here?"

"You'll see in 'n hour from now."

"Are they coming here?"

"Of course, de fust place. Bound to have shot and
powder and guns, and dey's in that store of your brudder's
yonder, and two barrels er whisky 'long wid 'em."

"Are you coming to the house?"

"Bound to sack and burn every house from here down
to Bronn's store. Dat's de word Levi give out."

"Are you goin' to kill as you go?"

"What else ought we to do to pay for what's been done
to us? Worst we could do wouldn't be nuff, Levi says.
He's goin' to tell 'em to jes' go ahead; do as you was done
by."

"A crime done by some outlaw ought not to be revenged
on innocent men and women. You would let them come
here to burn and kill us after all the kindness we have
shown you, Tom Ludd? You said I saved your child's
life when it had spasms two weeks ago; is this the return
you make?"

"How can I help what dey do? I'm a ossifer for true,
but Levi's our head; we must go by what he says. He
'lows nobody to interfere. I'm sorry for you all, and I'll
try to save your lives ef I can keep de giddy-headed ones
back; but dat'll be hard to do after dey've got to de
whisky in de store."

"They shan't get that. I'll stave in the heads of the
barrels myself."

His eyes sparkled with malicious triumph.

"Like to see you do it! Levi's got a guard over de store. When you go round to de front dere you can look over and see three cullurd men wid guns settin' on de store porch."

Zoe clasped her hands together—an involuntary gesture of distress and perplexity. The negro eyed her, well satisfied, a gleam of cunning in his face. He came near the paling.

"'Twould be mighty bad for you women and Vincent's little gal ef de men come over to you half drunk, as dey will do. I'll tell you what, I'll do my best to keep 'em away—or to git 'em jes' to rob de house and let you 'lone. I'll do it ef you'll give me your gold watch and chain and ten dollars beforehand; yes, and your gold bracelet wid de red—"

He was so intent he did not hear the panther-like step behind him.

"What are you doing here?" interrupted a voice, strong and harsh but not loud—Levi's peculiar voice; and as the frightened "Cuppural" turned round he confronted the tall form and scornful face of his leader.

"Blabbin' and boastin'—as it's your trade to do—you thick-headed fool. Clear out from here, and git to your business."

Tom slunk away, grumbling inaudibly. Levi came up to the paling, his tall, straight form towering above it, his gun on his shoulder, a pistol and a huge bowie-knife in his rough leather belt. His saturnine face was lit with suppressed excitement; a sneer curled his mouth as he watched Zoe. His face and form, instinct with savage power, filled her with terror.

"Levi," she said, "what is this you are going to do?"

"The long-tongued fool told you, I reckon."

"Surely it's not true that you mean to rob and destroy the few helpless whites left here?"

"You'll see for yourself what I'm going to do in less than an hour. My men are back there in the swamp, ready for anything. They remember Mose Clark, and they think of their own color lyin' in the jail up yonder and swinging to the trees to feast the buzzards."

"That was because one of them shot a man, and because the negroes had planned a riot."

"Who swung when Mose Clark was shot? And it's not true any riot was planned. I'd a known of it, wouldn't I? I'd a been around Cohatchie the night of the ball. 'Twas a got-up thing, that is what it was. But now, since we've had the blame, we'll have the game. We'll not disappoint 'em. But I've no time to waste. I come to git the key to your brother's store. Will you give it to me?"

"No."

"All right, we want to be civil; but there's other ways of gettin' in."

"Levi, can it be that you, whom we have never harmed, would bring a mob of drunken negroes into my brother's house and turn them loose on him and his helpless wife and children? Would you be so cruel? You have more sense than your fellows; you have complete power over them. O Levi! could you use your power so wickedly?"

"'Twa'n't cruel to hang Saul and Peter this morning without fair trial? 'Tain't cruel to kill the Radicals or drive 'em out of the country because they're friends to us? Why don't you look at that? My men shall do what they like. If any's killed, it's only tit for tat."

"One who would murder sick men and helpless women is a fiend and a coward," Zoe exclaimed, vehemently.

He turned on her glaring.

"You'll repent that," he muttered. Then, as he still

looked at her, "You hate us, you white-skinned women," he said. "You speak to us kindly as you do to dogs, but you scringe if we chance to come close to you. It would do me good to humble you; to see you kneel to me. I'll see it, too, before another sun shall set, my pretty one."

He laughed sardonically at the white horror his words brought into her face. Still laughing his low, Indian-like chuckle, he strode way.

Zoe stood where he left her—fear and perplexity seeming to root her to the spot.

"What can I do?" was the ever-recurring thought. "There are none within reach to apply to, no one to send if there was. Escape is impossible; resistance out of our power. Jim Nolan can not come; his brother is not able to make any continued exertion. What must be done? I have no one that I can go to with this dreadful news but Dan Nolan. He may be a thief and a murderer himself; he acknowledges that he is a criminal, but he is all I have to look to for help and advice."

She started for the house, and stopped as she saw young Nolan coming toward her.

"What's the matter? What's happened?" he exclaimed as soon as he caught sight of her face. In a few words she told him what she had just heard.

"Why on earth didn't you call me when that fellow Levi was talking to you? I'd a put a bullet in his smart body and put a stop to all of it. It's his getting up. The first thing we must do is to go over to the store, burst open the whisky barrels, and throw the powder and shot in the river."

"Too late," she said; "look there."

They had walked to a point where they could see a part of the store-front. Three negroes with guns sat on the porch watching them.

"I could take 'em off one after the other with my re-peater," Dan cried.

"No, you must not," Zoe interrupted, quickly. "It would hasten the attack and make them more savage. There are plenty others to supply the places of those if you killed them. Look at that head above the cotton! There are spies all around us."

"I see only this to be done. Go and get up your valu-ables and put them in the securest place you can think of. Tell your sister a part of what you apprehend, and tell your brother if he is conscious. Let Mrs. Vincent, you and the children, get into the small room where your brother lies. I will bolt the doors and windows as strong-ly as I can. Then I will make the outer room secure, and take my stand there with all the guns and pistols the house affords. A good number of the wretches will have to bite the dust before they get to you. Does that suit?"

"In all except that I will stay with you. I can load, and I can shoot a little. A well woman ought to be nearly as good as a sick man."

She spoke more hopefully than she felt. She followed out Dan's suggestions, but she worked with a heavy heart. She put the money and jewelry and important papers into a small iron box, and, as there was no chance to bury it outside with all those spies around, she hit upon the expedient of putting it on a board that fitted into the dining-room chim-ney, and pushing the board so far up the flue as to be almost out of reach. Even if the house is burned these may not be destroyed, she thought; chimneys are often left standing. Her brother was awake and conscious. His little daughter was feeding him with soup. Zoe's heart was almost broken when the girl turned her innocent, rose-bud face to her, smiling as she announced that papa had swallowed six spoonfuls of soup. What a fate might soon overtake that lovely child !

But Zoe would not give way. She nerved herself with all the courage that was in her. Very composedly she told her brother and sister that she had some reason to fear an attack from a few excited negroes. It was possible her fears were ungrounded, but she thought it better to take precautions and fasten the doors and windows securely. Her quiet manner had its effect, and injurious agitation was in a great measure forestalled.

When all was done that could be, she went into the outer room where Dan had just finished loading the guns and pistols. He was whistling gayly ; he looked as if the danger was an elixir to him. He expressed no regret, except that Jim was not here to share the fun.

Zoe went to the door. The afternoon sun steeped the luxuriant landscape in light and heat. The cicala sung in the shade of the tall grass, the silver-winged grossbeaks floated dreamlike across the sky. All was quiet and at rest ; nothing indicative of violence except those three men with guns lying on the gallery of the store, and negroes with guns had often lounged there before.

" Do you see any sign of anything wrong ? " she asked.

" Only this : the negro women in those tenant cabins are all standing at their doors looking down the river. They know what is coming, and from what quarter."

Five minutes passed. Zoe was at the lower end of the piazza. She uttered an exclamation.

" What do you see, sister Ann ? The very cloud of dust of the Blue Beard tale, on my word," he added, seeing that she could not speak. " Courage ! remember that we are to fight together. Don't let heroism ebb out of these throbbing little veins."

He took her hand as he spoke. It was cold as marble.

With strained, terror-fascinated eyes she watched the cloud of dust that grew into dusky ranks of negroes rapidly turning the curve in the road following the river bend. Nearer they came. The women at the cabin doors gave no sign, but stood and watched, still as statues. Levi rode at the head. A few others were mounted, the rest were on foot; about half of them were armed with guns, the others had various weapons. Some carried fish-gigs, some axes and hoes.

"Not more than fifty or sixty of them," Dan said, running his rapid eye down the motley ranks. "Not bad odds to fight against when you consider the cowardice of the beast."

They reached the store, and Levi ordered a halt. Flinging himself from his horse and giving his gun to one of the men, he came alone toward the house. Zoe had already retreated into the room and fastened the door. Levi came up, entered the gallery, and, glancing haughtily at Dan, asked aloud for Zoe.

"She's within. What do you want with her? I'm here to answer for her," Dan said, carelessly continuing to pull the ears of Zoe's pet dog.

"You can't answer for yourself yet," sneered the negro leader, and, striding past him, he knocked at the door, calling out for Zoe. She opened the door and stood before him pale as death, but calm.

"I am here," she said. "What do you want?"

He looked at her in evident surprise before he said:

"First I want the key to the store; do you still refuse to give it up?"

"I do! You may break the store open if you will. I will give you no help to get liquor and arms to use for a lawless purpose."

He pushed past her and entered the room, partly closing the door upon him.

"I see you are stubborn and proud still," he said. "Do you understand what is about to come to you? You are here in our power; no help can come to you; we have things in our own hands. In half an hour this house will swarm with men—*niggers*, you call them—mad, drunk, furious, ripe for anything. This floor will run with blood, the roof will blaze over your head. With this before you, you hold a stiff neck still. You must beg for mercy.

"I have pleaded with you for mercy, I do so again. Levi, as you hope for pardon from God, do not harm my sick brother and his helpless wife and children!"

"And you?"

"Yes, me too. I love honor and life too well not to plead with you to spare me. Keep your men from this house; do this, and all the money and jewels I have I will give to you."

"I don't want your jewelry, and I'll have all the money I need before this night is over. Your begging is too luke-warm. Kneel to me; remember, I have your life, and more, in my power. Seize my hands here in your soft palms, hug my knees with your arms, look up in my face with tears dropping from your eyes. Kneel to me, I say."

She looked at him with an eye that did not quail. "No," she said, "I will not humble myself to please you. It would be useless; I see that in your face. Our doom is sealed. I will not kneel to receive insult. Go; I have no more to say to you. I will die by my own hand before you shall touch me."

Cries of "Bring on the key"; "Break down the door," came from the mob at the store.

"You'll see when the time comes," he cried with fury in his looks; "you shall feel my touch then. It shall clamp you like iron."

He seized her wrist as she said the last words, his nails

pressed into her flesh till the blood came. "Dan Nolan," she called, but not loudly. She heard the click of Dan's pistol close to her. Suddenly Levi Adams loosed his hold of her, and leaped upon young Nolan like a tiger-cat, trying to wrench the pistol from him. It went off in the struggle. A shout from the negroes on the bank echoed the report. Zoe reeled back against the wall. "It is all over," she thought. "They will rush upon us in a moment."

The scuffle between the two men ended in Levi's getting the pistol in his possession and dashing Nolan to the farther end of the room. Once more Zoe heard the cries of the negroes, but she was too far gone with terror to notice that these cries differed from the others—to understand that these confused exclamations expressed alarm and dismay. Through a side window she saw several black forms rush by.

"They are surrounding the house," was her thought.

But through a back window she caught glimpses of negroes running wildly for the swamp, leaping the paling, crashing through the tall cotton. What did it mean? She flew to the front door. The negroes were all gone from the store, from the river bank. She looked down the road. There she saw a body of armed men riding swiftly toward her. Were they more negroes? No, thank God! there, under the dusty hats, were *white* faces—blessed white faces.

"We are saved; there are armed white men coming to our rescue," she said to Dan, who had staggered to the door, breathless from his struggle with the negro bully.

"Hooray! they are from the Texas line, some of 'em, I'll bet," cried the young fellow, with a feeble attempt at a cheer. "They came by the Bayou Prince road. Jim said Alver had sent messengers to Sabine County."

Waving his old red silk handkerchief, he shouted "Hoo-

ray, boys !" as loudly as he could, as the cavalcade swept
round the last river bend and came in front of the house.
Neither he nor Zoe had noticed Levi Adams. At first the
negro chief failed to take in the situation. When he did
comprehend it, he leaped out of the house by the back way
and strove, with voice and gesture, to stop the flight of his
demoralized band. He shouted to them to hold, he cursed
them, he implored them to come back and make a stand,
but to no purpose; they ran as only terrified negroes or
scared sheep *can* run. They had no whisky in them to
impart a fictitious courage. The sight of all these armed
white men rounding the bend in such dashing style struck
terror to their souls, broke up their ranks as though a
shower of shell from a near battery had burst among them,
and sent them helter-skelter in a wild race for the swamp.
Levi saw that not one would stand to back him. He saw
the soldiers close to the store. His horse stood there—the
yellow mustang that carried him like the wind. He made
a flying leap over the palings; a few more bounds and he
reached his horse's side. He jumped into the saddle and
caught the reins. Too late ! Half a dozen horsemen surrounded him, a dozen guns were pointed at him. He was
forced to surrender. Sullen and stoical, his bronze face
unmoved, he stood and submitted to the tying of his
hands.

A guard was left over him, and the others hastened to
pursue the fugitive negroes. Just as well hunt the "coon"
or the "opossum" in their woodland coverts without the
keen-nosed dog as to hunt in these thick jungles, these
vine-matted forests, for Levi's scattered flock. The soldiers
rode back an hour afterward, with only one captive—Tom
Ludd, the negro who had undertaken to negotiate with
Zoe concerning her safety. Tom's vanity, like Absalom's,
had occasioned his capture. Feeling his importance as an

"ossifer," he had donned an ancient long-tailed coat, and the impalement of that coat on the back fence of the field had caused him to be taken prisoner. Pitiful enough he looked now. He was shaking with terror, his black face had a gray look, his eyes stood out like a trapped rabbit's, he begged incessantly, piteously protesting his innocence. Levi flashed at him a single look of scorn. "Hush, fool," he muttered in his harsh, guttural tones.

The negro leader seemed to notice nothing, but not a movement escaped his panther eye. He did not seem to stir in a limb, but he had cunningly managed to untie the cord that bound his hands and was fastened to one of his feet. The sight of some mounted men on the opposite bank of the river drew the attention of the guard, and. taking advantage of the moment, Levi made a desperate effort to escape. With that wonderful agility none had ever seen surpassed, he cleared the half-circle of men with a bound and ran for the swamp. Before the men, who had dismounted, could spring upon their horses, he had reached the cotton, and with bent head was scudding down the rows, when a horseman, who seemed chief of the armed white party, came galloping from the swamp, and, riding before the fugitive, ordered him to halt. For answer, Levi snatched out a derringer he had kept hid in his bosom, and fired it, the ball grazing the white man's shoulder. In an instant the negro bully was seized by an arm more powerful than his own, and the sharp click of a pistol at his head warned him to be quiet.

A number of men rode up, and, giving orders to "tie the negro, take him to the swamp, and make short work of him," the horseman rode on to the house. He was a superb rider, and, as he removed his straw hat that the wind might cool his heated head, he looked one's ideal of the guerrilla chief; long-haired, with flowing beard, a falcon eye, a grand throat, and a broad chest and shoulders, which showed well in the easy gray hunting shirt.

He rode to the store and sat on his horse, looking at the miserable, cringing figure of Tom Ludd. That brave "ossifer" was calling God to witness that he never "had no han' in dese here wicked doin's. He was a peaceable, hard-wuckin', stay-at-home nigger. He was jes' stirrin' his wife's pot uv big hom'ly before de cabin when he seed de soldiers comin' and seen t'other niggers runnin' for de woods, and he, like a skeered fool, must run too, and de soldiers cotch him and think him guilty; but it's all mistake."

"But you had a gun in your hand," said one of the men.

"A gun?—me?"

"Certainly, you had a loaded gun. What were you going to do with that, you hypocritical Ethiopian?"

"Oh!" chattered the terrified darky, forgetting his former story. "I tell you 'bout dat gun. I was jes' goin' to de woods to shoot a squ'el for my poor, sick wife. Dat's all, my good master; 'pon my sacred word and honor, and I hope thunder strike me dead dis minite ef it ain't de sollum truth. Mandy—O-o-o-o Mandy!" he called to his wife, who, with her baby in her arms, had started from her cabin toward him with timid, hesitating steps, "come here and beg for your dear husband's life."

"Now," he went on as she hurried up, crying, "git down on your knees wid me and beg dese good, kind, fine-looking gentlemen to spare me dis onct and dey'll never kotch me nowhere atter dis, 'cept in de cotton patch at de eend uv a hoe. Jes' tell 'em how it was. I was stirrin' de hom'ly pot—no, I was gwine to de woods to kill squ'el for your soup case you was delicaty, and I never had no han' in dis no mor'n dat chile dere on his mudder's breast, what's goin' to be lef' 'thout a pappy ef you don't spar dis poor innercent nigger to his restracted fam'ly."

This allusion to her distressed condition, and to the round-faced baby that sucked its thumb serenely and stared in big-eyed pleasure at the scene, brought hysterical sobs and shrieks from Mandy. Tom encouraged her grief by groans.

"Hush your screeching and get up from here," commanded the man at whose feet the pair had dropped upon their knees, and whose commanding looks and the deference shown him entitled him to be thought Captain of the party.

At this instant successive reports of fire-arms were heard coming from some distance in the swamp. Echo sent them back with startling distinctness from the opposite bank of the river.

The men looked at each other significantly.

"They've settled with the nigger ringleader," observed one of them, laconically.

"Oh! good Lord!" howled Tom Ludd in despair. "Mandy, run to Miss Zoe; git her to come here and beg for me; run, Mandy, ef you love me."

His wife darted for the house. A minute afterward she came back and spoke a few words to the Captain. He set his gun against the side of the store and followed her to the house.

Zoe, standing on the front piazza, trembled as she leaned against a post, her face blanched with horror. She had just understood the meaning of that volley she had heard fired in the swamp. Those shots had riddled the negro leader, an hour before so exultant in strength and power. A sickening sensation overpowered her. She hardly looked at the man as he came up to her, his straw hat pulled over his face.

"Sir," she said, "I sent for you to entreat you to spare that miserable negro yonder. He was led into this. He has not sense enough to look to consequences. There are extenuating circumstances connected with this action of the negroes that should lead you to be merciful. The leader is killed; let that suffice, and spare the life of this poor, ignorant creature. He has always been inoffensive and humble till to-day."

"He shall be spared. I would grant a far greater request to *you*."

She looked up amazed. He stood before her, looking at her with the eyes whose melancholy intensity she could never forget. It was Hirne.

"I swore never to come back, never to see you again," he said, taking her hand and coming close to her. "I could not help it. Fate draws irresistibly. Destiny must be accomplished. Are you not married yet?"

She shook her head; she could not well have spoken.

"Thank Fate for this much! But how pale you are, sweetest! You are ill, or you have passed through some cruel trial; you have been frightened to death. How glad I am that we came up when we did! How glad that I happened to get word of this outbreak here! I knew that you lived here, and I urged the men on without a moment's stopping. Had we been ten minutes later—"

"Do not speak of it," Zoe cried, shuddering. "You have saved our lives. The negroes were about to break open the store, brutalize themselves with liquor, and come over here. My brother is sick, and confined to his bed."

"And you without a protector? No wonder you are pale as a flower that the storm has drenched. But you are safe now. A part of the men have gone on to Cohatchie; the others will stay here and protect you. I will stay if the disturbance is quelled in Cohatchie. If I might only protect you through life," he said, looking at her, as though he longed to clasp her.

"Is dey gwine to spar' Tom, Miss Zoe?" interposed a piteous voice in the yard just below. They had forgotten Mandy. Hirne glanced down through the vines, and laughed as he saw the distressed black face and the round-eyed baby.

"Yes," he said, "I don't doubt that Tom ought to hang, but he shall go free—not for his sake or yours, but for this lady's here. Go and make yourself easy. He sha'n't get his deserts this time, if he'll promise to stick to his hoe, and have no more military aspirations. Go and cook all the eggs and chickens you've got, and make any number of corn pones for my men. They are hungry as wolves. Here, hold your apron."

He threw a handful of Mexican dollars into her lap. "Get some dinner, or supper rather, quick as you can, or the soldiers may hang your Tom after all. Hungry men are savage."

"It'll be hard to persuade the men to set the scamp free," he said, as the woman moved briskly off. "Yet he hardly deserves to die—ignorant tool that he is—put up to what he tried to do by others. I hear your citizens have arrested the parish officers, and are keeping them under guard. Why did they not hang them with their negro dupes? The plot they tried to carry out was a fiendish one."

"Are you sure it was a plot of the Radicals? I have strong reason to think not."

"It is hard for your tender heart to believe that men can be so base, but you do not know their capacity for baseness. If you had my experience—! I can not believe that the citizens of this parish will let these men go unpunished, and there is no punishment sufficient for them but death."

His eyes, that had been so soft a moment before, emitted a savage flash, his mouth grew stern in an instant. Zoe did not venture to pursue the subject then. She saw in him once more that sudden transition into gloomy fierceness. It was as if he possessed two natures—one magnanimous and tender, the other bitter, relentless. Again she said to herself, "Some great wrong has warped this noble nature."

CHAPTER XXIX.

WHEN she went in she found her little niece Nelly deep in consultation with Mrs. Vincent about getting up a sumptuous dinner for the men who had so opportunely come to their rescue. Several negro women stood by, eager to help, as humble now as they had previously been insolent. They thought in their hearts that "slave time" had come again; they did not know but their husbands and sons would be hunted and shot down in the swamps; but all this would not prevent them from eating a hearty dinner, and enjoying a pipe or a nap afterward. Such is the African nature.

A long table was set on the back piazza, and spread with a varied abundance—dishes of fried ham and eggs, of bacon and greens (the national dish), mounds of biscuits and potatoes, a huge peach pie, baked fowl, and sardines and crackers from the store. To this table a part of the hungry men sat down, while the others had their dinner on the porch of the store—a dinner cooked in her best style by Mandy, who flew around with an alacrity born of her anxiety for Tom. That prisoner had not yet been released, but his wife had contrived to whisper a word of hope in his ear. After dinner was over, all being satisfied with what they had eaten, Hirne proposed to release the cook's hus-

13

band out of compliment to his wife's skill and good-nature, adding that Tom was simply a numbskull who had let himself be led, and was ready now to swear on his knees to his future good conduct. Tom was set free, and his voluble gratitude was ludicrous to hear. He trotted off with his baby in his arms, the gladdest darky in the parish.

It was now sunset, and the men who had gone to Cohatchie had not returned. The others were eager to cross the river and see what had become of their comrades, and what was being done in Cohatchie.

"Go on," said Hirne. "I and four others will be enough to stay and guard this place. I apprehend no further trouble here. Send word to me immediately what they have decided to do with the carpet-baggers."

The men crossed the river, the last red sunbeam glinting on them as they rode up the bank on the opposite side. The four men who were left sat talking and smoking on the gallery of the store, while the quiet dusk came down.

Hirne went over to the house. Zoe was sitting on a cool little side-porch, rocking to sleep the two-years-old baby which the new-comer had deposed. She was crooning softly a cradle-song :

> "Sleep, baby, sleep—
> Thy rest shall angels keep."

The picture she made was beautiful to the soul of the man so long used to bloody and turbulent scenes. He stood unseen, listening to the soothing strain, looking at the girl's sweet face, flecked with moonlight and leaf-shadows.

The sigh that escaped him betrayed his presence. She stopped singing, and asked him to come in. He sat down on the steps at her feet. The stars were coming out—pale in the lingering sunset radiance.

"How still and sweet it is !" Zoe said, breaking the silence. "I can hardly realize that a few hours ago such confusion and terror and such evil passions were at work, or that in the woods yonder, so dim and solemn in the moonlight, lies a mangled human body to bear witness to the violence the day's sun has shone upon. When will such violence and evil passion be done away with? We see so much of it here. I am heart-sick of it. Better the dreamy monotony of a lotus-land. But that would be no Eden to you men. Your restless spirits would not endure the quiet. I think men invented politics as an excuse for endless strife."

He said nothing for a moment, only looking up into her face, so fair in the moonlight. Then he said, slowly:

"The nearest I knew of happiness for many a day came from change and strife. But now, somehow, these fail to quench the thirst in my breast. I feel myself growing out of taste for them. To-night, as I sit here, facing the evening-star, with your sweet hush-a-by song in my ears, it seems to me it would be happiness to sit at the feet of one sweet woman and know her to be yours."

Zoe made no answer. She had not heart to rebuke the man she secretly liked so well—the man who had just been the cause of.saving her, it might be, from a terrible fate; but this passion, so suddenly grown bold and rash, needed checking. She sat and thought how she might most gently administer the check. It was Hirne who spoke first.

"Yes, mine has been a storm-tossed bark; it's little better than a wreck; there is no hope for it unless—it might be anchored to this little hand"—suddenly turning, taking up her hand that lay lightly across the sleeping child and pressing it fervently to his bearded lips—"the hand that belongs to another. Does it? Tell me, are you still bound to that man?"

"Yes."

"And you love him, and will marry him ?"

"I do not kn—I mean, you have no right to ask such questions."

"No right ! Why, my happiness for life is bound up in your answer. Tell me you do not love him best. You are silent. What a fool I am ! Of course you love him best. Doubtless he is one of fortune's darlings. His person is slick and fair as his fortune, while I—I am rugged as my fate. I would be mad to think that you could love me better. Yet I have been guilty of that very madness at times. Only for a minute, though. Way out on the plains, when the norther chilled my marrow as I rode, I have pictured a home and a lighted hearth, and within its ruddy radiance a woman with a dainty shape and soft, dark eyes, and the sweetest mouth this side of angel-land, sitting, waiting to smile when she heard my step, to spring to kiss me—to clasp my rugged neck with her soft arms, to—pshaw ! it was the merest mirage, that picture which rose before me as I rode in the cold and dusk with miles of tall, dry grass bending and roaring under the wild trampling of the north wind. But—I feel like fighting with fate for your possession. I don't deserve you, only by my love. I have loved you ever since your eyes looked on me with such divine pity as I sat chained in the hold of the Lavaca. I never could bear pity before. It grew almost as sweet as love when it shone out of your eyes. Long afterward, when I carried you in my arms, wet and shivering in deadly ague, when I held you to my heart for warmth, and covered your little, cold hands with hot kisses, I fancied when you were reviving you called my name—called it tenderly, as if you loved it. You think it presumption in me—a stranger, a rough Texas ranger—to talk to you so. You think in your gentle heart this man has done me a favor, he is unhappy, he is foolishly infatuated ; I hate to repulse him unkindly, but I know nothing of him except that he is an escaped Government prisoner, that he gambles, fights, gets into scrapes, is an alien from society. A black array of disreputables, certainly. She were a rash girl who would let such a man woo her; and for a dainty, proud, sweet woman like you! —And yet, Miss Vincent, had not circumstances thwarted my life and twisted my nature, I would not have been so mean a rival of that other man whom you will bless with your hand. My birth is good. My parents were honorable. I am not poor, vagabond though I seem, and I am not devoid of talent. I have been called a genius by my comrades to whom I sang my wild rhymes by a camp-fire. Some of these it may amuse you to read sometimes. I have them here in my pocket, scribbled in an old note-book— a blood-stained relic of war days. I was not a bad soldier, Miss Vincent, and I earned a rank of Major by good fighting. I have never done a deliberate wrong to any human being, though my hand has been ready to punish the oppressor and the cowardly imposer upon the weak. I am not such a foe to society either. I hate its shams, I care nothing for its applause, but I do not despise my fellow-men. I would like to do them good if I could. I am educating two boys—orphan sons of brave soldiers—and I pension two widows whose husbands fell fighting at my side. I don't tell you all this to praise myself, but I would like the woman I love to know my better side, that she might not shrink from me as an iniquitous monster—innately wicked. That I am what respectable and cold-blooded people call wicked is due as much to fate as to innate crookedness. If you knew my story—"

"Tell it to me; you promised once that I should hear it."

"You have not forgotten that? Then you *have* thought of me. I will tell you my story, though you will think still worse of me, maybe, but you shall hear it. I was born and reared in Texas. My parents had lost a large property in Virginia, and had come to Texas as much to hide their poverty as to retrieve their fortune. I was a passionate, willful child, but kindness could control me. My parents did not understand this; their plan was to quell the offending Adam in me by harsh rule. My brothers, who were cast in a gentler mold, they loved and praised. I was looked upon as a black sheep, punished inordinately in childhood, given over to my own devices as I sprang into precocious manhood. As a consequence, I felt myself an alien. I hunted and fished by myself or with the overseer's son—a dissolute youth. I read every book in the queer, miscellaneous library my father brought with him from the States. 'Rinaldo Rinaldini' and 'Byron's Corsair,' as well as 'Rasselas' and 'Pilgrim's Progress.' I carried the battered books with me when I went stock-minding on the prairies; I read them at night by the light of a tallow dip, I scribbled verses on the fly-leaves, and saw visions and dreamed dreams. At seventeen I fell in love; gave up my whole crude, fermenting nature to a mad passion for a girl with blue eyes and long lashes—one of those blushing, dimpled creatures that near-sighted fools imagine artless and angelic. I thought her truly an angel, and lived in elysium when she promised to marry me—boy that I was, not yet eighteen. On the very night before we were to have eloped she had promised to marry another man. I had heard that day that the marriage would be, but I would not believe it. That evening I went to her house. As I opened the door, I saw lights, an unusual gathering of friends, and my angel dressed in celestial white, standing before the priest, her hand in my rival's. I hardly know what I did, but my madness broke up the wedding. The only thing I remember distinctly after that sight of the white-robed bride is standing by the roadside at night with my brother holding a saddled horse. He was roughly shaking me.

"'Get to your senses; mount and ride,' he said. And in answer to my inquiry, 'What has happened?' he said, 'Look at your bloody hands. You have had a fight with McIvor. He has given you a scratch on the shoulder, and you have stabbed him, maybe, to death. They'll be after you; mount and go; there's money in your pocket.'

"At first I refused, but he prevailed on me to go. Neither he nor I thought I was seriously wounded, but before the day dawned I fell off my horse through faintness from loss of blood, and was picked up by a Spanish half-breed and nursed till my strength came back. Then I mounted my horse again and went on, hardly caring where, but with my face toward the setting sun. I passed over into Mexico and got among the Indians. They were friendly, but I did not stay with them. I built me a hut and camped to myself, and for over a year led a sort of hermit's life, not once seeing a white face. Once I helped the Indians in their fight with a tribe that encroached on their rights. At last I grew restless. I wanted to hear my native tongue, and to look into a white face. I had a little store of gold nuggets and some stones I knew to be of value. I left my hermitage and started eastward. As I neared the borders of my native State my heart beat faster. I heard the sound of running water, and rode to the boundary river just as a horseman on the opposite side approached its banks. He greeted me with a halloo, spurred his horse down the bank and across the stream, and dismounted and shook hands with me where I stood. I drank from the river and pledged him 'Our Country, the United States for ever.'

"'Take back the toast,' he cried, 'there's no United States,' and then for the first time I learned that the South had severed from the Union and was fighting for her independence. He himself was in the service, and had been sent on a secret mission to Mexico. The news of war stirred my blood. I pressed on to join the army. Stopping at home, I found changes there. I had not killed the man Laura was to have married. He recovered, but, before he was well, news came that he was an impostor, that he had already a wife. So my rash act had saved her from that marriage.

"But she was unhappy. Her father had died—she had lost her mother long before—and she was left without money, dependent upon relations who made her a drudge, and grudged her the bread she ate. It hurt me to hear this, though the girl had deceived me so. I would not see her, but I begged my father to offer her a home with him. I was going straight to the seat of war, and I asked him to take her into his family in my place. He did so, and I went to Missouri and joined General Price's division. Afterward my two brothers went to Virginia and fought under Lee. My father followed them—went back to his native country and bought back his old home, taking Laura with him. I went home once severely wounded, and remained three months before I was strong enough to sit in the saddle. When I returned to the army Laura was my wife. She made me believe that she had always been true to me, that her father had forced her to do as she had done. I believed her, trusted her, married her the night before I left, and tore myself from her arms in a passion of grief and tenderness, to return to my duty. I thought only of her in weary marches, in camps and battles, in the long days of pain and loneliness, and when I lay a prisoner in a Northern hospital. I had been taken up wounded and insensible from the battle-field. In the same battle my two brothers were killed. One fell by my side; as I stooped to put the canteen of water to his dying lips, a fragment of shell struck me in the breast, and another here where this lock covers the scar on my temple.

"When I was free again the war was over; our cause was lost. I hurried home, or to the place where my home had been. I found only a heap of ashes. I asked for my wife, my parents; the neighbors told a sickening tale. A party of marauders—an irregular offshoot from the Federal army —had burned my home, and maltreated the old man, my father, so that he died soon after. My mother died a few weeks later from the shock of grief and terror, and the exposure to the winter night. 'But, my wife! my wife!' I cried. The people looked at each other and shook their heads. 'She is dead, then? they killed her?' Still they shook their heads. At last one said: 'It is a pity she had not died, friend. The troops occupied the town afterward, and she went off with one of the officers.'

"Could a man hear these words and keep his brain cool? Mine was on fire, yet outwardly I was calm. I hunted out the wretch who had headed the band that murdered my father. I ought to have shot him down without giving him a chance for his life, but I could never do that. I provoked him to fight, and I killed him in fair combat. I was taken and thrown into jail. I made no defense. I knew none would be admitted. I was a Southerner—a Confederate officer. I was tried, condemned to be hanged. Afterward the sentence was commuted to confinement in the penitentiary for life. I was three years an inmate of the prison. One night there was an attempt on the part of the prisoners to burn the building. I helped to save it. I saved the life of the keeper when some of the incendiaries were about to kill him. For this I was recommended to mercy, pardoned, set free. Pardoned after suffering three years of misery and disgrace for having done a just deed. I had rather they had hung me, but for one thing—the chance to get revenge."

"And the woman?" Zoe asked, "your—?"

"My wife? I saw her once afterward—the only time since I parted from her twelve hours after that ill-judged marriage. It was in New York. As I walked the streets one night a sound of music and dancing came to my ears. A silvery laugh made me look up to the open, lighted windows of the hall. At one of them stood a woman, the light full on her bare shoulders and jeweled arms. It was Laura. She was as blooming as ever ; no remorse or shame had changed her. Two hours after, the floor of the building in which the revel was held gave way ; Laura was among the hurt. She never walked again. I provided for her comfort until she died, though I could not bring myself to see her. She was a soulless siren ; a soft-eyed, pink-cheeked simulator of innocence. I am glad you are no way like her, my dark, proud little love. Don't be angry with me. One may love the Madonna and praise her, sitting at her feet, as I at yours.

"Well, I have told you the circumstances that made me what I am. You know that I have been condemned to die on the gallows, have lain in a State's prison, though I never harmed an innocent man or wronged a woman. But, ah ! mine were rough ways and a wild life ; and blood and chains will stain, though one be shed in a right cause and the other unjustly worn. I am not fit to be your associate, my white innocence."

He leaped to his feet as though the thought stung him to the quick.

"I know you are glad that your husband that is to be has no such stains ; that he is a reputable man who makes money and takes care of himself, and keeps to smooth, beaten ways. Society smiles on him ; so it might have smiled on me had I been as little tempted and made of colder stuff. Then you might have respected me—given me your hand as a sign that you took me for an honest man and a friend, if no more."

She stretched out her hand impulsively.

"I do take you for an honest man and a friend," she said. "You have passed through the furnace; you were more than mortal if you did not bear the scars. But scars are only skin-deep; you may yet—"

She was going to read him a homily; but she faltered, embarrassed. That clasp in which he held her hand, that look, were too fervent for the friendliness she wanted him to pledge her.

"Oh! my sweet," he said, bending over her, "that other man may be worthier of you, but he can never love you as I do. If you would be my saint, I would worship goodness—in you—for ever."

He had knelt at her feet, still holding her hand, as though it were a last hope. He started as he heard the gallop of horses. The riders drew up to the front gate and hallooed for Hirne.

"Here!" he cried, starting up. The horsemen rode around to the back gate, and Hirne went out to see them. Zoe carried her pretty, sleeping burden into the room. Hurrying back, she stood on the steps of the piazza and heard the answer to Hirne's question : "What news from Cohatchie ?"

"The Radical officers are to be sent out of the State to-morrow with an escort to protect them."

"Sent off! Were they not convicted of having incited the negroes to rob and murder the white people of the parish ?"

"Of course. One of the black rascals that was hanged owned to being put up to firing on the patrol by the Radicals."

"And all those frantic calls for armed men to help put

down a riot result in the hanging of a few negroes! The
real offenders to be sent safely away! Are the men here so
mortally afraid of prospective bayonets that they let murderers go free?"

"No, Cap'n, all are not such cowards," exclaimed a
coarse voice. Cobb rode out from among the others, and
went on speaking: "There's men yonder in Cohatchie
that are mad enough at the verdict of the committee.
They've got plenty of grit to break it up, but they want
somebody to go ahead. Let me have a word with you,
Cap'n."

He rode up close to Hirne and talked to him in low
tones. Zoe heard Hirne say:

"I'm with you; I'll saddle my horse and be ready in ten
minutes."

"The sooner the better," Cobb replied. "By the time
we cross the river and ride to Cohatchie it will be day-
break, and our foxes leave cover at sunrise."

Zoe shuddered. She knew now what was intended.

"I will see Hirne before he crosses the river," she resolved. "He must have nothing to do with this, unless to
prevent it if he can."

She called him softly as he was passing through the
yard on his way to saddle his horse, which had been fast-
tened near the store. He came to her, and she began with
trembling earnestness:

"Don't go on that mission to-night, Captain Hirne."

"Are you afraid to have me leave you? A guard will
stay here to protect you. I do not think the negroes will
attempt any harm."

"I know they will not. I would not be afraid to
stay here without protectors. Levi is dead. Only his
influence wrought the negroes up to making that hasty
show of violence—half-armed handful as they were, come

together with a crude notion of self-defense and retaliation."

"How is that ? You do not believe the disturbance here was a part of the riot planned by the Radical gang ?"

"Captain Hirne, what proof have we that a riot was planned by the Radicals ? Is it not a senseless act, for those belonging to a party that has already the balance of power in the parish to plan to ruin themselves and their cause by such a step ?"

" What, then, did this excitement in Cohatchie mean ? —this great hue and cry, and calling together of armed men to protect the town ?"

"Captain Hirne—it goes against my heart to say so— but I fear the demonstrations in Cohatchie meant a deep-laid plot on our side ; not a plot of the people's, though they were duped and led into it by a few men (perhaps only one man) who are mad to rid themselves of Radical rule. You will say that this is a just motive, and that these office-holders are corrupt and are aliens, unfit to represent our people. But surely you will not hold that they should be got rid of by assassination ! You must feel what a horrible wrong it would be to take the lives of those six men in Cohatchie when no crime has been proved upon them. There is nothing in their past lives to justify the darker charge brought against them. They have lived among us for years ; they have done many a kindly act to our citizens. One of them has just married a daughter of our people ; all of them but two have families. They have resigned their offices ; they only ask to leave the State in safety, and to have their wives and little ones sent after them. Captain Hirne, have nothing to do with killing these men, I beseech you. Prevent it if you can."

The Texas ranger stood like a bloodhound suddenly leashed in sight of the game. The wrongs he had received made him over-ready to believe evil of the people at whose hands he had suffered. He was fired by the picture of the horrible negro outbreak inspired by Radical oppressors. The old strife was stirred up in his breast, the smoldering fire of vengeance blazed up anew. But he would do no harm to innocent men ; he would only punish the guilty.

He listened in profound, startled attention to Zoe's words.

"This is a strange revelation," he said. "A political plot! One of our men the instigator! Miss Vincent, will you tell me why you believe this ?"

"I came to believe it partly from putting things together, but chiefly because of what I heard from the lips of a man who declares he was hired to bring on a disturbance in a different way. That plan failed. Afterward the man was dangerously wounded while on this place. While he was so ill he told me of his being employed to create a disturbance with the Radical office-holders. I knew that he received money and messages from the man who had employed him, as he said. Yet he was a stranger—an acknowledged desperado."

"Where is this man ?"

"He is here."

"Will you send him to me ?"

"I will. I believe he will repeat to you what he owned to me."

As she turned off she saw a dusky form slink closer into the shadow of a tree a few steps from the piazza. It was Cobb. Standing on the ground below them, he had caught the import of Zoe's appeal to Hirne, and he resolved to forestall her. He watched her, and saw her approach Dan, who was leading his horse from the stable.

"I'm going with them, if I die for it. I can't stand it any longer," Dan said.

She stopped him, and made her request that he would tell Hirne what he had told her of his being hired by Alver.

"Anything to please you," Cobb heard Nolan say. "I owe Alver a grudge, anyhow. If he has done anything to Jim, he won't plot much more."

Zoe went back to the house, and Cobb came up to Dan as he was fastening his horse.

"Where's your Captain?" Nolan asked him.

"Yonder," returned Cobb, pointing to the store. "But, look here, my friend, you had better think twice before you blab to him what's on your tongue's end. Keep what you know to yourself and it'll be a sword over Alver, and as good as a bank account to you. You can check on the Colonel whenever you are hard up. But let it out, and where's the good to you or anybody. Another thing: if you try to spoil sport to-night, you stand in your own light. Them prisoners don't start off from Cohatchie empty-handed; you understand?"

Dan did understand. "You're in the right," he said; "I'll not stand in the way of sport."

He hunted up Hirne, and said:

"I am the man Miss Vincent told you about. I'm sorry she brought up what I said, because it was only a hoax. I did say some foolish things when I was out of my head with fever; and, when she asked me about them afterward, I didn't retract. I added to them, just to seem big in her eyes. It was foolish, but I thought nothing would come of it. Now she's made a serious matter of it, I must out with the truth."

"Are you telling me the *truth*, man?" Hirne said, in his incisive way.

"Do you think I'd tell you anything else? I—"

Cobb came up.

"Not saddled up yet, Cap'n? Where's your horse? I'll get him ready for you."

"Thank you. I'll go over and say good-by to the people who have been so kind to us."

"They've all gone to bed, I believe," Cobb said. But Hirne went on to the house. Zoe was attending to her brother. He waited a while, and, thinking that she had retired, went back to the store.

"Women—at least gentle, innocent ones like that young girl—are too tender-hearted to judge rightly. And they can not comprehend the stern necessity of punishment," he said to himself.

A moment later he and Cobb, Dan Nolan and the two men who had brought the news from Cohatchie, rode down to the landing, where they put themselves across the river in the flat. Not till they had landed on the opposite bank did Zoe find out that they had gone.

CHAPTER XXX.

"If I could have seen him again; if I had only made him promise that he would not harm those men!" she thought as she watched the party spur their horses up the steep bank of the river and ride away in the direction of Cohatchie. "But surely Dan Nolan told him; he promised he would; and what Dan could tell him of Alver's former scheme to involve the office-holders in a disturbance must rouse the suspicion that there is some such secret design in this reported outbreak, and that these men may be innocent of the charge against them. Yet Captain Hirne has gone to Cohatchie; for what purpose? God forbid that it is to head a mob to lynch and murder these officers. No, no, he has gone to restrain violence, to prevent bloodshed. He would not be so unmindful of my entreaties."

A step broke upon her anxious musing. Mandy approached and handed her a scrap of paper.

"Cap'n Hirne give it to me," she said. "He tore de paper outer his hat-crown and writ on it by de moonlight. He's a fine man. I'll never forgit him for sparin' Tom; nor you nuther, Miss Zoe."

Zoe took the crumpled bit of paper to the light and read the words penciled upon it.

"I waited to see you again before I went away, but you did not come out, and I was afraid of disturbing you. I know how sorely you need rest. I will see you some time to-morrow.   Yours,   HIRNE."

Mandy had followed Zoe into the room.

"Here's Cap'n Hirne's coat," she said. "He lef' it on de store gallery and ax me to give it to you to keep for him. Some papers in de pocket and a book. He say he tol' you about de book."

The note somewhat quieted Zoe's anxiety. Hirne would not have written to her so calmly, she reasoned, if he had been setting out on a bloody mission in disregard of her prayers. She had gained a hold upon this wild nature, but was it strong enough to overpower the long-indulged passion for strife and revenge that seized him at times with almost maniacal frenzy? More than once she had seen him in the grasp of this demon. An hour ago she had shuddered at the sudden change which came over him on hearing the news Cobb brought from Cohatchie; the grimly-set mouth, the lurid light that leaped into his eyes. That look haunted her when she at last lay upon her bed. But the long strain on brain and body soon reacted into rest, and she slept profoundly.

She woke from that deep sleep to see the sun shining brightly through the vines at the window, and hear the birds twittering in the trees outside. For a moment she lay in delicious oblivion of everything but present sensation ; then the recollection of yesterday's wild drama rushed over her, with the thought that it was not yet ended, and the dread that the darkest scene was yet to be unfolded.

The dread clung to her as she went about her domestic duties, helped by grateful Mandy. It was increased by a communication from Tom Ludd. Hugh, who was now free of fever, and eager for news from Cohatchie, had the negro at his bedside, plying him with questions. He learned that the four men whom Hirne had left to guard the place had crossed the river at daybreak on their way to Alver's head-quarters, and that one of them had said in Tom's hearing that there would be "wild work before the sun went down, for Hirne was on the Radicals' track, and they'd find he wasn't one like the Cohatchie folks—to make a big fuss and then draw back scared like a settin' goose."

"It's my opinion the officers will be lynched as they come out of prison," Vincent said. "It can be done without much fear of consequences. With all that mob they've got together there'll be no telling who did the mischief. An investigation of it will be another edition of ' Who struck Billy Patterson.' "

Zoe turned away, sickened by the horror these words suggested. And *he* would be foremost in this foul massacre—the man she loved. No, not loved. She said to herself that she did not love Hirne. She would not suffer herself to love such a man—but she felt in her heart that his words and looks lived in her as none others' did.

The long summer day wore on. How quiet it was! The broad fields lay green under the sun, no negroes at work in them, no negroes sauntering along the river bank, or hanging about the store. The echoing volley that had announced the fate of their leader had made them cower still closer in their coverts. They would not stir out even for food. Tom was the only negro man to be seen on this side the river for miles; and he kept as close to Zoe as possible. Presently, with his round eyes dilated with fright, he reported that a party of armed horsemen were on the other side of the river preparing to cross.

"'Tain't de ones dat was here yistiddy," he said. "Mebbe dese here won't know I done had my trial and got clar, do I got papers to show for it. Mighty strong papers, too; so dat young fellow dat laugh so tol' me. He gin me one paper, and when I showed it to Cap'n Hirne de Cap'n kinder frown and laugh to onct, an' gin me anuther one. I wish you'd jes' zamine 'em, Miss Zoe."

He took two folded scraps of paper from a flabby old pocket-book and handed them to Zoe. One of these to-bacco-scented slips, dated "Head-quarters, Hirne's Division," called upon all men "to know by these presents that Tom Ludd, a citizen of the African persuasion, had been pardoned for his share in the late disturbance through the following considerations: First, that a young lady, pretty as red shoes, had begged for him; second, that he was a *non-compos* of the first degree; and, third, that his wife could cook a chicken-pie fit to set before an emperor, or Sam Houston, if he was alive."

The other one of Tom's "strong papers" was a certificate that he had been taken up and acquitted. It was signed by Hirne, representing volunteers from Sabine County, Texas, and De Soto Parish, La.

As Zoe looked up from reading it she saw a negro

woman coming toward the house through the cotton, a tin bucket on her arm. Her wild look drew forth the inquiry :

" What is the matter ? "

The woman shook her head and muttered incoherently at first; then, coming nearer, she held up her hand and said, in a strange half whisper :

" I've seen a sight I'll never forgit to my dyin' day. I slipped out in de swamp to take some vittles to my George. I see a colored man standin' up aginst a tree. I call out, ' Who's dar ? ' No answer. I call agin. I see de limb close to him shake, and dat's all. I went closter. I see it's Levi. Nobody else so tall, and I see his lip turn up in dat scornin' way. I tought him 'live standin' dere till I got clost up, and, flop ! a buzzard flew out from de limb by his head ; an' den I see he's tied to a tree, an' his face an' bress full o' bloody holes where de shots tore, an' de buzzards done picked—"

" Hush ! " cried Zoe, covering her eyes with her hands as though to shut out the horrid vision conjured up before her. Tom rolled over and groaned in mortal fright. The next moment he caught sight of the horsemen who had crossed the river, and were now riding up to the house. He dashed into the kitchen, darted at a nearly empty flour-barrel, and turned it up over him. Under this defense he squatted, while the men dismounted, quenched their thirst at the cistern, and, filling their pockets with peaches, sat on the edge of the piazza eating fruit and talking to Vincent, who got up and came to the window in his shirt-sleeves. Tom did not venture from his hiding-place, and Mandy, coming to hunt for him, answered his sepulchral whisper, " Is dey gone ? " by overturning the barrel and revealing his motley figure.

" Go out and shake yerself, yer scary goose ! " she said.

"You've got a mess er biskitts in that wool o' yourn, let alone the rest of yer body."

The news from Cohatchie was better than Zoe had dared to hope for. The prisoners had been allowed to go safely away, accompanied by a guard they had chosen themselves. Among these was Hayne, the young Southerner, who had been such a pet with the Witchells, and Henry Bronn, Zoe's shy admirer. The Captain of the guard was a man who had lately insinuated himself into the favor of the Radical officers.

It was something that the prisoners had been suffered to depart, but the man who told Vincent of it laughed sardonically, as he added that he'd advise them not to crow until they were out of the woods.

"They took money enough to get them through all right," said another; "and they've got fine horses."

"They'll get through none the quicker for that," muttered the first speaker, significantly, whereat one, who seemed to be in command, called out:

"You had better hold your tongue, unless you know what you are talking about," at the same time directing a meaning glance at Vincent. The same man had brought Hugh an order from Alver to report to him at Cohatchie, and had questioned Vincent closely about his illness, as though he suspected it to be a sham. He volunteered the information that Alver was going "to keep things straight from now out, and that, more than ever, his motto would be, ' Those who are not with us are against us.' "

"We shall have some news before to-morrow," Hugh said as the reconnoitring party rode gayly away through the fields and along the river-bank, never once penetrating the swamp, where they might have found what they professed to be seeking—the negroes that had been in arms.

"There's more in the wind than these fellows will let

on," continued Vincent ; "more than they really know of, maybe, though one of them seems to suspect."

Still Zoe was hopeful that the worst was over. She found herself looking eagerly across the river for a sight of Hirne's returning figure. The old note-book he had wanted her to see had fallen from the pocket of his coat while that garment was being shaken and brushed by Mandy.

"It must a' gone through the war," was her comment. "Its all battered like as a bullet or a bay'net's come afoul of it. And here's a stain dat looks like blood. 'Tain't much of a thing to be totin' about."

But the book was "much" to Zoe. She took it out with her under the trees. Lying in a russet hammock— a-swing, like an oriole's nest, from a sycamore limb—she turned the pages of the old book, and read the fragments of verses he had scribbled in the saddle, on the prairie bivouac, or by the lonely watch-fire. They gave her broken, panoramic pictures of his wild, sad life, and strange, two-sided being. And she traced through them the growth of the shadow that overcast his better nature ; and also, as it seemed to her, the gradual passing of the shadow—a struggling out of the lurid mists of strife—a strong aspiration for a pure and more peaceful atmosphere. Zoe said to herself what a miserable thing it would be if this political agitation should draw him back into the old, turbulent vortex.

The verses at the beginning of the book were crude outpourings of boyish enthusiasm and passion, together with rhapsodies over the vast freedom of the prairies and mountains. Then came outbursts of patriotism—a clash of war cymbals—songs that stirred like bugle blasts, and that had been sung by his comrades on the march and by camp fires.

Blotted pages followed—the fierce, raving utterances of despair and revenge. They were too painful for Zoe to read.

In the group of poems that preceded these she found a dramatic colloquy that embodied the incident Hirne had related to her—his meeting the Confederate Secret Service messenger on the banks of a Mexican river, and hearing from him the startling news of the rupture between the States. In the poem the self-exile welcomes the tidings of war. It offers an outlet for the energies of his disturbed being. Seizing his gun and turning his face to the scenes of civilization, now the scenes of strife, he says :

" A woman's treachery drove me here, half maddened by despair,
 Like a wild, wounded beast, to make in loneliness my lair.
 I shunned my kind, and sought to find in trackless solitude,
 In savage sport and perils wild, cure for my bitter mood.
 But this is better; this is rare. Hail! glorious news of war!
 Hail! rattling challenge of the guns! Sweeter your music far
 Than the betraying song of love. I'll drown in battle's roar
 All memory of the siren voice that I shall hear no more.
 And life and death are one to me, for not an eye would weep
 If in my soldier's blanket wrapped I slept a bloody sleep.
 Welcome the tidings of the war! My wild blood bounds apace.
 Come, tried and trusty rifle-friend; give us a foremost place.
 Here's better game for you and me than buffalo or deer;
 We'll laugh at death we've faced before, and mock at coward fear."

Farther on he wrote of that four years' madness, so ill-judged in its beginning, so bloody in its issues :

" Down on the mighty drama rushed
  The midnight curtain of despair.
 Its lights are quenched, its music hushed,
  Not one wild echo stirs the air.
 Dried are the tears its pathos woke,
  Still'd are the plaudits of its power,
 Cold are the loving hearts it broke,
  And green its graves—the mournful dower
  It left to this forgetful hour."

Into the later poems had stolen a gentler spirit, though veined with the melancholy fatalism which he had told Zoe was born of his persistent ill-fortune. One little love song, which by its date had been written since he had known Zoe, was called "Parted."

> "We met; it was when laughing Spring
>   Her earliest wreath was twining,
> When birds were out on dewy wing,
>   And skies were blue and shining.
> I little reck'd of sunny skies,
>   Or April bloom beguiling,
>   My sunshine was your radiant eyes,
>   My spring your tender smiling.
>
> "I said to Fate, 'I will not fear
>   Your voice of cruel scorning';
> I said to Memory, 'Flap not here
>   Your raven wing of warning.
> The days *must* be for you and me,
>   The *nights*, all wild and lonely;
> But *now* I bid your shadow flee,
>   *This* hour is mine, mine only.'
>
> "Alas! I heard upon the hill
>   Fate's low, defiant laughter;
> Ah! felt you not my heart grow still,
>   My lips grow cold thereafter?
> I saw, and knew it for a sign,
>   The breezeless poplar quiver,
> And felt, even with your heart to mine,
>   We'd met to part for ever.
>
> "Dear love, the saintly sages tell
>   A wild and wondrous story,
> That death shall not the spirit quell,
>   Nor quench its fadeless glory;

I heed not these, but in my soul
  A prophet voice is telling
That love knows never mortal goal,
  Nor ever earthly knelling.
Beyond the stars, whose silver feet
  Through heaven's blue pathways quiver,
In some fair Aidenn we shall meet
  Who have parted here for ever."

A tear fell upon the old note-book.

"The passionate heart that throbs through these poems is mine," thought Zoe. There was a bitter-sweet thrill in the thought, and in the echo of the words:

"Oh! my sweet, that other man may be worthier of you, but he can never love you as I do."

The leaves whispered to the wind, the young orioles chirped in their hanging nests, and Zoe lay in her russet swing, her eyes fixed on the blue distance, her hands unconsciously clasping Hirne's book to her breast.

She did not know that a party of horsemen were approaching the house until they drew rein before the gate and hallooed. She started up. One of the men was Henry Bronn. Two others were men she had heard named as being of the guard who had gone to take the prisoners safely out of the State. Why were they here?

Zoe went up to the paling and returned their greeting.

"How is it you have returned so soon?" she asked.

There was a short hesitation; then one of the men said, with a forced laugh:

"They got away from us."

"Got away! Henry, how is this?"

The young man's round, stolid face was pale, and his eyes had a dazed expression. He shifted his glance away from Zoe's penetrating look. He hesitated, and his comrade caught up the answer.

14

"They got away from us, I tell you, Miss Zoe; didn't they, Henry?"

"Yes, they got away," the boy said, trying to imitate his companion's off-hand way of speaking. But Zoe saw that he seemed stunned. Only some great horror could have so affected his commonplace nature.

"How did they get away?" she asked, sternly.

"Oh! just got away; it's too long a story to tell right now. We are in a mighty hurry; just called to know if there's a fellow here named Dan Nolan. Alver wants him to report to him right away. His brother's in the calaboose at Cohatchie for cutting up."

"Dan Nolan is not here. He went last night to Cohatchie with some men who came from the Texas border."

"Then Alver'll probably see him some time to-day. Thanks and good-day to you, Miss Zoe. Come, boys."

Henry was riding away with the others, when Zoe detained him by a word.

"One moment," she said; "Henry, what became of those men you went to guard? They did not get away; I know what that expression means. They were killed. Henry Bronn, did you murder the men that were under your care?"

"I did not, Miss Zoe. I will come back in an hour if I can slip away and tell you all."

CHAPTER XXXI.

An hour afterward it was again dark. Zoe sat where she had been sitting last night when Hirne had thrown himself at her feet and told her the story of his turbulent

life. She had been looking for him every hour of the day.
She craved his coming that she might hear from him the
solution of a doubt that ached at her heart. She longed
to hear from his own lips that he had not disregarded her
prayer, that, if it was true these men were murdered, he
had no hand in their massacre. She jumped up eagerly
when she heard some one ride up to the gate. But it was
Henry Bronn's low, sturdy figure that came up the walk
and stood before her, holding out his hand. She grasped
it and looked hard in his face.

"You have come to answer my question, Henry?" she
said. "What has become of the officers you went to
guard?"

His hand shook as she held it, his eyes dropped.

"Miss Zoe, they got what they deserved, I reckon," he
said at last.

"Henry, do you mean to tell me they were killed?"

"They are dead, Miss Zoe."

"O God! all of them killed? Omar Witchell too—
that gentle-hearted, inoffensive soul, and young Edgeville,
and Devene, who has just married one of our Southern
girls, gray-haired Howard, and Wallace and Hollin, who
have wives here in our midst and little children, were all
these killed?"

"All of them."

"God have mercy on the soul that planned this dreadful deed, and upon those who executed it."

"They deserved it, Miss Zoe. They tried to stir up a
riot among the blacks."

"I am glad you believe so. I am glad to think that
most of these men-slayers believed they were doing a just
act, that they were executing rightful punishment upon
criminals. I fear it was a dreadful mistake. I fear a great
wrong has been done."

"Miss Zoe, you know that Captain Witchell extortioned upon the people."

"Should his sins be visited upon the heads of these men? Should a suspicion be punished as if it was a certainty? But all discussion is wasted breath now. The deed is done. There is one thing I must know. You say the guard did not kill the men—who did?"

"A mob that followed us."

"And who composed that mob?"

He shook his head. "There were so many strangers here," he said, evasively, "no telling who did anything."

"Why did not the guard try to defend the men that were in their charge?"

Again he shook his head. "They never helped; none of them that I saw," he said, "but—I mustn't say, though; I won't accuse anybody, for I don't know. But it was very strange. I know I never once suspected. It came so sudden and awful; it makes my head whirl to think of it. I see it all before me every minute; I see Omar's face, I hear their groans in my ears. Oh! Miss Zoe, it served 'em right, I s'pose, but it was awful."

"Henry, will you not tell me who did it?" Zoe cried, trembling. The thought that Hirne might be the leader in the assassination was agony to her.

"I will tell you all I know. We started to carry the men out of the State. We started in good faith; at least I did. I don't answer for anybody else, because I don't know. I hardly knew the Captain of the guard; he seemed a clever enough fellow. The officers picked us out; Omar chose me. I knew him right well; we had camped out on Lake Clear, and fished and hunted together. He was a first-rate fellow to camp with—so good-humored and so full of dry fun. Edgeville was with us too. He was a splendid shot, and could tell such tales of wild adventure around the camp fire. Oh! to think of how I saw him this morning—"

"Go on."

"The sun was an hour high when we started. The men had sat up all night, fixing up their business and writing letters. I carried the letters up to their wives, and brought back the things they wanted to take with them."

"Did they not see their families to say good-by?"

"No, it was against orders. The women had hoped to see them up to the last. It was right pitiful to hear them cry over the letters. I sat down on the gallery while they read 'em and packed up the things. I knew Mark Hollin's wife. They stopped at our house when they first came to this country. She came out to me, and took my hand and said: 'Henry, stand by my husband. Keep good faith with them all, and we will pray for you for ever,' Her little boy knew me and threw his arms around my neck. 'I send this kiss to my pa,' he said; 'tell him we're comin' to him soon. Ma has sent him my picture and hers, and I put his diamond buttons in his shirt myself. Mamma, what makes you cry so? you know we are going where pa is right soon.' I think Witchell's sisters had fears of what would happen. But the men seemed in pretty good spirits when we started. They looked pale and anxious, but Omar spoke to us pleasantly, and so did Devene, though he kept his eyes looking over the heads of the crowd at the house we could just see, where his wife stood at the window kissing her hand to him. She had been bent on coming to see him, and he had to send a special messenger to tell her not to try it. Edgeville joked and laughed. He had sent a letter by me to Auzete Blair the night before, and I had brought back an answer to it and her picture; I saw her crying as she wrote. There was a crowd round the door when the prisoners came out and mounted, but they all fell back, and we rode out quietly, nobody following us. Alver pledged them that they should be taken care of. Then he came up and took Rick Waldon—the Captain of the guard—aside and talked to him for some minutes, and then a big, dark-looking fellow they called Cobb spoke a few words to the Captain and laughed; I saw that same man afterward with the mob that did the killing. He had his hat slouched over his eyes, but I knew him.

"We took the road up the river to S——. The officers were riding fast horses; they were fresh, and wanted to go. 'Not too fast,' the Captain said, and we checked in a little. We had put a good many miles between us and Cohatchie. When we mounted a hill Wallace looked back and pointed to a cloud of dust way behind us, half a mile off, I reckon, and asked: 'What's that?' and Rick told him it was some of the boys of the guard whose horses could not keep up. Every time we mounted a rise we saw that cloud of dust, and once we saw men on horseback through it, and Howard said: 'Let's ride faster, boys,' and they rode on at a quicker pace, and we were forced to keep up with them. At last Rick Waldon said he was tired, and our horses were getting blown. He would not go a step farther until he rested. Here was a watermelon patch, and yonder, a little farther off, was a store and a cistern. We'd strike a halt and send for water and melons while the horses took a rest. So we got down. It was just beyond our parish line; I remember that, for I heard somebody say so, and Devene looked quickly at Witchell and seemed disturbed, but Omar didn't seem to mind his look. He was sitting on the grass, and was pale and absent-minded. Edgeville was as gay as ever, but I saw him, when he had his back to the men pretending to stroke his horse's neck, take Miss Blair's picture out and look at it, and his face got sober as he looked. Some of the men were cutting watermelons. Waldon was standing by his horse, looking down the road we had just come over. Omar was telling me not to go away after we got to S——without seeing him first, as he would have a letter for his wife he wanted to trust to my care, when, suddenly, Howard cried out : 'Look ! see all those men with guns ; what does that mean ?' We turned our heads and saw a posse of armed men on horseback turn the bend in the road and come galloping up to us. Devene cried out : 'Mount and ride for your lives.' They ran for their horses and jumped into the saddles as quick as thought, but their pursuers were upon them. The foremost man cried out : 'Surrender !' and the others yelled the word after him. The mob began firing. Omar turned in his saddle, with the blood running out of a wound in his neck.

"'Give me a gun ; I don't want to die like a dog,' he cried. The bullets rained upon him, and he fell under the horses' feet. Edgeville cried out : 'I'll die before I surrender.' He dashed ahead and reached the top of the hill ; a bullet struck him in the head ; he leaped up out of his saddle and fell to the ground dead. Devene was killed at this same place. Wallace and Hollin and Howard got some distance away, but they were caught and taken to Bard's store, a mile or so beyond, and there put an end to. Howard was shot first. The old man trembled like a leaf. He got down on his knees and begged them to spare him. Wallace, too, prayed to be spared. He said : 'God is my witness, I have never done a wrong to any man in this country. I am only a magistrate. Witchell sent for me here to superintend his business. He gave me a home in his house and this office. I have held the office only a little while. I have tried to do what was right.'

"They shot both of them. I counted the places where ninety buckshot had entered Howard's body. Mark Hollin

stood and saw them shot. When his turn came he said:
'Let me say a prayer.' They suffered him to kneel down,
and he prayed in silence a little while. Then he rose up,
and said, calmly: 'There is only one thing I ask of you;
that is, for God's sake don't harm my wife and my little
child. Let them go away in safety. That is all.'

"He was so cool and brave they stood with their re-
loaded guns in their hands as if they thought it almost a
pity to kill him. As they were going to shoot, a man
galloped up and cried out: 'A thousand dollars if you
will spare the prisoner's life!' They turned on him, and
he said: 'I don't make the offer myself; I do it for another man. He's got a fall from his horse back yonder,
and he's not able to come on. But he's got the money,
for I know him. He said he'd give a thousand dollars for
every life you spared, and I am only in time for one, I
see.'

"Some cried 'Humbug!' and some 'Plank down your
money; let's see the color of it!' and several called out
to Mark Hollin to run into the cotton-field, they'd give
him a chance for his life. But he stood still and said:
'You have killed all my friends, now kill me. I will not
run for my life.' Well, they shot him. I went up and
looked at him. His face was as calm as if he had dropped
to sleep. I don't know what they did with the bodies; I
went away. I felt sick and numbed, as if a bullet had
entered my own head. The looks of those dead men will
never get out of my mind. As I rode back and passed
where the others were lying, I saw one of the men taking
off Edgeville's watch and chain. His pocket-book was on
the ground open, and close to it was Miss Auzete's letter
and picture. I picked them up, and I've got them here in
my pocket. I'll give them to you to return to her. I saw
one man taking out the diamond stud-buttons from Mark

Hollin's shirt—the same his little boy told me he had put in. I couldn't help feeling awful bad about the wives and children of the men, who were praying and hoping they were safe, while they lay there dead. They deserved to be punished, I know, but it looked like a bad day's work, Miss Zoe." *

CHAPTER XXXII.

ZOE had not once interrupted his recital. Horror had held her mute. When at last she spoke her voice was unnaturally calm.

"You said the party of lynchers had a leader. Who was he?"

"They said he was a Texan. I don't remember his name. They called him Captain—something."

"Was it—was it—Hirne?"

"Something like that, I think. A man with long hair and a keen eye; rides like an Indian; wore a hunting-shirt and no coat. Do you know him?"

"I — I believe I do," she articulated faintly. Her hands were tightly locked, her features drawn and pale. Henry Bronn looked at her with distress in his good-natured face.

"I ought not to have told you this dreadful tale," he said. "I see how it shocks you, and no wonder. Miss Zoe, you don't blame me, do you?"

---

* The circumstances of the pursuit and killing of these six office-holders are given almost word for word as they were told me by one of the men who accompanied the prisoners as a guard. The man who offered a thousand dollars for every life the mob would spare was a Southerner.

He put out his hand to touch hers. Involuntarily, she shuddered and drew away.

"Why did not you—why did not the guard defend the men they were sent to protect ?" she asked.

"The pursuers swooped down upon us so sudden, and went through their work so quick, we were all taken aback; I was at least; I hardly had time to wonder what it meant before it was all over. Then, too, the Captain of the guard gave us no orders to defend the men. And you know they were Radicals, and were found guilty of stirring up the negroes to rob and murder us. Do you blame me, Miss Zoe ?"

"O Henry! do not ask me," she cried, lifting her white face from her hands. "There has been terrible blame somewhere. I can not reason about it. I am stunned. But I hope—I believe that our people went into this blind-fold. They were deceived."

"The wives of these men," she said, presently, "have they heard the fate of their husbands ?"

"Not yet. Some one will be sent this evening to tell them. All the money in the parish treasury could not hire me to be the one."

Zoe turned away and walked to the end of the veranda. The picture of the murdered men, the shrieking wives, and frightened, weeping children seemed present before her, seemed shaped in fire upon her brain. And there, too, burned the words : "*He* was the leader in this dark work. *He* was the chief of the assassins—he, the man you love."

She knew now by the sharp pang at her heart that she did love him. It was for his sake she had so often disap-pointed her betrothed. It was his image that had driven Royal's from her breast—Royal, her kind, true lover.

She had been false to him for the sake of this man who had proved so unworthy ; who had turned a deaf ear to her prayers, and gratified his passion for revenge in defiance of her warning that the blood he would shed might be innocent blood.

"He is a savage, a monomaniac!" cried Zoe. "His courage is only an instinct for blood. Oh! I hate him. I *must* hate him!"

She had controlled herself enough to ask Henry Bronn to go in to supper, and see him seated at the table, talking to Hugh. Then, no longer able to bear the restraint of another's presence, she went out into the orchard. She threw herself on the ground at the foot of the old apple-tree and pressed her forehead to its vine-muffled trunk, that the dewy coolness might quench the burning in her brain and enable her to think more calmly.

Before she rose to her feet again she had made her resolve. She would not see this man again, she would not trust herself to look another time into his eyes, to listen to his voice that had such power over her. This night she would write to Royal. She had not replied to his last letter in which he had urged her to name a day for the marriage she had so long put off. She would write to-night and name the day—an early day it must be. She must put the irrevocable vow between herself and this man who had gained such a hold upon her. When she was the wife of Royal West—that amiable, law-abiding, honored gentleman—she would forget this wandering barbarian. Her regard for him was only a romantic fancy; Roy had assured her that it was—a wild seed, passion blown, that had dropped into her heart's garden in some unguarded hour.

But ah! what root it had taken! What a pang it cost to pluck it up!

When she rose next morning after a restless night she was completely unnerved. The terrible shock of the evening before, coming upon her after the days of anxiety and

nights of watching she had endured, had so unnerved her
that she found her hand shaking as she returned Hirne's
note-book to the pocket of his coat. If she was so weak,
could she trust herself to resist his importunities to see her
when he came ?

Parties of horsemen, coming from Cohatchie, crossed
the river from time to time. Some of these were the Texans who had been with Hirne, now returning to their
homes. She longed to ask them if their leader had really
been one of the assassins, but the dread of having her slender hope swept away held her silent. The men appeared
discontented and gloomy, indisposed to talk. The fever of
excitement had died out. Their hasty rush to the rescue
of Cohatchie seemed to them a mere fool's errand.

At last Zoe heard one of them speak of Hirne. He had
stopped to get a drink of water, and, while he was still on
his horse at the gate, two other men rode up.

"Where is Hirne ?" asked the first comer.

"Don't know," was the response. "Haven't laid eyes
on him since he and the others followed the fellows that had
the Rads in tow."

"You didn't go with 'em then ? Neither did I, and I
ain't sorry I kept out of that scrape."

A dead weight of certainty crushed out the feeble hope
Zoe had cherished. To see him now would be unmixed
pain. Speak to him she would not. Yet, with an inconsistency that was followed by keen self-rebuke, she caught
herself looking among the horsemen for that leonine head
and proud, easy figure which would be seen above them
all.

"If I could go away before he came !" she said, with
tears of self-contempt springing to her eyes.

Chance favored her wish. Shortly after ten o'clock a
boat coming down the river blew the three-whistle signal

for stopping as she rounded the bend just above Vincent's house.

"It is mother," Mrs. Vincent called out, joyfully. "She said she would come to nurse me as soon as father's rheumatism was better."

The boat stopped. A little roly-poly matron, with numerous bags and bundles, was handed ashore, and soon Mrs. Hugh and the new baby were hugged by a pair of fat, motherly arms.

A sudden resolve came to Zoe. The boat had made fast to a great ash tree, and the deck hands were running up the steep bank to take on wood. Zoe said to her sister-in-law:

"Monde, you and Hugh are improving so fast now, and you have your mother with you, I believe I will run away for a little change. I'll go down with Captain Link as far as N—— to see Mother Doremus. You know she is Mother Superior at the Sacred Heart now. I have not seen her since I left St. Joseph's."

"Go, by all means, my dear. You certainly need change, and rest. Get yourself ready while Mandy packs up the things you will need."

Before the last cord of wood had been piled on the steamer's lower deck Zoe was on board for her trip to the convent at N—— thirty miles below.

Scarcely was the smoke of the boat out of sight when Captain Hirne rode down to the river at the ferry opposite Vincent's house. He looked pale and grave; there were lines of bodily pain about his mouth, but his eye lighted as he caught a glimpse of a lady's dress on the piazza.

"Are all safe and well?" he asked of Tom Ludd, who came in the flat to put him across.

"Yes, sir. Mr. Hugh is up; Miss Zoe is jes' gone away."

"Gone!" The light died out of the Captain's face. "Where did she go?"

"She went on de steamboat Mabel to de city, I b'lieve. Heap uv her frien's live dere, an' de gen'leman she's goin' to marry. Him and his sister come up here las' spring. Mighty handsome, high-flyin' gen'leman, and rich as Crishus. Won't you go by de house, Cap'n, and have a glass er claret wid Mars Hugh? Mandy done carried your coat up dere."

"No, Tom, I am tired, and must get on. I hurt my leg by a fall yesterday. Bring the coat out to the gate for me.

Tom brought the coat.

"God bless you, Cap'n Hirne! Me and Mandy 'll never forgit you," he said as his fingers closed over the half dollars Hirne put into his hand.

"So that's all over," the Texan said to himself as he rode away. "What else could I expect? What is there in me for a woman like her to care for? But I would have loved her. O God! how I love her!"

A quiver passed over his face, and his eyes grew misty. Then, setting his lips firmly, he shook his head backward and put spurs to his horse.

"I'll shut down on this nonsense at once and for ever," he muttered.

But the thunder-cloud then gathering in the west was not gloomier than his face as he rode on and entered the swamp.

CHAPTER XXXIII.

THERE is a legend of a man who wrested from a wizard the magic word for invoking spirits. With it he summoned a familiar imp and set it to doing menial work for him—bringing water for his cabbage-beds. But the cunning wizard had withheld a portion of the spell. The man had no power to dismiss the spirit he had called up; so water continued to be brought until not only was the cabbage-bed flooded, but the man and his house were swept away.

Both Alver and Witchell had invoked the demon of Lawlessness to assist them in their purposes, and the results had gone beyond their intentions. The imp, once summoned, would not down at their bidding. Witchell had thought that by causing a few mischievous, but not malignant, acts to be done to the negroes he would create the impression that Ku-klux were abroad in the parish, and obtain the military force he wanted for the protection of himself and his friends, and his ballots at the time of the election. But his unlawful scheme had recoiled upon his head. His intercepted instructions had suggested the very plot which had eventuated in the death of his friends and the downfall of his hopes of supremacy in the State.

Alver had summoned the fiend of Riot to work his purpose of freeing the parish from carpet-bag rule. He found himself unable to control the evil force he had invoked. It had swept on until its fury was quenched in blood. His female accomplice had foreseen this, and counted upon it, when she said to him : "Set the ball in motion and leave its course to chance."

Yet even she seemed appalled at the horror of the climax she had worked to attain. She was on horseback returning from a ride when the news of the massacre reached her. At the same moment her ears were filled with the agonized screams of the bereaved women who had gathered like frightened doves in Omar's cottage. Her face blanched ; she wheeled her horse and rode at wild speed back from the town.

When the terrible tidings reached Witchell, it utterly crushed him at first. Resentment was drowned in remorseful anguish, and the stern, cold man sat for long minutes with bowed head and shaking frame. Omar's faithfulness, Omar's simple-hearted devotion, rushed over him with the keen sense of loss, and he groaned out :

" My brother, my brother ! would to God I had died in your place ! "

He started up at last. His hands were clenched, his features convulsed. He called down fearful curses on the slayers of his friends.

" They shall suffer for it, they shall suffer for it ! " he swore. " The laggards at Washington can not now refuse me the troops. With the cavalry at my back, I will hunt down the last murderer among them and bring him to punishment."

The news of the Cohatchie tragedy flashed over the country from end to end. It roused the fury of the North, the grief and indignation of the conservative South. The Northern press denounced the people of the revolutionized parish as a "pack of cold-blooded murderers." They forgot that in small as in large revolutions the people are mere instruments played upon by some designing leader—some schemer, who has industriously collected all the explosive material, laid the train, and fired it by a bold or cunning stroke. Had those who sweepingly denounced the people as murderers looked upon the little town a few days after the bloody drama, they would have realized that men may be led blindly into doing deeds that they look back upon with horror when the short frenzy is over. An awful calm succeeded the tumult. Men sat silent in their homes, or gathered in the streets in gloomy groups. They sickened with the fear that now stole upon them that they had brought about the shedding of innocent blood.

A more active fear quickened their pulses. They looked daily for punishment at the hands of the Government. They expected the long-talked-of cavalry to swoop down upon them, capturing right and left. But days went by, and no soldiers came, no arrests were made. What could cause the delay?

There had been indignation meetings at the North, councils at Washington, an investigating committee appointed to inquire into all the particulars of the alarming affair, but no active steps had been taken to punish the rebellious parish, or to arrest the ringleader of the revolution.

Did the Government, in spite of its outward show of indignation, entertain a secret misgiving that the six office-holders had deserved their fate? Did they lend credence to the widely-copied version of the tragedy which was published in the "Cohatchie Times" (Alver's organ)? In that account it was elaborately shown that the six office-holders were guilty of having incited the negroes to a bloody outrage, and had deserved the doom which the excited mob had visited upon them, in defiance of the committee's magnanimous sentence that the men should only resign their offices and leave the State.

No doubt the heads of the Administration had a secret fear that much of this might be true. Conscious of having, in so many instances, put vile men in power through the South, they hesitated to punish an outrage that had possibly been provoked.

Else why the long period of inaction that lulled the parish into fancied security?

Alver took advantage of the interval to forward his cause. For days after the bloody culmination of his plot he was gloomy and inactive. Then he roused; he realized that it needed promptness and energy to carry out the advantage his bold *coup* had gained. Many things troubled him. In pursuit of his ambitious scheme he had neglected his legitimate business, and his interests had suffered. The ten thousand dollars which were in the parish treasury at the time of the killing of young Witchell, the tax-receiver, he refused to touch, though he could have done so without fear during the time that the parish was wholly under his control. But he was not a mercenary man. He valued money only as a means to attain power. But he had honorable instincts still; he resisted the temptation to appropriate some of the treasury funds to paying off the men who had helped to bring about the late crisis, and who were now clamorous to be rewarded. His haughty temper ill brooked being under obligation to them, and with difficulty he restrained himself when they pressed their claims for office and money. He feared them more than he did the coming of the troops. If disappointed, their rough natures would grow unmanageable and everything would be bruited abroad.

And Alver saw a prospect of making smooth water for himself. He could not be held responsible for the action of a miscellaneous mob, gathered from various quarters. He could show that he had tried to calm this mob. He ought not to suffer for its misdoing. He had never intended, never foreseen, this tragic termination to his plot. He had schemed to free his portion of the State from corrupt, alien rule, and secure to the people representation by their own citizens. It was a patriotic motive, and the end justified the means he had used to attain it. So he reasoned to calm his conscience and lull his fears.

Chief among these thorns in his side was Cobb. Another wished Cobb out of the way as heartily as Alver did. He had become a Damocles's sword over Floyd Reese. He claimed her as his reward. He had twice served her pur-

pose in the accomplishment of her designs ; he had her
doubly in his power. She knew that, if exasperated, he was
reckless enough to betray her, though it should cost him
his life ; and so she strove to conciliate him, while she
loathed herself for doing so.   Bad as she was, hard and
cruel, wearing without shame the diamond ring Cobb had
taken from the mutilated finger of one of the murdered
men, she was woman enough to shrink from giving herself
to the arms of a ruffian.   But she feared him more and
more.   He was growing impatient and jealous, and she was
forced to grant him interviews, in which she soothed and
coaxed him with all the art in her power.   Some of these
interviews took place in Alver's parlor.   Cobb was more
presentable now, since he had exchanged his shabby disguise
for a decent suit, and trimmed his hair and beard ; still that
rough figure, that sensual mouth and lowering brow, seemed
greatly out of place beside the beautiful face and superb
shape of the adventuress. Usually it was arranged that
he should meet her when she was out riding.   In some of
the wild bridle-paths that ran through deep forests, or along
steep-banked bayous, he would be waiting for her.   Rarely
they rode where there was a chance of meeting others ; but
one afternoon as they left an unfrequented "cattle-trail,"
and came out into the riverside road, they saw a gentleman
approaching on horseback, riding beside a lady dressed in a
black habit with a black crape veil thrown back from her
very fair face.   It was Mrs. Hollin going down to her plantation, and her escort was Alver.   He had shown every attention to the widows of the dead officers, had called upon
them, expressed his deep regrets at the fatal extent to which
the excitement had gone, had persisted, in spite of cold
looks and words, in doing everything for their comfort and
rendering them every assistance in their business, until the
poor ladies, too troubled to arrange anything for themselves,

and too frightened to venture out, began to give him their
confidence, and believe he must be the one friend they had
in this stranger land, and that he had done all he could to
avert the fury of the mob from their ill-fated husbands.

The parties were embarrassed on encountering each
other—all but Mrs. Hollin. Her pale, pensive face did not
change, but Floyd blanched as she met Alver's eye. Cobb
put on his look of swaggering assurance, and Alver's face
darkened and his mouth curled with mingled displeasure
and disdain. When they had passed, Cobb, twirling his
long mustache, said :

"My lordly Colonel that likes dirty work to be done
for him, but don't want it named before him, seems to be
flirting with the lemon-haired widow. That's rather fast,
ain't it ? He's up with that hump-backed chap—what's his
name—that had the king put out of the way and courted
the queen as she was following her husband's coffin. I've
seen it played. Well, the Colonel's his match, ain't he ?"

"No," said Floyd, haughtily. "He feels a sympathy
for those lonely ladies. He would do all in his power to
help them. *You* can not understand his feelings."

"Not being a gentleman like him, you mean. Well, I
can see his motives. He hears breakers ahead. He thinks
the troops may come, and he wants to make fair weather
with these women before they get here. He makes out his
case to them. There's nobody to contradict it. The darkies
are afraid, and the women never see anybody except him.
He's the plausiblest scamp in creation. He's got *you* under
his thumb. You're miserable now, for fear he don't care
for you. You're jealous of that yellow-haired woman, and
you're holding back from me on his account."

He had blundered on the truth, or he had watched
Floyd with such jealous scrutiny that he had discovered it.
She was made half frantic at times by the consciousness

that she was losing hold upon Alver. Ever since those two days in which he had secluded himself after the death of the six officers he had sent off under guard, he had seemed to feel a constraint in Floyd's presence. He answered her abruptly, he kept his brow bent and moody in her presence, and, with a woman's singular inconsistency, she now became, for the first time, deeply in love with the man she had before pretended to love for a purpose. His coldness was gall and bitterness to her; his slight shudder when she placed her hand upon his brow made her feel that he associated her always with the horror of that massacre.

The days went by. The widows of the dead officers went back to their relatives, and still no movement had been taken to punish the lawless action of the parish. "They believe the published statement," thought Alver. "Or they think it will be hard to disprove it. They will send their investigating committee to New Orleans and make a show of inquiry, but they will be afraid to stir deep, lest they turn up more offensive matter. They have sneaking fears that the statement of a plot to kill and rob may be true, and, while they make a pretense of inquiry, they will take no actual steps to search truly or to punish, for fear investigation may confirm the crime of their men. They will not send the troops."

This reasoning had much truth to found itself upon, and no action might have been taken but for one thing. Those who believed that Marshall Witchell would abandon his hold upon the parish, in the horror and dismay caused by the death of his brother and his friends, did not know the man. Grief held him paralyzed for a while; then his *will* aroused, made stronger by the opposition against him, made fierce by the revengeful thirst that now mixed with his desire to succeed. These people—these murderers of his brother—he said to himself, should feel his yoke as they

had never felt it before. He would show them that he
would succeed, and all who had conspired against his
friends should feel the full sting of punishment, if not directly at the hands of the Government, then indirectly
during his administration of office among them.

After persistent appeals he obtained the troops and
started with them up the river on one of the larger boats
now beginning to ply the rising stream.

They arrived without warning. The boat stopped at the
landing, and the uniformed men and horses came out in
numbers that struck dismay to the towns-people. Captain
Witchell was among them. Floyd chanced to see him before Alver did. His cold, determined eye filled her with
dread. She hurried to Alver and begged him to fly at
once. "If you had seen Witchell's face you would know
that he means to sift this matter to the bottom, and to
punish every man connected with it."

" He has not that power," answered Alver. " He may
arrest and try ; he has no proof to convict. I will not run
away. I will stand my ground. Let them put me in
prison, let them try me. They can not find me guilty. I
am not guilty of those men's deaths. I will nominate my
ticket in prison and win the day, if any fair election can be
held in the land."

" Alver, for heaven's sake leave at once. I ordered your
horse to be saddled as I came by the stable. Every one is
running away. I saw Cobb, Waldon, and Hayne on the
top of the hill with their horses at full speed. The troops
have begun arresting already. At least keep out of the
way until I can find out for you the extent of the danger
that is to be feared. They say Witchell has every man
down on his black list."

"I know that. I know every man has been spotted.
They have had spies and detectives among us for a month."

"And you will not go?"

"No; to go will be giving up all we have been working for. Strange that *you* advise it."

"True, for the moment I thought only of your safety," the woman said, with tears springing into her eyes. "Perhaps it is best you should remain and be cool and fearless, as you know how to be. Arrest and imprisonment will endear you to the people; and, when the trial comes, nothing can be proved against you. Circumstances favor you. You can show that it was right to arrest and dismiss the officers. You can show proofs of their guilt strong enough to authorize this; with their killing *you* had nothing to do. That was the work of a mob of strange men, over which you had no—Oh—see! they are coming." She broke off, catching her breath as a party of cavalrymen with an officer at their head rode up to the gate.

Alver received them with graceful urbanity. When arrested he smilingly signified his willingness to accompany them, and going in, followed by two soldiers, soothed his wife, clasped her and his children in his arms, kissed them, and said: "Now I am ready." His papers had all been secured and his business arrangements made beforehand in fear of his being suddenly taken up.

Floyd came to the door as the three were passing out along the corridor. Turning to the soldiers with her persuasive smile, she said: "Gentlemen, allow me a private word with your prisoner while you stand guard here at the door. You see, there is but one door to this room."

They bowed low, struck with admiration, such as all men conceived for this fair woman. She laid her hand upon Alver's and drew him into the room; her fingers closed upon his with a firm, cheering grasp.

"Courage," she said. "I will be outside to work for you; I will write and report to you, or I will come and tell

you face to face how all is going. I will be permitted to
see you. How glad I am that you are not to be taken away !
I heard them tell you so."

"We are only to be confined in the Court House and
guarded, though I fear that we will be taken to New Orleans
to be tried there. I don't fear the issue, but I regret to
lose time from my affairs here. I shall nominate my ticket,
and hope to be out in time to carry the election. If I am
not, my friends must work for our cause. I know that you
will, my brave heart. Keep a watch upon Cobb and Yent ;
they may turn traitors. Keep them silent by frightening
or coaxing, as you think best. Don't expose yourself to
danger or comment, and do not forget that my hopes are,
in a great measure, in your hands."

He had not spoken so kindly to her in weeks. But now
her face was close to his, her eyes wet, her mouth tremu-
lous. She looked womanly. He touched her cheek with
his hand ; a warm tear fell upon it. He shuddered ; the
thought of warm, dropping blood came into his mind.

He hastily unloosed her hands from their hold of him,
saying : "I must not tax their patience ; good-by," and
just touching his lips to her forehead, he rejoined the waiting guard.

"He is beginning to hate me," she cried to herself.
"It was for him I did it, and he hates me for it."

This was part of her punishment. The man she had
schemed and sinned for turned from her with a feeling of
repulsion. He was not of her moral caliber. If thirst for
power, and a fierce hatred of Radical rule, and a woman's
influence, had made him do a wrong, they had not debased
him. His remorse for the terrible issue of the excitement
in Cohatchie was none the less keen, that its working was
hid in his own heart. It was now pride and unrest that
urged him on to accomplish his purpose. But for these

he would have thrown up the game that had cost him so many sleepless nights.

Fifteen minutes later saw Alver a prisoner, with several others, in the handsome Court House that was Cohatchie's pride—a prisoner, but unshackled, allowed the freedom of the room, and permitted to receive and converse with his friends.

CHAPTER XXXIV.

THE work of arresting went vigorously on. Day and night parties of cavalry, with negroes to pilot them, scoured the country, surrounded houses without warning, and searched them from top to bottom. The Court House became like a hotel, so numerous were its inmates, while many, to escape capture, had taken refuge in flight. Young boys and gray-haired men fled the country in haste, or hid in the miasmatic swamps and thick woods, and fought musquitoes and lived by fishing and hunting, together with such food as their friends could manage to convey to them. Sometimes their hiding-places would be betrayed by negroes, and the ubiquitous cavalry would sweep down upon them in a hot chase across the country, their superior knowledge of the woods and their more dashing horsemanship usually enabling the pursued to escape.

The hot days were over ; the Indian summer wrapped the land in dreamy, colorful beauty. Zoe's wedding-day was near. Royal's sister, Kate, was with her—an affectionate, lively girl. Zoe had put aside the cloud that had so long hung between her and her betrothed. It was a mist of romance, she said to herself ; the breath of common sense must blow it aside. She went dutifully about her daily work ; she schooled herself into thinking cheerfully

15

of her marriage with Royal. He was to come on the next boat, and preparations were made for a quiet wedding. Quiet it must necessarily be, since society here was wofully broken up, hardly a male member being left in any of the households in Cohatchie, or for miles along the river, above and below the town. The men had been captured from time to time by the troops and confined in the strongly guarded walls of the Court House. A few nights before, an old gentleman, neighbor to the Vincents, had had his house surrounded at midnight by the cavalry. He had managed to get out and crawl into the garden, where he singularly escaped discovery. The garden was tramped from end to end, but the old gentleman, squatting close among his vegetables, was overlooked, or his bald white poll was taken for a cabbage-head.

Another house in sight of the Vincent place was surrounded the same night—a large, dark, old building which a yellow-fever scourge had left with one solitary occupant— a young man. Leaping from the window when he was waked by the clank of cavalry spurs outside his door, he found himself encircled with bayonets, and laughing recklessly and saying, "Why couldn't you let a fellow finish his morning nap?" he had given himself up. Two nights afterward some young men, who were in hiding, rode from their place of concealment through the fields, avoiding the roads and negro quarters, and came to see Zoe and Miss West. Zoe, listening anxiously at the window, heard the muffled sound of oars a few hours after their arrival, and gave the alarm in time for the young visitors to make good their escape. Fifteen minutes afterward a cordon of Federal cavalry was drawn up around the house in the moonlight, and the building was thoroughly overhauled. All who had carried arms during the riot were hunted down, the negroes being the chief informants.

Tom Ludd was expatiating to Zoe on the "meddlesomeness of niggers" in this particular one afternoon as she stood on the bank, watching the puffs of smoke ascending from a steamer coming up the river, but still miles below, around the bends of the crooked stream. She knew that Royal West was on the boat—the man that in two days was to be her husband, and she tried to believe that the flutter at her heart was joy. Kate was busy crimping her fair hair, for Roy's "best man," whom he was to bring with him, was her favorite admirer. Tom had been drawing in Mandy's "fish line," with a good-sized "cat" attached, and now, with his prize at his feet, stood where he had stopped on the bank near Zoe. With his eyes on the curls of smoke staining the horizon, he pronounced the approaching boat to be "de ole Bartable' comin' 'round Blair's Bend."

"Dere'll be more soljers on her, I hearn," he said, not quite able to hide the pride he felt in the fact. "De calv'ry cotch anuther man below here yisterday. I wuz down dat way huntin' my hoss and I seed 'em take him, and I wuz mity sorry to see who it was. I'd a warned *him* ef I'd had a chance, ef dey *had* tuck my vote away fur doin' it, for he wuz dat Cap'n what spared my life de time er de foolishness las' summer. 'Twas Cap'n—Cap'n Hirne. You 'member him, Miss Zoe."

"Remember him!" Zoe's white face bore witness that she did.

"Hirne captured! How came he here?" she controlled herself to say.

"I can't tell you about dat. He was comin' from Texas, maybe; was on dat route when he was tuck. He staid all night somewhere de night before, and some smart nigger reformed upon him to de calv'ry. Dey said he had a big han' in de 'sturbance, and de soljers was mity glad to git him. I got a chance to speak a word wid him, and he axed straight about you, Miss Zoe. 'Is she well?' he said, and den, 'Is she married?' and I tell him, 'Not yet. De weddin' will be performed next Thursday night; de cake done made and all.' He look mity down in de mouth, and no wonder. 'Tain't no fun to hear tell of weddin's and sich when you're in a scrape like he is."

And after hearing this, Zoe had to go and put on smiles and pretty attire to welcome the lover who came later. So pale was she that Kate insisted on touching her cheeks with rouge. The black brows looked like arches of jet on her ivory forehead, and the eyes beneath dropped their long lashes when Roy tried to read the meanings they held.

Winter Lareau, Royal's friend who had come to be "best man" at the wedding, had his eyes seemingly filled by the blonde beauty of Kate West—a fairy in pale blue, with moonlight-colored hair and a wild-rose complexion; so the engaged pair were left to themselves. How hard Zoe struggled to hide all she felt, and to seem interested in Roy's plans and happy in his praises! She succeeded as only a woman with tact and self-control could do. If Roy noted any lack of her usual variety and sprightliness, the plea of headache explained and excused it. But she was glad to take refuge in music, and she sat down to the cottage piano and played fragments of favorite compositions and sang snatches of songs to the delight of Royal, who liked music that was not too "artistic," and loved the simple melody of Zoe's songs. After all, though, the playing was not a wise move. The music brought its own atmosphere of romance and tenderness that was dangerous to one who had set bounds upon her emotions, and said, "Thou shalt not overleap them." Half unconsciously, she played the prelude to an air to which she had set Hirne's little song,

"We met to part for ever." Then giving herself up to the spell of the moment, she sang the piece to the end. When she reached the last two lines a voice caught up air and words—a voice so low it seemed an echo—and sang with her :

> "In some fair Aidenn we shall meet
> Who have parted here for ever."

She turned around, pale, as if she expected to see a ghost.

"Was it you that sang?" she asked Royal.

"No; I never heard those words before. It was some one outside. Hugh, perhaps," he said, wondering at the agitation of her looks. "You don't think it was the spirits?"

"Certainly not, unless you have brought them," she laughed, recovering her self-possession. "It was likely Hugh; he has heard me sing the piece before; or one of the negroes; they are wonderful at catching up anything musical."

But she was not candid in what she said; she walked presently to the back window, through which the sounds had seemed to come, and looked out. She saw no one, but the thick foliage of the cedar-trees close by rustled, though there was no wind. She was about to lean out and whisper a name into the dusk, when Royal, who was turning over music at a stand, called to her from the other end of the room.

"Ah! Zoe, here is that pretty little duet, 'Under the Stars,' we used to sing together. Come, let us sing it now."

She answered quickly :

"It has been so long since I tried it I have forgotten it; but Kate sings it, and your voices blend well together. I'll call her over and ask her to sing it with you."

Kate put down the pretty fancy work she had been trifling over and came to the piano, at which Royal sat down to play the accompaniment. Young Lareau stood by them to turn the leaves of the music. After the first few bars of the song, Zoe quitted her stand by the piano and went to the window at the back part of the room. Dropping the curtain behind her, she leaned out, listened, and looked. Nothing out there but the trees, motionless in the breezeless night, the chirp of insects, and, farther back, the white cotton-fields lying under the moonlight. She turned off with a sigh, and was leaving the window, when she again heard a rustling outside. Once more she looked ; she suppressed a cry that rose almost to her lips. There in the dim light, just below the window, stood Hirne. Startled, she stretched out her hand, half believing it was an illusion. He caught it in his firm clasp and pressed it to his lips. Drawing it hastily away, she found voice to say low :

"I thought you were a prisoner ?"

"I was. I got away from them. They followed me into the swamp, and I eluded them there. They went back without their game."

"Why did you not go on and put youself out of the reach of danger ? Why are you here, where they may come upon you at any moment ?"

"I am here to see you ; I came back to this place to see you. I have no intention of being balked of my purpose."

"But you will go now ?"

"Not until I have had one last interview with you."

"But every moment is full of danger. The negroes may see you and inform against you."

"I know it ; still I must see you."

"Come in then. Come to the back door through the shrubbery. The servants will not be so apt to see you."

"No, I will not go in. I know who is there. Do you think I want to meet *him?* Do you think I could bear to see him look at you as if you were his already? No. In a little while he will have you all to himself. All I ask of you before that time comes is a few moments of your society—a little while to look at you, and listen to you, and feel you near me. Then I will go away and you shall never hear of me again. But I will not go now until you have granted me this much."

"How can I? It is very dangerous for you to be here. Parties of cavalry cross nearly every night and patrol the river up and down."

"I have my horse fastened at the foot of the lane there in a clump of bushes, just beyond the great pecan-tree. Will you come to that tree to-night? There is something I must say to you. Will you come and tell me good-by for ever?"

She hesitated.

"I shall wait there until daylight, unless you come."

His voice was determined. She knew he would do as he said, and she feared he would be captured and that it would go hard with him, for she believed that he had been that "long-haired, keen-eyed Texan" who led the mob of lynchers. Believing it, however, she still found it hard to resist his pleading for a last interview, in which he had something to say to her. It might be important she should hear the something, she reasoned, and it was right to try and save him from the consequences of his own imprudence in exposing himself to capture on her account. It was her duty.

The last verse of the song was being sung. She must speak before the notes that had drowned their low talk should cease.

"I will come," she said, and stepped out from behind the curtain as Royal rose from the piano.

"Roy is in splendid voice," cried Kate. "Don't you think so, Zoe? Why, what is the matter? You look almost ready to cry. Does music affect you so? I thought you more matter-of-fact."

"'I am never merry when I hear sweet music.'"

"Bringing in Shakespeare to excuse yourself. Little sentimentalist! I suppose all people in love are sentimental, though. Head grows soft to sympathize with heart; is that not so, Mr. Lareau?"

CHAPTER XXXV.

She had promised rashly. She said so to herself as she stood at the window of her room and looked obliquely across the moonlighted field to the great pecan-tree that guarded the entrance of the lane. Should she go there to-night to see this man for the last time—this man she had been trying so long to put out of her heart?

And, after all, she had promised to meet him to-night—the night before her marriage. It was very wrong. She hesitated to go in spite of her promise. She lingered now, when at last she could go unobserved. She had left Kate asleep, her head with its golden plaits and crimps lying on the laced pillow, her eyes having closed while she was still talking of Winter Lareau. Royal and his friend were taking their night-cap smoke at the window below. The odor of the cigars and the murmur of the men's talk floated up to her where she sat. Presently Royal threw his half-smoked cigar out among the bushes, hummed a snatch from "La Duchesse," and said: "Well, 'get thee to bed,' as my Lady Macbeth has it."

"This place is awfully lonesome. I wonder how Zoe

has endured it so long. It is not strange she looks a little sad. I shall take her straight to Saratoga. The waters will do her good, though the season is nearly over. She needs brightening up, dear little girl."

They moved from the window, but directly Zoe heard Roy's mellow laugh.

"How happy he is !" she thought, "while I—well, when I am married it will be better. Surely this restless aching will leave me. I will forget this man whom fate has strangely mixed up with my life. It was wrong to promise to meet him to-night. But how could I help it ? He was looking at me so ; I was afraid he would grow excited and Royal would hear him, and there might be a difficulty between them. He is so reckless ; he will certainly expose himself to capture, unless I see him and persuade him to go away. I am afraid that he has already been seen by some of the negroes, they are always slipping about, and that the troops will be over to-night after him."

These thoughts ran through her mind as she hastily put on a dark-brown dress and knotted a veil of the same color about her head.

She looked at her watch as she was leaving the room ; it was eleven o'clock. Noiselessly she quitted the house by the back door, opened the gate of the rear yard, and hurried down into the little path that ran along outside the paling which divided the garden from the cotton-field. This path led past the stables to a lane between two fields. She stood, hesitating, looking down the lane that led to the swamp — the lane at whose foot was the pecan-tree — a black blot on the moonlight. She dreaded that negroes might be awake, who would see and follow her and discover Hirne. It was a time of suspicion and danger, and the troops had their dusky spies everywhere. Getting on the shadow side of the lane, she walked resolutely on. It was not more than four hundred yards to the pecan-tree, but it seemed a full mile to the girl who walked the distance with rapid steps, her heart beating wildly with conflicting feelings—fear and self-reproach, and agitation at meeting Hirne again. She was too breathless to speak when at last she stopped within the deep circle of shade cast by the wide, down-sweeping limbs of the pecan-tree. From its great trunk Hirne stepped out, and, taking her hand, said :

"You have come. It was kind of you. I thank you."

Then, seeing her agitation, he said, hurriedly :

"Have I asked too much ? You are trembling like a lamb under the butcher's knife. Do not be afraid to be alone with me. I would not harm one hair of your dear head. I will not even hold this little hand. I will keep my tongue from uttering one tender word—if I can. But you must not be too hard on me if I say a word that it is not right to address to another man's bride ; I am not used to schooling myself ; I am but a barbarian, you know, and you must pardon any lack of etiquette. God knows I mean no lack of respect—of reverence even. You are to me as a saint—as the Virgin Mother herself, looking down pityingly from her shrine. I could be content to think of you so, to look up to you in my thoughts and never ask you to come down to me, but I am not content to see another embrace my saint. The thought that you are going to marry fills me with gall and bitterness."

There was no answer Zoe could make to this, and presently he went on.

"Do you know, though, that you gave me a faint hope that you might not marry him after all—a faint, half hope that you might care for—me ? I know now that it was not so, and it was nothing you said, but that night on the porch you let me say wild things, tender things, to you without rebuke. You let me hold your hand for a sweet moment and sit near you, and—yes, your tones and your looks were kinder than you would have used, my sweet, had you known that you were throwing out mocking straws to a drowning man. It was a bitter disappointment when I came back and found you gone, and not a line, not a message for me."

"Did I think you would have cared for line or message when you had shown such disregard of my entreaties, my prayers?"

"Entreaties? prayers? What do you mean?"

"Did I not implore you to have nothing to do with the killing of those men?"

"You did, and your request was sacred. I had nothing to do with the killing of the officers."

"You had not? You were not that Texas captain that headed the lynchers?"

"I was not. It was another man, resembling me only in the long hair and beard, and in the horse he rode. He was called Captain Dick; who he really was I can not find out. Doubtless some fellow, though, who, like me, has had wrongs enough to make him desperate."

"And you had nothing to do with the killing of the men?"

"I was not on the spot. I even did what I could to prevent bloodshed. I had no idea of taking a hand in any violence when I crossed the river that night, because you had said what you did, though, let me tell you, Nolan denied that what he told you was true. He said he only told it to make himself important in your eyes."

"He said that to you? Why, he made the statement to me as a confession when he thought he would die from the cut on his head."

"He said he was delirious when he first declared he had been hired to create a row, and that afterward he deceived you purposely. I came back to the house that night to tell you this, and to see if it altered your views as to what should be done to the officers, but you had retired. I did not see you. I went on to Cohatchie to see what they were doing. On the way I cross-questioned the man Cobb. He was drinking freely, and told more than he would otherwise have done. I thought from his talk there might be a plot to overthrow the Radicals, and that, if there was any dark work in it, he was the agent, if not the planner. When the officers were sent away under guard, I determined to follow, and, if possible, prevent violence. I told my intention to several of my friends, and they said they were with me, and we started together. A mile or so out of town we came up with a party who seemed to come together by some preconcerted plan. Men rode up and joined them from time to time, and no questions were asked. They were, most of them, men I did not know. Cobb was among them. He shunned me, and tried to muffle up his face. He had found out from my talk that I did not favor lynching the men. We rode on, until my horse, that had got a shoe loose and was going fast down a hill, fell and hurt himself and me. I was compelled to stop by the way, but two of my friends went on, and I charged them to keep our boys from having any hand in the killing that I was afraid was going to be."

Zoe was silent. "Oh! if I had only known this before!" she was thinking. Presently she said :

"We heard that a man, who had been prevented from going on by a fall, sent a message to the lynchers, offering a thousand dollars for every man who should be spared. Was it you who made that offer ?"

"It was, and I meant it, and was sorry it came too late. I offered the reward for your sake, because you had begged to have these men spared."

"I thank you. Oh! I might have known you would never have had a hand in so bloody a deed."

"Yes, I might. I can't take praise that is not mine. There were men among those lynchers as good as I am—better, perhaps. I never did kill a defenseless man, but I might have felt as they had I lived in this parish and been saddled so long by extortioners, and had at last been led to believe I was about to be victimized by them and their negro tools."

"You can not tell me that you would have killed them?"

"Well, no; I could not have taken the life of an unarmed man. As for one begging me to spare him, kneeling, praying— But I don't like to remember that day—and it was not to listen to such gloomy talk I asked you to come here to-night. But I seem always doomed to say and do things to make you think me a blood-thirsty monster, while this moment, and for months—ever since I knew you—the better spirit within me has been longing for peace; I told you so once, and I told you that only your love could save me. That was a piece of mad presumption; but I am better for having known you, and I want to promise you, my good angel, this night, that I will renounce the wild life you found fault with. I will settle down in a quiet home I have, with the two boys I told you I was educating, and another orphan—the little daughter of the brother officer's widow I also spoke to you of. The mother died last month, and the little girl, ten years old, is my ward. I shall try to make a home for these three, and to make them happy. Does this please you?"

Emotion made Zoe's voice husky.

"It does," she said. "It pleases me best of all because in trying to make those orphans happy you will become happy yourself. Here is my hand; you have given me your promise, and I pledge you my sympathy, my best wishes, my prayers for your happiness."

"Happiness!" he echoed, bitterly. "I hope for no happiness." Then, recovering himself, he thanked her gently.

"And you," he said, "no need to wish you happiness. The good and beautiful can not but be happy. Yet griefs may come. I wish I could bear all yours for you. He is blest who has the privilege of sharing them. If Fate had given *me* that privilege—do not draw your hand away, sweetest. I only hold it because we are parting—saying good-by for ever. I have seen you, you have spoken kindly to me, and now it is time—"

"Hush!" cried Zoe, starting. "Do you hear that noise?"

"Where? what noise?"

"The tramp of horses, and a man's voice calling. It came from the river. Oh! what if the cavalry have crossed and are searching for you?"

They listened in breathless silence for a moment, straining their eyes in the direction of the river.

"Don't be frightened for me," he said low. "I have my horse here ready to spring upon him at an instant's warning, and there is the swamp behind us. They would not have caught me yesterday had I been upon my good Mort. I had dismounted to drink, and they surprised me."

"How was it that you got away?"

"The soldiers were in a cane patch stealing sugar-cane—all but one, who was guarding me. When he was not looking I gave him the slip and was off in a flash. He shouted to his comrades; but before they came and mounted I was in the woods. There Mort and I were at home. They will not penetrate far in the swamp, being afraid of an ambush."

"If they should arrest you, you could prove that you had no part in the murders? You would be in no danger?"

"Not if the trial was conducted with any fairness—unless something else came up, my old Alabama scrape, for instance. They might find I never paid that debt. I took French leave of the Dry Tortugas, remember. A trial would unearth all those old offences against this delectable Government."

"It would; I never thought of that. Oh! how imprudent it was for you to come here, knowing the troops were scouring the country!"

"I wanted to see you once more."

"Then go—go, my friend. Promise to leave here this very night. Return to Texas. Promise me."

"I will. Do not agitate yourself on my account. If they turned that lane this moment I could escape—but *you!*" he broke off, struck by a sudden and startling thought. "*You* are here! If they come they must not find you here alone. And to find you with me! Oh! it is you who run the worst risk to-night. And I have exposed you to it! I thought only of seeing you again. I did not think once of the danger to you. I was selfishly thoughtless. Forgive me, and go at once. Good-by, my dearest; my good angel; God bless you!"

He dropped the hand he had pressed in his, and she turned to leave him.

Suddenly, before she could get beyond the circle of deep shadow, he caught her and drew her back.

"Look!" he whispered, hoarsely. "The cavalry! They are coming!"

There in the moonlight, at the head of the lane, she saw a party of horsemen riding down upon them. She uttered a faint cry of dismay; then she said, firmly:

"Lose no time; mount your horse; go! go!"

"And leave you? Never!"

"They will not arrest *me.*"

"You will be exposed to their insults, their coarse jests, their rough questions and comments. Curses on my selfishness for having brought this upon you!"

"Think of yourself. Never mind me. I am not afraid to face them; or I can hide."

"You can not. They will search everywhere."

Indeed, there was little place for concealment. The strip of land had once been partially cleared. The large trees were gone. There were clumps of bushes here and there. The fence of either field was very high, and within, the corn, stripped of its leaf-blades, afforded little concealment. Then the moon was shining brilliantly, and the fence and fields were in full view of the approaching soldiers. A noise to the right turned Hirne's eye in that direction. There, just coming into sight around a curve in the rear fence, was another party of soldiers, and it was probable that yet another detachment was approaching around the lower field. They had divided to make more sure of finding their prey. Hirne turned quickly to the trembling girl.

"There is but one way," he said, in a firm whisper. "I can not leave you here alone; they must not find you here with me; they will not follow us far in the swamp. Come."

His horse—a fine black, that had answered his whistle a moment ago with a low neigh—stood waiting for him, his ears quivering with eagerness. As Hirne spoke he lifted Zoe to a seat upon the powerful animal. He sprang into the saddle before her, and at a word and a touch of the spur the horse bounded off. It was but a few leaps to the deep shadow of the swamp, but the horsemen on the right saw him, and with a loud shout they gave chase. He felt a tremor run through the arm of the girl who clung to him ; he dreaded that she would swoon.

"Don't be frightened," he said, as they flew on. "They will soon quit the pursuit ; they are afraid of an ambush. Bend your head, that the limbs may not strike you."

On they rushed through the silent woods. There was no underbrush, only the great trees and their clasping vines. The horse, well used to the woods, avoided these without slackening the long, sweeping gallop which kept the pursuers out of sight. They came to a low, marshy place—the bed of a dried-up bayou, now a mass of mud, mantled with deceptive green mold.

"Here's something that will stop them if I don't mistake," cried Hirne. "This will bog a bird—I found out to-day—everywhere but at one spot."

He turned his horse suddenly to the right, rode down the boggy ravine a few rods, and then crossed it on a kind of causeway formed of "chunks" and logs, but so hidden by water-grass that it was not easily perceived even in the light of day. He kept on in his changed direction, the horse holding a steady course, as though he had a certain goal in view. Presently they heard cries behind them. Hirne checked his horse and listened. Loud exclamations, oaths, expressive of anger and disgust, came to their ears.

"They are floundering in a bog equal to that of Killarney," Hirne said, with his low laugh.

"They won't pass that Rubicon to-night, but we will ride on farther to make sure. I know of a hiding-place they'll not be apt to find."

On they went. An opening in the woods appeared before them : a waste field, its fence nearly gone, a deserted log-cabin, half hid by weeds, standing lonely and black-looking upon the bank of the bayou which formed the farther boundary of the field. Riding across the field, Hirne drew rein on the steep bank of bayou Vincey.

"They would never venture to cross this fierce current," he said. "I should not like to swim it myself; but if they come here they will think I have crossed, for, see, here underneath the bank, where these two great trees have fallen into the bayou and their torn-up roots are overrun by a mass of wild vines, there is a natural hiding-place—a kind of cave hollowed out in the bank by the current at high water and roofed over by the tree-roots, the matted vines, and the earth together. A man and a horse can ride in under those hanging vines and be securely hid. I will ride a little way down the bank so that the horse can not be seen by any one coming, and we will wait and listen. If they come, we will conceal ourselves under the ledge; but I imagine they will have enough to do to get out of the bog, and will be glad to go back empty-handed."

Moments passed while they waited anxiously, but no sound broke the silence save the ripple of the bayou and the swish of the willows that dipped in the stream.

Hirne turned his horse and rode up the bank again, saying:

"I am sure they have given up the chase and gone back, but I think it is safer to wait awhile before we return, and give them time to cross the river."

He rode up to the deserted cabin. It was overgrown with gourd-vines and wild morning-glories; a single old ash-tree stood guard over it; in the yard stray marigolds and bunches of catnip struggled with weeds and bushes.

"I staid here last night," said Hirne. "The owls hooted me to sleep. As I broiled my dried-beef supper on the moldy hearth the lizards woke and peeped at me curiously from the cracks, and the bats whizzed around me like insulted witches."

Zoe knew the place well. She had gathered dewberries in the waste field last spring. It was a place cleared and cultivated, but deserted when the overflow of back-lands of a year or two ago had driven the settlers in the swamps from their inundated homes.

Hirne had spoken gayly to reassure Zoe; it had pained him so to hear the loud beating of her heart, and to feel how she trembled.

"Will you let me help you down, and rest here a moment on the porch?" he asked.

She faintly assented, and he lifted her gently to the floor and seated her upon a bench that was on the porch. At the same instant a harsh cry made her start with a scream. A great owl flew out of the big ash-tree and sailed across the bayou. The fright, slight compared to what she had passed through, was the final experience needed to overthrow her tottering self-control. She had borne up well; now she gave way. She covered her face with her hands and sobbed.

Hirne threw himself at her feet.

"For God's sake, don't distress yourself, Miss Zoe! All will be well. No harm shall come to you. It can not be an hour past midnight. In an hour more you shall be safe in your own room. I wish to heaven you had not left it! It was selfish, cruel in me to put this trial upon you. I see it now. I did not then. I fought with the mad craving to see you and have you near me for the last time. My dearest, do not fret yourself so. You will be ill. Forgive me, say you forgive me."

The sight of his distress quieted her.

"I have nothing to forgive," she said. "We could not foresee that the soldiers would come."

"And you will not hate me for this?"

"I could never hate you," she said; then, looking up

and smiling, though her wet cheeks and lashes glistened in the moon-rays, " never, unless you do some wicked, revengeful thing, and that you have promised never to do."

" Never. That is a little thing to do for you. Only to restrain my own wild will that never was curbed enough. Do you know I have never thrown a card or tasted liquor since that night I won Vincent's money, not knowing he was your brother—that night when I bore you from the burning boat, and held your chilled form in my arms. I shall never forget that day. It was the turning-point in my life. I have been a different being since then. My old pursuits give me no pleasure. To rove here and there seeking chances to revenge my wrongs has lost the feverish charm it had. Instead, I have a thirst to be loved. Oh ! what a thirst ! like a fire consuming my heart ; and it will never be satisfied."

" It will. You will love some good woman, and be loved by her."

" No. I shall never love any woman but you ; never, my dearest. I must try to make that little child love me as a father, and be satisfied. I am glad her eyes are dark like yours. She says her prayers at night. I will ask her to pray for you, my guardian angel, if only that I may hear your name."

Zoe made no answer. They sat near each other ; the moonlight was on her face, and one hand, lily white, drooped at her side. It tempted him, but he did not touch it. The Indian summer night was about them, with its faint fragrance and mystical beauty. The moon rode high ; the shadows hardly stirred ; the cypress-trees stood tall and solemn upon the banks between which the bayou flowed and eddied with low gurgling. That sound and the chirp of the night insects in the dewy grass kept the silence here in the swamp from being oppressive.

In spite of her anxiety and self-reproach, the situation held a spell for Zoe. To sit here in the depth of the autumn wood, with the man she loved and who loved her so well, had a charm of wild sweetness like that of a flower gathered from the brink of a precipice. She had no fear in being alone with Hirne. Impetuous, passionate as he was, she knew she could trust perfectly in his honor, in his love, that, with all its unconventional fervor, was of that fine, poetic quality that would not sully its object even in thought. He would have died rather than *startle* the modesty of the woman he loved. This moment was sweet to him, but he put aside the temptation to prolong its sweetness.

"I think we will be safe now in going back," he said.

He would put her in the saddle and walk beside her. "I like it better," he said. "I am tired of riding. I am a capital walker. Few horses can beat me." Which was no vain boast.

Cautiously, and with little noise, they retraced their way through the silent woods. Hirne, in low tones, talked cheerfully to keep up Zoe's spirits. Walking at her side, his tall figure, his careless hair, his free step, giving him a Robin Hood look; watchful of her comfort, careful the boughs should not incommode her, making merry over small mishaps and saying picturesque things in his quaint way, half jocular, half earnest, he made the way seem so short that she looked around amazed when they came out into the open strip of woods and saw the pecan-tree and the fields beyond, and the house in its tree shadows, all lying quiet and silent in the moonlight.

"No sight or sound of the troops," Hirne said. "Will you not ride to the end of the lane before dismounting? Mort will come back to me."

But this she would not do. It might draw notice to

him. She preferred to walk from the pecan-tree. So under the shadow he helped her from the horse. Her hands were cold, for the latter hours of the October night were touched with chill, and the malarial night air, the anxiety and fatigue, sent premonitory shivers through her frame. Her quick-sighted lover noted it as he helped her to alight.

"Your hands are almost as cold as they were that night I held them to my breast to warm them," he said. "If you should be ill from this night's experience I will never forgive myself. I shall for ever think with self-rebuke of the trial I have brought on you to-night. Your tender heart made you listen to my selfish prayer. Then, I was mean enough to play upon your fears for me."

"You must not talk so. I do not regret having seen you. My only regret is the danger you exposed yourself to."

"That is nothing—nothing to having made you pale and unhappy, and on the night before your wedding. I have come like a death's head at your feast of joy to make your sweet cheeks shed their roses. Don't think too hard of me. I did not mean it. I meant to have looked at you unseen and gone away, but when I saw *him* sitting by you, so proud and happy, and you smiling in his face, I thought bitterly : 'She might spare me one hour, to have her near me, to look at and listen to her for the last time—one hour from that man who is going to have her all her sweet life.' It seemed a small thing then for you. I feel now that it was a sacrifice I ought never to have asked."

"I do not feel it so since I have received your promise to quit a life of roving and violence and live in peace. And you have promised, too, to leave here, and not to come back till the troops have left Cohatchie. Have you not ?"

"Yes, I will go ; I will not try to see you again until— I have become resigned to thinking of you as another man's wife. Now I am not resigned. Don't shed a tear over *me*, my sweetest; I will get the better of this madness, and some day I will bring my little ward to see the fair woman she has heard me call my good angel. Good-by."

He pressed her hands between his own, repressing the passion whose thrill she could feel in that lingering clasp. A tear fell from his eyes upon her hand. She, too, was weeping as she turned away.

He leaned his arm on his faithful horse and watched her until her dark-robed form was lost in the silvery dusk of the night. Then, sighing heavily, he mounted and rode back into the woods. He was full of regret for the danger he had exposed her to, the pain of sympathy he had cost her. He did not dream the full extent of her trial to-night; he did not dream that she loved him. Pity for him, the sympathy of a womanly heart—this was all he thought she felt for him. He could not know that she, too, had struggled to preserve her self-control—that duty and honor had fought with the wild longing to speak words that would have made him happy; to say, "I love you. You are more to me than the man I was going to marry. I will fly with you to the wilds of Texas—anywhere to be with you."

She thanked God that strength had been given her to keep back this revelation; yet how happy it would have made him! She let herself fancy for a moment what a light would have leaped into those deep-set, wistful eyes.

She felt he had spoken truly. Her love could help him to be a good and useful man. Those strong energies, that ill-fortune had swerved from the right, she could help turn into worthy channels. Her love would be rest to him, and for herself, she felt that one year with Hirne in the Texas wilderness would be richer in happiness than an existence spent in the gay city with Royal West.

Yet she owed allegiance to Royal West. She must marry him. He had waited so long, so faithfully, for the fulfillment of her promise. He was here to marry her on the morrow. There was no honorable escape. To play him false at this late hour would be basest cruelty. No, she must marry him ; she must put out of her mind for ever the image of the man she had just parted with.

With these thoughts coursing through her brain she sat for an hour after she had softly entered her room. Day was streaking the east when she at last undressed and lay down upon her bed. She drew the coverlet about her. She was hot and shivering by turns; wild thrills ran through her brain and body—symptoms premonitory of fever. That hour of miserable watching had completed the work half done by the anxiety and terror of the night and the malarial breath of the beautiful but baleful swamp.

CHAPTER XXXVI.

Zoe's marriage day opened fair. A blue mist clung to the distant landscape, and a soft haze diffused itself through the atmosphere and chastened the splendors of the sun. The household at the Vincent cottage were early astir. Little Mrs. Hugh was in her pantry inspecting the bride's cake, about whose frosting she had been doubtful. Kate, fresh as a lily in her pretty blue morning dress, was up not long after sunrise and tapped at Zoe's door, calling out :

" Wake, laggard ! "

There was no answer, and the girl thought she heard a moan within. She opened the door in haste. There lay the bride-elect, her cheeks and lips carmine, her eyes glassy bright, turning with the vacant stare of unconsciousness upon her frightened friend.

A physician was sent for in haste ; he pronounced her illness to be malarial fever. For days she was unconscious, part of the time lying in a stupor, but often delirious. None guessed the immediate cause of her illness. Fortunately, her going and coming the night before had not been seen. When the soldiers surrounded and searched the house to find the escaped prisoner, they had been informed was lurking about the premises, they had been less thorough in ransacking than usual, owing to the presence of Roy and Lareau, whom the officer in command had known in New Orleans. The rooms of the young ladies were not molested, and Zoe's absence was not discovered. Immediately after searching the house and grounds they had ridden down the lane, having been told by a negro that, at dusk, he had seen a big black horse fastened under the pecan by a Texas hair lariat. The glimpse the soldiers had of the flying form of Hirne and his horse before the friendly shadows of the swamp received them was not sufficient to show them the female form beside him. So Zoe's night adventure was known to none but herself and Hirne. Her wild talk about being pursued through the woods, leaping fallen logs and ravines on horseback, riding down bayous to dark hiding-places, and her piteous appeals of "Do not leave me, take me with you," were regarded as incoherent ravings. And when, holding fast to Roy's hand and looking into his face, she said : "I love you ; I can't bear for you to leave me for ever ; I will go with you anywhere," he answered, tenderly, with tears in his eyes, " My darling, I will not leave you," and turning to Hugh, said, " You see she is not altogether out of her mind ; she knows me, and begs me not to leave her."

He and Kate were her faithful nurses, and when the
16

crisis was past she opened her conscious eyes upon their relieved and smiling faces. But she gathered strength slowly, and before she was well enough to walk about the room Roy was obliged to return to the city. A letter from his partner reminded him that a highly important case demanded his attention. His absence would cause him to suffer in his professional reputation as well as his purse. Zoe urged him to go at once. She was out of danger, and improving daily. It was at last decided that he should go. He had pressed her to let the marriage take place before he went. The day fixed for his departure he came in to see her, and found her sitting up for the first time. Her delicately featured face, with its dark penciled brows and exquisite outlines of chin and cheek, showed white as carven ivory in the setting of violet-purple dressing gown. Kate's deft hands had braided her hair into two loose, girlish plaits that hung down her shoulders.

"You look so sweet this morning!" Roy said as he lifted one of the little hands to his lips. "Are you sure you will not retract your decision of yesterday? Zoe, don't you think it would be better for us to be married before I go away? I would not feel so bad at leaving you then. Let the ceremony take place here, with only Kate and Hugh and his wife present, and you in that pretty purple gown in which you look like a pansy, my love?"

She shook her head, trying to laugh, as she said: "You know it is bad luck to marry a bride on her sick-bed, Roy."

"Bother such old woman's signs! Though I am growing almost superstitious about this marriage. It has been delayed so often by untoward circumstances, and, forgive me, by your caprice, my own, until it seems it is fated never to be. Do you intend making me a second Jacob, my dark-eyed Rachel?"

"Not so bad as that, Roy; listen to me. Let me get

well and look a little more like a bride ; then when Hugh
goes down with his cotton I will go with him, and—"

"And we will be married at once, quietly at church,
and will go on to Cuba to receive your father's blessing,
then from there to New York, Niagara, and the Lakes—the
stereotyped bridal tour—and back to New Orleans in time to
eat mother's Christmas turkey at our unfailing family reunion.   Well, that programme will do, my darling, second
best to the one I first proposed—that of marrying right
now, which I still think best, for I remember that 'there's
often a slip 'twixt the cup and the lip,' and my cup has so
often been put aside that I am naturally impatient."

Zoe did not encourage him to dwell upon this view of
the matter.   She said, as cheerily as she could :

"Perhaps we will have Kate's company in the trip you
have mapped out.   Mr. Lareau wants their marriage to
take place in a month or two."

"So they are really going to marry ; and that little co-
quette has got captured at last !   I was glad to see that she
laid aside her airs in Lareau's company.   He's too good a
fellow to be blown about by the capricious breath of a flirt.
He has interests in Cuba, so it is likely enough he would be
of our party."

It was decided that Zoe should go down to the city with
her brother and be married there in church, and after this
point was settled, Roy sat talking till Kate declared her
patient needed a rest after his "infliction of tongue," and
would not be satisfied till she had put her in bed and seen
her smiling at them from the pillows, sweetly, but with
eyes that seemed to have much ado to hold back their tears.
They flowed freely when she was alone.

"Oh ! how mean and ungrateful I am !" she said to herself, "to deceive him so ; to marry him loving another
man, thinking always of that other one, as I can not help

doing. But I told him once, and he said it was a romantic fancy I would get over. I have not gotten over it, and now I shrink from speaking of it again, since I have renewed my promise, and have come so near marrying him that it almost seems that I am his wife. Oh! how will it end, I wonder? It can not go on like this; I should feel guilty and wretched all the time. If marriage does not cure me, I shall despair. They say that, once married, a woman is sure to love her husband, provided he is at all lovable; Roy is kind, and I am truly attached to him; I thought I loved him until I met Hirne; I have caused him so much annoyance and trouble; I have disconcerted his plans so often by putting off this marriage, and now I am again begging for delay. But it must be the last time. I have the best of excuses now; I am really too ill to be excited by a marriage ceremony. As soon as I recover strength I will go down with Hugh and—oh! I wish Roy *would* be happy and pleased with me to let things stay as they are."

Royal returned to the city, and the next week Kate followed him. She had preparations to make for her own marriage. The days went by, Zoe recovered her health, but she was so grave that Mrs. Hugh grieved over her lack of spirits, and the children missed their romps with their pretty and agile aunty. She heard nothing of Hirne. True to his promise, he had gone away. The troops were still quartered in Cohatchie, greatly to the annoyance of the town and the disappointment of the party who had hoped to carry the election, now near at hand. They had expected the troops would be withdrawn, and the men who had been arrested would be released on their giving bond to appear when their trial was held. Alver nominated his ticket in prison, and still hoped to be out in time to rally his friends to the polls. He was disappointed; the troops remained after they had made all the arrests they seemed able or anxious to make, and when the election came their presence defeated the hopes of Alver. Men from the surrounding neighborhood would not come in to vote for fear of being arrested, while the negroes and the poorer whites from the "Hills," who were known as Witchell's friends, came to a man, and many, who had been won over to Alver's cause by his eloquence and energy, now voted with the other side through fear or policy, or because the presence of the dashing and powerful cavalry influenced their ignorant imaginations.

When the election came, the prisoners, strongly guarded, went to the polls and voted, and returned to prison. But their presence and their efforts on the election ground availed nothing. Their ticket was defeated.

Witchell was reëlected, but his success gave him no pleasure beyond a fierce feeling of triumph over these people who had shown themselves so determinedly opposed to him. His feelings toward them, which had never been bitter before, were now full of revenge. He seemed to see in every man the slayer of his brother.

To add to his bitterness there was the disappointment he felt in the action of the Government in regard to the murderers of his friends. He had looked for and demanded summary punishment, and he had met with delay and indefiniteness. He feared that the action of the Government upon the case would amount to nothing after all, and it was galling to him to know that the reason was because the party in power, conscious of the number of incompetent and unworthy men it had put in office through the South, was afraid to prosecute inquiries lest blacker developments should be brought to light to the damage of the party. "Stir not a dung-hill," says a coarse old proverb.

Evil reacts on itself. In this case evil had begotten

evil which it was afraid to punish, lest its own wickedness should be more fully exposed. The license permitted to those who administered rule at the South had tempted Marshall Witchell's ambition and love of gain, and the people had pushed their protest against his exactions to the deplorable extreme of mob and murder.

Nor did the wave of evil stop here. A spirit of strife was now engendered in the town that had been the scene of the riot. Suspicion and dissension poisoned social intercourse. Men who had been friends now looked upon each other as traitors or spies; the little community was broken into cliques, each of which suspected the other of intriguing against it.

It was now known that the prisoners would be tried in New Orleans by commissioners appointed by the Government. Meantime the actual leaders of the mob of lynchers had never been captured, though large rewards were offered for their arrest. Yet two of them, Cobb and Captain Dick (who was no other than Lanier), were in hiding not far from Cohatchie, and occasionally, in different disguises, they would slip into the town or dash in recklessly past the guard on dark nights, speak to their friends, throw letters, and receive packages of eatables or papers, and escape by outrunning and baffling their pursuers. Lanier had managed to obtain possession of the uniform of a United States soldier, and in this dress he had more than once rode into town, looked around, and got away without being found out. He had his eye upon Witchell, and he watched for an opportunity to "pick him off," as he said, without exposing himself to capture. But no such opportunity presented itself. Witchell kept within the protection of the troops. For the first time in his life he was cautious. "They shall not have the pleasure of killing me yet," he said, "not till I have wrought my will upon them." La-

nier had stealthy glimpses of him sometimes as he rode
about with officers of the cavalry, his figure erect, his eye
still cold and keen, his pride apparently unchecked, his
prosperity undiminished. None knew of the disappointed
feeling that gnawed in secret on his heart.

"Curse him!" muttered Lanier, "I'll be even with him
yet. All the while I was away something kept telling me
to come back and kill him—the villain that stole my love
from me and made me a vagabond. I came at last to find
her dead, no doubt through him, and to find revenge possible to me now, for the people will protect me in what I
may do to him. I've killed one of the brood, but that only
whets my appetite. I'll never rest till I've put him out of
the world."

He would utter some of these savage threats to Cobb as
the two broiled their game over the camp fire in their
hiding-place—an out-of-the-way nook in the heart of a
swamp back of Clear Lake—a nook surrounded by bayous
(with mud, alligators, and quicksand), whose fordable
places were known only to the initiated. Cobb encouraged
his ferocity and laughed, well pleased. He himself was
growing more irritated and impatient every day. His hope
of office had proved a delusion, and he was unable to
carry away the prize for which he had worked in such dark
ways—the woman who had so long been the object of his
fierce passion, whom he would have seized and carried off,
only he stood in awe of her strong will, and feared to make
her hate him. He did not know she already hated him,
and only hid her feelings lest she should excite him to desperation, and make him betray her secret. He was eager
to hold her to her promise that she would go away with
him if he did the work she required. He had done the
work—more than she had named at first; it was no fault of
his if it had failed of its expected result. But now she

showed no inclination to fulfill her promise. The presence of the troops gave him little opportunity to urge it upon her. In his stealthy or flying trips into town he could barely get a glimpse at or a word with her, hardly ever in private, and she refused to meet him in the woods for the sake of his safety, she said, as well as her own reputation. She, at least, dreaded the time when the withdrawal of the troops would put her in his power, and give him the opportunity to force her to close her bargain with him—the ex-overseer, the murderer of her husband, the man she loathed more every day as she grew to care more passionately for Alver. She showed herself womanly in this, at least, that she did not forsake Alver after his failure. She attached herself all the more closely to him and to his cause. She sought to console and cheer him, refusing to see how such consolation from her seemed to irritate and madden him.

"This failure is nothing," she said as she arranged in a jar on his table the flowers his little girl had brought to the prison for him. "This defeat is only the stepping-stone to success in future. These very troops who have caused your failure here will help you in the end. Already their arrogance and impositions disgust the common people, and even the negroes who are the Radical strength. Next time your success will be sure. And long before next election, Witchell's place will be vacant. Only the troops protect him now. When they are withdrawn he will come here sometime to see after his interests, for he is daring enough, and whenever he comes he will be killed."

"Talk no more to me of killing, for God's sake! I am sick of bloodshed," he exclaimed, turning away with a gesture of such distaste for her words and for her that she grew pale. She controlled herself, saying only in a tone of gentle reproach:

"I merely wanted to speak of how near you might be,

in spite of this failure, to the end you have been working for."

"I had better make sure of my neck or my liberty before I begin to think again of political honors," he said, with a sneer. "I have this trial before me, and, perhaps, a gallows or a State-prison. The commissioners appointed to try us are now in the city. We go down Thursday on the Alma."

It was the steamboat in which Zoe and her brother were going to the city. Thursday night Zoe sat opposite the chief prisoner at the tea-table. Very little like a prisoner he looked. His clear-cut face was paler and thinner than it had been before, and a shade of care, and of something darker and more restless than care, was in his eyes; but his old high-bred politeness, dashed with haughtiness, still distinguished his manners; his smile had its old charm, and his voice its tone of command. Zoe and her brother listened to him talk to a group of men that gathered around him after supper. He was wary and reticent at first, but presently something was said that touched his quick spirit, and his eye flashed and his tones rang out rapid and imperious.

"The commissioners will get the better of him," said Hugh to his sister. "He is too proud, and not wily enough to stand their cross-examination. He will betray himself. The only hope is that they will not care to press the investigation far just now. If it was before instead of just after a Presidential and other important elections, no pains would be spared to make large electioneering capital out of it; but the battle has been won, and it is not worth while working this up. It could not be put to much use just now."

Affairs of his own had called Hugh to town several days earlier than he had intended. The change in the time of starting was rather suddenly decided upon, and Zoe had not written to Roy to apprise him of it. He was not there to meet them, therefore, when the boat steamed into the harbor through the anchored vessels of all kinds and countries, their masts and chimneys reddened by the setting sun. Taking a carriage, Hugh and his sister drove to the house of Dr. Melvin, whose wife—a handsome society lady—was Zoe's cousin, and gave her a cordial welcome. Hugh, preferring the freedom of the hotel, went to take possession of his old room at the St. Charles. Mrs. Melvin carried Zoe to her room, lit the wax candles on the toilet table, and examined her critically.

"You are paler than you were last spring; but brides should be a little pale, and you are pretty as a white camellia. Take a bath and a cup of tea, and then get yourself into full dress, ready for going out. You are fortunate in having come this evening. It is an opera night, and we have a new tenor who is perfectly ravishing."

"That is tempting after months of starvation in music, but—ought I not to let Roy know I am here, and see him to-night?"

"To-morrow will do as well. I am sure he will be at the theatre to-night. He was there last evening in his partner's, Judge Taylor's, box, with the Judge's daughter Florence. She has been back from boarding-school only a few weeks, and is very pretty. *Chere,* I would give Royal a lecture; he was devoted to Miss Taylor."

"Was he?" smiled Zoe, absently, as she let fall the dark mass of her hair.

"Yes, and the Taylor family would be delighted to make a match between them. You are a thousand times lovelier than Florence—what hair you have!—but these young *débutantes* are irresistible to men somehow. *We* can only see bread-and-butter crudeness, or vanity that has not the art to hide itself. Make yourself splendid, Zoe ; I will send Lousette to help you. She will take delight in handling this lovely hair again."

Zoe had handsome dresses, for she had a taste for elegance, and had some means of her own ; besides, her father and brother had been liberal in the matter of her trousseau. She laid out some rich silks, trimmed profusely with Spanish laces—sent by her father from Cuba—before she decided to wear something that would make her least conspicuous —a black silk, relieved by delicate lace with pearl and coral jewelry, and a little pearl-gray hat and plume. Thus dressed, she accompanied Dr. and Mrs. Melvin to the opera. There was a crowd, but her party occupied reserved seats in a position that enabled them to see without themselves being conspicuous.

"There is Roy now, in the box with Miss Taylor," whispered Mrs. Melvin as soon as she had swept the room with her lorgnette.

Zoe turned her head and saw him seated by a pretty, fresh-looking girl in white. She held herself in readiness to catch his eye, and smile at his stare of surprise and pleasure, but he did not look in her direction. He was occupied with his partner, fanning her, bending to talk to her or to listen when she spoke. Zoe changed her mind. She pulled a corner of her light, pearl-tinted veil so as to shade her face, and watched those two in the lace-curtained box.

Before the ravishing tenor had bowed over his final ovation of flowers she had made a discovery. She saw that Roy loved this fresh young school-girl, and that the admiration was mutual. The girl, unconsciously it might be, was fascinated by her father's handsome young partner. Roy's attentions to her were by no means so exigeant as to attract notice ; Zoe even saw tokens of self-restraint on his part, but her quick eye and her woman's intuition showed her a dozen subtile indications of love.

After the first shock of surprise and mortified vanity there came a feeling of relief. The marriage might be annulled and no wrong done to Roy or to her own honor. He had not seen, or seeing had not recognized, her under that light gauze, and she would not permit Mrs. Melvin to make any sign to draw his notice to her.

"To-morrow will be quite soon enough," she said. "I will send him a note to-morrow."

Mrs. Melvin, who secretly thought Zoe had a right to be a bit jealous, was surprised at her gay spirits that night. After the opera she sang and talked for Dr. Melvin, who was a charming, gray-haired old gentleman, twenty years older than his wife, and so gallantly devoted to Zoe that Mrs. Melvin declared he had no eyes for any one else when she was by.

Before Zoe could send her note next morning Roy was at the door. He had met Hugh on the street, and came full of reproaches that she had not let him know of her arrival the evening before. Through all his fluency of talk Zoe detected the nervous embarrassment he tried to hide. She herself was cool and smiling, and, with perfect self-possession and easy flow of question and comment, she did her best to restore his composure. He did not know that she had been at the opera the night before, and she made no allusion to it. He had brought her a basket of grapes, on the top of which lay a roll of music—a new waltz, he said ; and Zoe, in the lull of the conversation, sat down and tried a few bars. Then she said :

"It is a wonder you did not bring a song; you always do. I have not forgotten your partiality for simple melodies, and have fitted one, for you especially, to a little poem you have read."

She struck a few chords and sang a few verses of "Mrs. Proctor's Woman's Question":

> "Before I trust my fate to thee,
>   Or place my hand in thine,
> Before I let thy future give
>   Color and form to mine,
> Before I peril all for thee,
> Question thy soul to-day for me."

Glancing at him now and then as she sang, she saw how restless the song with its searching questions, and her own earnest tones, made him. His color fluctuated, and at last, as if unable to bear the probe upon his feelings, he rose and walked the room. Her eye arrested him and drew him to her as she sang one special verse. She looked at him steadily, and it was a question, heart to heart, direct as if spoken, and more solemn and impressive, when she sang:

> "Is there within thy heart a need
>   That mine can not fulfill?
> One chord that any other hand
>   Could better wake or still?
> Speak now, lest at some future day
> My whole life wither and decay."

The fresh color that was natural to him was gone out of his face when she had finished. He looked troubled and conscience-stricken. He walked aimlessly about the room, and then came and stood by her and looked at her without speaking.

"There is something you want to tell me; what is it?" she asked, looking up and smiling.

He was very grave. "No," he said, "there is nothing I *want* to tell you."

"Then there is something you do not want to tell me, but feel that you ought. I can guess what it is."

"You can not guess," he said, hoarsely.

"Then there *is* something."

"Nothing except—except that I liked your song. Your voice has improved."

"Thank you. But you are not candid. There *is* something else, and I have guessed it. You love Miss Taylor—your partner's daughter."

He started from his seat.

"Who said so? Who has dared to tell you such a thing?"

"No one. I saw it myself. I was at the opera last night, and I watched you unseen. I saw as plainly, as if his heart had been bared to me, that the man who was betrothed to me, whom I came here to marry, loved another."

"O Zoe! I had hoped—I mean you must not think such a thing. It is absurd."

"It is true."

"And you tell me so with such kind looks! Though you must feel that I am a base wretch without truth or honor. But, Zoe, I swear I never dreamed of wronging you. This came on me unlooked for. I never thought there was danger until the mischief was well begun. I went with Florence because her father asked it. He never goes into society, likes his comfort at home when he is not engaged with his business, and he requested me to attend his young daughter. I found her attractive from the first. I was with her often; she knew scarcely any one, and she clung to me in a timid, girlish way. She liked me—"

"She loves you," Zoe interrupted.

"I believe she does," he groaned. "Yet I told her of my engagement to you. I have never said a word of love to her. God knows I had no intention of playing the villain. I tried to keep away from her, but her father would send for me, and seemed hurt if I did not come as I had been in the habit of coming while she was at school. For a long time I deceived myself into the belief that it was mere friendly interest I felt in Florence; I thought so until a few nights ago, and then— But no matter; Zoe, can you forgive me? After all, you are partly to blame. Those miserable, long engagements! they never end well. You *would* put off our marriage."

"I am glad I did."

"Glad! My God! Glad that I have been tempted to become unworthy of your confidence! But I will deserve it better in future. Bear with me, Zoe—my love, my *only* love. Yes, it shall be. I will get the better of this folly. You shall have no fault to find with me when we are married, dear. I will be worthy of your true heart."

"True? You forget that I once confessed a similar folly to you."

"When? Ah! that was only a passing fancy, a romantic dream."

"It was a lasting reality. It has lived in my heart ever since."

"Zoe?"

"Yes, my friend. You will not blame me now for saying I am glad this marriage was put off. Fate has had a hand in it. I love another better than I do you. I had trusted to marriage to conquer it. I could not bear to wound you by breaking a promise you had waited so long and faithfully for me to fulfill. Now I know I shall do you no harm by refusing to marry you. And so I do refuse you—now."

"But, Zoe, I can not permit— Are you sure—"

"I am sure I will not marry you; sure it does not break my heart to give you up; sure another girl would be happier as your wife than I would be; sure you will be happier with that one than with me, and sure that we shall yet have a wedding, although I now give you back your ring—a wedding with a fairer and more loving bride than I, who has my heartiest good wishes for her happiness, and whom I hope to know, and am sure that I shall love."

She never looked prettier in her life than when she stood before him delivering this little speech, with her black eyes sparkling roguishly, a flush on her cheek, and the little silky rings of hair trembling on her forehead. She was dressed with care; she was willing to give up her lover; but, with a pardonable womanly weakness, she wanted to make him feel what he had lost, and regret being given up just a little. He did feel the value of what he had lost. He thought as he looked at her that Florence Taylor could never be such a woman, and that he would always miss in her that variety, that quick sympathy, and that *spirituelle* charm which had kept him at Zoe's feet so long. But it was too late to encourage any such regret. Confessions had been made upon both sides that would rise up awkwardly at the marriage altar. He looked at her with a moment's longing. How adorable she seemed, now that she was not his any longer! He would get over this in a little while—when he met Florence again—but now he felt, most unreasonably, a jealous pang.

" And you— ? " he said.

" I shall probably never marry—never, certainly, unless I meet again the hero of my 'romantic dream,' as you call it."

" Who is he? I do not believe he is worthy of you. Where is he ? "

" I do not know. I never may see him again. But I will not anticipate evil. Do you know we have been talking nearly three hours ? " (consulting her tiny watch) " and I must dress to go on Canal Street with Cousin Clara. Will Kate come to see me this afternoon ? "

"Yes. She is in Carrollton visiting Maude Blake. I have sent for her. Zoe, what will Kate think, what will all our friends think, of our marriage being broken off?"

"Tell them the truth—that it is broken off by mutual consent. It may excite wonder and a little gossip; but what is that to a marriage in which our hearts do not wholly enter? And, Roy, go and tell Miss Florence that you are free and that you love her."

CHAPTER XXXVIII.

KATE came to see Zoe in the afternoon, but there was other company, and the two girls had no opportunity for a word in private.

"I will call round this evening with Roy," Kate said as she was going away.

"Come to tea," Mrs. Melvin urged, not caring to add that she had planned a kind of family party, having invited Hugh and Winter Lareau, whom she met on the street, to come and partake of oysters and champagne. Later in the afternoon she invited another person, no other than little Florence Taylor herself, not as properly belonging to the family party, but for a purpose of her own. Quite unexpectedly, Miss Florence called just before sunset, sending her card to Zoe, who received her cordially and did her best to put her visitor at ease. "She was curious to see Roy's betrothed," thought imaginative Mrs. Melvin, and she was sure it was jealousy that made the girl watch the face and follow the movements of the beautiful woman with such intentness.

Zoe saw otherwise. She pitied Florence's embarrassment, she saw dejection in her intent look, and she felt the quiver of hopelessness in the girl's voice when, taking Zoe's offered hand at parting and looking into her face, she said :

"Your picture is like you, only you are much lovelier. No wonder Mr. West loves you so."

"Have you seen Royal to-day ?" Zoe asked.

"Yes ; he dined with us. He had promised several days ago. This is my father's birthday."

"And did he tell you anything—anything *very* particular ?" Zoe asked, looking at her and holding the little gloved hand between her warm palms.

"He told me you had come and he had seen you."

"Nothing else ?"

She shook her head.

"He talked but little ; he said he was not well."

"There is something more that he ought to have told you—that he will tell you," Zoe said, smiling caressingly into the wondering young face.

She would have said more, so sorry was she to see that fair face clouded with despondency, but Mrs. Melvin came in at this moment with her invitation for Florence to come to tea.

"There will only be two or three friends," she said. "Mr. Larcau, Royal West, and his sister. Zoe and her brother are only home folks."

The girl hesitated. She knew it would give her pain to see Royal's devotion to this lovely lady, but the human heart, especially the heart of the young, has a perverse desire to inflict pain on itself. Then she could not help wishing to see the betrothed pair together, and to watch Roy's manner to the lady of his love. *Could* his looks be much more tender than some he had bestowed upon her ?

"I will come, Mrs. Melvin," she said, "if I can get any one to accompany me. My father never goes out, you know."

"I'll send my Doctor," Mrs. Melvin said, gayly, "and a handsomer beau can not be found in the city."

Florence laughed and thanked her, and so the question was settled. There was a spice of malice in Mrs. Melvin's motives for this cordial invitation. She was Zoe's devoted adherent, and resented in her behalf the attentions Royal had lately paid to Miss Taylor. "He looked glum this morning when he came to see Zoe," she thought. "The new face has something to do with it. Like most men, he is a ninny over every fresh, new face. Can't he compare these two and see how superior my Zoe is to the other? He shall have an opportunity to make the comparison to-night. Mr. Lareau is a fine singer, and the Doctor is a splendid conversationalist. He will draw Zoe out into talking as she *can* talk, and she and Winter will sing together, and Miss Florence, who neither sings nor talks well, will be eclipsed so far that Roy West will see what a simpleton he is to waste a thought upon her when such a girl as Zoe has condescended to love him."

They all came. Zoe was radiant, and contributed greatly to the pleasure of the evening by her tact in amusing people and making them feel pleased with themselves. But she set herself quietly against being "*drawn out*" in order to overshadow Miss Taylor. She was very attentive to Florence; took pains to lead her into conversation and make her appear well. Roy had not expected to meet Florence here; had not prepared himself to be in the room at the same time with the woman he was expected to marry and the girl who had stolen into his heart, and to whom he felt his manner had been over-tender for a preëngaged man. He was in a dilemma. He half believed Zoe would retract what she had said, that she had been prompted by pride and jealous pique to break off with him as she had done. He thought this lover of the "romantic dream" a myth, or a bygone delusion brought up now to make him believe she was not hurt by his unfaithfulness. He had adroitly sounded Hugh on the subject, and found that he knew nothing of any mysterious lover of his sister. He was not fully prepared to give Zoe up. Her attractions had never seemed so great to him as now. What a pride a man would feel in having such a handsome creature at the head of his establishment! And then if the marriage was broken off, it would create gossip, and he had a proud man's dislike to have his affairs talked about. Yet dear little Florence! how sweet and loving she was! Zoe understood pretty much what was passing in his mind, and she determined to put an end to his indecision. She would take the initiative herself, and let it be known that the marriage was not to be.

An opportunity presented itself. Hugh was describing an elaborately designed piece of silver-plate that Larcau had ordered as a gift to some friends—a fruit-dish—the design a chariot drawn by doves and ornamented with wreaths of myrtle and grape.

"A wedding present, of course, and we can guess for whom intended," Mrs. Melvin said, looking from Zoe to Royal.

"And when is it to be presented, may we ask?" questioned Dr. Melvin, taking off his gold-rimmed spectacles and smiling benevolently around. "We are all in the family, as it were, and take a family interest in our two young friends here; may we not know when the happy day is to be, Royal?"

Roy colored and looked confused.

"I refer you to the lady, sir," he said. "I shall abide by her decision."

"Why, is it not yet decided? Zoe, are you another 'Sallie of the Valley,' who had

" ' So great a mind
It took a long time making up ? ' "

"Yes, it is decided," Zoe said, leaning slightly forward, her elbow resting upon a stand bearing a vase of cut flowers. Her cheeks had flushed, but her mouth, though almost smiling, expressed firmness ; her look was clear and earnest. "It is decided that it is not to be at all."

She waited until the exclamations of surprise had subsided, and continued : "It is not to be at all. Such is the mutual and amicable agreement. Both of us discovered at last that a friendship, warm and true though it was, was hardly the basis a marriage ought to be built upon. It was better to have found it out before than after the irrevocable vows had passed ; was it not ?"

"Zoe, you are not in earnest, surely ?" came indignantly from Kate, while Hugh stared at his sister in speechless amazement.

"Never more so. Come, my friend," turning to Roy,

" ' We must confirm this doubting maid.'

Is it not so that by mutual consent and in all amity we have set aside our proposed partnership and agreed to remain only friends ?"

She went up to him and held out her hand as she spoke. He took it, got up, and stood by her. "It is," he said.

Before he spoke his eye had fallen on Florence, had met her eager, wistful eyes looking at him from a face white as marble, and leant forward in her unconscious intentness. When he said "It is," she drew her breath quickly with a little convulsive exclamation. Then recollecting herself, and fearing she had betrayed her secret, she colored crimson and buried her face in her hands. Zoe went up to her and kissed her on the forehead. Dr. Melvin was on his feet making a playful little speech to the effect that he was greatly relieved to find his "queen rose of the rose-bud garden of girls" was not going to be plucked by the ruthless hand of Hymen. He had long had his eye upon Miss Zoe as a second partner, in case Mrs. M.——"—nodding his iron-gray head over to his wife—"should accommodatingly leave him a fascinating young widower. He congratulated the pair on their moral courage and good sense in drawing back even at the altar's foot, he might say, when they became convinced that a marriage would not promote their happiness.

Then he opened a bottle of champagne on the center-table by him, and proposed the health and prosperity of the two who had dissolved partnership.

"O Zoe! how could you ?" asked Kate, reproachfully, when she could get a moment apart with her friend.

"He did not love me, Kate; he loved another. Could you not see it ?"

"That Taylor girl ? So she is the cause of this ? I thought so. I shall always hate her for it."

"No, you must not. She is a sensible, affectionate girl, just suited to Roy, and she loves him dearly."

"She is unprincipled, or she never would have tempted him away from you—tempted him to break his honorable word and wrong a girl worth a hundred Florence Taylors."

"The temptation was unconscious on her part. Don't be unjust, Kate. And Roy has not wronged me, dear. Let me tell you a secret. I was the first offender. I loved some one else better than Roy."

"You ? Zoe, I don't believe you. It's impossible, or I should have known it. Why, who is he ?"

"Some day I may tell you—if I ever meet him again. If I never do, why, then,

"'Dear fatal name, rest ever unrevealed.'"

CHAPTER XXXIX.

ZOE had been several weeks in New Orleans. Pleasant weeks they were, though she felt a little queer at seeing Roy, to whom she had always been a first consideration, now giving to another that homage she had so long been accustomed to receive from him. The November weather was as mild as spring, just frosty enough to give sparkle to the autumn sunshine. Amusements were plentiful, and Zoe enjoyed the opera and theatre, the drives to the lake, and the walks through the public gardens and parks. In one of these walks Zoe encountered her old acquaintance, Floyd Reese, accompanying a showy woman, highly rouged and youthfully dressed, but no longer young. Floyd, with a nod and smile, passed on.

"Why, that is Miss Reese, Colonel Alver's governess," said Kate.

"Do you recognize the lady she is with?" asked Winter Lareau. "You saw her last night in 'East Lynne,' but these stage stars look quite differently by daylight. She is Miss Duprez, the leading actress at the Varieties."

"How came Floyd Reese to know her so well, I wonder?"

"I have seen the same lady with Miss Duprez several times. Lance tells me she is an enthusiastic friend of Miss Duprez—writes poetry in her praise for the morning papers, and superintends her stage toilets. Pity she could not give her some of her freshness. It would be worth more than the dress accessories."

The next evening they went again to the Varieties; the play was still "East Lynne," and being then a new and popular piece, the house was full. When the heroine of the play came on the stage the audience were too much surprised to greet her with the applause usually given to a star on her appearance. They saw, instead of Miss Duprez, with her carefully-made-up face and form, a new face, fresh and beautiful; the neck and arms of a Greek goddess, hair in sun-hued waves over superb shoulders—a shape at once seductive and commanding. Zoe let fall her opera-glass in her surprise.

"It is Floyd Reese," she said to Kate.

"How in the world did she manage to get in here ?—a leading part, too. I can't understand it," said Roy, who was with them.

"Hush!" whispered Kate, "she is speaking; she has enough of the *débutante* to make her voice tremble a little."

There were other signs of the *débutante*—signs, too, of being new to her part—a want of ease and readiness, a hesitation and nervousness, but her natural grace, her self-reliance, her fine voice, and her beauty tided her over these, and her acting was successful. The witchery of the woman triumphed over the inexperience of the actress. Her power increased as her nervousness wore off, and when the curtain fell on the first act she was loudly called for.

"Yonder's Lance coming to us with Lareau," Roy said. "Now we shall hear how it comes that we have a new star instead of Miss Duprez."

Lance, a slender, long-limbed young fellow, with light hair parted in the middle, and fuzzy mustache, came up, following Lareau, and was immediately questioned about the new appearance. He was dramatic critic of a daily pa-

per, and occasionally earned a few dollars by polishing up or
paring down plays to suit managers' requirements. Hence
he knew all theatre people, sympathized with the managers,
was permitted behind the scenes, where he offered suggestions to the actresses about their "make-up," and drank
beer and sherry with the leading ladies and gentlemen between the acts. Usually Mr. Lance's printed opinion of
these leading ladies and gentlemen was regulated by the
amount and quality of the wine, or of the supper to which
he was treated after the play. He took pride in being familiar with all green-room gossip.

"Plays pretty well, doesn't she?" he said, in answer to
Roy's questions about Miss Reese. "Wonderful well when
you know that she has had but one rehearsal of this piece,
and never acted before in her life. Fact. She and Miss
Duprez are Damon and Pythias in petticoats. The Reese
made her acquaintance one night and won her lasting
gratitude by being equal to a great emergency, fixing the
refractory train of a Worth dress that refused to work well
at the last moment. They became inseparable. The Duprez thinks she couldn't make a stage toilet without her
friend's taste to direct it. Miss Reese came with her to
all rehearsals, and must have paid strict attention to this
part, for she claims to have learned it at these rehearsals.
They went out driving this morning, and stopped at a res-
taurant. Miss Duprez drank some beer, and ate some German *Kuchen* that must have been too buttery, for immediately after she was taken ill, and had to send word to the
manager that she couldn't play to-night. It was too late
to supply her place—too late to change the piece for another. Old Knox was in despair, when in comes Miss Reese
with the quiet assertion that she can take the part. The
manager stares incredulous, Miss Reese persists, a rehearsal
is hurriedly called, and it proves that she can go through

17

the part more than creditably, as you see to-night. It
may end in an engagement if the young lady has aspirations for the stage, and is not too devoted to her dear friend
to supplant her, which I think possible, as the manager
tells me she refuses to be paid for playing to-night ; says
the money must go to Miss Duprez. He is delighted with
her, swears she is the handsomest woman in the world, and
worth a dozen of poor *passée* Miss Duprez. Such eyes and
shoulders may dazzle even a manager and make him see
talent where none exists, though I am far from saying—"

"Excuse me," said a voice. A gentleman leaned forward from the seat behind and touched the dramatic critic
on the arm. "Is the actress—Miss Duprez—dangerously
ill ?"

Zoe recognized the voice (though there was a huskiness
in it), and turned round to speak to Colonel Alver, noting
that, though he bowed to her with his usual smile, there
was a troubled look on his face. She thought it cleared
somewhat when he heard that the illness of the actress
was not thought very serious—an attack of cholera morbus,
the physician had pronounced it. "Why should it concern Colonel Alver ?" thought Zoe. She could not guess
that, knowing Floyd Reese as he did, a suspicion had entered his mind while he listened to Lance's story, a suspicion that Floyd had schemed to get the place she occupied
to-night, and had got it by foul play. Had desperation at
being repulsed by him driven her to commit a new crime ?
For he had shaken her off at last. She had followed him
to New Orleans. When the trial was over, and the prisoners
set free on their bond to "appear when called for"—equiva-
lent to an acquittal—she came to him with her congratula-
tions and her suggestions of ambitious plans for the future.
He listened to her with anger and impatience. How utterly heartless she was ! He owed the darkest regret of his

life to her. She it was, he now knew, whose schemes had given a bloody ending to his plot. He would have no more to do with political scheming. The recollection of that awful tragedy which he had inaugurated was like a smoldering fire within him. It dried up the springs of ambition for ever. When she intimated that she knew for a surety that Witchell would be killed before six months, he turned upon her with flashing eyes and forbade her to speak to him on such a subject.

"Cursed be the day that I ever dipped my hands into the foul stream of political intrigue !" he said. And then, looking at her coldly : "You ask what I am going to do now ? I answer, I am going to return to my senses if possible ; I am going to attend to my legitimate business that neglect has nearly ruined. I am going to care for the interests and happiness of my wife and children, who are more to me than all the world. I am going to pray them and my God to pardon me for having followed an *ignus fatuus* that I now know was kindled at the fires of hell and waved by a tempting fiend."

His words fell as blows upon her heart. In his angry scorn of himself and her he did not dream what terrible force his words possessed. He had come to think of her as a hardened adventuress, unscrupulous as to crime, caring only for money and power. He thought her passion for him was a mere pretense to gain her ends, as he knew her professed regard for Cobb to be. He had no conception of its intensity—that it was the one true thing in the woman's nature. She had felt death trampling behind her in hot pursuit ; she had faced threats and insults, and horrible fears of discovery and ever-recurring torture of remorse, but despair had never seized her as it did at this moment, when she felt herself scorned and condemned by the man she loved and had sinned for. Yet, wrecked as she felt herself, she did not lose her self-command, or she lost it for a moment only. For a moment she stood white and rigid as stone, then she smiled in cold derision and made him a mocking obeisance.

"Include me in your prayer, pious sir," she said. Then, with a bitter sarcasm in her tone, she flung him the rebuke of Mephistopheles to Faust. "The devil that acts, commands respect; the devil that repents, I know of no more mawkish thing."

She gathered up her shawl and rose. "Farewell; I shall never trouble you again," she said, and she was gone from his sight before he could detain her.

"Floyd!" he cried, but she had passed out of the hall and down the steps of the boarding-house, and was hurrying along the street as swiftly as though pursued. He caught up his hat and followed her. A revulsion of feeling had come over him. He had not meant wholly to abandon her. She had devoted herself to his interest. For the sake of this devotion he would not let her suffer through want; and though he was no longer controlled by the spell of her intellect and her physical fascinations, these had not wholly lost their power over him. At a turn of the street he caught sight of her figure flying rapidly before him in the gray November twilight. A picture of her face rose before him as he had seen it just now, when she bent to him in mock reverence, her beautiful mouth quivering with anguish more than sarcasm, her eyes wild and woful behind their mask of flashing scorn. Though he believed this woman to be a beautiful incarnation of evil, he still followed her in the drizzly twilight, and felt a keen uneasiness when he saw her steps were directed toward the river. He was detained a moment by an acquaintance; he broke from him unceremoniously, but he had lost her, and for a time he looked for her in vain. When at last he caught sight of her she was standing on a dilapidated, unfrequented part of the wharf, looking down at the black water below her feet. He stood off and watched her. The wind that moaned round the pier lifted her hair and drove a fine mist of rain into her face.

She stood motionless. A wild impulse to end her life had led her here, but this impulse had been quenched, as it had many times before, by a fear of death, or what might possibly wait behind death. It was probably nothingness, but what if it were not—and if one might meet in the Beyond the rebuking eyes of those who had been wronged and foully dealt with here! As she looked down into the dark water *hope* looked up to her from the reflection of her own figure. She could see its outlines there—faint but still fair. The beautiful need never despair. There is always love for them—love which is power and hope. Because she had failed more than once, must she despair of success while she had that face, those resources of mind, this will-force, that even Alver had bent to? She would not give up. The world was wide; there were many doors that would open to courage, to cunning, and persistence. She would begin a new career; she would crush out this passion for a man who had shown himself weak and unworthy the prizes to be won by the bold. She had next to nothing in her purse; no matter, her brain was rich in schemes, fertile in resources that might be coined into money. She would succeed. She would show Alver that she could live in spite of his cruelty. His scorn should not kill her.

She did not see him as she turned in an opposite direction and signaled a solitary cab that was passing. As she was getting into it, Alver walked rapidly toward her. "Floyd!" he called again. She saw him; fierce resolve nerved every feature.

"I said to you just now, Farewell for ever. I shall never step across your path again."

The cab drove away. He was left standing on the wharf, hardly knowing whether he felt more relief or disappointment at being thus freed from the woman who had exercised such control over him.

He found afterward that she took up her abode at a fashionable hotel. He wrote to her and inclosed a banknote. Letter and money came back to him. She would scheme in various ways to get money, but she would not accept it from him. She won her place on the Varieties' stage by stratagem, as he suspected. But she had not meant a crime this time ; only a trick. It was not poison, but only tartar emetic, which she had dropped in her companion's drink. She had determined to do this when she insinuated herself by flattery and delicate service into the actress's confidence, and when she had studied with secret assiduity and rehearsed in the privacy of her own room the favorite *rôle* of Miss Duprez. She was radiant with triumph to-night. Even small success stimulated her intellect and filled her with electric power. Plot and intrigue were vital air to her.

"She was born without a conscience," thought Alver as he watched her.

Another watched her. Her Nemesis was there, and she did not know it. Had she lifted her eyes to the gallery, they would have met a pair peering from under a slouched hat that would have made her quail and falter in her most telling speech. Cobb had remained in concealment until the news came to him that the Cohatchie prisoners were released, and then, unable longer to restrain his impatience to get possession of Floyd, he had followed her to the city, hiring as a deck-hand on a steamboat, and sitting there to-night in the red blouse and wool hat of the roustabout.

He chewed his tobacco fast and fiercely as he watched the stage. He shifted his feet restlessly ; drops of sweat stood on his forehead. He would have liked to have leaped on the stage and torn her away from it—this white-armed siren that men were flinging flowers to and admiring through their jeweled lorgnettes. If they dared to interfere with him, he could turn on them and say, "She is mine," and defy her to deny it. She would not, in the face of the hold he had upon her—his knowledge of her true name and the crime in which she was implicated. He believed now that she had been deceiving him ; he believed that it was she who had betrayed his hiding-place to the cavalry and led him the closest race for life he had ever had ; but he never thought of giving her up for this. It only stimulated him more in his pursuit of her. He was as fierce in his resentment as in the brute passion he called love. He said to himself that when he had her in his power he would make her pay dearly for all this. He would carry her off to the wilds of Mexico or the Indian Territory, where there would be no men to take her part and go mad over her, and she should see no one but him, know no will but his. He would laugh to scorn her intellectual pretensions, and make her feel himself her master. She had better have lain low if she wanted to escape him. He had hunted for her through the city, wherever he dared, during the two days he had been here.

He had dogged Alver's steps without daring to speak to him, and he was here to-night to look out for his prey, and, lo ! there she was flashing behind the foot-lights.

"What cheek she has !" he said, grimly. "Wouldn't it cut her down at the knees, though, if some Texan or Louisianian in this crowd that had knowed her in times past was to get up and hollow out ' Mabel Waters ' ?"

The thought had scarcely passed through his mind when

a voice behind him—a gruff voice that was familiar to him—said :

"If I didn't know that Mabel Waters was dead and paying the penalty of her sins, if there is any punishment hereafter, I'd say that woman was she. You've heard me speak of her, Hirne—Jim Waters's wife, that helped a fellow to kill her husband after they refugeed to Texas the last years of the war. She and a young Texan, and Waters's overseer, who came with them from bayou Teche, were all implicated in the deed. The young man was lynched, the overseer ran off to Mexico, and the woman got drowned in trying to make her escape ; but that actress just gone off the stage is almost her image."

Cobb trembled and slouched his wool hat farther over his eyes. In spite of his disguise—the black dye on his red hair and whiskers and his changed appearance—he was afraid he might be recognized by the old steamboat captain, who had known him on the Teche. But nobody noticed him. The play proceeded, and absorbed the attention of the two behind him, or at least of the sailor, for the former steamboatsman had since taken to the sea and had a steamship plying between this port and Honduras. Hirne's eyes wandered often from the stage to the profile of a lovely woman occupying one of the seats below. He had come here to-night hoping to get a glimpse of her. He had seen her walking with Royal and Kate the day before—the same day of his arrival, and though he believed her to be Roy's wife, he could not resist the longing to look at her again. On the next day but one he was going away. He saw them go into an office where tickets were for sale, found out that they bought tickets for the Varieties that night, and got one for himself and another for an old friend who was with him. He chose a seat in the gallery ; there he could see her with little fear of being seen by her.

When the curtain fell on the third act Cobb heard the gruff-voiced sea captain say :

"Hirne, you're not in earnest about settling down and turning granger ?   Better go out to Honduras in the Southern Queen with me.   We sail next Thursday."

"Don't you think it's time I was done sowing wild oats ?" returned Hirne.   "I saw a gray hair in my beard this morning.   If you had seen the money I paid out for farm supplies, implements, etc., to-day, you'd think I was in earnest about turning granger.   My farm—stock ranche and grain plantation combined—can not be beat in the section where I live.   Settle down ! why, a man with a family can't play the Wild Rover well, can he ?"

"Family ! You don't mean to say you're married, comrade ? "

"No, I'm not, worse luck for me, but I shall have three children to keep me company—two fine, stalwart boys, and a little girl with dark, sweet eyes and a rose-bud mouth—a little beauty."

"Not your own children, surely ?"

"No ; their fathers were better men than I ever was or will be.   Two of them are poor Parkinson's boys—you remember he fell at Elkhorn at the head of his company.   My Jeannie's father was a young adjutant who was killed near Richmond in the last year of the war.   Her mother died a few months ago."

"You'll have to marry some good woman for the child's sake, if for no other.   I know you've no use for the craft since the one you had in tow wrecked you, and—I beg your pardon, comrade, I didn't mean—I remember—"

"No harm done," said Hirne, gently.   "I've got over that since I saw you last.   And I'm not a woman hater any more, Lawrence.   I almost wish I was," he added in thought, as at that instant Zoe turned her face to Royal and replied to something he had said with a little nod and a smile so sweet that Hirne inwardly groaned in bitterness of heart.

CHAPTER XL.

The December sunshine, bright as in April, sparkled over Lake Pontchartrain. A light breeze wrinkled its surface, dotted here and there with sailing craft — fishing smacks, trim yachts, and gayly painted pleasure boats. Hirne, standing on the shore, drew a deep breath and lifted his hat as he looked out over the silvery expanse of water. He had sickened of the city, as he was apt to do. This time its atmosphere seemed more than usually stifling, and he was impatient because his business detained him two days longer. He had come out here where the breadth of sky and water and the fresh air were some substitute for the wild freedom of his own home. A sober family carriage, drawn by two fat bay horses, bowled up to the lake shore and stopped near the unheeding man. A bright-faced girl looked out and spoke to a man riding on horseback alongside the carriage.

"Oh! look at the lake; how lovely! All crinkling and sparkling. Wouldn't it be nice to take a sail on it? Couldn't we, Roy? Wouldn't you like it, Zoe?"

At the mention of that name the gloomy man on the bank turned suddenly and saw the dark eyes, not seeing him, gaze out over the lake with something of weariness in their look. And there was a ring not altogether true in the voice that answered:

"Yes, it would be delightful."

"Then I will go and get a boat—just a little cockle-shell that I can manage myself—and we'll take a short row.

The carriage can wait for us at your Aunt Margaret's, Florence."

Hirne recognized the speaker who bent in the saddle to speak to Zoe and her companion in the carriage. This was the man whose happiness he could not help envying—the man he vainly tried not to hate.

He wheeled abruptly and walked a few steps away. Royal rode off, but returned in a few minutes to say that he had obtained a boat.

"It carries four," he said, "and I thought of taking the owner of it with us to help row, as I am a very poor oarsman, but I didn't like his looks. He had a villainous countenance. I guess I can manage the boat myself, especially while the lake is so calm."

"Certainly you can," Florence asserted with a confidence Roy himself was far from feeling. They got out of the carriage. Roy gave his horse in charge of the little black monkey of a footman who sat behind the carriage, his gay suit and gilt cap-band contrasting oddly with the sober, respectable vehicle of which he was an ornament.

The villainous-looking boatman brought round his boat, a narrow, sharp-nosed little trick gayly painted, and with "Flirt" in red letters on her side.

"She has a tricksy name," Roy said as he handed in the two girls. "I hope she'll belie it and be steady-going. For, I tell you again, I am a novice at the oars."

"I'll show you," Zoe said, laughing, "but we must go only a short way."

They pushed off, and the man from whom the boat had been hired came up to where Hirne was standing.

"That younker dips the oars in like he was afeard they'd stir up somethin'. He's not much used to them, sure, but he wouldn't let me go along. I warn't nice-enough-looking, I reckon. I only hope nothin' will happen to my boat.

She's a good enough boat when you know how to handle her, but she's narrow, and sets light on the water, and that sail makes her top sorter heavy, so if the wind rises, as it's sure to do toward evenin', he'll have his hands full to keep her right side up."

Hirne looked thoughtful. He made some unimportant response, and walked away, with more animation than he had shown before. He had not intended to go on the water, but he now went and hired a boat with a boy to accompany him.

Royal's party was tempted farther from shore than they had meant to go. A little sail attached to the boat was spread to catch the favorable wind, and the party was in fine spirits until it came time to return. The wind had greatly freshened, and now it was no longer in their favor. The pretty "crinkles," as Florence had called the infant waves, were now large enough to excite her apprehension as they broke against the side of the tiny Flirt, and scattered their spray over her gunwales, which were so low she seemed constantly in danger of dipping water as she rocked and tossed about. The little sail was taken down, and Royal gave all his attention to the oars, but he found difficulty in making his boat behave, and he saw he made no headway.

He grew hot and confused. Florence's frightened face and exclamations of alarm, as the boat careened this side and that, increased his annoyance.

Zoe was so busy trying to quiet Florence, and to retain her own composure as she saw the wind increasing and Royal losing his self-possession, that she did not notice a boat that came straight toward them and drew up alongside the Flirt.

"Can I help you?" asked a man's voice, curtly but not unkindly.

Royal looked around sharply. Mortified and annoyed, he was about to give a testy reply, but the stranger's manly face made him think better of it.

"I believe I *have* got more than I can manage," he said, with a short, vexed laugh. "These oars seem bewitched. I wish you had them. I've just been admiring your oar-stroke."

"I'll take them," the stranger said. "Here's your money, boy; take your boat back. Hold her steady a minute, till I can scramble over her side; keep the two boats together one second. There!"

With a quick stride he transferred himself into the Flirt. The little boat rocked wildly for a minute, and Florence clutched Zoe with a nervous grasp, but she gathered confidence from the looks of the new man, and the cool, prompt manner in which he seated himself and took the oars that Roy was so glad to relinquish. He showed at once that he knew what he was doing by the way in which he righted the boat and sent her steadily ahead with a firm sweep of the oars. Getting over the fright, Florence began to forestall the teasing she expected by turning upon Zoe.

"Why, how pale you are!" she said. "And you pretended you were not frightened at all, and were so good at scolding me. I never saw you half so white."

It was true, but the paleness did not come from fright. Hirne had not once looked around, nor did he glance at Zoe as he stepped into the boat. His voice had sounded familiar to her, but she did not realize it was he until she looked up as he stood a second in the middle of the boat—a tall, strong figure, in carelessly fitting gray clothes, with bronzed neck and gray-blue eyes. How her heart throbbed as the blood rushed to it, leaving her with the paleness Florence had commented on!

Not a word did Hirne speak to her during the time he

was pulling for the shore. He seemed taken up with what he was doing, and only addressed a few necessary words to Roy. When the bank was reached he stepped out first, only touching his hat to those in the boat, and hardly listening to Royal's thanks. But he did not go away, as he seemed about to do. He had caught one glance from the dark eyes that held him against his will. He stood a few steps off, irresolute, pretending to look after a jaunty red and black oyster smack that was putting out from the shore. Zoe stepped from the boat and went straight up to him and held out her hand. As he took it his own shook, his face changed color under its sun-bronze.

"Were you going away without speaking to me?" she asked, her smile beaming upon him. He stammered an apology. She had no time to talk to him; her friends were waiting, wondering at her effusive gratitude to a stranger. She said: "Come to see me; come this evening." She put a card with her address on it into his hand, and before he could speak she turned back and joined her friends, looking so flushed and bright that Roy wondered, and Florence said:

"Well, you are rosy enough *now* at all events."

CHAPTER XLI.

WHEN Zoe said to Hirne, "Come to see me this evening," she had forgotten that she was due at a party the same evening. As the party was given to her, and Mrs. Melvin was going with her, an excuse would be out of the question. She determined to be ready early that she might have a half-hour for Hirne, if he should come (his cold behavior made it doubtful) before her cousin, who lingered at her toilet, like all *passée* belles, should be dressed.

She lit her candles at dusk and dressed rapidly, though with even more than her usual care. She wore a dress of lusterless silk, canary-colored, with black lace and velvet; a few pale yellow Japan lilies in the dark, looped curls of her hair. Her hand trembled as she fastened them in. What if he should not come to-night? if she should never see him again?

A ring at the door brought a rush of color to her cheeks. Lousette came in.

"A gentleman to see you, Miss Zoe; he would not send up his card."

"It is Mr. Terrance, very likely; he was coming to go with Cousin and me."

"It's not Mr. Terrance, miss. He's not a city man."

"What does he look like?" asked Zoe, lingering a moment to calm her happy flutter of spirits.

"He looks gentlemanly, but he's not what I call a fine gentleman, like your other beaus, miss."

"Why, Lousette, what is the difference?"

"He ain't got a slim waist, miss, and his hair ain't barberized fancy, and it's pretty rough. Then his hands ain't none of the whitest, and he ain't got any seal-ring on."

Zoe laughed her old, merry, musical peal.

"Evidently my visitor is not a fine gentleman," she said; "thanks to God who made him a man."

She went down stairs and glided unheard into the parlor. There stood the hero of her heart—no fine gentleman surely, but a noble specimen of the strong, free-limbed *man!* He did not see her at first; he was standing at the chimney-place, leaning his arm on the mantel-piece with his bent head upon it. She came toward him; her dress rustling softly made him turn.

He half staggered. He had never seen her in evening dress ; never seen her beautiful round arms and neck bare. She dazzled him. He drew back the hand he had meant to offer, and bowed stiffly as he stepped back. But she came on.to him, her eyes shining, her lips glowing, the diamond pendants trembling at her tiny ears, her white hand held out to him.

The strong man trembled.

" Don't," he said, motioning her back from him.

" You will not shake hands with me ? "

" I— Forgive me, madam, I will shake hands."

He touched her hand with ice-cold fingers.

Zoe understood.

" Is this our covenant of friendship ? You were not even coming to see me, and yet you said you would surely come."

" There was a condition. And the condition, unfortunately, is not fulfilled. I was first to get over my folly—my madness. And I have not. 'I am as mad as ever. I ought not to have come here to-night. You were kind to ask me, but you did not know. We can not be friends ; I could not be harmless as your friend, so it is best we do not meet again. I knew it to-night, but I said to myself, 'I must come once to see if she is happy. She did not look altogether so at the theatre. And if it should be that he does not prize her as she deserves—' But it's all right ; you are happy ; your eyes tell me so. Oh ! sweet eyes !—I must go now—I must go at once. You are going out, I see. I will not keep you."

" Stay," she said, detaining him, laying her ungloved hand on his arm and looking into his face with those earnest yet half-smiling eyes.

He drew away from her almost rudely.

" For God's sake, don't touch me ! don't come near me !

Do you want to drive me mad? I am trying to be a good and peaceable man, as you desired, but if you look at me like that—you will make me a murderer at heart. This moment I could almost kill the man who claims you as his own."

"No man claims me as his own."

"What! Where is your husband? Where is West?"

"Royal West loves another woman. He does not care for me."

"Not for *you?* Impossible. Yet—was that the secret of your sad looks the other night? Has he dared to make you suffer? to desert you—to love another better than you —who are the queen of all women? Then he deserves to have me kill him."

"No, he does not, for I am quite willing he should love another woman. Indeed, I connived at it."

"Zoe, is it *you* can speak this way? And you a wife?"

"There again you mistake. I am no wife."

"Not married yet? Then your engagement to West—"

"Is broken off for ever. He loved another, and will marry her soon—and I—"

"And you?"

"I had long loved another—ever since he saved my life, risking his own; ever since he held me, fainting and freezing, in his arms and infused his own strong, warm life into my frame. Yes, even before that, when I saw him, though wounded and in the power of his enemies, spring to defend a woman."

"Zoe, speak to me; tell me, do you mean to give me hope?"

He was standing before her, pale, panting. He had seized her hands and was half crushing them in his unconscious grasp.

"Do you mean you could love *me?*"

Under his look she became suddenly calm, her eyes dropped, the warm color dyed her face, her neck, and bosom, and she said low :

"I have always loved you ! "

He did not clasp her in his arms as another would have done. Down he dropped on his knees. Still holding her hands, he put them over his bowed face, and she felt the hot tears on her fingers. A single sob shook his manly chest. Then he rose and stood up to his full, proud height. He shook the hair back from his forehead ; his eyes shone misty and splendid, filled with unutterable tenderness. He took her in his arms; he showered kisses on the lips he had never hoped to touch !

"My own," he said at last. "May God bless your life as you have blessed mine to-night ! "

CHAPTER XLII.

THREE weeks afterward they were married—a quiet wedding at Mrs. Melvin's, with only a few friends to witness the ceremony, and no relatives but Hugh and his wife and the children, whom Zoe in her letter to Hugh had especially enjoined him to bring. The marriage was a great surprise. Some of Zoe's friends declared she was throwing herself away on an adventurer. Wild tales were told of Hirne's past life, but his proud look, his open brow, contradicted anything that would have called his honor in question, while in his eyes a certain kindly, even tender expression, shading into melancholy, told of generous and affectionate impulses, upon which circumstances had fallen with the effect to chill but not to destroy. Hugh, who thought Zoe good enough for a prince, demurred at first at

this marriage with a stranger, but he was won over by the
manliness of the man, no less than by the numerous certifi-
cates of respectability, and even of high standing, which he
brought forward. Hugh found that Hirne had friends in
the city among the best of the old proud families—friends
who knew him, knew of all his eccentricities and their
source, knew of the generous and gentle nature which lay
under a surface that had been lashed into turbulence by
wrong. They rejoiced in the fair prospect there was now
that the current of his life would become clear and flow
calmly and beneficently to the end.

Hirne's pecuniary circumstances came to light in the
insight into his affairs which he gave to Zoe's brother. She
found that, instead of marrying a man of small means, as
she had thought, her lover had large possessions in lands
and cattle.

Two days before Zoe's modest wedding she had been
first bridesmaid at a large and fashionable one, where she
had seen her merry friend Kate transformed into Mrs.
Winter Lareau. Florence Taylor was second bridesmaid,
looking extremely pretty in her dress of peach-bloom silk,
with peach-buds in her blonde hair.

Prettier still she looked when, two weeks later, she
stood before the priest, a bride herself, little and childlike
in contrast to Roy's tall stature, but with a woman's sweet
earnestness on her young brow.

Hirne and his wife sailed for Cuba to pay a visit to Zoe's
father. Afterward they would go to New York, take a
look at the Great Lakes, the Falls, etc., as bridal pairs are
in fashion bound to do, and then return to New Orleans
via the great Mississippi and a luxurious steamboat. From
New Orleans they would go to Hirne's Texas home. The
supplies, to purchase which he had come to the city, had
already preceded him ; the provisions, farming imple-

ments, etc., had been shipped, together with a big box of
presents chosen by him and Zoe for the boys and the little
girl Jeannie, whom a good neighbor was taking care of.

As Zoe was being driven to the levee to take passage on
the steamer Citrus for Cuba, she passed an almost close
carriage containing a veiled lady. The passing of a funeral
procession along a cross-street delayed the two carriages a
few moments ; the lady's veil was inadvertently pulled to
one side, and Zoe caught a glimpse of Floyd Reese's brilliant eyes. In that brief glance the eyes of the adventuress
seemed somewhat hollow and anxious. She hurriedly ad-
justed her veil and signaled that the carriage should be
driven on.

Zoe had heard of Floyd as being regularly engaged by
the theatrical company in which she had played during the
illness of Miss Duprez. That actress, after a protracted
indisposition, had found herself so coldly treated by the
manager that, in a fit of anger, she threw up her engagement. This was just what the manager desired ; and he
immediately offered her place to Floyd. The new leading
lady became a favorite at once. She played with a freshness and enthusiasm wanting in hackneyed actors. Then
romance threw its rose-colored mist around her history and
her present life, enhancing the attractions of her beauty
and talents. It was said that she was followed and watched
by a jealous husband or a revengeful lover, and was constantly in fear of her life. She kept her rooms always
locked. She saw no company, visited no public places,
took no pleasure drives or sails, though invitations poured
upon her from her admirers.

She drove to the theatre to rehearsals in the day in a
close carriage. In the evenings when she was to play a
policeman rode beside her carriage, being assigned that
duty on her representing that she was threatened with vio-

lence from a certain party. When upon the stage her companions had more than once seen her shudder and turn pale. It was when her look had been drawn irresistibly to the gallery, and she had seen there a dreaded face—eyes that watched her with a sinister blending of hate and sensual passion. That face made her life a perpetual dread. Each night her heart stood still as the curtain rose upon her lest she should hear his voice cry, "Mabel Waters, your career is ended!" There was the constant fear, too, that some one among the audience might recognize her and proclaim her identity with the Texas refugee, the woman who had been accessory to her husband's murder, and who was believed to have been drowned in flying from the Texas avengers.

Each night, when Cobb's steady stare drew her eyes to his with a horrid fascination, she saw that his bloated visage and bloodshot eyes had grown more malignant. She had refused to see him or to allow him to speak to her, and on several nights he had been repulsed by the police when he attempted to stop her on her way to the carriage which waited for her near the private entrance of the theatre. Once he had resented this, and received five days in the lock-up.

These things had worked in his revengeful blood, inflamed to fiercer madness by the hard drinking he had taken to. She feared he would be wrought to the desperate point of giving himself up to justice that he might denounce her and secure her punishment. He was further maddened by finding he could get no more money from Alver, who, before he had left the city, had thrown him a bill as he would a bone to a dog, and told him to keep out of his sight for ever.

He found himself unable to carry out his design of getting Floyd in his possession. Pinched by necessity, and forced to work on the levee to get money to buy liquor and a ticket for the gallery of the theatre, the man was like a snake pinned to the earth, writhing and lashing himself impotently, and ready to turn his fangs upon himself in his rage and despair.

Floyd knew well what was passing in his mind, and her dread of him increased. She determined to abandon her present situation, throw away her hopes of fame and fortune, turn her back on the adulation that was sweet food to her vanity, take what money she had saved, and slip away somewhere—anywhere so that it was out of sight of her watchful enemy. He would not be looking for her to take this move. He knew the company to which she belonged was soon to leave for Mobile. He expected her to go with it. She had been warned by a dirty scrawled note, inclosed in a bouquet thrown to her on the stage, that she would not be suffered to leave with the company.

"'There's a slip 'tween the cup and the lip,' and you'll find the slip, my lady," he wrote. "Make your arrangements if you like, but you'll find me planted in your path. I've stood it long enough, and if you don't come and go with me, according to promise, we'll both go together to Uncle Sam's hotel, or to worse. That's all."

It was this note that had determined her to abandon her situation and make her escape secretly. She would go to Cuba, or to some other of the West India Islands, or she would stop at some lonesome, out-of-the-way point on the Florida coast—anywhere to be out of the way of Cobb, with the terrible vision of the gallows or the prison cell, which the sight of his watchful eyes brought up to haunt and torture her.

She reached the wharf five moments after Zoe and her husband had gone on board the Citrus. As she descended from the carriage two men, dirty and unshaven, were working near her on the levee. One looked up.

"Dommed if that woman ain't got a foine foot and leg of her own," he said.

The other looked, started, dropped his crow-bar, and stared at the veiled and muffed lady a moment. Then, as she passed them on her way down to the ship, he muttered to himself: "It's her. There's no other can walk like her. It's that she-devil, I'd almost swear. She's tryin' to get away from me, but I'll follow her. Let me see. Curse the luck! I've got but one dollar in the world. Well, I'll hire myself and work my passage—no; I'm tired of the cussed work; I hate it; but I've got so shabby that rogues won't have me in their ring. All through *her*. I've been dodgin' after her, doing black work for her, riskin' the rope and the chain-gang for her, and gettin' paid in deceitful smiles and kisses as long as she had use for me, and now she flings me off, spits on me, thinks I'm too low down to harm her. I'll show her. I'll pay her, if I have to swing with her, or rot with her in jail, though there's not a jail in Texas that could hold *me* long."

As these thoughts worked in his half-crazed brain he was watching the veiled woman greedily. The polite captain had assisted her on board the vessel. As she stepped on the lower deck a puff of wind blew aside her thick veil. She clutched it hastily and drew it over her face, but not before the sunlight had flashed on her white brow and golden hair. The sight maddened Cobb yet more. His eyes shot a baleful flash from their bloated sockets, he ground his teeth into his filthy dyed mustache; his companion spoke to him, but he made no answer. He sat down on a cotton bale, pulled out a dirty memorandum book, and wrote these lines:

To Captain Lawrence, of the Southern Queen:
Cobb Watson, the murderer of your old friend Waters,

and Mabel Waters, his wife, who was accessory to the murder, are both on board the Citrus bound for Cuba. If you would punish the guilty, take instant measures.

He folded this, and, with it in his hand, went up to the mate of the vessel, touched his hat respectfully, and asked if an experienced deck-hand was not needed on the Citrus. Hardly looking at him, the officer answered gruffly that the Citrus had all the hands she wanted.

"But if I give you work for nothing—such work as these here can do—" he said, stretching out his stalwart, hairy arms.

The mate cast his eye around, and was rather impressed by the muscular limbs.

"Nothing?" he repeated, gruffly. "Can you sleep in a rat-hole with a hard-tack for rations?"

The sailors within hearing burst into a laugh. Cobb, with a grin, answered: "Ay, ay, sir." The prompt response, and the laugh which he took as a compliment to his wit, put the old tar in a good humor.

"Tumble in, then; tumble in, my hearty. We'll give you a trial. If your work is as bad as your looks, though, we'll turn you into another Jonah sure."

Cobb went to the purser's office and bought an envelope, in which he put the slip of paper he held in his fist, and directed it to Captain Lawrence, of the Southern Queen.

Captain Lawrence had delayed sailing for Honduras owing to repairs that had to be made in his ship, which had been injured by being run into by another vessel while she was in the harbor.

"Ain't you a coming to finish this job?" asked Cobb's fellow-workman, a burly Irishman.

"No. I've got another. I've shipped on the Citrus. Comrade, where's your boy? He brought your breakfast a while ago. He's a sharp one, and I want him to do a bit of errand for me. Here he is now. Simps, here's a quarter for you if you'll take this letter to Captain Lawrence, at the Southern Queen. Do you know where she lies?"

"Sartain I do, and the cap'n's there a overseein' the workmen. I seen him a while ago."

"Well, take him this at once, so he'll get it before the Citrus pushes off."

The boy nodded, but he seemed in no hurry to go, and rung the quarter against his old jack-knife to test the silver. The Citrus whistled a warning for all to come on board.

"Go, I tell you," cried Cobb to the boy. "They'll follow us," he thought grimly as he hurried on board. Ten minutes after the steamship was on her way.

She had run for two hours. The "city of one vast plain" was out of sight; the shores, adorned with white villas and green orange groves, had given place to flat marshes and canebrakes; the river was broadening, sea-like, toward its mouth, when a little steam-tug was seen up stream, puffing as it cut the waters like a teal. It bore down on the Citrus and signaled her to stop. In a few moments it was alongside the vessel; three men came on board and showed the commander a warrant to arrest two persons on board his ship: one, Cobb Watson, who had committed a murder, and Mabel Waters, who was accessory to it. Captain Lawrence was here to point out the accused, who were well known to him. The captain's usually ruddy visage was pale with excitement. He would not have been so ready to have a warrant of arrest sworn out on the strength of that anonymous note, had he not twice had a look at Cobb's features during the past week, and, in spite of his disguise, been impressed with his resemblance to Watson, the overseer and murderer, as he had been struck by the likeness of the beautiful actress to Floyd Reese. This resemblance had haunted

18

the mind of the worthy sailor, and troubled him no little. He hailed the note as a possible solution of the mystery, and was determined to pay all expenses in order to get at the facts in the case.

Cobb was found and identified as Watson, the criminal, and handcuffed at once.

"Now get the woman," he said. "She is up stairs in the cabin, being quality," and he laughed maliciously.

They started in search of her. She was on deck, enjoying the sunset and the admiration her beauty excited among the male passengers.

Miserable as she felt, full of forebodings that fevered her brain and thronged her sleep with horrible dreams, she yet found men's admiring looks a sweet elixir. She stood leaning on the railing, the sunset reflection making her fair skin more dazzling, her plenteous hair more like spun red gold. The fine molding of her bust, her arms, and limbs was apparent under the soft clinging dress of gray. She knew men were looking at her with quickened pulses. She was thinking, "Once in Cuba out of reach of that wretch, I will make all this white and red and gold of mine serve me in good stead. Those meager, swarthy Spaniards will lose their senses over my white, plump beauty. It shall buy me a rich old Don for a husband, and I will reign in the tropic capital a sort of queen."

Hanging over the railing, watching the sunset-painted waters, and building these gilded castles, she heard not the first tokens of the approaching Nemesis that would throw a black pall over castles and castle-builder. She heard not the hail of the steam-tug, and only wondered a little at the sound of confused voices below that presently drew the men away who had been watching her with lazy admiration as they stood or sauntered about. She was left alone upon the deck. An excited voice within broke her reverie, and brought her to the door of the cabin to find out what was the matter. A negro waiter, his eyes round and big with news, was telling that a tug had overtaken the ship, and the sheriff and some more men had come on board and arrested a man named Cobb for murder. "And now," he went on, "they're comin' up to git the other."

"Another man to be arrested, you say?" asked Floyd, in sharp, quick tones from the door.

"No, miss—no man at all; t'other one's a woman: Mabel Waters, I hear 'em call her. Here dey come up stairs now!"

Floyd glided from the door like a specter; round to the rear part of the boat she darted; looked one instant, with clinched hands and convulsed face, upon the dark, foam-streaked waters below, and crying, "God, if there be a God, have mercy on what you made!" she threw herself over the railing. There was an echoing plash, and the dark waters closed over the fair face for ever.

The officers of justice found no Mabel Waters on whom to serve their warrant. Cobb, when he learned her fate, dropped his head in his hands with a groan. The revengeful feeling that had driven him to betray her at his own cost died out, and left him gloomy and sullen. He never suffered on the gallows. He died of malignant fever ten days after he was committed to prison for trial.

CHAPTER XLIII.

WITCHELL had been disappointed in his efforts to punish the slayers of his brother and his friends. The disappointment was a keen blow to him, but he gave no sign. His pride and his stern determination forbade him to give up his office and have no more to do with the people who had shown such opposition to his rule. He determined to go back among them, to carry on his business as of old, to levy taxes, control courts, and be supreme in administrative matters as he had been before. Rule he would, as he had once said, "if not by good will, then by force." It was the only stimulus left for him, since Death had laid its destroying hand on the best of love and friendship that had been granted him—such love and such friendship as had seldom been given to a man. All that had been soft in his nature hardened into iron now, and the man who once more rode through the streets of Cohatchie was a stern and smileless man, whose eye had the cold flash of a bayonet, whose brow never relaxed, whose voice uttered only necessary words in hard, metallic accents.

He was here at this time to superintend the collecting of taxes. They should be placed in his hands as formerly; and he was rigid in exacting every dollar that could be claimed. He rode occasionally from his home to Cohatchie unarmed and unguarded, unless when, at his mother's intercession, some friend, armed with gun or pistol, joined him and rode beside him under some friendly pretext.

One heard that Witchell had at last returned unaccompanied by his guard of troops—one who had hoarded up revenge against him for years. Lanier had not gone back to Mexico. He had hidden in the lake swamp until discovered and forced to fly. But he had not gone far. He was just within the Texas border when he learned that the man he hated so vindictively had returned to Cohatchie and rode at large, unprotected by cavalry. He came back at once.

He lay in wait several days for his prey. At last he saw Witchell ride up to the opposite bank of the river with one Kane, who had married an elder sister of Witchell, long since dead. Through a screen of trees he watched the two leave their horses fastened to a tree on the upper bank, enter a boat that had a negro oarsman, and proceed to cross over to the Cohatchie side of the river. When they were in the middle of the stream, Lanier rode out from the trees, pointed his repeating gun at Witchell, and fired. The ball struck Witchell in the side with such force as to knock him backward into the water. Wounded, but not mortally, he clung to the side of the boat with both arms. Lanier took aim again and shattered one of his enemy's arms. Still he clung on with the other. Once more the gun was raised, but Kane had now recovered from his first shock, and, seizing his own gun, sent a bullet at Lanier. It grazed his forehead. He laughed derisively, shook back his wild hair, covered Kane with his weapon, and fired, killing him instantly. Another shot in quick succession shattered Witchell's other arm, and, loosing his hold, he dropped back into the water.

"For God's sake, don't shoot any more! Both de men's dead," the negro shouted.

The madman laughed again.

"Well, they'll make better buzzard's meat than State officers any day," he called back. He wheeled his horse and rode deliberately away.

Witchell was not dead. As soon as Lanier turned from the bank the negro drew the mangled man from the blood-dyed waters and laid him in the boat beside the corpse of Kane. He was taken back to his house and laid down in the same room where Adelle had closed her dark eyes for ever. Both arms had to be amputated, and for weeks he hovered on the border land between death and life. His suffering was borne with the stoicism that characterized the man. That his life was spared was due to woman's faithful nursing. Marshall Witchell could never lack the love and care of woman. Some strange magnetism in this cold, reserved man drew women to him.

This one, who nursed him for love as never a menial would have done for gold, was young and fair, with a delicate refinement in looks and manner. She hurried to his bedside across a distance of a thousand miles so soon as she knew that he was wounded. She sacrificed friends and reputation that she might keep life in his mutilated body. She hung over him day and night, turning aside her head to hide her tears when she saw his white lips crushed together with mortal pain, or saw his dreary smile as she put to his mouth the food or the water he had no hands to take for himself.

It was a bitter fate! He, who had so gloried in his strength and soundness of limb, who had been as active of body as of mind, who had so many proud purposes mapped out—to be henceforth helpless, dependent upon others even to raise his food to his lips, to wipe the sweat of anguish from his brow.

No arm to execute the prompting of that quick brain, that indomitable will! All his ambitious hopes for ever in the dust!

The woman who watched him so devotedly shuddered as she saw his lips writhe and his brow work with the bitterness of that thought. At such times she would fling herself on her knees by his bed and pray for him through her tears—pray to the Mother of Sorrows, in whose intercession she believed. Maimed as he was, he was dearer to her infatuated heart than friends or home or her own fair fame as a woman; and when she saw the faint hue of life stealing into his marble face she dropped tears of joy upon the locks she daily combed away from his temples.

He did not marry her; he was grateful, but his heart was too deeply seared for any tenderer feeling to take root in

WILD WORK.

it. He would bury himself in solitude; no eye should see his humiliation. He resigned his place in the State Senate; he went back to his New England home. But there was no balm in solitude; no rest in idleness. His spirit chafed at the inactivity of his lot; recollection embittered the lonely hours. At last he accepted an office he had before refused—that of minister to a foreign Court. He quitted his native shores, saying to himself, with grim satisfaction, that it was for ever.

Alver moved away from Cohatchie. The place was haunted by associations he could not bear to face. He set up his new vine and fig-tree in a remote portion of Texas. There he has retrieved his wrecked fortune. Few of those about him know his history. He is respected, looked up to; a group of noble boys are growing up around him. Abroad he wears the same proud, inscrutable face, though his cheek is worn and his eye hollow. At home he is subject to fits of gloom. Only his gentle wife can soothe him when these dark moods are upon him—when he hears the croaking of the raven that will not "take its form from off his door."

In the same grand State live Zoe and her "wild rover" —now a peace-loving citizen and a happy and useful man. The fire of his nature is subdued, not extinguished. Enough of the old vim and enthusiasm remain to make him a leader in those progressive movements in education, agriculture, and manufactures which are fast giving Texas a foremost place among the States. Hirne's marriage is a most happy one. His strong, rugged character finds its best supplement in the tender, yet vivid and elevated, nature of his wife.

It is just six years this summer of 1880 since the tragic event on which this story turns took place near the little river-side town of Cohatchie. In this brief time the spirit of Change has moved strongly over the South. The turbulent, transition period is over; the appeals to mob law have ceased. The people have learned to assert their rights more wisely; the Government to regard them more carefully. Bitter experience has taught these lessons. Mutual sympathy and understanding open a fair prospect of union in more than name between the two sections of the Republic. In a little while our children will look back with wonder to the "dark era of carpet-bag rule." A picture of that time, even imperfect as this, may then be of interest as a curious study; and, since history repeats itself, and governments and society move in circles, such a picture may be valuable as a warning.

THE END.

A STIRRING AMERICAN NOVEL.

MANCH.

A NOVEL.

By MARY E. BRYAN,

Editor of the "Sunny South."

One vol., 12mo. Cloth. - - - Price, $1.50.

"I regard it as one of the most interesting and thrilling stories I ever read."
—ALEXANDER H. STEPHENS.

"The story is strongly dramatic and admirably handled. It is told with great vigor and skill; its dramatic incidents are presented dramatically; the characters and its personages are cleverly discriminated; in a word the workmanship of the piece is in the main so good as to justify us in saying that the author has positive gifts as a novelist."—*New York Evening Post.*

"A story of wild border-life. It is sensational, working constantly to climaxes, thrilling in many portions, arousing the sympathies of the reader, and holding his attention to the end."—*Chicago Tribune.*

"The plot is intricate and the interest breathless."—*New York Herald.*

"The interest of the story is maintained until the close."—*New York Evening Express.*

"Its characters are made to stand out boldly and distinctly; its plot is a strong one with no minor parallel threads to detract from its power. Arousing interest at the beginning, it sustains and increases it to the *finale* without relaxation. Its motion is consistent, and at times intensely dramatic. In less skillful hands it might have been called sensational; in those of Mrs. Bryan it is an effective piece of art. The style is colored with the warm glow of the creole. It is tinged by the touch of a rich poetic temperament, and occasionally surprises one with a unique figure or a dainty fancy. But it is not weakly effeminate or florid; on the contrary, it is characterized by more of strength than accompanies the work of most women."—*Louisville Courier-Journal.*

"'Manch' is intensely dramatic from beginning to end, and while it is possible that the character of the child, whose name gives the book its title, might have been made more vividly picturesque, it is nevertheless invested with a pathetic interest all its own. In brief, 'Manch' is a strong story—strong in its plot, strong in its suggestions, and wholly original. We believe it will be one of the most marked literary successes of the season."—*Augusta Chronicle.*

For sale by all booksellers; or sent by mail, post-paid, on receipt of price.

D. APPLETON & CO., PUBLISHERS, 1, 3, & 5 BOND ST., NEW YORK.

MISCELLANEOUS PUBLICATIONS.

The Land of Gilead.

With Excursions in the Lebanon. By LAURENCE OLIPHANT. With Illustrations and Maps. Crown 8vo, cloth. $2.00.

"His journeys took him quite off the beaten tracks of tourists and archæological explorers; he got an 'inside view,' so to call it, of native life and manners; he saw something of the wandering Bedouins; and we know of no recent book on Palestine which is really so instructive, from which the reader can derive so large a fund of entertainment."—*Eclectic Magazine.*

Anecdotal History of the British Parliament.

From the Earliest Periods to the Present Time, with Notices of Eminent Parliamentary Men and Examples of their Oratory. Compiled by G. H. JENNINGS. Crown 8vo. Cloth, $2.50.

"As pleasant a companion for the leisure hours of a studious and thoughtful man as anything in book-shape since Selden.—*London Telegraph.*

"It would be sheer affectation to deny the fascination exercised by the 'Anecdotal History of Parliament.'"—*Saturday Review.*

Young Ireland.

A Fragment of Irish History, 1840–1850. By the Hon. Sir CHARLES GAVAN DUFFY, K. C. M. G. New cheap edition. 12mo, cloth, $1.50.

"Young Ireland" is a memoir of the few stormy years in Ireland during which O'Connell was tried and convicted of conspiracy, and Smith O'Brien tried and convicted of high treason, written by one who was in succession the fellow-prisoner of each of them, and has seen since a remarkable career in Australia. The book is founded on the private correspondence of the leading men of the period, and throws a searching light on the Irish politics of the present day.

"Never did any book appear so opportunely. But, whenever it had appeared, with so lucid and graphic a style, so large a knowledge of the Irish question, and so statesmanlike a grasp of its conditions, it would have been a book of great mark."—*London Spectator.*

A History of Greece.

From the Earliest Times to the Present. By T. T. TIMAYENIS. With Maps and Illustrations. 2 vols., 12mo, cloth, $3.50.

"While I cheerfully acknowledge my obligations to Gibbon and Grote—the most eminent of modern historians—a careful study of the Greek writers has led me to differ from them on many important matters. The peculiar feature of the present work, therefore, is that it is founded on Hellenic sources. I have not hesitated to follow the Father of History in portraying the heroism and the sacrifices of the Hellenes in their first war for independence, nor, in delineating the character of that epoch, to form my judgment largely from the records he has left us."—*Extract from Preface.*

History of Herodotus.

An English Version, edited, with Copious Notes and Appendices, by GEORGE RAWLINSON, M. A. With Maps and Illustrations. New edition. In four volumes, 8vo. Vellum cloth, $8.00.

D. APPLETON & CO., Publishers, 1, 3, & 5 Bond St., New York.

MISCELLANEOUS PUBLICATIONS.

The New Nobility.

A Story of Europe and America. By J. W. FORNEY, author of "Anecdotes of Public Men," etc. 12mo. Cloth, $1.50.

"Colonel Forney has written an exceedingly clever and entertaining story. The reader will have little difficulty in surmising the import of its title: he will hardly need to be told that the members of the new nobility are those able, energetic, dauntless, and self-made men who are the strength and glory of this Republic. The dialogue is particularly bright; the descriptions of European life are vivid and truthful, attesting the extensive acquaintance of the author with society and letters."—*Philadelphia North American.*

Lady Clara de Vere.

A Novelette. From the German of FRIEDRICH SPIELHAGEN. Appletons' "New Handy-Volume Series." 18mo. Paper, 25 cents.

The story was undoubtedly suggested by Tennyson's famous poem, "Lady Clara Vere de Vere."

All Alone.

A Novelette. By ANDRÉ THEURIET, author of "Gérard's Marriage," "The Two Barbels," etc. Appletons' "New Handy-Volume Series." 18mo. Paper, 25 cents.

Mary Marston.

A Novel. By GEORGE MACDONALD, author of "Robert Falconer," "Annals of a Quiet Neighborhood," etc. 12mo. Cloth, $1.50.

"The merit of the book does not lie in the plot, but in its thoughtful observation of the world we live in—what it is, and what it might be. 'Mary Marston' is a fine work, which may be read and pondered over with a view as much to improvement as amusement. There is nothing careless or slovenly about the drawing of any character, nor yet about any other part of the book. The author is evidently too thorough to send his work forth to the world in a condition less good than the best he can make it."—*London Spectator.*

Great Singers.

Second Series. MALIBRAN—SCHRÖDER-DEVRIENT—GRISI—VIARDOT—PERSIANI—ALBONI—JENNY LIND—CRUVELLI—TITIENS. By GEORGE T. FERRIS, author of "Great Singers," First Series, "The Great German Composers," etc. Appletons' "New Handy-Volume Series." 18mo. Paper, 30 cents; cloth, 60 cents.

D. APPLETON & CO., Publishers, 1, 3, & 5 Bond St., New York.

BIOGRAPHICAL SKETCHES.

Beaconsfield :

A Sketch of the Literary and Political Career of Benjamin Disraeli, late Earl of Beaconsfield. With Two Portraits, from a Sketch by Maclise, in 1830, and from a Drawing by Sir John Gilbert, in 1870. By GEORGE M. TOWLE. ("New Handy-Volume Series.") 18mo. Paper, 25 cents; cloth, 60 cents.

Thomas Carlyle :

His Life—his Books—his Theories. By ALFRED H. GUERNSEY. ("New Handy-Volume Series.") 18mo. Paper, 30 cents; cloth, 60 cents.

Ruskin on Painting.

With a Biographical Sketch. ("New Handy-Volume Series.") 18mo. Paper, 30 cents; cloth, 60 cents.

Stray Moments with Thackeray :

His Humor, Satire, and Characters. Being Selections from his Writings, prefaced with a Few Biographical Notes. By WILLIAM H. RIDE-ING. ("New Handy-Volume Series.") Paper, 30 cents; cloth, 60 cents.

The writings abound with delightful little essays and incisive bits of satire and humor, many of which in this volume have been brought together as a sort of literary banquet of Thackeraunian tidbits.

Lord Macaulay :

His Life—his Writings. By CHARLES H. JONES. ("New Handy-Volume Series.") 18mo. Paper, 30 cents; cloth, 60 cents.

A Short Life of Charles Dickens,

With Selections from his Letters. By CHARLES H. JONES, author of "Macaulay: his Life—his Writings." ("New Handy-Volume Series.") 18mo. Paper, 35 cents; cloth, 60 cents.

The work is an attempt to give, in a compact form, such an account of the life of Dickens as will meet the requirements of the general reader. Liberal extracts are made from the letters of Dickens, in order that, so far as possible, he may depict himself and tell his own story.

A Short Life of Gladstone.

By CHARLES H. JONES, author of "A Short Life of Charles Dickens," "Macaulay," etc. ("New Handy-Volume Series.") 18mo. Paper, 35 cents; cloth, 60 cents.

"In two hundred and fifty pages, the author has succeeded in giving a clear impression of Gladstone's career, and, what is better still, of his personality. Extracts from his speeches and estimates of his literary work are given, and an excellent feature of the book is its short but significant citations from the press, which help the reader to see the great statesman through the eyes of his contemporaries, both friend and foe."—*Boston Courier.*

D. APPLETON & CO., Publishers, 1, 3, & 5 *Bond St., New York.*

www.ingramcontent.com/pod-product-compliance
Lightning Source LLC
Chambersburg PA
CBHW032310280326
41932CB00009B/761